Planting the Faith in a New Land

The History of
the Church of the Brethren
in Indiana

Planting the Faith in a New Land
The History of the Church of the Brethren in Indiana
Copyright © 1992 by Indiana History Editorial Board

Typesetting notes:
Body text is set in Garamond Book type.
Headlines are set in Garamond Ultra Condensed type.

Dust jacket design: Gib Foster, Manchester College Printing
Book design: Steve Bowers

Printed by
Evangel Press
Nappanee, Ind.

 Printed on recycled, acid-free paper.

Foreword

I n our modern society, with its increasing mobility and pluriformity, we have become the subjects and often the victims of so many displacements that it is very hard to keep a sense of rootedness, and we are constantly tempted to become bitter and resentful ..."

"Where have I been asked to leave my father and mother; where have I already been invited to let the dead bury the dead; where am I challenged to keep my hand on the plow and not look back? God always calls, always asks us to take up our crosses and follow. Displacement is not primarily something to do or to accomplish, but something to recognize."

Seeds of Hope
Henri Nouwen

Some of us can resonate with feelings of displacement. We have experienced so many changes in our lives that rootedness may have been lost. Abram and Sarah likely had questions about their relocation described in the book of Genesis. Displacement occurs early and often in biblical accounts of life.

Planting the Faith in a New Land describes the establishment of the Church of the Brethren in the state of Indiana. God called these church planters to relocate, and some of them certainly wondered if they could ever feel at home as Hoosiers.

Despite the computer age and its technological impact upon you and me, we can read the history of our Brethren predecessors knowing that their experiences of call were not totally different from ours. God's call always is an invitation to move beyond what we have known.

We can be thankful for the dedication and insights of Steve Bowers as he pulled this story together. Thanks is also due the editorial board members who conceived the need for a new account of the development of the denominational and congregational life in Indiana.

As we read of our ancestors in the faith, let us reflect upon our willingness to be mobile, to be displaced, and to be followers of the God who continues to call the workers into the new fields of harvest.

Charles Boyer
LaVerne, California

Author's Note

I have often heard Christians speak of having a religious experience. If such a thing is possible, the writing of this book has been an 18-month religious experience for me. The true stories of the pioneer Dunkard families who tamed the Indiana wilderness are stories of drama and faith that are both inspiring and humbling.

Having been part of the Church of the Brethren in Indiana since birth, I thought I was fairly knowledgeable about my heritage. I now realize how little I actually understood. The more I have learned, the more questions I have about who these people were and what their lives were like.

This book was originally conceived in 1989 as a successor to the two previous Indiana histories: *History of the Church of the Brethren in Indiana* (1917) by Otho Winger, and *History of the Church of the Brethren in Indiana* (1952) written by historical committees of the three districts in Indiana. The boards of the South/Central District and Northern Indiana District approved the project in 1990 and an editorial board was formed.

My first direct involvement began when a letter arrived at my home in November 1990. Ferne Baldwin, chair of the editorial board, asked if I would meet with them to discuss the possibility of serving as the writer for the project.

My friends will testify that I am a firm believer in the direct intervention of God at certain times in all our lives. I can point to that letter from Ferne as one of those times in my own life.

After meeting with the board, they asked me to accept the assignment of writing this new history book. I agreed without really knowing what I was getting myself into. Ignorance, in this case, was fortunate.

One of the first things that appealed to me about this project was the editorial board's direction that they were not interested in a book that is simply a dry recitation of facts. Each of them is personally captivated and excited about the history of the church, and they wanted a book that transmitted that excitement to others. For that reason, those expecting to find a scholarly thesis in these pages will be disappointed. While we have done everything possible to make sure our stories are accurate and we are confident they are substantiated in fact, readers will not find every detail scrupulously footnoted and cross-referenced. We believe the book is historically accurate, but the buck stops with the author and any errors should be considered my own.

This is purposely designed to be a book for everyone. Our goal was to make the story of the Church of the Brethren accessible to a wide audience who might find new inspiration in the true stories of those who came before them.

While I am responsible for the writing, there are many other people who have contributed along the way. Dozens of people throughout Indiana have contributed the stories of their own congregations. The editorial board has spent many hours giving me advice, pouring over raw manuscripts, and directing the entire project. Their help has been invaluable and, through our regular meetings at Timbercrest in North Manchester, I came to value their enthusiasm and friendship as much as I valued their advice.

A special tribute goes to Ferne Baldwin, chair of the editorial board, who has been the real heart and soul of the project. She worked tirelessly, digging up fact after fact, and never failed to ask, "What else do you need?" If anyone's name should be written in gold in this book, it should certainly be hers. I have every confidence her name is already written in gold in a much more important book.

Thanks also go to my father, Elmer Bowers, who agreed at the last minute to help me in an odyssey to find and photograph every active congregation in the state. He photographed all of the South/Central District churches while I covered the Northern Indiana District, a project which took us several days and more than 2,000 miles.

I must also give personal thanks to my family: Ryan and Rachel who patiently understood when Dad had to turn down their requests for his time because he had to work on the book; and Jane who has supported and encouraged me even when it was not easy to do. Their love and support has meant more to me than words can express.

There were times when the writing of this book became a mystical experience. I sometimes stopped in mid-sentence to listen because I could almost hear the voices of Elder Jacob Miller, Elder Daniel Cripe, Elder Jacob Berkey, Otho Winger, and many others speaking to me across the years. Knowing more about these people and their families has given me a much greater appreciation for the responsibility we all bear by claiming the title "Brethren."

Finally, the ultimate in thanks must be given to my God. I have no doubt (S)He was peering over my shoulder (especially at the times when I wondered if there would ever be an end to the work), whispering it would be alright if I just typed one more page. If ever I needed proof of God's love for me, it certainly came during the writing of this book.

Steve Bowers
Goshen, Indiana
June 1992

Indiana History Editorial Board

Table of Contents

Book I:
The Indiana Story

1

Beginnings

Europe in the early 1700s was not a friendly place for independent thinkers, particularly when they were doing their thinking about religion. In spite of this, a small band of eight adults held a baptism service in the Eder River near Schwarzenau, Germany, in 1708. This small act, expressly forbidden by the law of the land, marks the beginning of the Church of the Brethren.

The historical currents that led to the founding of the Brethren had been washing over Europe for nearly two centuries. Wars regularly laid waste to wide areas. Most of the conflicts involved religion because there was no division between religion and politics.

The Thirty Years War is the classic example of a religious and political conflict of the period. Lasting from 1618 to 1648, it was the longest and most devastating of the many wars of that time. It began when Protestants revolted against Catholic authorities in Prague, Czechoslovakia, and soon spread throughout Europe. The combatants not only battled each other's military might, but regularly sent armies to destroy their opponents' economies as well. At a time when most economies were largely based on rural agriculture, this translated into the destruction of entire farming villages and towns. After 30 years of such bloodletting, the population had been decimated.

The Treaty of Westphalia, signed in 1648, brought the Thirty Years War to a close. The treaty guaranteed the right to exist for the three major religious groups (Catholic, Lutheran, and Reformed), but they could not mix. The result was that most of Europe was carved up into religious territories. The approved religion of each territory was determined by the loyalties of the king and the nobility. The residents of a given area had to declare allegiance to the religion of the monarch, or they were forced to move.

The area of Germany which cradled the early Brethren had barely recovered from the Thirty Years War when it was subjected to repeated invasions by the French during the War of the League of Augsburg (1688-1697). Additional misery was caused by drought, crop failures, and incompetent and uncaring government.

Unrest began to spread, sometimes breaking into violence against civil and religious authorities. These revolts were put down unmercifully, so a new alternative was emigration. So many people moved out (many to the new land in America) that the area known as the Palatinate began to resemble a deserted wasteland.

Because of the close relationship between religion and politics, it meant the state helped enforce religious doctrine and the church often enforced state laws. Taxes collected by the state supported the church and paid the salaries of the clergy. In return, the church supported government policies, including exhorting the people to support the many wars that swept across the land.

Religion had become cold and lifeless to many people. Worship services were dominated by ritual that was often not understood. Ministers were part of the ruling class, the aristocracy, and often viewed their uneducated parishioners with open contempt. Some were little more than corrupt drunkards.

Anabaptists and Pietists

It is small wonder that the atmosphere of 17th and 18th century Europe led to a number of religious reform movements. Such movements were not tolerated lightly by the church or the government. They were ruthlessly ferreted out and murderously put down. Imprisonment, torture, confiscation of property, and execution (frequently by burning at the stake) were common.

In spite of this persecution, the reform movements continued, often in secret, and they gained new adherents. Two of the reform schools of thought, the Pietists and the Anabaptists, were most influential on the early Brethren.

The one thing above all else that marked Anabaptists was their belief in adult baptism. The three state churches taught infant baptism, but the Anabaptists believed that baptism should only come through an informed choice made by the individual.

Anabaptists also believed the highest authority was the Bible, which was interpreted by the state churches as undercutting the authority of the clergy and church tradition. They spent much time studying the Bible which led to a number of beliefs and practices counter to the teachings and actions of the state churches.

A primary point of contention (other than adult baptism) was the Anabaptist belief that an individual's highest allegiance belonged to God and God alone, not the state. Therefore, they refused to swear oaths of allegiance as required by the state. Coupled with their refusal to go to war because it meant killing, the churches and states viewed Anabaptists as a threat to their established order and power.

However, the common people were drawn by their commitment to support each other in a simple lifestyle. In spite of severe persecution in the 17th century, the Anabaptist movement grew and spread rapidly throughout Europe. Persecution actually helped spread the movement as believers fled intolerance. In some areas, they fared quite well and even prospered.

They became known as "People of the Book," studying it diligently as individuals and in small groups. Not only did they believe in it, they actively tried to live out its dictates. This was a major difference that separated them from other Protestant groups.

The Pietists held many beliefs similar to those of the Anabaptists, but there were also differences. Pietist extremists, for example, believed the church was entirely spiritual which meant no formal church organization was required.

The foundation of Pietism was built around the belief that the key to faith was a close, personal relationship with Jesus. They placed much emphasis on meditation, prayer, fasting, and repentance, and their aim was to become as much like Christ as possible.

They were known as "good people" because they believed their relationship with Christ must carry over into everyday life. Pietists were quick to point out that they were not trying to win salvation through good works—only to be more like Christ. They did believe it was possible to lose salvation by not living a life that measured up to Christ's standards.

Mack and the Brethren

Alexander Mack was born into a solidly middle-class family which owned vineyards and a mill. The family home was near Schriesheim, a small town just north of Heidelberg in the Rhine Valley. He married Anna Margaret Kling, the daughter of a solid citizen of Schriesheim, Jan. 18, 1701.

Mack's family was firmly entrenched in the German Reformed Church. Although it is not clear how he first became acquainted with the Pietists and Anabaptists, Mack was deeply involved with them soon after his marriage.

In 1706, Mack invited Ernest Christoph Hochmann von Hochenau, a Radical Pietist leader, to speak at the Mack mill. Hochmann came from a noble family, had studied at several universities, and seemed destined for a distinguished career in law or diplomacy. However, he was converted while at the University of Halle and turned down a number of appealing job offers, opting instead to lead the life of an itinerant preacher.

Hochmann was described by friends as an extremely likeable and persuasive man. His efforts gained support among both the common people and the nobility, but he also had powerful enemies. He taught that separation from the state churches (which he referred to as Babylon) was necessary for true salvation, which was more than enough to earn the wrath of established authorities.

Mack became one of Hochmann's close allies and accompanied him on several trips, but it wasn't long before the group found themselves in real trouble. Hochmann and nine of his followers were arrested in Mannheim and were sentenced to hard labor.

Although Mack was not with Hochmann at the time of his arrest, the Mack family was persecuted and threatened because of their association with him. Rather than compromise his beliefs, Mack sold his share of the mill and other holdings to his brother, John, and left Schriesheim with his wife, family, and a few followers.

The small group wandered for a few months before settling at Schwarzenau in the county of Wittgenstein, a region bordered by the Eder and Lahn rivers. The area was under the control of the Sayn-Wittgenstein family, and had become notorious as a place of refuge for all sorts of religious dissenters under the tolerant rule of Count Henrich Albrecht.

Count Albrecht and his sisters regularly shocked the nobility of the region by associating with many of the radical commoners of Wittgenstein. The Count was a man interested in all kinds of new ideas who seemed to relish the debates fostered by his tolerant attitudes.

Another reason for his tolerance may have been that many of those who moved in were industrious farmers and craftsmen. Ruling over a territory devastated by wars, he desperately needed their skills and labor to rebuild the Wittgenstein economy.

Mack and others spent a great deal of time studying the New Testament. They came to dislike the extremist position of some Pietists, including Hochmann, which completely rejected church structure. Another major issue which divided them was baptism.

A group of those around Schwarzenau became convinced that the only way to be completely obedient to the teachings of Christ was to form a congregation through baptism. They wrote an open letter to others of their acquaintance announcing their intention to proceed. Hochmann's opinion was that while water baptism was biblical, they should not demand it of everyone because it would make them too sectarian.

In the late summer of 1708, eight adults gathered at the Eder Brook. Drawing lots, one member was selected to baptize Mack. Mack then baptized this brother and the other six men and women. This simple act marks the beginning of the Brethren. They did not adopt a formal name, but referred to themselves simply as "the Brethren," a term which in German refers equally to men and women.

Although the baptism was held quietly as a private service, news of the event spread rapidly and criticism was just as swift. Authorities from neighboring territories saw the event as a new rise of both the Anabaptist and Pietist troublemakers. Hochmann saw it as a return to the errors of the state churches. Count Albrecht, however, held off the critics, and Mack, as the leader of the new group, wrote two treatises (*Basic Questions,* 1713, and *Rights and Ordinances,* 1715) in an attempt to answer the criticisms.

Early Beliefs

These early Brethren were often confused by outsiders with Mennonites. But they held a number of distinctive beliefs. They could best be described as a combination of Anabaptist and Pietist thought.

The Brethren agreed with the Pietists when they rejected the state churches. They were committed to the Bible, particularly the New Testament and the life of Christ it describes

Unlike the Pietists, however, they saw dangers in individual interpretations of the New Testament. This was balanced through group study and prayer. When there was conflict within the group, the Holy Spirit was asked for guidance to bring them to common agreement.

They agreed with the Pietist vision of a close, personal relationship with Christ. They also agreed with the Anabaptist stance on nonviolence, which is not surprising given their experience with the regular warfare of the time.

Another position which may have related closely to their experience with the state churches of the time was that there should be no force in religion. While they demanded conformity within their own group of believers, no one was forced to join them.

They attempted to imitate as closely as possible the church described in the New Testament. This led to a number of unique practices including adult baptism by trine immersion; a regular re-enactment of the Lord's Supper, including feet washing and communion, which they called the love feast; the laying on of hands; anointing for healing; separateness from and nonconformity to the world; and the holy kiss of brotherhood and sisterhood.

They were humble people who worshipped in homes and barns and refused to elevate their ministers above the common lay people, either organizationally or physically. All preaching was done from a table placed at the same level as the congregation.

They adopted a common pattern of plain dress and personal appearance as a bulwark against envy, lust, and pride.

Church discipline was strict, but was viewed as a way to keep members in the faith rather than exclude them.

The early Brethren were particularly vocal about rejecting any attempts at developing a creed. A creed, they said, could be used against them by state church authorities who would try to entrap them with their own beliefs. Even more important, they felt a creed might make Brethren beliefs so inflexible that any further enlightenment through the Holy Spirit would be rejected.

Their only creed, they insisted, was the New Testament—a stance that has remained consistent throughout Brethren history.

Expansion and Emigration

The early Brethren were excited about their new faith and wanted to share it with others. This process began almost immediately after the first baptism, and friends and neighbors all over Wittgenstein began hearing about it. They gained many converts—so many that no building in Schwarzenau could hold them, so the meetings were moved outdoors.

Ministers were sent on evangelistic journeys to Switzerland, the Netherlands, and other parts of Germany where new congregations were formed. A major group was formed in the Marienborn area of Germany, but it was forced to leave in 1715 and moved to Krefeld.

This expansion was not taken lightly by the state churches. Missionaries and their converts were sometimes prosecuted resulting in imprisonment and confiscation of property.

A combination of religious persecution and economic problems led the Krefeld community to a decision to emigrate to Pennsylvania in 1719. It was an attractive destination because there was already a considerable German population located there, and the Quakers who governed it were well known for their religious tolerance.

Although the exact reasons are murky, the original Schwarzenau congregation moved from Wittgenstein in 1720. They settled in West Friesland in the Netherlands but remained there for only nine years. At the urging of the Krefeld group, Mack led most of these Brethren to

Pennsylvania in 1729. The remaining Brethren in Europe left periodically during the 1730s and only small, isolated groups were left by 1740. Because most of the leadership was gone, the Brethren in Europe soon died out completely.

The Brethren in America

The Brethren from Krefeld arrived in America in 1719. They and the groups who followed settled primarily in the Germantown area north of Philadelphia and farther west in Pennsylvania.

Their first concern was to establish a way of supporting themselves. Some were craftsmen and took up their old trades in the New World. Many others were attracted by cheap land and became farmers, including some who had never before farmed. A few small groups met from time to time for Bible study, but there were no organized worship services.

In 1722, Peter Becker and others came up with a plan to hold regular worship services in the fall. They spent several weeks visiting all the Brethren in the area to tell them of the meetings.

Even though travel was difficult, these first worship services in Germantown were well attended. Bad weather during the winter months forced a pause, but the meetings were taken up again in the late spring of 1723 with renewed vigor.

The Brethren eagerly shared their faith with neighbors and friends who also began attending the services. Some of these newcomers asked to be baptized, but there were no ministers in Pennsylvania authorized to conduct the service. The Pennsylvania Brethren were in a quandary, so they wrote to Mack and his group in the Netherlands asking how they should proceed. The European Brethren replied that the Pennsylvanians should select one of their number as minister and go ahead with the baptism.

Becker was the logical choice, and he became the first minister in America. The baptism service was held Dec. 23, 1723, in Germantown in conjunction with a love feast. It was the first time either event had been held in the New World, and the date is generally accepted as the official establishment of the Brethren in America. It paved the way for expansion of the Brethren farther west in Pennsylvania, south to Virginia, and even farther west into Ohio and, about 80 years later, into a new land known as Indiana.

2

The Way West

Within their German-speaking communities, they were known as Tunkers or Tunkards. Their English-speaking neighbors adopted an Anglicized version of the word and called them Dunkers or Dunkards.

By the late 1700s, the Dunkards had expanded widely west and south from their home base near Germantown, Pa. Many of the original immigrants from Germany were craftsmen, but they quickly adopted the role of frontier farmers. They were often among the first settlers pushing into new lands in the West as the frontier steadily marched across the continent.

As early as the mid-1700s, there were Dunkard congregations in Virginia, Maryland, North Carolina, South Carolina, western Pennsylvania, and even as far southwest as Georgia.

Morgan Edwards, a Baptist historian, wrote about the Brethren in his book *Materials Toward a History of the Baptists.* He compared them with the Quakers in their simplicity of language and dress, although the Brethren wore beards and the Quakers did not. They also opposed the use of military force, would not take oaths nor swear, and would not lend money for interest. In addition to their strict adherence to baptism by immersion three times forward, they were also distinguished for their observance of the love feast which included washing of feet, a fellowship meal, the bread and the cup, and the kiss of brotherhood and sisterhood (also known as the kiss of charity).

Ministers were elected by congregations from among their own members and usually had no formal training. Many of those chosen for ministry began their work as first degree ministers or licensed exhorters. They were given a period of time, something like a trial period, to develop their gifts before being ordained.

An ordained minister was the second degree of ministry and was generally bestowed on someone who was considered a good teacher as well as being spiritually mature.

The third degree of ministry was reserved for those who exhibited strong leadership qualities. These elders (sometimes known as bishops) were generally considered to be the leaders of the local congregation. Elders sometimes were given oversight of more than one congregation. This was particularly true in frontier areas where populations were small and scattered.

The tradition of an Annual Meeting was begun in 1742. Congregations were expected to send representatives to these meetings, often the elders or ministers. By the late 1700s, Annual Meeting had become a place where decisions were made about congregational life and orthodoxy for the entire denomination.

The United States at this time included the inhabited areas along the East Coast plus the great wilderness in the West which included the land from the Great Lakes to the Gulf Coast and bounded on the west by the Mississippi River. Between wild animals, such as wolves and bears, and hostile Native Americans, it was a dangerous place to be.

Down The Ohio

About 1800, possibly a few years before, Brethren settlers began moving into Kentucky and southern Ohio. They followed the two great migration routes used by almost all of the settlers of this period: the Ohio River and the Cumberland Gap.

Roads into the wilderness were few and far between. Where they did exist, they were often little more than cart paths. With conditions like these, the rivers became the interstate highways of their time, and the Ohio was the most frequently traveled. Its great waters flowed past West Virginia, Ohio, Kentucky, Indiana, and Illinois, and poured into the mighty Mississippi where travelers could go all the way south to New Orleans.

Settlers from Pennsylvania primarily used this major river artery as a way to get into the interior of the country, and their most common method of travel was by flatboat. A number of boat builders went into business in western Pennsylvania building large floating platforms which families used to transport their entire farms, including livestock, to the West.

One of the early Brethren families involved in this craft was that of Elder George Wolfe Sr. Elder John Henry Moore in his book *Some Brethren Pathfinders* wrote that Elder Wolfe, who was born in Lancaster County, Pa., moved his family to an area along the Monongahela River about 40 miles south of what is now Pittsburgh. At the time, the tiny town had just been incorporated and was little more than a military outpost.

Settlers moving west from Pennsylvania and Maryland usually began their trips over land. They loaded all their possessions and provisions into Conestoga wagons, often trailing livestock behind them, as they crossed the Allegheny Mountains into western Pennsylvania. Some continued overland pushing deeper into Pennsylvania, but many chose the river as a quicker and easier way of pushing deep into the western wilderness.

These pioneers quickly adopted the flat bottom boat, or flatboat, as the preferred method of travel. They were long, ungainly craft, but their redeeming features included the fact that they were cheap and could hold an enormous quantity of goods for their size. They were commonly 12-15 feet wide and about 50 feet long. A portion of the boat, usually in the rear third, was enclosed to provide shelter during bad weather. A large steering oar, which operated somewhat like a rudder, was located in the rear, and oars (sweeps) were located on either side to propel the craft through calm water. Long poles were also kept on the deck, both as a method of steering the boats and as a way of propelling them through shallow water.

A cooking area was often created near the stern. Logs formed the boundary of a small space which was then lined with stones and filled with dirt about 12-18 inches deep. A small cook fire could be built here without too much danger of catching the rest of the boat on fire, although such mishaps did happen to the uncautious.

Entire farming families, sometimes more than one family, were literally loaded aboard these river craft along with everything they would need to survive in the wilderness. Farming tools, enough food to last for several weeks, rifles, lead for shot, gunpowder, and seeds (usually corn) were crowded onto the flat deck and tied down. In some cases, even the wagons that had originally brought them to the river were wheeled on board for the trip down the river.

Livestock presented some especially ticklish problems, particularly when a cantankerous ox decided a land-based animal had no business going on a river cruise. Experienced farmers were careful to keep unruly animals away from each other and away from areas of the boat where quick access might be needed to avert navigation catastrophes. Some boats included pens for the animals.

Most voyages began in April or May—late enough in the year to avoid problems caused by spring flooding but early enough to give the settlers a head start on building shelter when they reached their destinations before winter came howling down from the North. The entire trip would take several weeks, depending on just how far west the family decided to go.

It was a one-way trip. Flatboats were excellent, stable platforms for floating with the current, but it was practically impossible to move them upstream. When a destination was reached, the boats were broken apart and the lumber either sold or taken inland with the settlers and used to build homes and barns.

Elder Wolfe and his family eventually made this river trip to Kentucky in 1800. Pushing off from the Monongahela shore, they floated west into the unknown. Depending on the current, they could travel from just a few miles a day up to 20 or 30 miles.

Life aboard a flatboat soon settled into a routine, usually with a helmsman at the rear and a lookout in front. Most of the trip was fairly placid but could quickly turn exciting, even dangerous, when encountering fast-moving water and rapids. More than one flatboat came to grief by foundering on rocks in the middle of a rapids or by being dashed into an unforgiving shoreline by a swift current.

It was not unusual to encounter other boats traveling north and east. The travelers would often stop and tell each other the news from opposite ends of the river and share information about what lay ahead.

Food was plentiful in the form of fish from the river and game from the shore, usually venison or, a frontier favorite, wild turkey. While the men were guiding the boat or hunting for food, the women usually spent their time knitting and cooking.

At dusk, the flatboats were guided toward the shore to be tied to trees lining the bank. Night, when the boats were stationary, was often the most hazardous time. Wild animals roaming the woods were drawn by the sounds and smells of the farm animals on the boats. It was not unusual for a bear, panther, or wolf to leap onto the deck from the shore. Hostile Indians were also in the area, and it was not unknown for a flatboat to be attacked. Stories of families losing their scalps this way traveled quickly up and down the river, frequently embellished with gory details along the way.

For these reasons, a sentry was usually posted throughout the night. Some of the very best sentries were dogs which often accompanied the families as much for protection as for companionship.

Knowing exactly where you were along the river was a problem. The surest way was when a settlement was encountered. A stopping-off point for many on their way to Kentucky was the small community of

Cincinnati on the Ohio side of the river. Settlers often stopped here to stock up on provisions before making their final push into the wilderness farther south. Very few ventured west and north into what is now Indiana. It was still too wild and too difficult a place to enter with any reasonable chance of survival.

The Final Leg

The final leg of the trip into Kentucky was often the most difficult and hazardous. The area around Louisville, 130 miles beyond Cincinnati, was infamous for its white water where the river dropped over 25 feet within a span of two miles.

Having survived that sometimes thrilling, sometimes disastrous, ride, the pioneers then faced the arduous task of pulling a flatboat against the current to get into the interior of Kentucky. The best way of moving inland for any distance was to stay on the water and travel up the tributaries pouring into the Ohio. This required straining at the oars on the sides of the boat. In areas where the current was swift, ropes were tied to trees and the boat was pulled forward. In rare instances when the shore was clear of trees and brush, oxen or horses might be used to pull the boat ahead.

This was exactly the trip that Elder Wolfe and his family made in 1800. They traveled up the Green River from the Ohio and then overland to Logan County in the southern part of Kentucky where a few other Brethren were already living.

Other Brethren entered Kentucky from settlements in North Carolina. These people largely made their way into the state through the Cumberland Gap over what was known as the Mission Road where Kentucky joins Virginia and Tennessee in the Cumberland Mountains. Daniel Boone and about 30 other men were hired in 1775 to cut a road into Kentucky at this point. In spite of the fact that several members of the road crew were killed in Indian attacks, they managed to construct a path wide enough for foot travel and pack animals. The road was finally widened in 1795 and made passable for wagons and carts. This was the key to opening up Kentucky for settlement by an overland route.

Many Brethren families from North Carolina traveled this route into Kentucky. The preferred method of travel was usually by Conestoga wagon, sometimes in groups and sometimes alone. Most of the Indians were moved out of the Kentucky area by the early 1800s, so it was deemed relatively safe. The pioneers still faced dangers from wild animals and weather, however, and endured many hardships.

David B. Eller, in his thesis *The Brethren in the Western Ohio Valley, 1790-1850*, identifies five areas of Kentucky that were settled by the Brethren between 1790 and 1820. However, he notes that it is impossible to know exactly how many congregations were established from available records. All of these congregations had ceased to exist as part of the Brethren by 1840.

When Elder Wolfe moved his family to Kentucky in 1800, Brethren were also moving to Ohio, although at a slower pace. Kentucky had already joined the United States as a state while Ohio was still part of the Indiana territory. The population of Kentucky in 1800 was listed in the U.S. census as 400,000 while there were only 45,000 in Ohio.

Tradition holds that Elder John Countryman was the first Brethren minister to settle in Ohio. Born in Rockingham County, Va., he crossed the Ohio River from Kentucky in 1793 and settled in Adams County, Ohio. Other Brethren families soon began building communities around Dayton, 50 miles north of Cincinnati. Strong Brethren settlements were soon thriving in Hamilton, Warren, Montgomery, and Darke counties.

While much of the settlement in Kentucky came from those moving from North Carolina and Virginia, Brethren pioneers in Ohio were primarily from Virginia and Pennsylvania. This difference would later play a significant part in the way the church developed in Indiana as settlers from Kentucky and Ohio became the first to enter the new land.

3.

Coming To Indiana

T he great area that now comprises the states of Ohio, Indiana, Illinois, and Michigan was a vast wilderness in 1800 filled with fertile land, huge stands of virgin timber, abundant game, and hostile Native Americans.

A number of important measures were adopted by the federal government during this period which encouraged settlement of the new land. An ordinance was passed in 1785 mandating that the territory be surveyed. The land was blocked off in squares six miles on a side called townships. The townships were then divided into one-mile squares called sections. Each section containing 640 acres was made available for sale for about $1 to $2 per acre. One progressive section of the ordinance which would have far-reaching consequences was a provision that set aside the profit from the sale of Section 16 in each township for public education.

The Land Act of 1800 made land even more readily available. It reduced the minimum purchase to a half section (320 acres) and allowed the sale of the land on credit with a down payment of only 25 percent. This meant a 320-acre section could be purchased for as little as $80 which made the land available to many more people.

The Northwest Ordinance of 1787 established a territorial government for the area northwest of the Ohio River. It provided for the division of the territory into smaller segments when the population of a given area reached 5,000 adult males. These areas could then petition for statehood when the population reached 60,000. Although it wasn't spelled out in the law, it was understood these population figures referred to white men only and didn't include Native Americans or freed slaves.

The territory was initially divided in 1800 with Ohio on the east and the Indiana territory on the west. A territorial government for the Indiana territory was established at Vincennes.

Further reductions came when Michigan was split off in 1805 and Illinois in 1809. Ohio was officially admitted into the Union as a state in 1803.

Equally important were developments with several Indian tribes. General "Mad" Anthony Wayne led a U.S. force to victory in The Battle of the Fallen Timbers near the Maumee River in 1794. This led to the Treaty of Greenville in 1795 which was signed by a number of tribes. Part of the land ceded to the United States by this treaty was an area which included the southern two-thirds of Ohio and a narrow strip of south-eastern Indiana. Tribes who were part of this treaty were the Wyandots, Delawares, Shawnees, Miamis, Ottawas, Chippewas, Potawatomis, Kickapoos, Weas, Eel River Miamis, Piankashaws, and Kaskaskias.

Even though Indian raids continued to be a threat until about 1815, the Treaty of Greenville marked the turning point. United Indian resistance ceased and thousands of pioneers began pouring into Ohio.

William Henry Harrison was the governor of the Indiana Territory from 1800 to 1812. He pursued an aggressive policy of land acquisition from the Indians which resulted in a series of land cessation treaties between 1803 and 1809. Most of the treaties were signed at Vincennes, the territorial government headquarters, or Fort Wayne. These treaties covered most of the southern third of Indiana and nearly all of Illinois.

The settlement of Indiana began in earnest about 1800. Most of the early population moved north across the Ohio River from Kentucky or west from Ohio. The interior of the state was so densely wooded that it was nearly impossible to penetrate very far into the wilderness. The heavy undergrowth in the forests made it difficult for a horse and rider to travel, let alone a wagon. Many of the initial forays were made on foot, and most settlers followed rivers or military roads to make their way into the state.

The early settlement of the state occurred in a crescent shape across the southern part of Indiana running from Vincennes in the west to an area known as the White Water in the east.

Otho Winger in his landmark book *History of the Church of the Brethren in Indiana* identified settlers along the Four Mile Creek in Union County, Indiana, adjacent to Ohio as the first Brethren to come to Indiana beginning in 1804. He correctly identified the Four Mile Church as being the oldest organized church in the state in the area known as the White Water. It was officially organized in 1809 by Elder Jacob Miller from Montgomery County, Ohio, and Elder John Hart of Preble County, Ohio.

However, Winger and a subsequent 1952 history based on his book entirely missed a group of Brethren in southern Indiana. David B. Eller, in his thesis *The Brethren in the Western Ohio Valley, 1790-1850,* has identified another group of Brethren who moved into Indiana as early as 1802.

Jacob Stutzman Sr. and three of his sons purchased 400 acres in an area along the Ohio River known as Clark's Grant (now Clark County) in 1802. This area covered 150,000 acres and was originally reserved for soldiers who had served with George Rogers Clark during the American Revolution.

Stutzman came to Indiana from North Carolina where he was a Dunkard minister near the headwaters of the Uwharrie River. His three sons joined him in the Hoosier state from Henry County, Kentucky. Three other sons and three sons-in-law and their families had moved into the area by 1806.

Eller indicates records from the time are unclear, but Stutzman may have founded what was known later as the Olive Branch Christian Church. Surviving records are inconclusive, but local tradition says Olive Branch was originally a Dunkard congregation.

Settlement of this area remained very slow, however, until the War of 1812 was concluded with a treaty in 1814. At the conclusion of that war, the threat of Indian attacks on settlers was, for the most part, removed. This resulted in a rush of settlement by Brethren from Kentucky and North Carolina beginning about 1816. In addition to the Grant County settlements, Brethren located in communities in Orange, Lawrence, Knox and Washington counties by 1820.

These southern Indiana Brethren apparently had little or no contact with the Brethren who were moving into the mid-sections of the state at about the same time. The story of what eventually happened to these southern Indiana churches will be addressed in the next chapter.

Life on the Four Mile

The first Brethren community in Indiana which took root and remains to the current day was centered around Four Mile Creek in Union County next to the Ohio border. Although most of the early settlers in the area came from Ohio, most were born in Virginia, and the area they settled in Indiana was known to many as the Virginia Colony.

John Miller, son of the well-known Elder Jacob Miller Sr., was one of the first to settle along the Four Mile Creek on the Indiana side in either 1804 or 1805. His land was near what is now College Corner, Ohio. He found good clay on the land and established a kiln where he made pottery and brick. He became known as Potter John to distinguish him from another John Miller (possibly a cousin) who settled in the area and was known as Col. John.

Philip Lybrook came to the Four Mile in 1806 north of Potter John. He left his two oldest sons there during the winter and brought the rest of his family the following spring. His wife, Anna, was a daughter of Elder Jacob Miller.

Others who settled during this period were Tobias, Abraham, and Daniel Miller (all sons of Elder Jacob Miller), Daniel Hart, Daniel Brower, Edmund Moss Sr., David Rinehart, Christopher and John Witter, Joseph Kingery (whose wife, Eve, was a daughter of Elder Jacob Miller), Peter Eikenberry Jr., and John Moyer.

Although there are few records of these people, their lives on the frontier would have been little different from other Indiana pioneers. Most came to Indiana on horseback and by wagon following the few trails that had been carved into the wilderness. Sometimes there were no trails at all and a way through the heavy undergrowth had to literally be cut, foot by foot. Crossing streams and rivers was often a tricky business, especially after heavy rains, and swampy areas could quickly bog down even the strongest team of oxen.

Once they had arrived at their new home, one of the first requirements a family faced was shelter. A common first home was a lean-to with one side open which could quickly be built from small trees and branches. The open end usually faced south, and a fire was usually built here for cooking and to provide warmth.

The second need was to provide food. There was abundant game, but this offered a limited diet. Many families timed their trips to arrive in the spring so they could quickly plant a few crops, usually corn and perhaps a few vegetables. This was not as simple as it sounds because the land was frequently in the middle of a forest which had to first be cleared before anything would grow.

The next order of business was to improve their shelter which meant construction of a log cabin. Trees about a foot in diameter, often tulip poplar which was plentiful, were cut down and notched at the ends. The logs were stacked and the spaces between the logs were filled (chinked) with clay, mud, and small pieces of wood. The roof was constructed of clapboards hand-cut at the site, and the floor remained dirt, sometimes covered with clay or sand. A door was cut into one wall and a fireplace built on another wall. A window was sometimes cut into a third wall. The doorway was covered only with a blanket until time could be found to build a more substantial door.

Construction of these early log cabins was usually accomplished with the help of neighbors. Not only was help necessary to get the work done, but the events also served as social functions which tied the families together as a community.

Most families brought some iron cookware with them, but nearly all furniture was made from wood after they arrived. Bedding was often brought in, but the beds themselves were made from local materials. Utensils were also made of wood or gourds.

The need for food drove much of early pioneer life. A rifle was a necessity for the Dunkards just as it was for all other settlers. Wild game supplied most of the early diet with deer and squirrel common items on the pioneer table. Wild turkey was especially prized for its flavor, and fish were abundant in the local rivers and streams.

Nuts, berries, grapes, crab apples, pawpaws, and persimmons were plentiful in the forests when they were in season. These were often gathered by the women and children while the men and older boys were out hunting or fishing.

Whatever time could be spared from gathering food was spent clearing land so it could be farmed. Trees were an important natural resource, but they were also a problem. Nothing could be planted until tall stands of virgin timber were cleared.

Many trees were felled with an ax, but some (up to 10 feet in diameter) were too large. The bark of these trees was removed all the way around which caused them to die. They were then either burned while standing or left to fall. Regardless, the tree no longer produced leaves so the sun could shine to the ground and get to newly planted crops.

The resulting fields were filled with stumps. Some farmers removed them, but others didn't wait to get their crop in and simply planted around them.

In almost every case, the first seeds planted were corn. It grew abundantly in the rich, Indiana soil and was especially suited to the climate. It produced more food per acre than any other crop and quickly became a mainstay of the pioneer diet. Women ground it into meal to make johnny cake, mush, and corn pone. With the outer shell removed, it became hominy.

A bonus was that corn not used to feed the family could be used to feed the livestock. Many families brought with them a milk cow and a few chickens, but the most common frontier farm animal was the pig, although these animals were much different than the pigs we know today. They were often referred to as razorbacks or landsharks. They had long legs and were very fast. They had a great ability to find food on their own in the forests. Most pigs, in fact, were allowed to roam free until just a few weeks before butchering. Then they were penned and fattened on corn. Most pioneer families did hog butchering in late fall after the harvest. The fresh meat was devoured with relish, but most of it was preserved with salt and smoked.

Once the family had established itself, vegetable gardens and fruit trees were added which provided more variety to their diets. Women and children were primarily responsible for the gardens and preserving the food after harvest.

Winter slowed the pace of life somewhat, but there was still much work to be done. This was the time of year when men built furniture for the house. They also worked with leather to make their own shoes, belts, and harnesses. The women spent many hours with needle and thread making clothes and bedding for the entire family. Of course, there was always cooking to be done. Nearly everything in the pioneer diet was either boiled or fried over the open fire in the fireplace.

Medicine was practically unknown on the frontier, and disease and accidents often took a heavy toll. A cholera epidemic hit the Brethren settlers on the Four Mile in 1821 and again in 1832. It was said every family lost at least one member. Typhoid was another common hazard that was often fatal.

Indians were still part of the landscape. There are few records of encounters between the Dunkards and Indians, although Elder Jacob Miller, living in Montgomery County, Ohio, is said to have visited Indian encampments where he became a welcome visitor with his prayers and songs. Otho Winger records that the Indians called Elder Miller "The Good Man the Great Spirit sent from the East."

John Wagoner of Anderson tells of a tradition in his family about some of his Indiana ancestors who encountered Indians. Indians on hunting trips occasionally entered the area where this family lived in central Indiana and sometimes stopped at the log cabin to ask for food. The family always welcomed them and gave them something to eat.

The father of this pioneer family had to take some corn to market, a journey of several days. He was careful to make sure they had enough food for the time he would be gone, but heavy rains set in soon after he left. When he tried to return, he found the creeks and rivers had gushed over their banks, and he was unable to cross them for some time. The family's food supply soon began to dwindle without the father there to supply fresh game.

After a few weeks, a band of Indians knocked on the family's log cabin door and asked for food. The wife tried to explain her predicament and told them she had very little food. The Indians forced their way inside to see for themselves, but left after they were satisfied she was telling the truth. The Indians returned later, but did not stop at the cabin to ask for food. After they left, the family found a large piece of fresh venison left for them on a nearby tree stump.

The First Church is Organized

With so much time and effort required simply to survive, we may wonder how the families on the Four Mile had time for a spiritual life. But they would no more have thought of venturing into the wilderness without their special brand of faith than they would have gone without an ax or a rifle. They gathered in small groups whenever possible on Sundays for Bible study and worship. When travel was not possible, individual families held their own services, usually led by the father.

Elder Jacob Miller numbered several sons, daughters, and many grandchildren among these early settlers on the Four Mile. He visited as often as he could from 1805 to 1809, not only to see his family but to bring preaching as well. Elder Miller and Elder John Hart from Preble County, Ohio, organized the first church in Indiana among these settlers in 1809. It was quite naturally called the Four Mile Church. John Moyer and Daniel Miller were called as the first ministers, and Christopher Witter and Joseph Kingery were selected as the first deacons.

The Four Mile congregation was extremely successful and grew rapidly, both from immigration and by conversion. Baltzer Lybrook was called to the ministry in 1813. He lived in the northern part of the Four Mile territory while Moyer and Miller lived toward the southern end. The membership was widely scattered over the length of the territory, and it was decided travel would be much easier if two congregations were formed. The resulting congregation in the south was called the Lower Four Mile, and the congregation in the north was called the Upper Four Mile.

The first church building erected in Indiana by the Brethren was built by the members of the Lower Four Mile in the 1840s. It was located about two miles north of College Corner, Ohio, on the Indiana side of the state line near Four Mile Creek. The wood frame structure was about 40 feet wide by 50 feet long and had a raised floor that gave the congregation elevated seats. It followed the Brethren tradition of having separate entrances for men and women.

Many of the original settlers on the Four Mile and some of their children remained only a few years before pushing farther on into the Indiana wilderness and beyond. Jacob Huston moved to the area of northern Indiana near St. Joseph County in 1824. Philip and Edmon Moss moved to Carroll County where the Bachelor Run Church was started in Edmon's home. Philip later moved on to Butler County, Iowa, in 1855.

Potter John Miller used the bricks he made in his kiln to construct the first brick house in the area in 1815. Potter John and seven of his children moved across the state to Parke County in 1824, but he returned to the Four Mile about 20 years later. He and his wife, Phoebe, were buried in the Kingery Cemetery in Preble County, Ohio.

Several sons of Abraham Miller (grandsons of Elder Jacob Miller Sr.) moved to northwest Indiana around St. Joseph County.

Daniel Miller moved to Putnam County near Potter John in 1830, then moved on to Monroe County, Iowa, in 1847. Some of his children went with him to Iowa while others remained in Putnam and Parke counties in Indiana.

One of the key factors to all this migration and settlement was the typically large pioneer family. Elder Jacob Miller Sr., for example, was the father of 12 children. Just one of his sons, Abraham, was the father of 15 children and nine of these children also raised large families. Another son of Elder Jacob, Aaron, had a family of 11 children. At the time of his death in 1816, Elder Jacob Miller numbered his grandchildren by the dozen. Many of his descendants would become church leaders throughout Indiana and other states.

Families of eight to 15 children were not unusual on the frontier. Pioneer women often married young, and it was not at all unusual for them to begin having children at age 18 and to have a child every other year after that until their mid-40s. It was not unknown for a mother and her oldest daughters to be pregnant at the same time.

As the children grew up and ventured out on their own, they wanted land of their own just like their parents. As the population of an area increased, land became more and more scarce, so it was quite natural for them to look farther and farther west. A common event was the migration of whole sets of sisters and brothers at the same time with one or two siblings, often the youngest, left behind to care for aging parents and take over the family homestead.

It was just such a migration that led to the founding of a church near New Paris in southern Elkhart County in 1837. Six Whitehead brothers and three sisters moved to the area from Montgomery County, Ohio. They included brothers Samuel, Peter, Adam, Valentine, John, and Lewis, with sisters Esther Stutzman, Mary Conrad, and Margaret Lentz. The area they settled west of New Paris was part of the Elkhart (later West Goshen) territory, but it was split off in 1838 to become the Turkey Creek district. When it was decided to build a church in 1854, two brothers donated land for the church, a third donated timber, and a fourth donated land across the road from the church for a cemetery. The building they constructed now forms the basis of the Maple Grove Church of the Brethren and is the oldest church building still in use in the Northern Indiana District. Many of the Whiteheads and their descendants are buried in the cemetery across the road from the church.

The pattern of settlement described at Four Mile was typical of other Dunkard migrations into Indiana as the state was settled from south to north. The Dunkards were among the most active groups in the settlement of Indiana, and some historians have indicated that at one time one of every seven Indiana residents was a Dunkard. They not only established settlements, but also established churches based on their special religious understanding and faith that continue to be some of the strongest and most active in the entire denomination.

4

The Lost Dunkards

What happened to the Dunkards in southern Indiana?

Looking at a map today, the New Hope Church of the Brethren near Seymour is the southernmost congregation in the state. Next in line are the new Christ Our Shepherd congregation at Greenwood on the south side of Indianapolis and the Four Mile Church, the oldest congregation in the state, southeast of Richmond.

In the early 1800s, however, there were several active Dunkard groups all the way from the Bedford area to the Ohio River. What became of these early Brethren? The answer can be found in looking at where these early settlers originated and the attitudes and associations they brought with them when they crossed the Ohio River into Indiana.

The Brethren who located in Kentucky, Illinois, and southern Indiana were primarily of southern background and outlook. These "Far Western Brethren" often had few ties to the Annual Meeting Brethren in the East and were often not in harmony with Annual Meeting. This was the exact opposite of the Brethren who settled central and northern Indiana, and who came primarily from Ohio, although many were originally from Virginia and could be considered to have a southern background.

Between 1790 and 1800, a group of Brethren in North and South Carolina began openly preaching a doctrine known as universalism or final restoration, which is the belief that God will one day restore all souls from hell. Alexander Mack, himself, believed in a form of universalism. He wrote that he could not find the idea of eternal damnation sustained by the scriptures, and that all people would someday be united with God. However, Mack also believed that those united with God after death would never attain the high state of those who chose to follow Christ in life.

Ardent universalists went much farther than Mack. Some even suggested there is no hell except that devised in the minds of men.

David Martin, the most influential Dunkard minister in the South, became the leader of the universalist faction in South Carolina. He eventually led nearly all the Brethren in that state into universalism, ending their identification with the denomination.

In 1798, a minister from North Carolina was expelled by Annual Meeting for openly preaching universalism. The Annual Meeting minutes identify this man only as Brother John H. Other sources identify him as John Ham, although irrefutable identification may never be possible.

Many of those who pioneered the settlement of Kentucky came from the area of North Carolina where Ham was active. In fact, some historians have reasoned that one of the driving forces behind the westward movement was because some ministers wanted to get away from the discipline and doctrine with which they were confronted in the East. Whatever the reasons, many of the Kentucky congregations have been closely identified with the universalist movement in North and South Carolina. Even though these congregations were not always in fellowship with Annual Meeting, they continued their Brethren identity well into the 1800s.

The Kentucky settlers were primarily the Brethren who later pioneered the settlement of Illinois, Missouri, and southern Indiana. As they moved farther into the wilderness, they became even more isolated from the doctrine of Annual Meeting. The differences continued to grow and included differences in the practices of love feast and, eventually, baptism. By the time the Brethren moved into southern Indiana, they already had a considerable record of ignoring the official pronouncements of Annual Meeting and going their own way.

The Early Leaders

The loss of the Dunkards in southern Indiana cannot be assigned to a single place and time. It was a gradual process that occurred over several years. However, there are certain events and specific people that stand out.

One of the first of these events was a meeting held in Muhlenberg County, Kentucky, concerning some difficulties with the churches in that region and a Dunkard minister named Adam Hostetler. The most likely date for this meeting seems to be 1820, although some sources say

1816. Attending were two elders from the East plus George Wolfe Jr. and James Hendricks. Wolfe, whose family migration from Pennsylvania to Kentucky was described in an earlier chapter, had by this time pioneered the settlement of Illinois. He had, in fact, been ordained in 1814 by Adam Hostetler and either Peter Hon (Hawn, Hahn) or Joseph Rowland. Hendricks was from Cape Girardeau County, Missouri. He was the son of the man who baptized Wolfe, and Wolfe had ordained James in 1818.

Although there is evidence Hostetler was associated with universalism, this does not seem to be the primary issue of the meeting in Kentucky. Wolfe and Hendricks both, for at least some period in their ministry, were also advocates of universalist ideas.

Wolfe, writing a number of years later, identified differences in feet washing as a major issue which was not resolved. He also noted that Hostetler and his followers were excommunicated the following year in Ohio.

Abraham Cassel, writing in 1886, also focused on feet washing during love feast as the primary issue at the Kentucky meeting. The Annual Meeting Brethren advocated a method in which one person would wash the feet of several people in a row while another person followed behind to dry. The towel and basin were then turned over to another pair who would serve several more people. This method became known as dual mode. The Far Western Brethren, however, practiced single mode in which one person both washed and dried the feet of one person, then turned the towel and basin over to the next person in line.

There was also disagreement over the order of the service. The Far Western Brethren first ate a fellowship meal, then washed feet, and finally observed the bread and the cup. Annual Meeting Brethren insisted that washing feet must come before the fellowship meal.

Cassel wrote that there were seven issues discussed in all at the Muhlenberg meeting. However, the only additional issue he specifically identified was slavery.

While Wolfe wrote that Hostetler was excommunicated the following year (probably 1821) in Ohio, Cassel wrote that a committee of 12 elders met at Hostetler's home in Shelby County, Kentucky, in 1821, and it was at this meeting that Hostetler and his group were disfellowshipped. Cassel said the charges included nonconformity to the traditional garb of the Brethren, being too worldly, and being too "zealous in religious excitements." He placed the number of people lost in this process at about 1,500, although that number was later disputed as being too high by other Brethren writers.

David Eller, in his thesis *The Brethren in the Western Ohio Valley,*

1790-1850, writes that he does not believe that either universalism or feet washing was the central issue in this split. Evidence which backs this idea includes the fact that universalism and the mode of washing feet continued to be issues for the eastern and western factions for many years after the Kentucky schism. Wolfe, himself, was in the thick of many of these debates. The mode of feet washing, in particular, was a hotly debated issue at Annual Meetings for many years. Although single mode came to be the dominant practice by the late 1800s, it was not adopted as an official position of the church until the early 20th century.

Eller believes Cassel may have identified the real reason for the Kentucky split when he wrote about "religious excitements." This is probably a reference to a strong revivalism movement which was occurring on the frontier at that time. Frontier preachers began holding revival meetings shortly after 1800, but the practice gained real momentum with the great earthquake on the New Madrid Fault in 1811.

J.H. Moore in *Some Brethren Pathfinders* wrote that the first steamboat (the New Orleans) to ply the Ohio River was launched at Pittsburgh in early December 1811. Word of the amazing "fire boat" spread rapidly throughout the Ohio Valley, and large crowds turned out to see it pass by belching a great cloud of black smoke and white steam. Just as the hissing, fire-breathing monster was making its way into the waters of the Mississippi River on Dec. 18, the largest earthquake ever recorded east of the Rocky Mountains struck. Near Cairo, Ill., a huge lake 60 miles long and up to 30 miles wide was created as the earth sank, taking with it a large virgin forest.

For three days, the earth trembled, and the tremors were felt all through the Ohio Valley across southern Indiana and even into Ohio. Aftershocks were reported for another six months.

Those of a superstitious nature were convinced that the great quake was caused by the fire boat, either through some natural calamity or because it had made God angry.

Revivalist preachers were quick to take advantage of the situation and took up the cry that the world would soon end. They advised, often by shouting at the top of their lungs, that every man, woman, and child needed to get right with God and do it in a hurry. Converts by the hundred were made in this fashion, often accompanied by frenzied outpourings of emotion.

As the months passed, the immediate threat seemed to diminish, but the popularity of revivalism did not. Moore even indicates that Wolfe and his brother, Jacob, were baptized by a Methodist revival preacher about 1812 in Illinois. They soon sent for a Dunkard minister from Kentucky. That man was John Hendricks (father of George Hendricks) who baptized the Wolfe brothers and several others in Illinois.

Frontier revivalism, however, was frowned upon by the Dunkards in the East and could well have been at the heart of the ouster of Adam Hostetler and his group in Kentucky. The position of the eastern Brethren was that baptism should be undertaken only after serious thought and prayer and not as the result of an outpouring of emotion at a revival meeting.

The Kentucky-Indiana Association

At about the same time the Hostetler group was disfellowshipped (and possibly in response to this action), congregations on both sides of the Ohio River joined together in a Kentucky-Indiana Association (sometimes known as the Hostetler Brethren). Several Indiana congregations were part of this group including White River (later known as Old Union) in Lawrence County, Lost River (later known as Liberty) in Orange County, Bethel in Harrison County, and Olive Branch in Clark County. There may have been as many as 15 congregations in Indiana and Kentucky which were part of the association.

Another minister closely associated with Hostetler during this period was Peter Hon. Hon and Abraham Kern of the White River Church began preaching and practicing single-immersion baptism, similar to the Baptists in the same area. This was apparently not immediately accepted within the Kentucky-Indiana Association, and there was much controversy over the issue. By 1826, however, baptism by single immersion had become the dominant practice of most of the churches in the association.

During this same period, Joseph Hostetler, Adam's nephew, became one of the most influential of the Dunkard ministers in the association. Joseph was a licensed minister when he moved to Indiana in 1817 or 1818 and was ordained by Adam in 1821 during an annual meeting of the association. He was known as "the boy preacher" and was reputedly one of the most persuasive speakers to ever stand before a Dunkard crowd.

Sometime prior to 1825, Joseph came into contact with the thinking of Alexander Campbell through Campbell's monthly *Christian Baptist,* which was published from 1823 to 1829. Campbell and his followers (known as Campbellites) were early members of what came to be known as the Restoration movement. They emphasized a primitive, New Testament form of Christianity and rejected denominational names. They fervently supported the independence and authority of local congregations and said higher church organizations should operate only in an advisory capacity.

Hostetler first wrote to Campbell in 1825 identifying himself as a member of a church called "German Baptists, sometimes Dunkards."

The letter questioned Campbell on several points. Campbell printed both Hostetler's letter and his own reply in the *Christian Baptist.*

In the spring of 1826, Hostetler publicly announced he would preach on primitive Christianity at Orleans in Orange County, Indiana. Madison Evans in *Biographical Sketches of the Pioneer Preachers of Indiana* reports Hostetler spoke for 90 minutes to a crowd numbering up to 1,000, including a number of Dunkard ministers. There was no doubt his message put him firmly in the camp of Campbell and the Restorationists.

While many in the crowd that day were convinced, especially on the point of discarding denominational names, a number of the ministers were not. Hostetler soon learned that he would be facing serious charges at the next meeting of the Kentucky-Indiana Association. He quickly launched into a tour of every congregation in the association to personally explain his beliefs.

The association meeting of 1826 was held in Nicholas County, Kentucky, at the Somerset Creek (East Union) Church. Hostetler was so eloquent in defending himself that not only were all charges against him dropped, but he was asked to be the main speaker at the 1827 annual meeting.

The 1827 meeting was attended by John Wright and his brother, Peter, of Washington County, Indiana. They were leaders of a small group of free will Baptist churches in that area. John Wright issued a plea for unity between the two groups. Hostetler and the Brethren agreed and the new group agreed to call themselves "Christians." Wright also suggested they seek a merger with the New Light Christians, and he was authorized to contact them. The New Lights came from various backgrounds, but one major name connected with a group of New Light churches in Kentucky was Barton Stone. Stone's movement began with an event known as the Great Kentucky Revival of 1800 which was held at Cane Ridge Presbyterian Church in Bourbon County, Kentucky, where Stone was pastor. He and his followers (Stonites) left the Presbytery in 1804 and continued as Christian or New Light churches. They referred to the Bible as their only rule of faith and practice.

A unity meeting was held in July 1828 near Edinburgh in Bartholomew County, Indiana. Some sources indicate this meeting was attended by Dunkards, Baptists, and New Lights. Other sources cast doubt on this assertion. It is almost impossible to know since no minutes were kept due to the fear of giving the appearance of forming a new denomination.

Regardless of who attended the meeting and what agreements were made, it is known that the 1827 meeting of the Kentucky-Indiana Association was the last ever held. Joseph Hostetler and Hon, along with

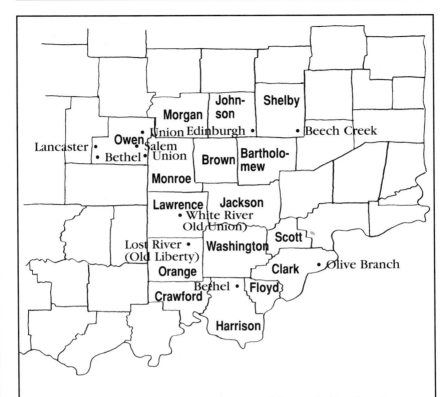

This map shows the locations of some of the early Dunkard congregations in southern Indiana prior to 1840. These congregations can be positively identified as having a Dunkard origin, and there may have been others. The map was originally drawn by David B. Eller. Additional congregations have been added through research by Ferne Baldwin.

a few others, traveled extensively throughout Indiana, Kentucky, and Ohio during the next few years urging congregations in those areas to become part of the Restoration movement and change their identity to Christian. Members of churches who were convinced by Hon even, for a time, were referred to as "Honites."

All of this was going on against a background of other mergers of independent groups, including those led by Alexander Campbell and Barton Stone in 1832. These mergers led to the formation of a group which came to be known as the Disciples of Christ. In spite of their strong feelings against denominationalism, the leaders of the movement ended up creating a new denomination.

The change of the southern Indiana congregations from Dunkard to Disciples occurred over a period of about 10 years beginning in the late 1820s. It was complete by 1839 when the Disciples of Christ held their first state convention in Indianapolis. Barton Stone was the featured speaker at the event which was attended by many former Dunkards. Among the churches listed as participating in this event were Lost River and White River. Joseph Hostetler, Peter Hon, and Abraham Kern all became influential leaders for the Disciples of Christ (known as the Christian Church since 1968).

The Dunkards in southern Indiana had ceased to exist.

5

Life In The Early Church

Life in the Indiana wilderness was harsh and beautiful at the same time—endlessly demanding and endlessly freeing. Making sure you and your family were protected from the elements and had enough to eat was paramount and depended upon your wits and skills with the plow, the fishing line, the hunting rifle, and the ax, and knowledge of the beasts and plants of the woods. There was little time for anything except activities that made survival possible. It is important to note that among the things the early Dunkard pioneers considered necessary for survival was their special brand of the Christian faith.

The Dunkards in Indiana were usually at the very leading edge of settlement. They were often among the first white settlers in a new territory. Most of these very early pioneers moved as small groups of families. Individual families came later and often intentionally moved to an area where the Dunkards had already established themselves.

Like other Indiana pioneers, the Dunkards devoted the first few weeks and months in the wilderness primarily to their need for food and shelter. But they also believed strongly in the necessity of taking time to worship their God. This quickly led to groups of people meeting in each other's homes on a regular basis to read the Bible, pray, and sing hymns.

Preaching depended upon the availability of an ordained minister or elder. In some communities, like Four Mile in Union County, this happened on an irregular basis. From 1804 until the church was organized in 1809, formal preaching only occurred when men like Elder

Jacob Miller Sr. made trips into the wilderness from Ohio. It was only later that they had their own ministers who supplied regular preaching.

Other Brethren communities were lucky enough to have a minister or an elder in their midst. This was true in Elkhart County where Elder Daniel Cripe was among the first settlers in 1829.

Regardless of their circumstances, Dunkard settlers were quick to establish regular Sunday gatherings. These early meetings were always in someone's home or barn because there were no meeting houses. As circumstances improved, some of the wealthier settlers actually designed their homes to accommodate such gatherings. Movable walls were part of the building plans so that two or more rooms could be joined.

Going to Sunday meeting became a ritual. On foot, on horseback, and by wagon, they traveled over trails through thick stands of woods, across prairies, and through streams and swamps on journeys that sometimes took several hours and often began before dawn. Sometimes an extra stop would be made to give a ride to neighbors who did not have horses and a wagon.

Arriving at the designated home, they were warmly greeted by those who had already arrived. Horses were tended and food which had been brought was temporarily stored.

Seating for men and women was separate, with men on the right and women on the left. In some congregations, the front bench was reserved for the deacons; in others, it was reserved for children who were old enough to be seated by themselves. The deacons were usually responsible for maintaining discipline among the children seated on this bench. There was often a pitcher of water nearby for restless and thirsty youngsters. If all else failed, a deacon might use a long stick to administer a sharp rap to the back of the head.

The service usually began with singing. Since there were few if any hymn books, a deacon often led hymns by "lining" them—singing a phrase or a few words at a time which were then repeated by the rest of the people. The earliest hymn books were printed in German and contained only words and the name of a hymn tune. Later versions used shaped notes.

The practice of lining hymns went on for many years; in some churches, well into the 20th century. Willis Maugans, a long-time pastor at Pipe Creek Church, wrote about the practice in a congregational history he compiled in 1986. "Usually one minister would line, another lead the tune, and the congregation would sing each line as it was read to them. Grandma (Barbara) Mills told of one time the minister who was to line the hymn forgot his glasses, had started the first line and discovered his dilemma. Looking out the window, he saw his son coming late to service and said, 'Across the field comes my son John, I hope he has my specks along,' and they sang it. Astonished at this, he said, 'I didn't mean to sing at all, I think the devil's in you all,' and they sang it."

Most Dunkards knelt during prayers led by deacons and ministers. This practice could be quite uncomfortable, particularly during the prayer of a long-winded brother. Older members were sometimes excused from kneeling when they were physically unable.

The sermon (delivered in German) was given by an elder or minister and was always based on scripture. It was not unusual for such an oration to last an hour or more. The sermon was followed by "exhorting" from other ministers in the group or the deacons. Each one elaborated on the ideas presented in the sermon as he felt led by the Holy Spirit. The net effect was like listening to three or four sermons in a row.

After two or three hours, the meeting generally ended with more singing and a final prayer.

The women then adjourned to prepare the noon meal while children played and the men gathered to talk. The food was blessed by the elder or minister and the group enjoyed what, for many, was the most substantial meal of the week.

Most families timed their departure carefully so they could arrive home by nightfall. Travel at any time was difficult but was especially hazardous in the dark. An unseen hole or rut could snap a wagon axle and strand an entire family in the woods overnight.

Sunday gatherings could not always be held every week due to the difficulty of travel. This was especially true during the winter months. But the early Dunkards made every effort to meet as often as possible. It was a way to strengthen their sense of community as well as a way to strengthen their faith.

The First Meeting Houses

Within a few years the members of the first Indiana churches felt the need to construct meeting houses for their Sunday services. Some were opposed for several reasons. They were afraid a meeting house would lead to a loss of the sense of community that was developed by meeting in homes. There was also some fear that a meeting house would lead to unseemly pride. Meeting houses were common in the East, however, and those in favor inevitably won out.

The early German Baptist Brethren did not speak of building a church. They were building a meeting house. And that is precisely what these buildings were.

Most were simple, wood frame buildings built on a field stone foundation, exactly like most barns. Huge framing timbers were cut and shaped by hand from the virgin stands of timber widely available

throughout the state. Some of these monstrous beams are still supporting church buildings in use today. A classic example is the Howard
Church of the Brethren west of Kokomo. Originally built in 1865, the
underlying framework is made of hand-hewn beams measuring a foot
square. The crossbeams are 40 feet long and the beams running the
length of the building are 60 feet long.

Once the frame was in place, the entire exterior was covered by
sawn boards. The roof was finished with wooden shingles, and plain
windows were cut into the sides. Most of the earliest churches were
built with two entrances: one for women and one for men. The entire
building was finished off with a coat of whitewash.

An important element for any meeting house was a place to tether
horses. Most congregations initially installed hitching posts or rails.
Some later built sheds or barns where the teams could be sheltered.

The interior was just as plain as the outside. There was only one,
large room. Pegs sticking out of horizontal boards often lined the back
and sides of the room where members could hang their coats, shawls,
bonnets, and hats. Light was furnished by candles or kerosene lamps.
Heat was supplied by one or two wood stoves. Seating yourself just the
right distance from a wood stove so you were neither too hot nor too
cold became a refined art. Two rows of backless benches were set up,
and a table was placed at one end of the room on the same level as the
benches. The elder, ministers, or deacons were seated around this table
during worship services. In some churches, this table was placed
between the two entrances. This provided considerable incentive for
people not to be late because they had to enter in front of the entire
church.

Typical of the self-reliant nature of these early settlers, most of the
material for the construction of a meeting house came from the members. The land itself was usually donated or deeded for a token amount
of money. Stones for the foundation were plentiful in the surrounding
fields. Trees to supply the beams and boards came from the woods of
one or more members. About the only items which had to be purchased
were mortar for the stone foundation, nails, and windows.

All of the labor was donated. Most men had at least rudimentary
carpentry skills, and community building projects were a way of life.
Construction of a meeting house was not unlike building a barn. Church
members gathered at the building site, and the women cooked while
the men worked. Boys helped their fathers wherever they could, while
girls were included in preparing the food. It was a time for building
personal relationships as well as a meeting house.

Most of the early churches could comfortably seat about 50 to 100
people. Because of their large territories, often covering more than one

county, it was not unusual for the membership to number 200 to 300. This may seem incongruous until the difficulty of travel is taken into account. Many members lived far enough away from these early meeting houses that they could only make it to Sunday meeting once every few weeks or even months. About the only time the entire congregation gathered was at love feast and communion once or twice a year, and these services were generally held in large barns, not at the meeting house. As a result, there were often several meetings going on in different locations every Sunday: one was at the meeting house, and one or more smaller gatherings at homes throughout the territory.

This difficulty with travel is illustrated well in a story written by Geroby Stump as part of the 125th anniversary at Pine Creek in 1979. "How well I remember when John Nisely and John Hoover came to our place one Saturday to be at the meeting over Sunday. They walked from Union about 14 miles away. They walked back home on Monday. The roads were rough at that time. I remember them saying a man was on his way to Plymouth. He caught up with a man who was driving a team hitched to a wagon. The man said he should get on and ride. The man who was walking said, 'No, I am in a hurry,' and went on around."

Worship in a meeting house changed little from the first meetings held in homes. The location may have changed, but the attitudes of reverence, simplicity, and humility remained.

Baptism

Many of the early churches were located near rivers, streams, and creeks. A list of church names shows how true this was: Bear Creek, Cedar Creek, Loon Creek, Lower Deer Creek, Pike Creek, Pine Creek, Pipe Creek, Spring Creek, Sugar Creek, Turkey Creek, Upper Fall Creek, Yellow Creek, and others.

This affinity for water had several roots. One was a need in the very early churches for a ready supply of fresh water. But one of the primary reasons was for baptism.

Baptism for believers is at the very heart of who the Brethren are—the bedrock of their faith foundation. This tradition stems from the very beginning of the Brethren in Schwarzenau, Germany.

The traditional Brethren baptism ordinance has remained basically the same throughout the church's history. The believer enters the water with a minister and kneels. The minister asks the believer three questions. Although the wording may vary slightly, they are always similar to the following:

> *Do you believe Jesus is God's Son, and do you receive and trust*
> *him as your Savior and Lord?*
> *Do you turn away from all sin, and will you endeavor by God's*

May 21.
Pipe creek   1869
curch

Miame county Indiand
this is to sertify our sister Westhas
mouved from us and She is amember
of the Jermanbabtist church and is
in full fellowship as fare as we no
and we hope whane ever these fue
tines will be handed that you will
receve hur as euch dand bild hur up in ehrist
and may the grass of god be with
all the true isreal of god in
~~Jeses~~ Jaeses Crist and may the
communian of the holey gost be
with ous all amen } sined in behalf of
the church   Abraham Shepler
                    godlope Heller
                    Phillip Earebaugh
                    Daniel Bowser
Bengemin Kinsey } John E cripe
                 Jonathan Shhepler
              David R Shiveley
              David B Shiveley

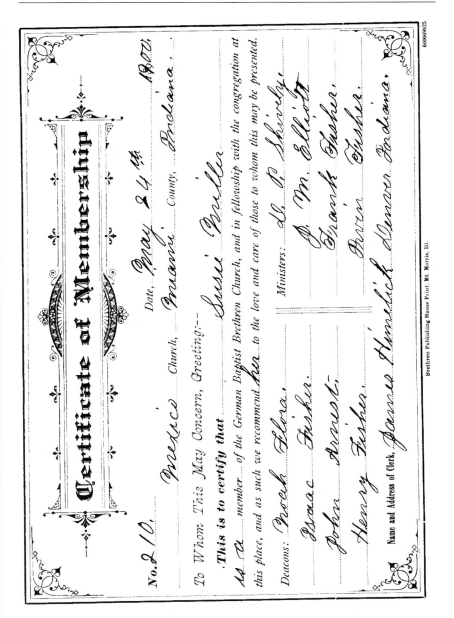

The membership certificate on the page at left is from the Pipe Creek congregation and is dated May 21, 1869. By 1900, when the membership certificate on this page was used, the church at Mexico was using pre-printed forms. This particular form was printed at the Brethren Publishing House in Mt. Morris, Ill.

grace to live according to the example and teachings of Jesus Christ?

Will you be loyal to the church by upholding her by your prayers and presence, your substance and service?

After answering these questions, the believer is then completely immersed three times (in the name of the Father, Son, and Holy Spirit) by bowing forward. The minister then lays hands on the believer's head and prays.

The one major change in baptism from the early Indiana Brethren is the location. Baptism in the 1800s was nearly always held in a stream. This was true regardless of the time of year, and there are many stories about the deacons chopping through ice to make a place for the baptism to be held.

In many congregations, it was important to locate the meeting house near a stream for this reason alone. Salamonie, for example, was originally located near the banks of the Salamonie River. On the day of a baptism, the entire congregation trekked to the river bank located behind the church to witness the service. In cold weather, those who participated in the baptism were quickly wrapped in horse blankets and taken inside the church building where they changed into dry clothes and sat beside the wood stoves to warm up.

In the late 1800s, several congregations began to use horse tanks for baptisms as an intermediate step to installing indoor baptistries. Many people felt this was a terrible mistake; that the only true baptism was held in flowing water.

Love Feast and Communion

For the early Brethren in Indiana, love feast and communion was much more than the observance of a religious rite—it was a time of renewal and rededication to their baptismal vows and to the church.

In most congregations love feast was held in late summer or early fall. Only a few held the observance twice a year, with the second one coming in the spring.

The observance was preceded by the annual visit. Initially handled by the ministers, the duties for this process were quickly expanded to the deacons as membership grew. This was especially true in the earliest years when travel was extremely difficult.

Visitors were dispatched in teams of two who usually traveled on horseback, sometimes on foot, to the homes of members they had been assigned. The reason for these visits was to be sure there was harmony within the church before love feast and communion was celebrated.

Three questions were always asked. They were variations of the following:

Are you still in the faith of the gospel as you declared when you were baptized?

Are you, as far as you know, in peace and union with the church?

Will you still labor with the Brethren for an increase of holiness, both in yourself and others?

If it was discovered there was difficulty between members, or between members and the rest of the church, the ministers and deacons moved as quickly as possible to resolve the conflict. This sometimes resulted in a rupture and the loss of a member. More often, however, it served as a healing process that did not allow old wounds to fester and cause even more harm months or years later.

In some congregations, those who were being visited made it a point to make a special gift to the church beyond their usual support.

Also during the annual visit, each member was given an opportunity to present suggestions or concerns to be taken before a council meeting. This meeting was usually held between the conclusion of the annual visit and the onset of love feast and communion. It often turned out to be the liveliest council meeting of the year because of the many issues raised during the annual visit.

Organizational details for love feast were also worked out at this meeting, including how much meat and bread were needed and how much grain should be supplied for the many horses which needed to be quartered and fed. Meat was usually purchased, while the grain and bread (often made by the wives of deacons) were often donated. Old council minutes from many churches list the actual quantities of these items for each love feast. A typical example is from the Bethel Church at Milford. For a love feast held in November 1897, 275 pounds of beef were ordered along with nine pounds of butter and three gallons of apple butter. Each member was expected to bring three loaves of bread. Six bushels of corn were donated for the horses.

The observance of love feast and communion was often the largest gathering of the church all year. This was the one service that all members did their best to attend, no matter how difficult travel was.

The location was announced several weeks in advance and word was spread during the annual visit. For nearly all churches founded prior to about 1875, these services were universally held in the barn of a member for a couple of reasons: many congregations had no meeting house, so meeting at a member's home was already standard procedure; even if the congregation had a meeting house, it was seldom large enough to handle the large crowd that gathered for this service.

In selecting a location, consideration was given to the size of the barn available and its location. It was generally located somewhere in the middle of the congregation's territory to make it as easy as possible for the most members to attend.

Hosting such a gathering could entail considerable expense and sacrifice for a family. Nevertheless, there was no shortage of volunteers because it was considered a great honor to be chosen. Traditional Brethren humility, however, limited any prideful displays.

The love feast and communion gathering was at least a two-day affair. Families often left home on Thursday or Friday to make it to the site by Saturday morning. They usually carried with them enough food to feed the family for several days as well as feed for the horses and bedding.

Upon arrival, the boys were put in charge of tending the teams of horses while their fathers gathered to cut and split wood needed for cooking. The women and girls immediately began the cooking chores. Beef or mutton for the communion meal was cooked in large iron kettles over outdoor fires.

After enough wood had been laid in, the men began preparing the barn to handle the service. The main floor was cleared and swept. Rude tables were built by laying planks on sawbucks. Seating was supplied by hay bales or by laying planks on low blocks of wood or whatever else might be handy. A few congregations limited participation to only men, but most included women although seating was segregated. At times, women were consigned to a place off to the side. A separate set of tables was often set up nearby, sometimes just outside the barn, for those who were not members, primarily younger family members. They participated in the fellowship meal, but could only observe the remainder of the service.

In later years, the services were moved to the meeting houses. At Pipe Creek, for example, the first love feasts were held at the church after a brick building was constructed in 1871. Benches in the church were specially built so the backs could be flipped to a horizontal position to form tables.

Utensils were usually made of wood or tin—plates, bowls, cups, and spoons. In a few cases, the plates and bowls were made of granite. A cup of water and a slice of bread were set out at each place. Bowls of hot beef and broth were the last things to be set on the tables. This was often accomplished with a "soup line," which operated the same way as a bucket brigade at a fire. A line of people was formed, each two or three steps apart, and the bowls were passed from hand to hand. It was a quick and efficient way to quickly distribute the hot dishes and is still used in some congregations today.

At the appointed hour on Saturday evening, the brothers and sisters gathered at the tables illuminated by the flickering light of candles. A hymn often opened the service, a short sermon was given, and scripture was read.

The first action of the participants was washing feet. In the early days of the church in Indiana, most congregations followed the lead of the Annual Meeting Brethren in the East by observing dual mode. This called for a minister or deacon to wash the feet of several members. This man was followed by another minister or deacon who dried the feet. The feet of several members would be washed before the duties of washing and drying were transferred to two other people. This was continued until the feet of all members present were washed. Hymns were sung while the ritual was completed.

This was in contrast to most of the Far Western Brethren, particularly in Illinois, who practiced single mode, which is the method observed throughout the denomination today. In this practice, a single member washes and dries the feet of another. The two members then exchange a handshake and kiss of holy fellowship before the towel is transferred to the next member who continues the footwashing ritual.

The debate over which method (single mode or dual mode) was proper raged for many years. Church periodicals from the middle 1800s were often filled with emotional letters espousing the "correct" practice. The denomination finally settled on single mode in the 1880s. One of the influential facts which helped settle this debate was that the original congregation at Germantown, Pa., observed single mode.

Following the footwashing ritual, a fellowship meal was shared. This was usually bread which was dipped in the beef and broth soup. In some cases, mutton was used instead of beef.

Mutton was used at the first love feast and communion observed by the Elkhart (West Goshen) congregation in 1830. There was no beef to be had in the wilderness of Elkhart County when Elder Daniel Cripe gathered the 20 members of his fledgling church for the first love feast held in northern Indiana. The only animal large enough to feed everyone was the only ewe lamb owned by Elder Cripe, and he didn't hesitate to donate it for the service. This was a tremendous sacrifice for a settler trying to establish a new farm on the Elkhart Prairie.

Communion was observed once the fellowship meal was completed. This part of the service was subject to a number of local variations, but remained basically the same from place to place. Scripture was read and prayers were said followed by the breaking of unleavened bread with the words, "This bread which we break is the communion of the body of Christ."

The form of the bread often varied, but was always unleavened. In some places, it took the form of a long strip from which small pieces were broken as it passed from hand to hand. In other places, it was a short piece which was broken in half by two communicants. Some churches pierced the bread with a three-tined fork to represent the Trinity, while others pierced it with a five-tined fork to represent the piercing of Jesus' hands, feet, and side.

It may be a surprise that fermented wine was used in nearly all congregations in Indiana through most of the 1800s, as it was throughout the denomination. This, too, was subject to local variations. After scripture and prayer, the communicants repeated, "The cup of the New Testament is the communion of the blood of Christ." In most early services, a single cup was then passed from hand to hand.

The practice of using fermented wine continued until the temperance movement gained prominence in the 1870s. Annual Conference in 1875 discussed using unfermented grape juice instead of wine, but left the decision up to local congregations. The rule of using unfermented grape juice was finally adopted by Annual Conference in 1895.

Women were usually allowed to participate in communion, but often were not allowed to break bread with others or pass the cup. In these cases, a deacon handed each sister a piece of bread and the cup.

Love feast and communion ended with the singing of a hymn, and those present then filed out quietly. Everyone then pitched in to clean up.

It was not unusual to find several hundred people gathered for such a service. This presented some logistical problems in finding a place for everyone to sleep. Most people from a distance brought their own straw tick mattresses. Women and children were given the best accommodations in houses whenever possible. Many others slept in haylofts and other parts of the barn. Some slept in or under their wagons. When services were moved to church buildings, many of these buildings were designed with lofts where people could sleep.

Sunday morning included a big breakfast followed by a joyous worship service and a big noon fellowship meal. The members then took their leave, knowing they might not see some of those present until the next year.

The gathering of such a large crowd often created quite a sensation in a local community where such gatherings were unusual, to say the least. Geroby Stump of Pine Creek recalled this scene from his boyhood: "People used to come from Elkhart County, and from Union west of Plymouth. They came in big wagon loads. After the stables were full of horses, they would tie the horses to the wagons. There was maybe one acre full of teams."

Records at Pine Creek show attendance at communion services prior to 1900 ranged from 300 to 420. Between 400 and 500 pounds of beef were purchased each year.

It was common for a group of 300 Brethren to find themselves being observed by an even larger crowd of spectators. The Brethren did not seem to mind this and often used it as an opportunity for evangelism. However, there were, at times, a few people in the crowd intent on causing trouble. Hecklers sometimes tried to disrupt the service.

In some places, it became common for the Brethren to hire one or two men from outside the congregation to maintain order. At Salamonie, the sheriff was called in. In the 1880s, the Killbuck congregation (now Antioch) hired a young Methodist man named John Sherman Alldredge to perform this service. He later married a Brethren girl, joined the church, and became a prominent minister and state legislator in the early 1900s.

The problem was slightly different for other congregations. Such a large gathering of people, many of whom were far away from their homes, led some entrepreneurs to set up stands to sell food and almost anything else that could be bartered. In at least one case, an enterprising neighbor set up makeshift bleachers and sold seats. Most congregations quickly established rules which prohibited setting up these profit-making operations on church property, but there was little they could do about stands set up on adjoining land. They did what they could, however, to keep the crowd of observers from becoming so raucous they disrupted the service.

Anointing

The anointing service is the ordinance of the church which has changed least since it was brought to Indiana by the early Brethren settlers. It is often a very private service for a person in emotional or physical difficulty, or for people dedicating themselves to a specific church-related task. Those attending are frequently limited to the person being anointed, family members or close friends, a minister, and a deacon.

Following the New Testament tradition of anointing with oil, the service is conducted by a minister and a deacon who place a few drops of oil (usually olive oil) on the forehead of the person being anointed. Some ministers place the oil in the form of a cross in the name of the Father, Son, and Holy Spirit. Hands are then laid upon the head of the person being anointed and prayers are said.

Members of the early Indiana church conducted this service in a form nearly identical with that found today. The one major difference is that members of the church in the 1800s often limited requests for this service to cases of dire need due to the lack of communications and difficult travel conditions.

Unless the request for the service was made at a Sunday worship gathering, a family member had to travel on foot or horseback to the nearest minister or deacon. This was sometimes a considerable distance and might take up to a full day or more, especially during bad weather. The minister and deacon then had to make the same trip to the family's home where the service was conducted.

Although the service is a very serious one, many ministers and deacons have found themselves conducting it in less than ideal conditions. Joe Balsbaugh, a deacon at the Mexico church, wrote the following account of a service in which he assisted:

"The lady being anointed was in bed, with her husband standing at the foot of the bed, and my wife seated nearby. Another party in this service was the lady's dog, named Joe, who was under her bed. Just as I started to pour a few drops of oil into the pastor's hand, a long, rough growl came from Joe under the bed, and I jerked, pouring much more than a few drops of oil. The husband commanded, 'Joe, keep still! Shut up and get back under the bed!' Joe continued to growl periodically, poking his head out from under the bed and showing his teeth, while the husband scolded the dog throughout the service.

"James says, 'The prayer of a good person has a powerful effect.' One may wonder how powerful our prayers were as we prayed with one eye on Joe and the other eye directed toward God."

The difficulty of travel in the early church often meant that anointing was conducted only at a time when a person's life was in danger from illness or injury. The anointing service itself came to be widely viewed as appropriate only in these circumstances, a view which carried over into most of the 20th century. It has only been in the last few years that an emphasis has been placed on using the service in other situations as it was originally practiced by the Brethren founders.

Weddings and Funerals

Weddings and funerals were always held in homes in the early years. This custom prevailed even after many congregations had built meeting houses.

A wedding was a time for family and friends to gather to celebrate a new beginning. Since early Dunkards tended to exist in closed, German-speaking communities, a marriage often meant bringing together two families who had known each other through the church for many years. It was as close as German Baptist Brethren came to holding a church-sanctioned party, although there was certainly no dancing.

Long after congregations began to build meeting houses, weddings continued to be held in homes. The trend toward using churches as the setting occurred gradually over a period of many years. Some church weddings were being held as early as the 1870s, while other congregations can date their first large church weddings as late as the 1940s.

Funerals were also a time for families and friends to gather in the home. There were few funeral directors in the Indiana wilderness, so when someone died, friends would come to the home and take over. Usually the women would bathe the body and wrap it in a white sheet in a custom called "laying out" before it was placed in a wooden coffin, usually made of oak, ash, or pine. Toward the middle 1800s, it became more common to dress the body in the best clothes available.

Funeral services were large gatherings, and often presented opportunities for people to see each other who had not been together for many months. Scripture, a sermon, prayer, and hymns were all part of the service.

The coffin was taken to the burial ground carried on the shoulders of pallbearers, if the distance was not great, or by wagon. Mud boats, flat-bottomed wagons with no wheels that slid across the ground when pulled by horses, were used during wet weather.

Further services at the gravesite included scripture, prayer, hymn singing and, sometimes, a short sermon.

Funerals were gradually moved to the church buildings over a period of years, much like weddings. Families also began holding funerals at funeral homes during the 1900s. It has become the custom for most people to visit with the family prior to the funeral and not as many attend the actual funeral service.

Ministers officiated at both weddings and funerals from the very beginning. Most early congregations had more than one minister and the choice of who officiated was left to the family. Occasionally, a minister from another congregation might be brought in if there was a strong tie to the family.

The free ministry was in effect throughout the 1800s and well into the 1900s in many places. Families quite often offered the ministers at least token amounts to help pay for their time and expenses. Some ministers always performed these services without pay, viewing it as part of their service to the church, while others accepted a gratuity. This custom has continued to the present day.

6

Organization
and Discipline

The Church of the Brethren has always been democratic in its organization. Although Alexander Mack was the first person baptized into the new group and became the leader and first minister, the person who baptized him was chosen by lot. Major decisions are almost always made on the basis of a majority of the group. In the early church, decisions were often made by consensus rather than taking a vote.

By the time the Dunkards came to Indiana, the church was organized around three primary structures: Annual Conference (at that time known as Annual Meeting or the Big Meeting), local church councils, and a local church board which usually included elders, ministers, and deacons.

As has been discussed in a previous chapter (Chapter 4, *The Lost Dunkards*), the churches in the northern half of the state were closely affiliated with the Annual Meeting Brethren and recognized its authority. The large questions of doctrine and practice for the entire denomination were answered at this level. The southern Indiana churches were often not in harmony with decisions made at Annual Meeting, particularly over the issue of baptism. These congregations had broken completely with the denomination by about 1840.

The decisions of Annual Meeting were the principles which guided decisions at the congregational level. Elected representatives from each congregation (usually ministers and elders) were eligible to vote at

Annual Meeting, although any member could attend and speak. The same rules apply today, and each year delegates from Indiana churches participate in the decisions made at Annual Conference. The one major difference is that the majority of delegates are now lay people and not ministers.

Indiana has hosted a number of Annual Conferences over the years. The traditionally accepted date of the first Big Meeting hosted by Hoosiers was in 1852 at a farm owned by John Weiland near Baintertown, located between Goshen and New Paris in Elkhart County. The gathering of several thousand people created quite a stir among the local citizens, many of whom visited the site to see what the large crowd was all about.

However, there was a special General Conference held Sept. 23, 1848, at the home of John Koontz in Carroll County near Delphi. A General Conference was not the same as an Annual Meeting because it was limited to one issue, but it did involve representatives from the entire denomination. This particular General Conference was called in an attempt to settle the dispute which had gone on for a number of years between Peter Eyman and Peter Replogle, two elders in the Bachenlor Run congregation. Eyman and George Patton were among those singled out at this meeting for holding unacceptable views.

Although the General Council attempted to reconcile the matter, it was unsuccessful. Eyman, Patton, and others were later disfellow-shipped. They left the church and formed their own denomination which they called the Church of God, also known as the "Oimanites" and New Dunkards.

Indiana again hosted Annual Meeting in 1858 in Carroll County near Flora. Bachelor Run was the host congregation for this conference which was notable for its rainy, wet weather which turned the conference grounds into a sea of mud.

Nettle Creek hosted the next conference in Wayne County west of Hagerstown in 1864. The Civil War was raging which made travel to the conference difficult and even hazardous for many delegates. It was at this conference that Elder John Kline of Virginia served as moderator for the last time. Southern rebels who thought he was a spy assassinated Elder Kline shortly after his return to Virginia from Indiana.

Annual Meeting returned to Indiana just four years later in 1868 when Rock Run served as host southeast of Goshen in Elkhart County. Special arrangements were made to stop trains on the Lake Shore Railroad to allow passengers to get off at the conference site.

North Manchester in Wabash County has served as the site for Annual Conference on several occasions. The first time was in 1878 when Sarah Major created a local sensation by delivering a sermon. A crowd estimated at 15,000 to 20,000 converged on the site to witness the incredible event of a woman speaking to this large gathering of churchgoers.

North Manchester was again the site of Annual Conference in 1888. This conference was made noteworthy by the death of Elder James Quinter who died while giving the closing prayer of the conference. Elder Quinter had been a major force in the church for many years. Tradition says there were several people at the conference from Elder Quinter's home congregation at Huntingdon, Pa. One of them sent a telegraph back home informing them that "the body will arrive" by train at a particular time. However, he neglected to say whose body was arriving, which created quite a stir in Huntingdon.

North Manchester also hosted Annual Conferences in 1900, 1929, 1945, and 1949.

Annual Conference was held once in Muncie in Delaware County in 1893. The meeting site was about one mile outside the city and a special electric railroad line was built for transportation. This was at the height of the natural gas boom in the area, and many who attended the conference came away with tales of the first gas wells they had ever seen.

One of the most famous Annual Conferences in the history of the church was held in 1882 on the farm of John Arnold just north of Milford. It was at this conference that the final break occurred which eventually resulted in the Church of the Brethren and the Brethren Church. A more detailed account of this conference is given in Chapter 7, *The Great Divide.*

Several conferences were also held at Winona Lake in Kosciusko County in the early 1900s including 1910, 1913, 1916, 1919, 1922, 1925, and 1935. Anderson hosted Annual Conference in 1932 and 1939. More recently, Indianapolis has served as an Annual Conference site, including the conference scheduled to be held in 1993.

Local Ministry

For most of its history in Indiana, the Church of the Brethren recognized three degrees of ministry. Because early ministers were never paid for their service to the church, it often required several ministers to take care of a single congregation. This was especially true when the territory was spread over a wide area.

The first degree of ministry was considered a time of testing to determine if a person was suited to the task. A first-degree minister could preach and lead worship services. He could not on his own, however, legally perform marriages or conduct a funeral service, although he could assist in the presence of a second- or third-degree minister. This was how most people entered the ministry. It was equivalent to being licensed in the present-day church.

Each congregation was responsible for securing its own ministerial leadership. When a need for a minister was felt, the congregation called in one or two elders, often from outside the church territory, to conduct a special council meeting. These meetings took various forms, but a typical session often began with prayer followed by the reading of scripture. A favorite was I Timothy 3:1-11.

"The saying is sure: If anyone aspires to the office of bishop, he desires a noble task. Now a bishop must be above reproach, the husband of one wife, temperate, sensible, dignified, hospitable, an apt teacher, no drunkard, not violent but gentle, not quarrelsome, and no lover of money. He must manage his own household well, keeping his children submissive and respectful in every way; for if a man does not know how to manage his own household, how can he care for God's church? He must not be a recent convert, or he may be puffed up with conceit and fall into the condemnation of the devil; moreover he must be well thought of by outsiders, or he may fall into reproach and the snare of the devil." (RSV)

Other scriptures often used on this occasion included Acts 20:18-35, Titus 2:1-8, and I Peter 5:1-4.

One of the visiting elders would then offer a short sermon which included additional instruction on the qualifications for ministry. Another prayer was then said, usually asking specifically for the guidance of the Holy Spirit as they deliberated the calling of new leadership for the church.

The visiting elders would then go to a private part of the meeting house—sometimes outside if there was no other room available. Each member of the church, both men and women, went in alone to the elders and gave one or two names of people they thought would make a good minister.

After all the members present had been polled, the elders tallied the names. They could then take one of several actions depending on the outcome.

If one person received what the elders believed was enough votes, they could announce that person as having been called to the ministry.

If two names received a similar number of votes, both could be announced as being called to the ministry.

If the votes were widely scattered, the elders could declare that no one was called.

For many years, only men were called to the ministry, but such a call always included the man's wife. This was because devoting as much time to the ministry as the task required affected the entire family. Many couples asked for a few days to consider the call, and this request was nearly always granted.

Ministry was a high and holy calling and was considered a call not just from the congregation, but directly from the Holy Spirit. Not a few men initially shrank from the call, but it was a thing not easily dismissed. Men who seemed reluctant were likely to receive a visit from elders and deacons who urged them to seriously consider the magnitude of their decision.

Being called to the ministry was often as much an economic decision as a religious one. There is no record of any minister in Indiana being paid until just before 1900. Ministers were expected to follow the example of the Apostle Paul and provide for their own support. Most were farmers and, later, many were teachers.

Early frontier ministers were expected to travel to the homes of members when needed. This often meant a journey on horseback or on foot that might last several days or even a few weeks. Elder Samuel Murray was one of the leading early Dunkard preachers in Indiana. He settled in Miami County seven miles west of Peru in 1851 and was instrumental in establishing the Pipe Creek Church. He moved to Huntington County in 1864 and was active in the Salamonie Church. He was married five times and had 16 children. He died March 31, 1906, just one day short of his 100th birthday, at the home of his son in Indianapolis.

Otho Winger in his 1917 history of the Indiana church quoted from Elder Murray's autobiography giving the following account of one of his trips:

"I will now narrate a few facts from the very many of my first work in the ministry in Indiana. I soon had a circuit of about 30 miles square. The country was new, much more wild and uncleared land than cleared. The woods were very thick with brush and undergrowth; many places the roads were very bad; many of the roads had only a part of the undergrowth hacked out. Our traveling all had to be done afoot or on horseback; if we would have had buggies we could not have used them. I had seven different points to preach at. Very often our road or trails went through places that in the spring of the year were not safe to go through; then we had to go around through the brushy, thick woods. I often had my hat brushed off of my head and nearly filled with snow. Of course I had to get off in the snow to get it, then get on my horse and go on, thanking the Lord it was no worse.

"I well remember one Sunday morning I started for an appointment some eight miles distant. I soon got to a large pond with a thin plate of ice on it. I knew it was not safe to venture in with a horse, so I had to go around through the woods; did not go far till I had my hat brushed off again. Of course I got off and got it again. The brush was full of snow. I often put my head down as far as I could and held my hat with one hand; in this condition I crossed my path, a deep snow being on the ground, and the sky full of dark clouds. I got lost and could not tell where I was. I kept straight on and finally came to a very high fence around a small field. I noticed a cabin at the other side of the field; I got off in the snow, laid down the fence, got the horse over, then put it up; got my good horse and rode across the field, then had another fence to lay down and put up. I got on my horse and rode up to the cabin and called. The wife came to the door. I said, 'Can you tell me the road to the Baptist meeting house?' She said, "Back there.' I looked around. I then discovered that I had not got very far from home. I was now on a better road. I knew that road would take me to Deer Creek. I went on; presently the sun came out, which made it more cheerful.

"I then soon struck through the woods, hoping to strike my path, and did. I took my path again and finally got to a creek which I had to cross. It was so high I could not possibly ford it. I went down the creek to the first house and found the mother of the family at home. I asked where the men were. She said, 'They are over at the church house.' I asked how they got over. She said there was a high foot-log; if I thought I could walk it, I could put my horse in the stable and go over. I did so, and when I got over I found the house pretty well filled with attentive hearers.

"After preaching we again crossed over the high foot-log. When we got to the house the good mother had a good dinner of corn bread and bacon, etc. After eating a big dinner I went home, feeling well paid for my very toilsome and dangerous trip. I felt very thankful to the good Lord that brought me safe to my home where I could rest my body, and I felt happy in the Lord that I did my duty."

This sense of duty was felt heavily by those who accepted the call of ministry. This is reflected in another story from Elder Murray.

"One afternoon I started for my appointment 10 miles away; it was a very stormy afternoon. My wife and children did not want me to go. They thought it too dangerous to be out. I never did disappoint the people when I had an appointment, except in the case of sickness or death; nothing else would keep me from filling my appointments. So I went on my way, the wind blowing very fiercely, causing timbers to crack and fall.

"I finally got to the place where the road was not cleared out, only the brush and small timber were cut out; the large timber in and along the side of the road was deadened. I saw that the timber was occasionally falling. I halted a few minutes. The woods were very thick and brushy. I was now over half way through on my way; I could not think of turning back and disappointing the people. So I looked up to God and prayed for aid, and I soon felt perfectly safe and secure from all harm. I knew He would take me through. I moved on while the timber was falling before me and behind me, but the Lord took me through unhurt and I went on rejoicing unharmed to my appointment.

"The meeting was in Brother Enstine's cabin house, all in one room; stoves, beds and furniture all in the same room. Of course beds were used for seats. Small children were piled on the beds for both morning and evening meeting on Sunday. So we had two meetings.

"Friendly reader, do you ask if I enjoyed these meetings? I answer, 'Yes, indeed!' I sometimes wish we could have such glorious, happy meetings as we had in those times. People did not think of style and fashion. Nowadays the preacher tries to put on style in his preaching.

"The next day on my way home when I came to this fallen timber. I halted and looked. The road was covered with timber; no one would have thought that anything could have passed through alive while the timber was falling. I could not pass through. I had to circle around through the woods. I want to say here that I, in my lifetime, have experienced more than once that God is a prayer-hearing and a prayer-answering God."

Not all of these harrowing journeys ended so happily. Elder Jacob Berkey was a principle in the founding of the Rock Run Church in Elkhart County and several others in northern Indiana and southern Michigan. Late in his life, he moved to northeastern Texas about 1879 where he attempted to found new congregations. He was called to conduct an anointing service some distance away in 1881. He traveled by train as far as possible, then continued on horseback. He found a creek at Gainesville swollen by recent rains and was warned by a man on the other side not to cross. Elder Berkey, however, was not about to be deterred. He disregarded the warning and both he and his horse were swept downstream by the swift current. His body was recovered the following day.

The judge and lawyers of the county paid for Elder Berkey's burial clothes. They had heard him preach in the courtyard and were impressed with the man. Several hundred people attended his funeral.

Olden Mitchell, Elkhart, Ind., presented a historical paper at the 1991 Annual Conference in Portland, Ore., on the 100th anniversary of paid pastoral ministry. He identified three ministers as being the first to be paid for their services in 1891, and none of them was in Indiana. By 1928, however, more than 500 congregations were paying their pastors on at least a part-time basis, and a number of them were in Indiana. This change in ministry continued throughout the 20th century until now most pastors receive at least some kind of payment for their services.

Once a call to the ministry was accepted in the 1800s, the new minister was licensed for one year. At the end of that year, the congregation could vote to continue the license for another year, or, in a few cases, the license was rescinded or given up voluntarily.

If the man had proven himself capable in the task, another option was to approve him to ministry in the second degree. This usually occurred after several years of service as a first-degree minister and was equivalent to being ordained in the present-day church. A second-degree minister could perform all rites and ordinances, including marriages and funerals.

Eventually, a minister might be advanced to the third degree, more commonly known as elder or bishop. An elder was the highest ministerial position in the church and was reserved for those who had shown exceptionally good judgment and had performed well for a number of years. Elders presided at council meetings, love feasts, and baptisms. The elder with the longest tenure was called the presiding elder or the elder-in-charge. An elder was sometimes placed in charge of more than one congregation. One of the most valuable functions of an elder was in resolving disputes within a local congregation. An elder was responsible for making sure a local church followed the decisions of Annual Conference.

Deacons

Deacons were called in a process similar to that of ministers. They, too, were called by their congregations. After a trial period of one year, they were considered to be installed in the office for life. Deacons sometimes participated in worship services, but they could not officiate at weddings and funerals. Some of their prime duties included preparing for communion services, visiting the sick, visiting members who lived too far away to attend regularly, and providing care for the needy. They were also largely responsible for the annual visit prior to each love feast and communion.

In between church council meetings, the elders, ministers and deacons were responsible for the day-to-day decisions needed for the smooth operation of the church. They were usually referred to as the church board, and their authority varied from congregation to congregation, often depending upon the forcefulness of the personalities involved.

The advent of paid, professional clergy in the 20th century led to the demise of the elder system. Professional pastors gradually began to take over the duties which had been reserved for elders. In 1955, Annual Conference replaced the term "presiding elder" with "moderator," and it was decided lay people could hold the office. The office of elder was formally eliminated in 1967, although those who already held the title were allowed to keep it for life.

This change was accompanied by a change in local church organization. As churches began hiring part-time and full-time ministers and the elder system began to decline, the old model for a church board no longer worked well. In some places, the deacons continued to provide this leadership role in conjunction with the pastor. In others, a new kind of board was adopted composed of elected lay members of the congregation. This model, adapted from the secular world, was adopted by more and more churches until the denomination suggested in the early 1970s that it be adopted throughout the denomination.

The majority of congregations in Indiana now function in this manner, but a significant minority has retained a board which more closely resembles the old model. This is especially true in the South/Central District where nearly a third of the congregations have never adopted the new model.

Church Council

The church council was the final authority for all local matters. Members included all members of the local congregation, both men and women. Councils in the early 1800s made decisions by trying to reach a consensus without taking a vote. The practice was soon changed to accepting the vote of the majority. Anyone could speak to any issue raised, and each member had an equal vote. Most of the speakers, especially in the early years, were men, although there was no rule prohibiting women from speaking. This gradually changed over the years until, in at least some congregations, women were as likely to be heard as men. Meetings were conducted by the presiding elder.

How often council meetings were held was a decision left up to each congregation. Most councils met monthly or bimonthly throughout the 1800s and well into the 1900s. It has only been in the last half of the 20th century that councils have begun to meet more infrequently.

A prime point of business for these early councils, as it remains today, was finding local leadership. Every member was expected to contribute to the life of the congregation in some way, and a nomination for a position was considered a high calling. It was unusual for anyone to decline a nomination because it was expected they would respond to the call of the Holy Spirit.

One story from a central Indiana church illustrates this attitude well. A presiding elder was accepting nominations for a certain position when a member of the council offered a name. The elder accepted the nomination and the nominated person then quickly rose and said, "I decline." The elder, not used to hearing people turn down a nomination, responded with, "Ida (pronounced "Idy") Kline has been nominated. Are there other nominations?"

Minutes from congregations throughout Indiana show that by far the most time spent by local councils was on questions of behavior and dress. This was a pattern that persisted well into the 1900s. Such questions started becoming rare at many churches during the 1930s, although the practice continued in some congregations into the 1960s.

The early Dunkards were expected to hold to a strict code of behavior which most modern Brethren would find difficult if not intolerable. Obvious things like public drunkenness and gambling were taboo, but so were other activities now accepted without question. These included things like involvement in politics, attending fairs and festivals, and becoming a member of "secret societies" such as fraternal organizations and lodges.

The alcohol issue was one that surfaced early in the Indiana church. Because corn was the main source of income for most families, getting it to market was critical. That was a difficult task in an era when roads were nonexistent in some areas.

Some astute farmers quickly discovered that distilling their corn into whiskey increased their profits. There was a ready market for whiskey, and the distilling process reduced the volume of the corn dramatically. A lower quantity of product to carry to market eased the transportation problem, and profits were often better for whiskey than for corn meal.

Some early Dunkards evidently succumbed to this economic lure and began operating their own stills, even though a decision at Annual Meeting in 1781 clearly forbade the practice. This happened in the Nettle Creek congregation around 1840 when several members were called before the council for operating private distilleries. The results were mixed. Tradition says one brother claimed he was in debt and would be financially ruined if he gave up the business. He was disfellowshipped by the congregation and eventually died a poor man. Another brother admitted his error and chose to remain with the church. He closed his still, took up another business, and died a wealthy man.

Tobacco in the early church did not carry the same stigma as alcohol, although its use was not encouraged. Chewing tobacco and pipes were the most frequently accepted. One of the trademarks of Elder George Wolfe from Illinois was his pipe. There are also stories of members, including women, standing outside the meeting house smoking their pipes while Sunday school sessions were going on inside. Minutes from the Pleasant View Church show the council admonished members in the 1800s not to use tobacco in church; especially no spitting on the floor.

Pleasant View also switched to the use of unfermented wine for communion services on Oct. 17, 1890. One woman complained that it tasted like "slop." She was later admonished by the council for using improper language for a lady.

Members were often called before the council for questionable behavior. At Pine Creek, for example, 32 different cases were brought before the church council at a single meeting in 1881. The list of admonishments included such things as joining fraternal organizations, being involved in politics, fishing on Sunday, playing cards, playing certain musical instruments, dancing, attending fairs and other amusements, and being seen in a tavern.

At Anderson, the deacons were sent to visit a man who was seen in the vicinity of a political rally. He explained that he just happened to be walking past and did not take part in the rally, so the matter was quickly settled.

At Manchester, five men were called before the council on March 29, 1888, for attending a (live)stock show in Chicago. All five made an acknowledgment of their error and the minutes record, "The church counseled in the above cases—is satisfied."

The same year, two men were in trouble for joining secret societies. The minutes from a council meeting on Aug. 2 record, "A charge against E.S. and D.K. for joining the Grand Army (of the Republic). E.S. justifies himself in doing so. D.K. said he belongs and is not sorry for it. E.S. said if he could not belong to both, he would hold to the Grand Army. J.C. Murray gave them a hearty and warm admonition to be careful in the steps they are taking in the matter. R.H. Miller also admonished them to be very careful in what they are about to undertake to do as the Grand Army is only carnal and has no comfort nor solace in time to come, and said he hoped they would consider and return. The church counseled and decided as follows: to disown them, 94; give them time, 74; with the church, 19; neutral, 4. They are disowned."

Two years later, a woman was called to account for attending a local fair. The minutes state, "The case of J.S. before the church for not hearing the church. She said she was to the fair and would go again if she felt like going or any other place she felt like going. The church counseled. She is disowned for disobedience to the church."

The Order

The most frequent transgressions were over the mode of dress. The issue affected both men and women, but the minutes of most church councils indicate it was more frequently women who were called to task.

The style of dress was not an issue for the early Brethren in Europe, and it did not become an issue in the United States until about 1800. The Brethren desires to be frugal and to be separate from the world seem to have been motivating factors for rules regarding the clothing members could wear.

Questions about clothing and style of dress were queries addressed by Annual Conference almost every year from 1804 through the early 1900s, although there is nothing in the minutes about dress prior to 1800. Over time, the decisions of Annual Conference became more and more detailed until approved clothing nearly amounted to a standard uniform, although Dunkards would have been appalled at that description.

For men, standard dress included the following:
- a plain cutaway coat with standing collar, which was symbolic of a cleric and signified the belief in the priesthood of all believers;
- a white shirt with neck and wrist bands;
- broadfall trousers;
- heavy shoes or boots;
- a broadbrim black hat, which was a symbol of nonresistance;
- a shawl or cape overcoat;
- cropped hair and a beard with no mustache because mustaches were fashionable and often worn by military men;
- no gold jewelry.

Standard dress for women was as follows:
- a plain dress;
- a white cap or plain bonnet, which was a symbol of the priesthood of all believers;
- stockings;
- a neckerchief;
- a dress cape;
- an apron, which symbolized acts of service;
- a shawl;
- long hair;
- heavy shoes;
- no gold jewelry.

In general terms, dress was to show nonconformity to the world and avoidance of the evils associated with fashionable or worldly dress. Plain dress and avoidance of bright colors also avoided the sins of arrogance and pride. Life was serious and physical passions needed to be tempered with grace.

This description is only general. Modifications were made over the years, and approved dress varied from congregation to congregation.

These photos show good examples of the Order of Dress approved by the German Baptist Brethren. Sylvia Toney and Elizabeth Garver, students at Manchester College about the turn of the century, are shown at left. Another unknown young man who was a student at Manchester is shown at right.

There was never universal acceptance of any single type of dress.

The approved style of dress came to be known as "the order of dress," later shortened to "the order." In general, members were expected to wear the order to any church function, and the restrictions were especially stringent for deacons, ministers and elders who were expected to set an example. Over time, some congregations began to demand that the order be worn at all times.

The order was one of the basic issues which led to the three-way schism in 1881-83 which created the Old German Baptist Brethren and the Brethren Church. But even that major split did not bury the issue. Questions about dress continued to be troublesome for both local congregations and the entire denomination.

Persistent queries led to a number of special study committees in the late 1890s and early 1900s, but none of the actions settled the issue. More and more members discarded the order after 1900 and argued that it was an impediment to evangelism. Gradually the church came to see propriety in dress as a personal matter and not an issue which should determine membership.

The question of dress became a particularly troublesome issue at the Anderson Church where several members were employed as postal carriers. At one time, in fact, a majority of the staff in the Anderson Post Office was Brethren. These men were required to wear uniforms, and it became a subject of debate within the church over whether or not this was proper. The church council eventually decided the men could wear uniforms as terms of their employment.

Rules governing dress varied greatly from congregation to congregation in Indiana. In general, it can be said that conforming to the order relaxed considerably following World War I. By the 1940s, most congregations did not try to dictate a style of dress to their members, although they still preached the virtues of modesty and a simple lifestyle in general.

Perhaps the last bastion of rules on dress has been the covering for women. Most women continued to wear the covering at church services through the 1950s, although the practice dwindled considerably during the 1960s. Seldom worn outside a church setting, there still are some congregations where many women can be seen wearing coverings during church services. This is especially true at love feast and communion. For most congregations, however, questions of dress have ceased to be an issue.

Discipline

The early Brethren never viewed discipline as a form of punishment or exclusion. The ultimate hope and goal was that an erring member would be brought back into full fellowship with the rest of the church membership.

The two primary methods of discipline were avoidance and disfellowship. Both practices were viewed as last resorts and, at least originally, were reserved for only the most grievous sins. Even then, they were invoked only when the member refused to acknowledge the error and conform to behavior approved by the church.

Prior to about the middle of the 19th century, the most frequently used form of discipline was avoidance or "shunning." All members of the church were required to avoid contact with the person who had been excluded.

The Brethren came to recognize that some sins were worse than others. Complete avoidance, in which all members refused any contact, was reserved for only the most severe sins. Others guilty of lesser offenses might be prohibited from participating in love feast or council meetings. In other words, there was an attempt to make the punishment fit the transgression.

The practice could create terrible problems within families when only one member had been put in avoidance. It was nearly impossible for families to completely avoid another family member, particularly in the one-room cabins of the frontier. At times, family members who had previously been blameless found themselves placed under partial avoidance because they could not stop contact with another member of the family who was put under complete avoidance.

For this and a number of other reasons, the practice of disfellowship became more common than avoidance during the second half of the 19th century. Although the effect was similar, the Brethren did not use the term "excommunication." One explanation is that it sounded too much like force was being employed. Another is that it was often tied to the theology of churches from which the original Brethren had broken. Instead, the Dunkards talked of a brother or sister who had been disfellowshipped or "disowned."

Like avoidance, the practice of disfellowship was used only as a last resort—often after repeated attempts at reconciliation. Another excerpt from the Sept. 7, 1893, minutes of the Manchester Church council illustrates this point.

"Brother H.S. was again visited for attending saloons. This being the third visit and he refused to appear before the church. Church voted as follows: disown, 106; with the church 26."

One of the problems with church discipline was that what might be accepted by one congregation was subject to action by the church council in another. There was no universal code of conduct which was uniformly enforced everywhere.

To current church members, the practices of avoidance and disfellowship sometimes seem brutal and unforgiving. And in some cases they were.

Many of the old church elders insisted the real question was whether or not the person would listen to and follow the rules and the decisions of the church. In other words, were they willing to give up their personal rights and submit to the decision of the church body.

It must also be remembered that the goal behind discipline ultimately was reconciliation. It remains a fact, however, that there are few records which show cases where a church council disfellowshipped a member and then actively attempted to win them back to the fold. In the few cases where reconciliation occurred, it was almost always the disfellowshipped member who actively sought out the church. More often, a disfellowshipped member simply moved on to a different church or denomination, or left church life altogether.

In Indiana, active church discipline began to wane in the 20th century, particularly after about the 1930s. One of the last bastions of the practice was in the area of divorce and remarriage. Although formal disciplinary proceedings against divorced members became rare, many divorced members have experienced an informal sort of shunning, even to the present day. This is particularly true for ministers. Some Indiana congregations have welcomed ministers with a history of divorce. For others, however, it is too bitter a pill to swallow.

In general, Indiana churches in the last half of the 20th century have followed the lead of the majority of congregations in the denomination in emphasizing positive examples of the Christian life. They have focused more on repentance and forgiveness than on discipline and punishment.

Districts

A new organizational structure arose in the mid-1800s which came to be known as the district. Churches in Indiana and throughout the brotherhood had worked together on an informal basis for years, but there was no formal structure.

This began to change with a decision by Annual Meeting in 1856 which gave conditional approval to the formation of districts by groups of adjoining churches. Final approval to this structure was given in 1866.

The first meeting of this kind was held in 1857 at the Bethany Church, then known as Solomon's Creek. Another similar meeting was held in 1859 at a love feast near Goshen. This meeting was attended by 25 elders and ministers.

The first meetings which closely resembled today's district conferences were held in 1863. One was held near Goshen on April 6, 1863, and the other was held near Flora on May 1, 1863. The minutes from both of those meetings show that the business was almost exclusively devoted to questions of behavior. Remembering that these meetings were during the height of the Civil War, this query at the

PROCEEDINGS

--OF THE--

Brethren of the German Baptist Church,

--FOR THE--

Southern District of Indiana,

--HELD IN THE--

Howard Church, Howard County, Indiana,

--ON--

Thursday, April 19, 1877.

NEW CASTLE:
Courier Steam Print.
1877.

This was the program cover for the 1877 conference of the Southern Indiana District. The event was held at the Howard Church.

Goshen meeting serves as an example of the six which appeared on the agenda.

"Query 4: About attending political and war meetings and voting at political elections. Considered not to have anything to do with politics at all, much less with war affairs."

Among the 10 business items at Flora was this:

"Query 1: A soldier comes under conviction while in camp, requests of the brethren to be baptized, and if not permitted to come home, requests the brethren to come to the camp and baptize him, promising that he will leave the service as soon as he can honorably do so. What will the brethren in this meeting advise the brethren to do in this case? Answer: It is considered advisable that such applicant should be received into the church."

The actual division of the state into districts began at a statewide meeting held at the Andrews Church on Oct. 25, 1866. A committee was assigned the task of studying ways the congregations in the state might be grouped.

The report returned by the committee recommended that the state be divided into three districts: Southern Indiana, Middle Indiana, and Northern Indiana, with specific congregations assigned to each district. This recommendation was accepted and put into effect in 1868.

The original Northern Indiana district included the southern tier of counties in Michigan which bordered Indiana. The Florence congregation located near Constantine, Mich., is still a part of the Northern Indiana District and is the last remnant of this original boundary.

Records of district meetings prior to 1881 are either sketchy or nonexistent, but it seems likely such meetings were held at least annually and probably more often. One of their primary duties was to elect representatives to the Standing Committee of Annual Conference, a change which was adopted in 1868.

The work of the early district organizations can be roughly broken into three categories: mission, ministry, and education. Various committees were used to pursue these interests over the years.

Mission prior to the early 1900s was defined as expanding the church within the state. To that end, the districts established committees and programs which supported new congregations with both leadership and money. For a number of years, a handful of ministers were specifically appointed to do mission work at various places in Indiana, and funds were raised to defray their expenses. These efforts were highly successful, and many of today's churches owe their existence to the emphasis placed on local mission during these years.

Education was initially focused on Sunday school programs. Meetings were held to train and support teachers in local congregations.

Some of the districts also supported higher education through Manchester College.

Various committees were formed to support ministry in each district with functions ranging from discipline to education.

The district structure has been fluid over the years as the organization changed to meet the changing needs of the congregations. Perhaps the most dramatic change occurred on July 31, 1971, when the Middle Indiana and Southern Indiana districts merged to form the South/Central District. The day began at the Kokomo Church of the Brethren with representatives of each district meeting separately. During these meetings, they formally agreed to the merger. The two groups then met together in the afternoon at a school across the road from the church. Dr. Carroll (Kaydo) Petry was installed as the first district executive for the new district, a post which he continues to hold.

The current structure of the two Indiana districts is similar. Both hold district conferences to which congregations send delegates. The district board is made up of members elected at district conference, and each district board member serves on a commission. South/Central Indiana commissions include Evangelism/Church Development, Ministry, Nurture, Witness, and Stewards. Northern Indiana commissions include Stewards, Nurture, Witness, and Ministry.

Indiana Districts-1868

Southern Indiana

Four Mile
Nettle Creek
Buck Creek
Bush Creek
Mississinewa
Killbuck
Fall Creek
Arcadia
Jonesboro
Greentown
Howard County
North Fork of Wild Cat
Middle Fork of Wild Cat
Potato Creek
Ladoga
Owen County Lick Creek
Columbus

Middle Indiana

White County
Mexico
Squirrel Creek
Manchester
Clear Creek
Blue River
Beaver Dam
Eight Mile
Salamonie
Antioch
Eel River
Santa Fe
Pipe Creek
Upper Deer Creek
Lower Deer Creek
Wabash
Prairie Creek
Bachelor Run
Somerset
Winamac

Northern Indiana

Portage
Baugo
South Bend
Bremen
Pine Creek
Union
Yellow Creek
Elkhart
Turkey Creek
Union Center
Solomon's Creek
Rock Run
Springfield
Shipshewana
Washington
Cedar Creek
Tippecanoe
Pigeon River
Fawn River
English Prairie

Indiana Districts-1992

Northern Indiana

Agape
Baugo
Beacon Heights
Bethany
Bethel
Blissville
Blue River
Bremen
Camp Creek
Cedar Creek
Cedar Lake
Columbia City
Communion Fellowship
Crest Manor
Elkhart City
Elkhart Valley
English Prairie
Florence
Goshen City
Iglesia Evanelical Emanuel
LaPorte
Lincolnshire
Little Pine
Maple Grove
Michigan City
Middlebury
Mount Pleasant
Nappanee
New Paris
New Salem
North Liberty
North Webster
North Winona
Osceola
Pine Creek
Pleasant Chapel
Pleasant Valley
Plymouth
Prince of Peace

South/Central Indiana

Akron
Anderson
Andrews
Antioch
Arcadia
Bachelor Run
Beech Grove
Bethel Center
Buck Creek
Buffalo
Burnettsville
Christ Our Shepherd
Eel River
Flora
Four Mile
Guernsey
Hickory Grove
Howard
Huntington
Kokomo
Lafayette
Liberty Mills
Locust Grove
Logansport
Loon Creek
Lower Deer Creek
Manchester
Marion
Markle
Mexico
Muncie
Nettle Creek
New Hope
Northview
Peru
Pike Creek
Pipe Creek
Pittsburg
Pleasant Dale

Indiana Districts-1992 (cont.)

Northern Indiana

Rock Run
Southside Fellowship
Syracuse
Turkey Creek
Union
Union Center
Wakarusa
Walnut
Wawaka
West Goshen
Yellow Creek

Southern Indiana

Pleasant View
Portland
Pyrmont
Richmond
Roann
Rossville
Salamonie
South Whitley
Spring Creek
Sugar Creek
Union Grove
Upper Fall Creek
Wabash
West Eel River
West Mancester
White Branch
Windfall

7

The Great Divide

Anorthern Indiana farm field served as the stage for one of the greatest events in Brethren history. It was the site of the 1882 Annual Conference which was the final act in a great drama that became known as The Great Divide.

The Great Divide is a phrase that covers a three-way schism which eventually produced the Old German Baptist Brethren, Brethren Church (Ashland), and Church of the Brethren. The splits occurred over the period 1881-83, but the division was brewing for more than 30 years before the schisms actually happened.

While Dunkards generally held to the same core beliefs, there were conservative and liberal wings of the church with the majority of the members located somewhere between these two extremes. Over time, the left and right wings of theological belief began to grow farther and farther apart, and this created friction. The three major groups came to be known as the Old Orders (those who espoused the most conservative views), the Progressives (those who pushed the most liberal positions), and the Conservatives (those in the center).

As their name suggests, the Progressives believed there must be progress, movement, and advancement within the life of the church. They tended to support any idea that would advance the gospel as long as it did not violate the gospel. This led them to advocate many ideas which were anathema to the Old Orders. They included

• Sunday school programs;

- the use of musical instruments in worship;
- higher education;
- an educated and paid clergy;
- a deliberate policy of evangelism in the form of foreign and home missions;
- protracted (revival) meetings;
- open exchanges of opinions in church periodicals;
- plainness of dress, but not uniformity;
- less authority given to Annual Conference and more authority to individual congregations.

The Old Orders were opposed to every one of these positions. They believed that such innovations would lead to individualism and threaten the spirit of community (*Gemeinschaft*) that had been so important to the Dunkards. Central to their belief was that the individual should always submit to the wisdom of the group; that the mind of Christ should always be sought through consensus.

Beginning in the 1840s, Annual Meeting began hearing queries on issues later identified with the Progressives. The influence of the Old Orders was strong enough in the beginning that few of these queries received much support. That began to change as the years passed, however, and by the 1860s, many of the Progressive queries were receiving substantial support.

One of the keys to spreading the message of the Progressives was the founding in 1851 of *The Monthly Gospel Visiter,* the first paper published for Brethren. Henry Kurtz was the founder of the publication which soon was called *The Gospel Visiter.* Annual Meeting was asked about the appropriateness of such a publication in 1851, the same year it was founded, but it was two more years before an answer was handed down. The answer, that it was a private venture and should not be interfered with, was not what the Old Orders wanted to hear.

The Gospel Visiter (changed to *Visitor* in 1856) quickly became very popular. Kurtz saw his publication as a way to unify the widely scattered Dunkard congregations. While he was personally supportive of many of the views of the Progressives, he was very tactful about it within the pages of his magazine. He did support such things as Sunday schools, evangelism through missions, and higher education.

A man who served a brief apprenticeship with Kurtz was Henry Ritz Holsinger, who would later become the focus of the Progressive movement. After publishing a secular newspaper, *The Tyrone* (Pa.) *Herald,* from 1863 to 1865, he founded *Christian Family Companion* in 1865. It was this publication that he used as a pulpit to become the spokesman for the Progressives.

Unlike Kurtz, Holsinger was not a tactful man and often let his passions get the better of him. Writing in *Some Brethren Pathfinders* in 1929, Elder J.H. Moore described Holsinger this way:

"In his makeup, Brother Holsinger was decidedly aggressive, extremely so. He was mentally alert, quick, keen witted and outspoken. What he thought he wrote or spoke regardless of results. In a general way he was in accord with the outstanding doctrines and fundamentals of the church, but differed sharply with most of the leaders on policy and methods. He was a born editor, and our people probably never had in their ranks a man of finer editorial ability. But he was no diplomat. He compromised on nothing. In a sense, he was a clear-cut agitator. And still, getting on the right side of him, he was found to be one of the most pleasant of men. He made many friends, fast friends too, but he made twice as many enemies."

One of Holsinger's first major run-ins with church authority came at Annual Meeting in 1867 when he led a fiery argument about the installation of deacons by the laying on of hands. His arguments became so intemperate that he was later forced to acknowledge his error and apologize. Writing of this incident himself in *History of the Tunkers,* Holsinger said, "By this time the audience was excited to the highest pitch. I never before or since witnessed such intensity of feeling in an assembly. The council was held in a dense grove, and men and women wept out loud, and several voices shrieked so as to awaken the echo."

In spite of being forced to make an apology, Holsinger was not cowed. This incident began a long series of clashes with Annual Meeting's leaders which occurred almost every year. He was frequently the subject of special investigations, and he was often forced to acknowledge his errors and apologize.

The Old Orders

The Old Orders also rallied around a publication and a personality. In their case, the publication was *The Vindicator,* and the man was Peter Nead.

Nead was Lutheran by birth, but was later baptized by the Dunkards and became a minister in 1827. This was just about the same time that the Dunkards were shifting from the use of the German language to the English language. Nead, a native speaker of English, always preached in that language, but his devotion to Brethren doctrine gave him acceptance. He is often credited for helping to smooth the change in language.

While not a highly educated man, he did receive what was considered a good education for his time, and he was also a devoted reader. He began a series of publications in 1834 which were largely devoted to Brethren theology. His books and pamphlets were considered the best explanation of Brethren doctrine and thought of their day.

Nead moved to an area near Dayton, Ohio, in 1848. This area of the lower Miami Valley became a center for the Old Order movement with Nead at its head. Other strongholds were located in Maryland, Pennsylvania, and Iowa.

As the Progressives became more and more vocal about implementing change at Annual Meeting, the Old Orders saw their influence declining. This led to a meeting of elders in 1868 at the Lower Stillwater, Ohio, meeting house (where Peter Nead was elder) where a document known as the First Petition was drawn up. The petition asked that Annual Meeting take action to bring the Brethren back to their original standard. The petition was presented at the 1869 Annual Meeting.

The answer from Annual Meeting was a compromise which agreed some abuses were taking place and gave guidance in correcting these problems. But it also did not prohibit certain "innovations," and this was unacceptable to the Old Orders.

This rebuff led to the founding of *The Vindicator* in 1870. The publisher was Samuel Kinsey, the minister of the Lower Stillwater Church and also the son-in-law of Peter Nead. The purpose was to provide a voice for the Old Orders, and Nead was one of the most frequent contributors to its pages until his death in 1877.

Annual meetings throughout the 1870s became a tug-of-war with the Conservatives caught in the middle trying to seek compromise positions. They did their best, but the compromises only seemed to further alienate the opposing groups which edged farther and farther away from each other.

Finally, the Old Orders decided there had been too many compromises. A meeting of elders primarily from the Miami Valley area of Ohio met at the Salem, Ohio, meeting house in 1879 and formulated what became known as the Miami Valley Petition. The petition called for strict adherence to the "ancient apostolic order of the church in her humility, simplicity, and nonconformity to the world." The elders noted the troubles which had been plaguing the church and said the causes had to be removed before peace and union could be restored. They said they would not tolerate such innovations as salaried clergy, Sunday schools, higher education, protracted meetings, the single mode of foot washing, elaborate and fancy houses and barns, and expensive furniture and carriages.

This gauntlet was laid down at the Annual Meeting of 1880 after it had been approved at the Southern Ohio district meeting, although it was not supported by all the district delegates. Standing Committee of Annual Meeting again sought compromise by writing a substitute paper which attempted to correct abuses, but allowed some of the innovations the Old Order elders said they could never accept. One statement which incensed these elders read, "Hence, while we are conservative we are also progressive."

After this meeting, Old Order leaders were urged by a few prominent Annual Meeting elders to submit their petition again with a few modifications. This "Reconsidered Petition" was submitted at Annual Meeting in 1881, but it was rejected as ineligible because it had not first been approved by a district meeting.

This was the final blow. A few Old Order congregations had withdrawn from the German Baptist Brethren (the denominational name adopted in 1871), but the real break occurred following this 1881 Annual Meeting. An organizational meeting for Old Orders was held at the Salem meeting house in Ohio in December 1881, and the first Annual Meeting of the Old German Baptist Brethren was held in the Wolf Creek congregation in Montgomery County, Ohio, in 1882. Approximately 4,000 members left the German Baptist Brethren and joined the Old German Baptist Brethren.

This split had varying effects on the congregations in Indiana. The majority of churches lost just a few members, but there were pockets that were much more deeply affected.

Yellow Creek in Elkhart County was one of those places. Elder Samuel Leer and Benjamin Burkett, a minister in the second degree, left with 11 other church officials. The only official who decided to remain with the German Baptist Brethren was John Nusbaum, a deacon.

At that time, there was no church polity governing what happened to church property in the case of a division. The story is told locally that Nusbaum attended a meeting with those who were leaving to join the Old German Baptist Brethren. It was agreed that the first person at the church the following day would retain possession.

Nusbaum rose early and rode his horse to the Yellow Creek meeting house well before dawn. He found the church empty when he arrived and was standing in the doorway when the first of the Old Order representatives appeared. The Yellow Creek building thus remained with the German Baptist Brethren. The Old Orders formed a new congregation and built another meeting house a short distance away where the group is still active.

Bachelor Run and Flora (which were the same congregation at the time) lost 126 members. Of the 160 members in the Howard congregation, a third withdrew including two ministers and two of three deacons. Many members and much of the leadership left the Lower Deer Creek Church and formed a new congregation of the same name. The group remaining with the German Baptist Brethren renamed themselves Deer Creek to eliminate confusion.

The Progressive Split

Henry Holsinger and the Progressives had continued to pressure Annual Meeting to endorse their ideas at the same time the Old Orders were resisting any change. Holsinger, in particular, was extremely vocal, not just in pushing for reform but in criticism that the elders of Annual Meeting were not moving fast enough. Writing in *The Progressive Christian,* Holsinger compared Standing Committee of Annual Conference to secret societies and lodges. This outrageous comparison and several others led at least five districts to present charges against Holsinger at the 1881 Annual Meeting in Ashland, Ohio. Annual Meeting then appointed a committee to go to Holsinger in Berlin, Pa., to investigate the charges.

Holsinger had been ordained to the ministry by the Berlin congregation on Oct. 21, 1880, and was very popular there. When the Berlin Committee from Annual Meeting arrived in August 1881 to conduct Holsinger's hearing, Holsinger insisted on making the hearing public, including even those who were not members of the church. He also hired a stenographer to make a record of the proceedings which he intended to publish. The Berlin congregation backed Holsinger at every turn.

After two days of procedural wrangling, the Berlin Committee finally decided they could not accept all of Holsinger's conditions, and the attempt to hold a hearing was abandoned. The committee announced "that Brother H.R. Holsinger cannot be held in fellowship with the Brotherhood, and all who depart with him shall be held responsible to the action of the next Annual Meeting." In effect, Holsinger was excommunicated until Annual Meeting could act.

The next nine months were filled with malice. Holsinger's supporters attacked the action of the Berlin Committee while his detractors agitated for his permanent expulsion. Many people felt Holsinger and his group had gone too far, but they also felt the Berlin Committee's action was far too severe. Some suggested the committee had gone beyond its authority and should have withheld a decision until their report was presented at Annual Meeting. Even some of the members of the Berlin Committee itself came to this view.

Elder J.H. Moore, who was an eyewitness, wrote, "Public sentiment began to crystallize and every well informed member could observe that in the open conference the report of the committee would likely be approved. Even Brother Holsinger and his friends realized this and were much discouraged. They, along with everybody else, could see that the agitation had reached a critical point."

Annual Meeting in 1882 was located on an Indiana farm owned by John Arnold. The 35-acre site was located a short distance east of the present intersection of U.S. 6 and Ind. 15 in Elkhart County north of Milford.

The Big Four railroad ran north and south past the site, and the B&O railroad ran east and west a short distance to the south. Both railroads made special arrangements to transport passengers directly to the conference grounds. There was even a temporary U.S. Post Office built at the site.

The Solomon's Creek (now Bethany) congregation was in charge of arrangements. J.W. Rowdabaugh was 12 years old when the 1882 conference was held. He wrote about his memories in 1951 when he was 81 years old.

"A large tent was erected with a seating capacity of 5,000 inside and seats all around outside. A dining hall had a seating capacity of 1,500 at one time. There was also a large lunch room. A double furnace was installed for cooking 41 head of corn fed beeves (*sic*). The cooking continued day and night by Solomon Rowdabaugh and Cyrus Lantz as head cooks.

"A baggage room and ticket office were in the depot built by the Big Four. They also put in telegraph service and a switch. The B&O built one-and-one-half miles of new track from their main line so they could land their passengers on the meeting ground. The two railroads hauled passengers to the surrounding towns for night lodging, bringing them back to the meeting grounds in the morning.

"The church building (Solomon's Creek) and the houses and barns for miles around were also used for sleeping quarters. The Big Four did not have enough passenger coaches so they used a box car. I recently talked to Brother Milo Cripe of the West Goshen Church. He said he was one of the box car passengers, which was filled to capacity of standing room. Ira Shively of New Paris put down many driven wells about 20 feet deep into sheet water which furnished plenty of pure water for man and beast.

"One field was used for horses and wagons, as many people came for many miles and stayed for the entire nine-day series of services. Horse feed was furnished by the local Brethren free."

Supplying food for a gathering of thousands was a major undertaking. Meal tickets cost 15 cents each, and some of the food listed included 41 "beeves," 2,000 pies and 13 gallons of apple butter. Special arrangements were made for fresh bread each day. Quoting Rowdabaugh again, "The bread was baked in Chicago and shipped by the car load to Milford junction on the B&O railroad. The cases were lined with muslin. D.W. Weybright and Elmer Troup muslin-lined a sideboard wagon box and hauled the unwrapped and unsliced bread to the meeting ground. They said the bread was still warm when they opened the car.

They also testified to me that the bread with butter was good eating."

Later accounts of the 1882 conference have placed the attendance as high as 10,000, but an accurate estimate is nearly impossible. Rowdabaugh himself wrote, "No one ever knew the exact total of attendance at this conference ... Judging from the amount of food used, it is evident that this meeting was one among the largest in attendance of any Brethren conference. We quote Sol Dickery, who once said, 'We could not count them by the thousand, so we counted them by the acre.'"

There was a sense of foreboding in the air as the thousands gathered at the conference site. Enoch Eby, the moderator, had also served on the Berlin Committee, so when the committee's report was presented on June 1, he stepped aside and D.E. Cripe took over the chair. The committee report was read and explained, then a motion was made for its adoption.

Holsinger's opponents no doubt expected a bombastic tirade based on his past history at Annual Meeting. They were in for a surprise.

Friends of Holsinger presented a compromise paper which Holsinger had promised to sign if it was accepted. Its tone was surprisingly conciliatory given the past nine months of vitriolic rhetoric.

Holsinger made five points in the paper. "First, I humbly ask the pardon of the brethren for all my offenses, general and particular, committed in the past either through the *Progressive Christian* or otherwise. Second, I promise hereafter to administer the discipline of the church in harmony with the practices of the church and will cease to practice or teach any system of church government not in harmony with that prevailing in the church as set forth by A(nnual) M(eeting). Third, I promise to cease to speak or write in antagonism to the general order and union of its practices as now prevailing in the church. Fourth, I promise to cease the publishing of the *Progressive Christian* or any other paper or anything in fact in opposition to A(nnual) M(eeting). Fifth, I promise to publish these declarations in the *Progressive Christian* and to harmonize action with the church. I ask that they be placed upon the minutes of this meeting."

Viewed from the perspective of more than 100 years, Holsinger's promises seem quite reasonable, but emotions were high and, as Elder Moore had commented, Holsinger had made many enemies. The intemperate behavior of the past caught up with him.

Nearly the entire day was spent debating the question. Finally, the motion to accept the Berlin Committee's report was pressed, and a vote was called for. Elder Moore estimated there were 7,000 voting members present and all but about 100 stood to support the motion. Writing in 1929, Elder Moore recalled, "I have attended a good many Annual

Meetings, 43 of them, but I never before or since witnessed such an impressive moment. And while there were many sad hearts, still there seemed to be a feeling of relief."

Moore believed there were three points on which Holsinger continued to differ from the direction already being taken by the denomination. One was a denial of the authority of Annual Meeting to discipline individuals or churches. Another was requiring the use of the prayer veil by women and, finally, the whole question of uniform dress for every member.

Writing 47 years after the event, Moore's sadness was still evident. "Had he (Holsinger) been half as patient and one-third as diplomatic as were thousands of aggressive members who stayed by the mother church, he might have seen the day when most of the changes for which he contended were acceptable by the church without any noticeable opposition. And this not because he was contending for them, but because the church in a normal way was naturally moving out in that direction.

"It was unfortunate, very unfortunate we think, that the Milford Conference did not instruct Brother Holsinger to sign his declaration, and then have the committee incorporate it in their report, and then let the past be past. He would doubtless have lived up to the pledge thus made and that would have put an end to all further division sentiment. While some others were exceedingly radical none of them would have headed a movement for separation. But there were mistakes on both sides. There was too much excitement and too little diplomacy—too much zeal and not enough charity."

A number of historians have since agreed with Moore's assessment that the schism need not have occurred. The suggestion has been made that the Conservative elders were exhausted from all the years of trying to hold together the Old Orders and the Progressives and simply did not have the energy left to seek compromise one more time.

After the vote, Moore described Holsinger's mood as depressed. Still, he was able to rally his spirits enough to lead a group of his supporters to a nearby school house where they discussed what to do next. Rowdabaugh recalled, "On the afternoon of June 1, this writer saw Elder H.R. Holsinger and a number of others leaving the conference grounds and going west one mile on the public highway which is now federal road 6 to the Clayton school house, and there, with Elder R.P. Brown as chairman, organized the Progressive church. Some time later they changed the name to the First Brethren."

Holsinger's group eventually held a meeting in Dayton, Ohio, in June 1883 which marked the official formation of the new denomination.

The aftermath of this second schism was much like the first. Some churches lost only a few members while others were devastated. It is estimated some 5,000 members left the German Baptist Brethren to join the newly forming Brethren Church.

One of the Indiana congregations hardest hit was Eight-Mile (later Markle) where the Progressives were in the majority and took over the church building. They were unsuccessful at keeping their group together, however, and later abandoned the building which was eventually razed.

The members of the Eight-Mile congregation who remained German Baptist Brethren refused to give up and continued to meet regularly in homes. Their number increased, and they were able to purchase an existing church building in 1887.

A more accommodating solution was reached between the groups who were part of the Middle Fork congregation (a forerunner to Rossville). Middle Fork at that time had several meeting houses, one of which was at Edna Mills. This meeting house was used on alternate Sundays by the two groups until the late 1800s. This sharing of the building created some unique problems. For example, the Progressives purchased an organ and used it during their worship services. The next week when it was the turn of the Conservatives to use the house, the organ was unceremoniously shoved into a closet.

The wounds of the three-way split between the Old Orders, Conservatives, and Progressives were extremely deep and lasted for many years. Both the Old German Baptists and the Brethren Church have experienced division since their initial formation. Many who were brothers and sisters prior to 1881 were never able to completely forgive the experiences they lived through during that trying time.

The benefit of history shows that nearly all of the reforms sought by Holsinger and the Progressives were adopted by the German Baptist Brethren within a generation of the split. Paid clergy, higher education, Sunday school, intentional home and foreign missions, the use of musical instruments, and relaxation of the standards of dress were part of the evolutionary change in the church.

Ironically, the 20th century has seen a reversal in the perception of which group is liberal and which is conservative. The Conservatives who became the Church of the Brethren are now considered much more liberal in their programs than the Progressives who became the Brethren Church.

More recently, there have been some attempts at healing. At the Annual Conference in Cincinnati, Ohio, in 1987 it was announced that the Church of the Brethren and the Brethren Church were beginning to talk to each other about their similarities and their differences. These discussions are still continuing.

On May 19, 1991, a special service was organized at the 1882 Annual Conference site north of Milford to commemorate the event and to pray for healing of the breach. The event was labeled the "Arnold's Grove Revisited Prayer Meeting" and was organized by clergy from the Church of the Brethren and the Brethren Church. Sponsors included the Northern Indiana District's New Church Development Team, New Paris First Brethren Church, and New Paris Church of the Brethren. Appropriately, members from the Bethany Church assisted in preparing the site. Several dozen people attended the service which included symbolic foot washing and the bread and cup communion.

But more than 100 years after The Great Divide, all of the groups continue to pursue their separate courses.

8

Sisters Among The Brothers

Women have played a key role in the Church of the Brethren from the very beginning. Three of the original eight members (Anna Margaretha Mack, Johanna Kipping, and Johanna Nothiger Boni) were women.

For most of the denomination's history, leadership roles for women have been sharply defined and often severely limited. It was not always that way in the beginning, however.

The early European Brethren lived in a culture which expected women to be submissive, but records from the period indicate all eight of the original Brethren were active evangelists, witnessing publicly at every opportunity. Among the many charges levied against them, along with other Pietists and Anabaptists, was that they allowed wives to show disrespectful behavior toward their husbands and that women were allowed to teach just like men.

Women were involved in all areas of church life regardless of their marital status. One example of how far this was taken is that after the death of Elder Jacob Schneider, his widow was listed as serving as an elder for seven years.

The opportunities for women in leadership roles apparently continued after the Brethren came to America. Two women were among the first six people to be baptized in the Colonies in 1723. Margaret Bayer was elected a deaconess at Germantown in 1769 in her own right, not as the result of the election of a husband.

At the same time, however, a more traditional view of male dominance was becoming more and more prominent. Alexander Mack Sr. wrote that a wife should be obedient to her husband, although he baptized a woman against her husband's will on at least one occasion.

By the time the first Dunkards settled in Indiana, the pattern of leaderhip roles being reserved for men only was firmly entrenched. Women were not allowed to vote at Annual Meeting, and how much authority they were given in their own local church councils varied from congregation to congregation. Some churches did not allow women to speak; others allowed them to speak, but they couldn't vote; and some allowed women a full and equal voice and vote.

Ministry was a position strictly reserved for men. Women could become deaconesses, but only upon the election of their husbands as deacons. Wives had little choice in the matter, and about their only official duties were to prepare food for love feast.

Women were not allowed to break bread at communion. The elements of communion were distributed by male deacons and ministers under the leadership of an elder. The bread and cup were given to men as a group, and they then distributed the elements among themselves. Each woman was individually given the bread and cup by a deacon or minister.

There was a basic equality of expectation concerning moral behavior between the sexes, however. Lifelong, monogamous marriage to a fellow believer was the only accepted standard. Divorce was only allowed in cases of adultery, although the wife of an abusive husband might be allowed a divorce in some cases. Divorced persons were not allowed to remarry. Sex was permitted only within the bounds of marriage, and married partners were expected to live in harmony with each other. Both men and women were held equally responsible for meeting these standards or they were disowned.

Life On The Frontier

In spite of the severe limitations placed on them, Dunkard women in the early 19th century still managed to play a crucial role in the life and growth of the church. This was especially true on the frontier where traditional roles often had to be abandoned because the family's survival depended upon it. Many of the elders who traveled widely and are given much of the credit for the growth of the church during this period were only able to do so because they were married to strong, competent women who ran the family farm in their absence.

One of the best examples is the life of Sarah (Lint) Berkey. She married Jacob Berkey in Pennsylvania, and in 1848 moved to Elkhart County, Ind., with their five children. They settled on land just across the road from the present site of the Rock Run Church east of Goshen.

The Berkeys (who had three more children in Indiana) became part of the closest German Baptist Brethren congregation at the time, which was Elkhart (West Goshen). It wasn't long, however, until they began to actively organize a new group closer to their home.

The result was the organization of Rock Run in 1850. Jacob was elected to the ministry the same day the church was organized. He soon became an elder and was placed in charge of the infant church.

Jacob Berkey quickly developed a widely known reputation for his preaching and evangelism. He often spent days at a time traveling on horseback throughout northeast Indiana and southern Michigan. His trips resulted in the formation of a number of new congregations.

While Jacob was out doing church work, Sarah stayed behind and managed a highly successful farming operation in addition to caring for her family of eight children. But her work for the church extended far beyond supporting her husband.

When a proposal was made for the construction of the first Rock Run meeting house, some members objected because they would have to wait to eat their noon meal until they had traveled all the way home instead of enjoying a fellowship meal. Jacob Berkey stood up and volunteered to feed anyone in his home who felt this was a hardship. There is no record Sister Sarah raised an objection to this offer.

The Berkey household became a widely recognized stopping point for traveling Brethren where perhaps hundreds of people were welcomed, housed, and fed over the years. Annual Meeting was held on the Berkey farm in 1868 which must have presented formidable logistical problems for the lady of the household.

In 1879, Jacob and Sarah moved to Texas where Jacob drowned in the spring of 1881 while attempting to cross a rain-swollen stream on his way to an anointing service. Sister Sarah died in 1888.

Another example of the formidable character of Brethren pioneer women in Indiana is the story of Mrs. Phillip Hartman. The Hartmans came to Indiana in the fall of 1844 from Westmoreland County, Pa. They were the first German Baptist Brethren family to locate in Adams County, Ind., when they settled on the banks of Peterson Creek east of Peterson.

Phillip Hartman died only a year later, leaving Mrs. Hartman to care for her brood of seven and carve out a wilderness farm at the same time. Not only was she successful, she was the only Brethren member in the area for the next 15 years, faithfully holding onto her unique beliefs and handing them down to her children without the support of anyone else.

It wasn't until 1860 when Mr. and Mrs. Israel Stoneburner moved from Hocking County, Ohio, and established a farm just a mile from the Hartman property that she had any fellow believers nearby. These two families were the start of the Pleasant Dale Church which was eventually organized as a separate congregation in 1889.

Annual Meeting

Questions about the role of women began coming to Annual Meeting in the mid-1800s. One of the first was a query about women breaking bread for themselves at communion. The 1849 Annual Meeting upheld the practice of not allowing women to act as men did.

Another query in 1854 questioned the role women should play in local church council meetings. Annual Meeting responded with an action that upheld local congregations which had given women the right to vote.

The increasing debate over the role of women in the church was one of the contributing factors in the three-way schism of 1881-83. Old Order Brethren insisted the traditional role of women must be upheld while Progressives demanded a greater role for the female half of the membership.

It was during this period that the question of women voting at Annual Meeting was formally raised. The issue came out in 1881 during a debate over whether or not women could wear hats. It was noted by several speakers that the issue of wearing hats affected only those who had no voice.

At the 1882 Annual Meeting held in northern Indiana, delegates actually approved giving women a vote, but the action became virtually meaningless through a ruling by Standing Committee in 1883. Standing Committee ruled that women could only participate in a rising vote. Such votes had traditionally been open to any male member in attendance at Annual Meeting, not just delegates, and were generally limited to items which did not affect denominational policy. Since women could not be elected delegates, they were effectively shut out of the gain they had achieved just the year before. A more direct query about women being delegates was rejected by Annual Meeting in 1889.

Sarah Major

Women who were acting in ministerial leadership roles were also a troublesome area during this period. Much of the debate centered on the activity of Sarah Righter Major.

Sarah Righter was born in 1808 near Philadelphia. She was converted at the age of 18 while listening to Harriet Livermore preach. Soon after this, Sarah experienced a call to preach, and she was encouraged by her father and others. She began preaching and almost immediately experienced opposition. Annual Meeting in 1834 rejected the notion of women preaching, and Sarah defended herself in an 1835 letter.

She married Thomas Major, a Brethren minister, in 1842, and they moved to Highland County, Ohio, in 1843. The Majors preached in many areas throughout Ohio and Indiana. To head off some of the criticism, Thomas would often open the meeting, then invite Sarah to speak. In congregations where she was specifically asked not to speak, Sarah often led prayer.

The activity of the Majors did not go unnoticed. Annual Meeting received a number of complaints. At one point, a committee was assigned to investigate the situation and suggest that Sarah be silent. However, the committee was reluctant to take any action. One member said, "I could not give my vote to silence someone who could outpreach me."

In 1859, Annual Meeting made a distinction between teaching, preaching, and prophesying. Women were not permitted to preach or teach, but they could prophesy (exhort) or give testimonies about their spiritual experiences. This action left open the door for Sarah Major's activities, and she and Thomas continued to be an effective team.

Sarah become so well known that she was asked to speak at Annual Meeting in 1878 held at North Manchester. She was formally invited to speak by her husband, and it was made clear she would be prophesying, not preaching, but it was a fine detail indistinguishable to many of those present. The idea of a woman speaking at such a gathering created a local sensation, and the many thousands of Brethren who converged on the site were joined by several thousand more curious non-Brethren onlookers from miles around. It is estimated that 15,000 to 20,000 people gathered to witness the event.

Sarah Major died Sept. 18, 1884, but her name remains familiar to generations who have used Sarah Major Hall at Camp Mack.

An Indiana Pioneer

An early Indiana woman who carried on the tradition of Sarah Major was Bertha Miller Neher Stine. Born in Warrensburg County, Mo., in 1873, she moved with her parents to Wabash County, Ind., in 1874. She graduated from Mt. Morris Academy in 1893, and in 1894 married Levi Neher who was also from Wabash County, Ind.

The Nehers lived and taught school in Fruitdale, Ala., for three years, then moved to Chicago where Levi worked for a telephone company. They moved to Milford, Ind., about 1902 where Levi organized and operated a telephone company.

In Milford, they found a small Brethren group that had started a Sunday school program, and Levi (who was elected to the ministry in 1898) and Bertha helped organize them into a congregation. Their efforts led to the formation of the Bethel Church of the Brethren and the construction of a new church building which was dedicated Nov. 12, 1908.

Bertha and Levi had acted as full partners in the organization of the Bethel Church, and her work was officially recognized in 1910 when the Bethel congregation voted to make her a licensed minister. She was well known for her unusual speaking ability in the pulpit and was described as being able to preach with great power.

In addition to her preaching, Bertha became widely known as an author. She wrote a children's book, *Among The Giants,* in 1895, began writing for the *Brethren Teacher's Monthly* in 1907, and was editor and associate editor of the *Northern Indiana News Letter* for several years.

Levi had started an automobile business in Milford, and the Nehers moved to Warsaw in 1913 where he continued in the auto business. He was ordained to the eldership the same year and remained active in the church until his death in 1924.

Bertha continued to be active in the church including a short term as pastor at the Winona Lake (North Winona) Church. She traveled to the Holy Land in 1927 and used her experiences in a series of articles and sermons upon her return to Indiana.

She married Elder A.M. Stine in 1928 and died in 1948 at their home in North Manchester.

Mattie Dolby

One of the most interesting women in Brethren history was Martha (Mattie) Cunningham Dolby, a native Hoosier who struggled to work for the church against great odds—she was a woman and she was black.

Mattie Cunningham was born Oct. 28, 1878, in Cottage Grove, Ind. Both her parents were baptized German Baptist Brethren; her father at Cottage Grove and her mother at the Howard Church. Mattie was baptized when she was 16.

Mattie graduated from high school in 1899 and, in spite of the strong opposition of her father who thought only her brothers should go on to college, enrolled at Manchester College in 1900. She and her brother, Joe, cooked and ate their meals off campus that first year because of prejudice. In the second year, however, fellow student Otho Winger organized a group which supported Mattie and Joe and made them welcome in the college dining rooms.

Mattie worked as hard outside the classroom to support herself as she did on her regular studies, and she graduated in 1903. She joined James and Susan May in an effort sponsored by the General Mission Board to start a new church among the Afro-American people in Palestine, Ark. During that first year, Susan May died and James May left the mission after a small group had been baptized.

Mattie was left alone to continue the work. She successfully organized a Sunday school which provided more educational opportunities for her charges than did the public schools. She also worked tirelessly to secure funds for a new church building which her poverty-stricken charges could not afford.

Malaria was rampant in the South during this period, and it did not spare Mattie. Ill health caused by the disease forced her to leave Arkansas in 1906, and she moved to southern Ohio to work among several black congregations there. She met Newton Dolby, the son of a Brethren minister. They were married in 1907 and were installed as deacons of the Frankfort church near Jeffersonville, Ohio. It was here that she was elected to the ministry and installed in a ceremony Dec. 30, 1911.

Newton Dolby was a licensed engineer who worked at Wilberforce College. Mattie used the opportunity to study Greek during the two years they were there.

The family moved to Mt. Morris, Ill., in 1913, then returned to Ohio in 1917. They were living in Urbana, but there was no Brethren congregation located there. So the family made a 24-mile round trip to the Springfield Church every Sunday and often in the middle of the week as well. These trips lasted for seven years until a change of administration at the church caused the Dolby family to suddenly become outcasts. Mattie was told they were no longer welcome as before, and it was suggested they find someplace closer to their home to worship.

This act lost the Dolbys to the Brethren. The family joined a Methodist church where Mattie served as a minister for nine years.

Newton died in 1926. Otho Winger, the man who helped make Mattie and Joe feel welcome at Manchester College, was then the president of the school. His respect for Mattie was so strong that he traveled to Urbana to preach Newton's funeral sermon.

Newton's death created severe financial hardship for the family. Even though she had a college education, the only work Mattie could find was to take in washing and ironing; and even with the help of her six children, she was still unable to pay all the bills.

Mattie was forced to move her family back to the Cunningham family farm in Howard County, Ind., where her brother, John, operated a dairy farm. She lived there five years while her children grew up.

Several of her children moved to Chicago, and she joined them there for a short time. But in 1936, she returned to Urbana, Ohio, with two of her children. A few years later, a nearby Church of God congregation called her to be their pastor, a post she kept until her death in 1956. She was buried next to her husband at Oak Dale Cemetery in Urbana.

A tribute to her ministry occurred a short time after her death when the black congregation she served merged with the white

Northside Church of God in Urbana. The two congregations have worshiped together ever since.

Bertha Neher and Mattie Dolby were isolated cases, however. The struggle for an official role for women in the church continued at the national level throughout the late 1800s and well into the 20th century. At the 1885 Annual Meeting, a group of women met to discuss ways they could support the budding foreign mission effort. This led to the formation of a few women's mission societies in Pennsylvania and Illinois. However, a query to Annual Meeting in 1886 led to a vote which banned separate organizations for women. Persistence finally paid off in 1895 with permanent official recognition of women's groups to aid missions, and within a few years, most Indiana churches had organized such groups. Other votes taken during the 1890s, however, continued the pattern of male dominance.

A crack in this wall appeared in 1898 when Annual Meeting agreed that women could serve as delegates to district conferences. This action was interpreted by some to mean that women could also serve as official delegates to Annual Meeting, and Bertha Ryan, a former missionary to India, appeared as the first woman on the official list of delegates in 1899. By 1901, seven women were serving as Annual Meeting delegates, and one was from Indiana.

Women In Missions

It was on the foreign mission fields that many women found the freedom to serve the church they loved in ways they were not allowed to at home. Even without the formal titles, many women serving in foreign missions acted in pastoral roles. When these women returned home, it was difficult for them and for the church to say they could no longer perform the tasks they had performed so well in foreign lands.

The Brethren had forged a strong foreign mission effort by 1900. Many Indiana women were among those whose dedicated labor resulted in Brethren missions in China, India, and Africa.

Alice King Ebey was born near Laketon and attended Mt. Morris College, Manchester College, and the University of Chicago. She married Adam Ebey in 1900, and they went to India a short time later. She was in charge of a training school for workers and worked at evangelism. She wrote Bible commentaries in English which were then translated into Indian languages. The Ebeys returned to the U.S. in 1931, but Alice returned to India for two years in 1945 following her husband's death in 1939.

Winnie Cripe was born in Elkhart County and attended Bethany Seminary. In 1911 she went to China where she actively worked in the Sunday school program and other areas. She died in China in 1934 and was buried there.

Many other Indiana women worked actively on the mission fields as teachers, evangelists, and even physicians. Among them were Josephine Powell, Lillian Grisso, Minerva Metzger, Laura Shock, Ella Miller Brubaker, Anna Warstler, Josephine Keever Flory, Velma Ober, Ruby Frantz Rhoades, and Marguerite Burke.

Many of the women serving in foreign missions went with their husbands. One exception was Nettie Senger. A native of Fort Wayne, Ind., Nettie went to China in 1916 as a single woman. She had studied the Chinese language for about a year when she started developing a closer relationship with the villagers in her area of Shansai Province. This included arranging short overnight trips and staying in Chinese homes.

Nettie established special ties to the women of the villages and accepted Chinese customs as a way of getting closer to the people. She began wearing native Chinese dress and always carried knitting with her so she could join in the informal conversations among small groups of women.

A number of senior missionaries repeatedly admonished Nettie to stop identifying so closely with the Chinese people because she was demeaning the dignity of a Christian missionary. She ignored the warnings and moved ahead with projects she felt were important. She established a school for young mothers and wrote textbooks that were used in many schools all across China. During her years in the country, she earned a master's degree in Chinese philosophy and a doctorate studying the impact of Chinese civilization on women.

Nettie was forced to leave China in 1939 with the coming of war and revolution. She returned to Fort Wayne where she continued to be active as a Bible teacher and church worker. She was one of the charter members when the Beacon Heights Church was established in 1952 and remained active in the congregation until her death in 1969.

One of Nettie's hobbies was collecting old and rare Bibles. She gave her collection to Beacon Heights, and the church in 1975 turned over the collection to Bethany Theological Seminary. Among the many valuable items in the collection was one of the original Bibles printed in German by Christopher Sauer.

Other women found fulfillment working for the church in other capacities. Sunday school programs and music were primary areas where the church profited from the leadership of gifted women.

When the General Mission Board wanted to start a new congregation in Anderson in 1893, they sent Ella Raffensperger. She organized a Sunday school as the beginning of a mission point under the direction of the Lower Fall Creek congregation. She organized the first service on

June 22, 1893, and laid the foundation for a very successful congregation which remains active to this day.

When efforts were being made to support a fledgling congregation in Logansport, the Middle Indiana Mission Board sent Josephine Hanna and Dossie Webb who were instrumental in establishing a strong Sunday school program and boosting the evangelism effort.

Marguerite Bixler Garrett was born in Hartville Ohio and showed a great passion for music from an early age. She joined the church while leading singing for I.D. Parker who was conducting a series of evangelism meetings.

Marguerite enrolled at Mt. Morris College and soon after graduation became head of the music department. She was chosen to be the first music director at Manchester College when the school opened in 1895, and she became widely known in Indiana and beyond for her direction of congregational singing.

In 1906, she traveled to the Holy Land and, while on the trip, met O.D. Garrett who lived near Bluffton. They were married in 1908 and lived in Wells County for many years where they were members of the Prairie Creek Church. This congregation licensed her to the ministry which gave her authority to preach as well as lead hymns. She was active for many years in district and national activities until her death in 1963, and two of her hymns were included in the 1925 hymnal.

Cora Stahly

Another woman who found fulfillment in music was Cora Miller Stahly. She was born in Ohio in 1877 and showed signs of musical talent at a very early age. She finished high school and became a teacher in a German-language school when she was 16 years old. She entered Manchester College and graduated with the class of 1899 as the first student to receive a degree with a music major.

Cora then enrolled in the Chicago College of Music in 1900 and lived at the Hasting Street Mission which was operated by Brethren. Her father died while she was living in Chicago, and she helped her family move to Nappanee, Ind. She and the rest of her family joined the Nappanee Church in 1903, and Cora held her membership there for the rest of her life.

She married Clayton Stahly in 1904, and he supported her gift all his life. Over the next several years, she taught music at Smithville College in Ohio, was head of the music department at Manchester College from 1911 to 1920, and headed the music department at Bethany Bible School in Chicago from 1920 to 1922, commuting there from Nappanee by railroad.

Cora led singing at Annual Conference a number of times and was made secretary of the denominational music committee which developed a new hymnal in 1925. Soon after the hymnal's publication, the denomination realized many local congregations did not know how to use it, so Cora was asked to make a tour of churches in the West to teach them the proper skills. Clayton rented their farm, and the Stahlys spent the next 18 months traveling through Washington, Oregon, California, and other western states.

It was during this western trip that they fell in love with California and decided to spend their winters in that state. Beginning in 1926, they rented their Indiana home in October and drove to California where they spent the winter months. They followed this routine for the next 38 years. They sold their Indiana farm in 1940 and moved to a cottage on the eastern shore of Syracuse Lake.

In California, Cora was active in the Women's Christian Temperance Union and served as music director for the Los Angeles County WCTU for five years.

In October 1964, Cora and Clayton were honored by their friends in Nappanee and Syracuse on their 60th wedding anniversary. They left for California a few days later, and Clayton began remodeling their home. He was stricken just three weeks later and died. Cora returned to Nappanee where she lived until her death Jan. 1, 1971.

While women were able to find some avenues to express their faith through the church, they were still standing on the sidelines in many areas. Queries continued to come to Annual Conference, and 1910 proved to be a watershed year. At that conference, action was finally taken which allowed women to break bread at communion without an administrator, just as men did. At the same meeting, women were given permission to organize a permanent Sisters' Aid Society, which became the successor to the Sisters' Mission which was outlawed by conference in 1886. A half measure had been adopted in 1895 which permitted women to form sewing societies, but the 1910 action fully permitted a separate women's organization. The Sisters' Aid Society was recognized as an official organization of the Church of the Brethren in 1917. This evolved into the Women's Work program of the Church of the Brethren in 1930.

The activity of women like Bertha Neher and Mattie Dolby created serious questions throughout the Brotherhood. Queries began coming to Annual Conference asking by what authority some districts were allowing women to preach.

A ministerial statement was brought to the 1922 Annual Conference which included a provision for licensing sisters to preach. This provision caused a spirited debate, but it was passed. Licensing of women to the ministry was now officially sanctioned by the denomination, but women could not be ordained. In some cases, this created the awkward situation of a woman acting in a pastoral role who could not legally conduct weddings, nor were they officially sanctioned to conduct baptisms or communion.

This situation remained until 1952 when a paper was adopted which gave women pastors the privileges of an ordained minister in the congregations where they functioned as pastors. But it still did not give them the right to be ordained.

Annual Conference moved another step forward in 1956 when it was agreed that women could be elected to the office of deacon in their own right and not strictly as "helpmeets" to their husbands.

The final step came in 1958 when Annual Conference granted women "full and unrestricted rights in the ministry."

Taking this action did not mean automatic access to leadership and ministerial roles for women. In Indiana, as in other areas of the country, acceptance of women as ordained ministers has come slowly, although the state has often taken a leadership role in this area. While women have served in important leadership capacities, there are also congregations who still refuse to consider women as pastors, even on an interim basis, as a result of sincerely held beliefs about the role of women in the church.

In spite of obstacles, a number of Indiana women have made major contributions to the church in ministry over the last 30 years. A few outstanding examples provide snapshots of what life for them has been like.

Opal Nees

Opal Pence Nees vividly recalls the day she received her call to ministry: she was 15 years old in 1941, a sophomore in high school near her home at North Manchester, and in the middle of a history exam. "I had a religious experience," she says. "I knew I had to be either a missionary or a minister."

She was so deeply moved by the experience that she got up from her desk and went to a phone to call her church moderator Edward Kintner. He wisely advised the young girl to take her call seriously, but she needed to finish her exam, graduate from high school, and then go to college to prepare herself for what was ahead.

Opal followed Kintner's advice and attended Fort Wayne Bible College for three years. During that time, she was active in the old Fort Wayne congregation (predecessor to Lincolnshire) and found a great deal of encouragement there.

She then attended Manchester College, graduating in 1950. She was active in her home congregation, Pleasant View, during these years, and they responded to her work by voting to license her to the ministry in 1945.

Opal served in three summer pastorates while at Manchester. The first was at a Christian Church in Iowa where Dr. Edna Fellowes served as a role model and mentor. The following two summers, she acted on her own as a pastor at two tiny congregations in southern Illinois.

Her first permanent pastorate was at the Auburn Church from 1950 to 1954. Because women could not yet be ordained, Opal could not perform baptisms, marriages, or preside at communion. Those tasks were left to the district moderator. Arlo Gump and, later, Russell Sherman were called to Auburn to perform these functions during the four years Opal was there.

She was called to the Blissville congregation near Plymouth in 1954 and stayed there for the next eight years. They were eventful years. First, moderator Homer Kiracofe soon decided he didn't like it that Opal could not perform all ministerial tasks. He pushed the district board which agreed to Opal's ordination in 1955. The action was taken with the understanding that the ordination was only for Opal's term at Blissville, and she would have to seek ordination again if she moved to another congregation. This was in harmony with the 1952 action of Annual Conference.

Then in 1958, the denomination lifted all restrictions on women in ministry. A special ceremony was organized to confer permanent ordination on Opal.

In 1962, Opal began a two-year special assignment in South Bend to help with the transition as the congregation moved from being First Church of the Brethren to Crest Manor. She served as the second staff person and functioned as secretary and in Christian education.

It was in South Bend that she met and married John Nees in 1964. He died in 1974.

In 1964, Opal was offered a job at Elizabethtown College, Elizabethtown, Pa. She spent the next 12 years of her life there on the student personnel staff and as director of conferences. "It was an opportunity for me to be in touch with another segment of the work of the church," she explains.

In 1976, she decided to go back to the pastoral ministry and accepted a call at the Liberty Mills Church. She remained there until August 1989, and then embarked on a series of interim pastorates that took her to churches in Maryland, Ohio, Pennsylvania, and Indiana. She completed an interim assignment at Logansport in May 1992 and was serving at Pleasant Dale in the summer of 1992.

Opal has served the broader church as well. She is a member of the Manchester College Board of Trustees and is on the board of Brethren Benefit Trust. She also delivered a sermon at Annual Conference in 1989.

Opal says she has served as a woman in ministry in the Church of the Brethren with a minimum of complications. "There are a couple of reasons for that. I carried none of the baggage of the women's liberation movement. I started out long before that was an issue.

"Also, I started where people knew me. The people in the churches and the district leaders all knew who I was and were used to me," she said.

"I also think it made a big difference that I was at Elizabethtown (out of a direct pastoral role) during a very turbulent period of time. It's hard to say how things might have been different if I had stayed in the ministry then.

"The Church of the Brethren has been very good to me. I've had an empowered kind of ministry, and I owe that to the church."

"The longer I was at it, the easier it got. I've only really been challenged about my role a couple of times.

"My answer to people who question my role is that I'm a woman in ministry and there is nothing I can do about it. I can't change the fact that I'm a woman, and I can't deny my call."

Harriet Finney

Unlike Opal Nees, Harriet Wenger Finney does not remember a specific time when she felt a call to ministry. She describes it as a feeling that began growing during her teenage years when her family was at the Union Grove and Rossville churches. Harriet was a pastor's daughter. Unlike Opal, she did not receive a great deal of encouragement.

"I talked with my mother about it," Harriet says. "She didn't exactly discourage me, but she helped me understand that women who felt such a call usually married pastors and served with their husbands."

Harriet continued to feel the call to ministry, but it remained dormant for the next 15 to 20 years as she became a wife (married to Ron Finney) and mother. The Finneys were living in Colorado when she finally decided the time was right to actively pursue ministry. "I was about 35 years old, and I was the one who had to initiate the process," Harriet recalls.

This resulted in her licensing in 1978, and she began working in a part-time position as coordinator of ministries at the Northern Colorado Church of the Brethren, Windsor, Colo.

Two years later, Harriet received a call to accept a full-time position at the Plymouth, Ind., church. It was decided she would be ordained in Colorado in the Western Plains District since that was where she had originally been licensed.

Just two days before her scheduled ordination and three days before the Finneys were to move to Indiana, Harriet was admitted to a hospital in Fort Collins for surgery. The surgery occurred so abruptly that some members of the Western Plains District Board had already left home to travel to Colorado for the ordination service.

After some hasty arrangements were made, Harriet was wheeled into the hospital chapel on the originally scheduled Sunday, and she was ordained in the presence of a small group of people from the Northern Colorado Church.

In Indiana, Harriet took up the position of associate pastor at Plymouth in 1980. She was then called to be pastor at Plymouth in 1985 upon the retirement of Kenneth Yingst and continues to serve in that position.

When Harriet arrived in Plymouth as an associate in 1980, Opal Pence Nees was serving at Liberty Mills. Phyllis Carter had become pastor at Goshen City by the time Harriet became pastor at Plymouth. There were also a few women serving in pastoral roles in other denominations in the Plymouth area, which she found helpful. "There were no problems in my role as associate pastor at Plymouth," she says. "There were some who were opposed to my becoming pastor, but it was minimal."

More frustrating than outright opposition are attitudes that Harriet needs extra help in pastoral duties because she is a woman. "Sometimes people go out of their way to make sure I know how to do something. They think that my being a woman means I don't know how to handle some pastoral situations. Sometimes it would be easier if they would just come right out and say they are uncomfortable with a woman minister."

On the whole, however, Harriet's experience has been very positive. "I have felt very encouraged and supported by the people I've served," she says.

Phyllis Carter

Perhaps the best example of what Indiana women can now accomplish in the church is Phyllis Noland Carter. Many Indiana women seeking licensing and ordination over the past 20 years have listed Phyllis Carter as one of their role models.

Raised in southern Indiana, she grew up as part of the Church of God (Anderson). Married at age 17 to John Carter, they lived in Russiaville. Phyllis joined the church of her new husband, the Friends (Quakers), and became an elder at age 26.

In the late 1950s, John Carter attended a peace-making conference at Manchester College where he met Dan West. That meeting was to prove fateful about four years later when the Carter family experienced what Phyllis calls "a family crisis. I told John I had to have help," she recalled.

John remembered meeting Dan West and decided that if all Brethren were like him, Dan West's denomination might hold an answer. It was 1962 when the Carters first visited the Kokomo Church of the Brethren on a Sunday morning. Pastor Ron Petry paid a visit the following Tuesday, and Phyllis questioned him about Brethren beliefs for the next three hours.

John and Phyllis attended membership classes through the summer months and were guests at a love feast on World Communion Sunday in October 1962. Immediately after that event, they decided to transfer their letters of membership.

The Carters moved to a farm near Bryant, Ind., in 1966 and became part of the Hickory Grove congregation. Phyllis attended a Mission 12 event in Indianapolis the following year and encountered a spiritual experience which changed her life. She became involved in public speaking and publicly sharing her faith until one day in 1968 she felt she could no longer speak publicly. Together, the Carters decided they needed to be baptized in the Brethren tradition. Phyllis immediately resumed her speaking engagements after she and John were baptized at Kokomo by Ron Petry.

Phyllis and John were on a speaking tour in the East in 1968 when they were informed that Phyllis had been elected to the Church of the Brethren General Board. "I remember asking, 'What's that?'" she recalled.

The election had occurred at Annual Conference in Ocean Grove, N.J. At that time, it was not necessary to obtain a candidate's permission to be placed on the ballot. Phyllis was elected without any prior knowledge of her candidacy or any real understanding of the denomination's national structure.

In the fall of 1968, the Bethel Center congregation at Hartford City was seeking a pastor. The call went out to Phyllis Carter. She initially balked. "I told them Brethren don't have women pastors," she said.

But within a few weeks, her attitude changed. "I attended a joint communion service of Hickory Grove and Bethel Center at Bethel Center," she said. "When I picked up the cup, I started to cry because I knew it was a cup I couldn't put down."

At the time, Phyllis was a lay person. Although she initially was against being licensed, Middle Indiana District leaders convinced her it was important for a pastor, especially for a woman pastor, to have as much authority as possible. Two years later, she was ordained.

In 1968, Phyllis was one of the few Brethren women anywhere serving in a pastoral position. "I had a somewhat different attitude about it because of my background with the Friends. Women ministers are not unusual to them," she said.

She recalls having many contacts because of the novelty, but didn't feel she was the victim of much prejudice. "There was one deacon at Bethel Center who told me he didn't feel good about me being the pastor," she said. "I told him I hoped he would at least be my friend."

The first real test as a pastor came within a few weeks when nine people requested baptism. "I was scared to death, so I asked Ron Petry to come from Kokomo to do it," Phyllis said.

A few weeks later, 12 more people requested baptism. This time Petry was not available, so another minister was asked to perform the task. Unfortunately, this baptism turned out to be an unpleasant experience for those who participated, and Phyllis immediately went to visit each new member to apologize.

When she returned home, her deacon friend was waiting on her. "He told me, 'Phyllis, you aren't doing your job,'" she recalled. "He said, 'You are the person doing the calling. It's your responsibility to do the baptizing. I guess it doesn't matter that you're a woman.'"

Speaking with a group of male ministers from other denominations about her fear of performing baptisms, they all explained their own fears. "They helped me understand my fear wasn't because I was a woman; it was because I was treading on holy ground," she said.

After spending four years at Bethel Center as a part-time pastor, Phyllis was called to the Wabash Church where she served as the full-time pastor until 1978.

Throughout these years she continued to serve on the General Board, including serving as chair of the World Ministries Commission. She also became the first moderator of the newly merged South/Central Indiana District in 1971.

It was also during this period that Phyllis became the first woman to deliver a sermon in her own right at Annual Conference. The historic event occurred at Cincinatti in 1972. Sarah Major had delivered an address to Annual Conference nearly a century earlier, but she was invited to speak by her ordained husband, and it was made clear that Sarah was exhorting, not preaching. In contrast, Phyllis spoke on her own as an ordained Church of the Brethren minister.

During the late 1970s, denominational leaders were under pressure to move women into leadership roles. Attention focused on three women: Ruth Ann Johanson, Ruby Rhoades, and Phyllis Carter. The three met informally in North Manchester, Ind., at the home of Pat Helman, wife of Blair Helman, then president of Manchester College. "We knew how important it was for this to work out. We agreed we couldn't be in competition with each other like men often were and be successful," recalled Phyllis. "We knew what positions were being talked about, so we mutually agreed what direction each of us should go."

She enrolled at Bethany Theological Seminary and spent 1968 and 1969 there while also serving as interim pastor at York Center Church, Lombard, Ill. She became the district executive of the Florida-Puerto Rico District in 1980 and resigned from the General Board.

After three years, Phyllis felt a longing to get back into pastoral ministry. She heard the Goshen City congregation in Indiana was looking for a new pastor and, even though the church profile said the congregation would not accept a woman pastor, she moved ahead anyway. "I never paid attention to things like that," she laughed.

Within a few weeks, she received an overwhelming call and was installed as pastor of one of the largest Church of the Brethren congregations in Indiana.

While operating a successful pastorate at Goshen City, she continued to be active in district and national affairs. This culminated in January 1990 with a call to be placed on the ballot as moderator-elect of Annual Conference. Phyllis was in Puerto Rico as part of a work group from the Goshen City congregation when the call came from a Standing Committee representative. "I asked if I could have some time to think about it," she recalled. "They said, yes, I could have two hours."

Although she was reluctant, at the end of the two hours Phyllis returned the call to the United States and agreed to the nomination. She was consequently elected at the 1990 Annual Conference in Milwaukee six months later and installed as only the second woman moderator-elect in denominational history. (Elaine Sollenberger had served as moderator in 1989.)

Unlike most modern Annual Conference moderators, Phyllis chose to continue her full-time pastorate at Goshen City and serve as the spiritual leader of the denomination at the same time. Goshen City hired T. Wayne Reiman during 1991-92 to assist on an interim basis while Phyllis filled a heavy travel schedule.

Through all her travels as moderator, Phyllis said being a woman became a major event in only one place—Cuba. "They were deeply honored that our denomination sent a woman," she recalled. "They felt that if a woman was a denominational leader, then the Brethren must really mean what they say about all people being equal in the eyes of God."

Although her years of service to the church have led to the very pinnacles of denominational leadership, Phyllis has never forgotten where she came from, often describing herself as just an Indiana farm girl. "It's amazing how far an Indiana pig farmer can go," she often says.

An outward expression of this sincere belief was her use of a towel instead of a gavel during her term as moderator. It was a practice adopted from Dan West who also used a towel during his term as Annual Conference moderator. It was the influence of Dan West that originally brought the Carters into the Church of the Brethren. Phyllis chose to carry his spirit of service with her wherever she went.

9

From Sect To Denomination

For about the first 100 years after they came to America, the Dunkards more closely resembled the definition of a sect than a denomination. They lived in a controlled, somewhat closed society, although they never shut themselves off from the world; nor did they attempt to withdraw from it. Acceptable behavior was well defined and strictly enforced, right down to the manner of dress.

One of the first of the sectarian barriers to be breached was language. The close-knit Dunkard communities in Pennsylvania were almost exclusively German-speaking and were largely self-sufficient. It was entirely possible for a Dunkard to live, worship, make a living, and trade without being able to speak English. The first Bibles printed by the Sauer Press in America and the first Brethren hymnal were printed in German.

As the Brethren began to spread west and south, however, it became increasingly necessary for them to be able to speak English. By the time the first Dunkards reached Indiana, some congregations, particularly in the South, were already using English in their worship. The early Indiana churches initially used German almost exclusively, but they soon began using both languages and eventually switched to English.

The transition can be seen in the hymnals these Dunkard pioneers used. Between 1800 and 1850, hymnals were published either in German or in both English and German. After 1850, most hymnals used

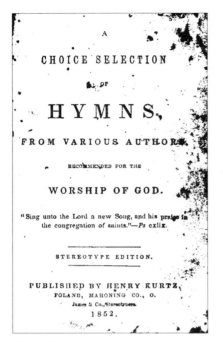
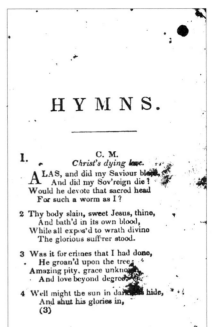

These hymnal pages show the changes that were taking place in the use of language in the church. Printed in 1852 by Henry Kurtz, the words were all in English. These reproductions are only slightly smaller than actual size which measure 2.5 by 4.25 inches.

English exclusively.

Ironically, one of the people who may have been most influential in the switch from German to English was Peter Nead, the man viewed widely as the leader of the Old Orders who split from the denomination in 1881 because they could no longer tolerate liberal reforms. Nead was raised in a German-speaking home, but he preached and wrote entirely in English.

Much of the support for the continued use of German came from the same people who supported Old Order positions on other issues. Nead became a chief spokesman for the Old Orders, both in the pulpit and in print. His consistently conservative positions put him in great favor with the most conservative elements of the church who became more and more willing to use English because that was the language Nead used.

It is also ironic that the leader of the Progressives, Henry Holsinger, included a regular column in his publication *The Pious Youth* devoted to instruction in the German language.

Although German culture continued to be a dominant influence well into the 20th century, the use of the German language had died out except for a few isolated pockets by the late 1800s.

Transportation

Improvements in transportation had a major impact on the church in Indiana.

The first settlers literally had to hack and carve paths through forests and swamps to get to the unsettled lands they were buying from the territorial government. It was just as difficult to get back out. Farmers who were resourceful enough to tame the wild land and grow crops were faced with major obstacles when trying to get their products (usually corn) to market. Initially, this could only be done on foot or on horseback. This method of travel was slow and severely limited the amount that could be carried. A few resourceful men built their own crude boats and rafts and floated down streams and rivers to the nearest market where the lumber from the rafts as well as the corn could be sold.

Eventually, footpaths became worn and widened into trails called traces that could sometimes accommodate wagons. Finally, the state became involved in providing improved gravel roads and highways which greatly improved a farmer's ability to market his crops. This process of early road building did not happen overnight, however, and it was well into the 20th century before improved roads had reached nearly every corner of the state.

For awhile in the 1830s and 1840s, there was a huge boom in building canals. A whole system combining canals and natural water-ways was envisioned which would link the major centers of commerce in the state and become watery highways for trade bringing untold wealth to the Hoosier state. A combination of private and public projects was undertaken, but most of these canals were never built. Those that were built never equaled the dreams of their promoters and many people who bought stock in private canal companies lost a great deal of money. Even the state government in Indiana nearly went bankrupt over broken canal dreams.

The coming of the railroads in the 1840s transformed the state economy and had far-reaching effects on the Dunkards. The canal bust quickly turned into a railroad-building boom as hundreds of miles of new tracks were laid across Indiana. The announcement that a railroad would be built through a town could turn a sleepy little community into a boom town almost overnight. In contrast, being bypassed by the railroad often meant economic ruin.

Most Dunkards in the 1800s were farmers. Initially, the railroads meant easier access to markets for their crops. There seems to have been little opposition to use of this new technology, especially when it came to improving farm income. In the late 1800s, however, the railroads brought an entirely new dimension to the church.

After the first continental railroad was finished in 1869, there was a tremendous rush of railroad building across the West. Within 25 years, there were five major transcontinental railroad lines. The federal government encouraged this frantic activity with generous land grants. Companies that built lines across the West were given huge tracts of free land as an incentive. Often, this amounted to alternating sections of land five to 10 miles deep on either side of the railroad line. The result was that railroad companies had tens of thousands of acres of land to sell.

The railroad companies were eager to find settlers to buy this land for two reasons. First, the sale of the land, even at rock bottom prices, helped offset the original cost of building the railroad. Second, the railroads needed steady income from customers who needed the transportation they provided. Settlers who turned bare land into thriving farms were the ideal targets—not only did they need to purchase fares for personal transportation, they also needed a way to get their crops to market, and trains were the best way.

Most railroad companies established land offices with agents who aggressively recruited settlers. Land was sold cheaply for $1 or $2 per acre and, in some instances, was actually given away.

Some land agents specialized in working on the East and West coasts where recent immigrants were arriving in droves looking for places to settle. This was how many Russian Mennonites settled in central Kansas.

Other land agents transplanted entire communities from the East along their western lines and specialized in persuading others like them to move west as well.

German Baptist Brethren were among those targeted by the railroad companies, and Indiana became a lucrative market. The Northern Pacific Railway was one of the most active railroad companies in recruiting Brethren settlers. Advertisements appeared regularly in Brethren publications touting the virtues and benefits of places like North Dakota, Idaho, and Washington. The ads often listed existing Brethren communities and the ministers who lived there. Potential settlers were invited to write to these ministers for unbiased opinions.

An ad in *Brethren's Family Almanac* in 1897 is a good example. The ad declared, "Farming in North Dakota is no experiment. Its record in 1895 was: wheat, 20 to 50 bushels to the acre; flax, 15 to 25 bushels; oats, 40 to 80 bushels; potatoes, 200 to 300 bushels, and other crops in proportion.

This ad promoting settlement in North Dakota appeared in Brethren's Family Almanac. It is typical of ads placed in the 1890s which influenced many Indiana residents to move west.

"It enjoys an enviable reputation for raising live stock (sic) and dairying. Its healthfulness is unquestionable. The summer heat never depresses and the winter cold never chills."

The ad listed more than a dozen Brethren settlements and gave a list of Brethren ministers already living there. The ad then appealed to the Brethren sense of community. "Churches have been organized at various points. The largest organization is perhaps that at Cando, where the membership is over 100. Services, however, are held at most of the places named above."

As late as 1914, an ad urged all Brethren attending Annual Conference in Seattle, Wash., to obtain a ticket on the Northern Pacific Railroad which would travel through these territories and give passengers a view of the farmland and a taste of the climate.

Land agents C.W. Mott based in St. Paul, Minn., and Max Bass based in Chicago were well known among the Brethren and trusted. Elder Amos B. Peters, who resided near Walkerton, Ind., became acquainted with Bass who represented the Great Northern Railroad. Bass persuaded Elder Peters to lead a group of Brethren to North Dakota to begin a settlement. In 1894, over 350 Brethren boarded a special train with Elder Peters that took them to their new homes near Cando, N.D. Elder Peters later assisted in establishing Brethren settlements in the Wenatchee Valley of Washington State along the Great Northern lines. It was largely through the efforts of these two men that literally hundreds of Brethren moved west into North Dakota and Washington, and the majority of them came from Indiana.

The railroads were more than accommodating in getting these settlers moved. Families who bought individual fares were often given free freight cars to transport all of their household goods, farm machinery, and livestock.

Brethren who moved west seldom did so alone. Entire family groups often moved together. Sometimes the groups reached beyond single extended families and included entire communities.

The movement of such large groups sometimes had devastating effects on the congregations they left behind, particularly when those moving away were among the leaders of the church. A large group moved from the Union Church in the 1890s, and it took the congregation a number of years to recover.

Another group left the Roann Church for North Dakota. A short time later, some came back to the Roann area, but soon left again to settle in the Wenatchee Valley in Washington. All of these moves created severe upheaval in the Roann congregation.

In a few cases, mass migrations weakened congregations so much that they never did recover and were eventually disorganized.

Urbanization And Education

Railroads were on the leading edge of a major social upheaval called the Industrial Revolution. The phenomenon changed the face of the United States, Indiana, and the Brethren.

The population of Indiana increased rapidly throughout the 19th century. Over the course of 100 years, the state had been transformed from a wilderness to a patchwork of cultivated farmland divided by roads and highways and dotted by towns and communities. The largely rural population was beginning to shift as more and more people found jobs in towns and cities where factories and retail establishments were springing up.

This change was reflected in the location of the largest and most active congregations. Prior to 1900, most of the Brethren churches were located in rural areas. Suddenly, new congregations were being organized in cities like Fort Wayne (1897), Elkhart City (1897), Huntington (1899), Goshen City (1905), Wabash (1913), Plymouth (1916), Second South Bend (1907), Anderson (1893), Indianapolis (1901), Kokomo (1916), and Muncie (1897).

At the same time, some rural congregations which had been large and vibrant began to decline and, in some cases, ceased to exist. A classic example is the old Portage Church organized in 1831. Portage was the second congregation organized in northern Indiana and built the first meeting house in the northern half of the state in 1851 about eight miles northwest of South Bend. It was home to such famous pioneer preachers as Elder David Miller and brothers Jacob and James Miller (also both elders). The congregation grew into one of the largest in Indiana during the 1860s and 1870s.

A series of divisions split off portions of the original Portage territory. Berrien was organized in 1867 taking Berrien County, Mich. This was followed by LaPorte in 1870 taking LaPorte County and Pokagon about 1870 taking Cass County, Mich. A large number of people left Portage in the 1882 split with the Progressives. Second South Bend was organized in the city of South Bend in 1907, further reducing the Portage territory.

All of these divisions resulted in a much smaller congregation with fewer leaders. Although the church struggled to regain what it had lost, the effort eventually proved futile. Portage was disorganized and the property sold in 1921.

Not only was the location of the church population changing, so was the makeup. Nearly the entire church membership in the early 1800s was made up of farm families. The small number who were not directly engaged in farming were nearly all related to farming in some way: millers, blacksmiths, and merchants.

The way people made a living began to shift in the mid- to late 1800s, and the pace of change accelerated rapidly with the coming of the 20th century. More and more people were employed in business and industry. In urban congregations, the balance shifted completely to the point that farmers became a minority, even a rarity in some cases.

A large part of this new pattern of living was another change in transportation—the automobile. Large numbers of people were suddenly able to travel much greater distances in much less time.

To the church, this meant the breakdown of territorial barriers. Brethren who resided within a particular congregation's territory were no longer constrained by travel to be part of that congregation. Church members became mobile and chose what church they wanted to attend based on the personality of the congregation, not strictly on how far away it was from their homes.

There were new attitudes and expectations about education. One of the major issues in The Great Divide of 1881-83 was whether or not it was proper for Brethren to pursue advanced education, which often meant beyond the eighth grade let alone college. The Old Orders were opposed to it while the Progressives went so far as to suggest there should be Brethren-sponsored colleges.

After the denominational split, many German Baptist Brethren (Church of the Brethren) openly supported the idea of higher education. Indiana was a leader in this area, which is covered in more detail in Chapter 10, *Institutions*.

This new emphasis on education created even more changes for the church. One small example was the struggle over the use of musical instruments in the church, particularly pianos and organs.

A number of Brethren had obtained musical training on their own from the mid-1800s on. Conservative Brethren condemned having musical instruments even in private homes, although many (including some elders) purchased pianos and pump organs. Some of these musicians wanted to use their talent in worship, but traditionalists would not allow it.

One of the best examples of the attitude at the time was at Middle Fork (later Rossville) where three meeting houses were in operation. After the 1882 split between the Progressives (Brethren Church) and the Conservatives (Church of the Brethren), the Edna Mills meeting house was used on alternate Sundays by the two groups until the late 1800s. The Progresssives purchased an organ and used it during their worship services. The next week when it was the turn of the Conservatives to use the house, the organ was unceremoniously shoved into a closet.

The first pianos began showing up in Indiana churches soon after the turn of the century, and the pace accelerated in the 1920s. It was not without controversy, however. Most congregations debated the issue over several years before the question was eventually resolved.

In some congregations, the question was resolved by a sort of default process. Pianos were sometimes donated by a particular family. Rather than offend these members or lose an excellent donation, congregations accepted them.

At Kokomo, the situation was slightly different. The debate over the use of a piano had gone on for several years when the youth of the church decided to take matters into their own hands. They managed to obtain a piano and, late one night, a group of young people lugged the heavy instrument up to a second floor classroom where it was covered with blankets. It wasn't until several weeks later that opponents to the use of a piano found out about its existence. They demanded its immediate removal. However, most of those against the piano were elderly and somehow there never seemed to be enough younger, able-bodied people around at the same time to haul the offending beast out. The piano stayed, and Kokomo still uses musical instruments today.

At West Goshen, questions about using a piano were raised repeatedly at council meetings beginning in the 1920s. After several years of debate, it was finally agreed in 1935 to use a piano in worship over the strong objections of some members. But that wasn't the end of the story.

Once the decision had been made to use a piano, a pianist had to be found. Several people in the congregation were capable, but they all declined because they were afraid of the possible repercussions.

Finally, a delegation went to Dean Henry on a Saturday evening and asked him if he would play the piano at the service the next day. He agreed and became the first person to play the instrument at West Goshen in a worship service.

Henry still vividly recalls the trepidation he felt as he manipulated the keys at the close of the service knowing that one of the strongest opponents would be waiting for him in the cloakroom. "I knew that as soon as I finished, he was going to collar me," Henry says. "Sure enough, when I went back to get my coat, there he was; but he was all smiles. He said, 'Dean, as long as everybody plays that piano like you did, it will be all right.' Boy, was I relieved."

Henry's piano-playing was so popular that he was asked to fill that role for the next 19 years until he finally asked to be relieved of some of the duties.

Pianos and organs began appearing in more and more churches until, by about 1950, they were commonly used almost everywhere. The use and variety of musical instruments expanded in the 1960s to cover a diversity of the musical spectrum. Guitars, horns, and drums became a part of worship. More recently, vocalists have used taped backgrounds featuring full orchestras. A church without a musical instrument has become an oddity.

With a new emphasis on higher education in the 20th century, the expectations of a minister increased. Free ministers had served the church since its inception, but seminary training, which had been nonexistent, now came to be a standard requirement. This led to the acceptance of paying salaries to ministers.

Burnetts Creek, which was officially organized in 1889, became one of the first churches in Indiana to begin paying its pastor. George Heeter was hired on a part-time basis in 1899 and was paid $200 a year. The congregation was heavily criticized by some of its neighbors at the time for having to hire someone to preach to them.

But the trend was unstoppable. The move toward a professional ministry was under way among the Brethren, and soon many other churches were paying their pastors, and a few were hired on a full-time basis. This was a change that occurred gradually. Some churches were served by the free ministry well into the 1940s and 1950s, but the majority of pastors in Indiana are now employed full time and the remainder receive at least some salary. A number of small congregations still operate on a part-time basis or share a pastor with another church in a yoked arrangement.

A symbol of the many changes that were occurring throughout the church at the turn of the century was the discussion surrounding the adoption of a new name. By the late 1800s, many people had become uncomfortable with German Baptist Brethren which had been adopted in 1871. Even though the last German-language hymnal was printed in 1903, the majority of Brethren could not use the language after 1900. The name was considered too limiting and was often cited as a hindrance to evangelistic efforts.

Even though the name of the denomination was officially German Baptist Brethren, they were still popularly known as Dunkards or Dunkers outside the church, and many members themselves clung to those terms. Annual Meeting came close to adopting the name Dunker Brethren Church in 1905. The discussion continued until 1908 when Annual Meeting adopted the name Church of the Brethren. It was the same year that the bicentennial of the original baptisms in Schwarzenau was being observed.

As with most other changes, some Indiana congregations immediately adopted the new name. For others, it took much longer.

One impetus to adopt the new name was World War I which made an affinity to anything German extremely unpopular. At West Goshen, for example, a stone marker identifying the church as German Baptist

Brethren was removed from the front wall and put into storage after the church and several individual members received threats. In 1933, the stone marker was taken out of storage and placed in a sidewalk. It was again moved and used as a cornerstone when an addition was constructed in 1955.

Mission Emphasis

Another new emphasis which thrust the Brethren into the world was the major effort put forward in foreign missions. The Foreign and Domestic Missionary Board had less than $10 in the treasury when it was created in 1884. By 1913, the General Mission Board (a successor agency) listed assets of nearly $1 million.

The Brethren mission in India, established in 1894, was highly successful. This success led to the opening of new mission fields in northern China (1908), Nigeria (1922), and Ecuador (1946).

Foreign mission work was seen throughout the church as a special calling. Indiana natives played important roles in all of the Brethren mission fields. Most received special support from their home congregations. Missionaries on leave thrilled Indiana church members with tales of the hundreds of people who were being won for Christ and the church.

This activity shifted suddenly about 1950. A major upheaval occurred following the revolution in China which brought Communist rule. All Brethren missionaries in the country were expelled in 1950.

In addition, there was a change in mission philosophy within the church. This led to the adoption of a mission strategy at the 1955 Annual Conference which called for the creation of independent, self-supporting churches indigenous to the countries in which they were located.

This new philosophy led to a number of major changes. The India mission became part of the Church of North India in 1970. Nigerian congregations became part of the Fellowship of Churches of Christ in Nigeria, then in 1973 became a fully independent Church of the Brethren in Nigeria (Ekklesiyar 'Yan'uwa a Nigeria).

This philosophy held sway for nearly 35 years until a query from an Indiana church once again lit the fire for foreign evangelistic mission efforts. The query originally came from the Goshen City congregation and was passed on to Annual Conference by the Northern Indiana District Board. It raised the question of foreign mission emphasis, specifically over the issue of establishing a mission in Korea.

The query was hotly debated in Standing Committee where some committee members felt it should not be considered because it had not come through the district council. Standing Committee voted to pass the query on to the entire delegate body at the 1990 Annual Conference in Milwaukee where it was once again the subject of intense debate. Many native Koreans who were Church of the Brethren members living on the West Coast were especially vocal in their support of a Brethren mission effort in their homeland.

The outcome of the debate at Milwaukee directed church officials to investigate the possibility of establishing a Church of the Brethren mission in Korea. A team sent to the country in 1991 recommended the establishment of a Brethren mission in Korea and efforts to do so have been launched.

Since then, there has been a flurry of potential mission activity, not only in Korea, but also in the Caribbean, especially Puerto Rico, Haiti, and the Dominican Republic. In 1992, it is still not clear what this new emphasis on mission will eventually lead to. What is clear is that the impetus for the change began with a query from Indiana.

Other Signs Of Change

Architecture was another symbol of the changing church. Dunkard meeting houses in the 19th century followed a similar pattern. They were simple, modest buildings. Most had two entrances, one for women and one for men, and the majority had only one large room.

The coming of Sunday school programs in the last half of the 1800s required the construction of multiple rooms to accommodate several classes. Many church entrances were also remodeled to include only one doorway which was used by both men and women.

A wonderful example of the changes that were occurring again comes from West Goshen. In 1885, the congregation decided to build a new, larger meeting house. The new church was built of brick and became a source of some minor controversy over an incident involving the windows.

Valentine Berkey, a prominent member, was appointed to secure materials for the project. He wanted arched, cathedral-type windows and doors for the new building, but also knew the conservative elements in the congregation would never approve them. He had the frames built in two sections—the lower section was of the standard rectangular shape and the top section was arched. These top sections were kept out of sight as construction progressed. When the bricks reached the tops of the rectangular sections, the arched tops were installed and bricked in place before anyone could voice an objection. Thus, the new church became the first German Baptist Brethren Church in Indiana to have cathedral-type windows and doors.

Even as late as 1951, church architecture was a controversial subject. The Plymouth congregation approved construction of a new building Jan. 12, 1951. It was also agreed to hire an Episcopalian architect to design the new church. This move was highly controversial and drew criticism from around the state from those who felt Plymouth was building a church that was far too fancy and expensive.

Church buildings in Indiana today reflect the varied tastes of their congregations. While some buildings still have the plain simple look of Brethren congregations from 100 years ago, others are indistinguishable from their Methodist and Baptist neighbors, including stained glass windows. A common thread which binds them all together, however, is a baptistry.

The Order

Not only did their buildings change, but so did the look of Brethren themselves as they abandoned the traditional garb (The Order). The issue of prescribed dress was another of the major issues that led to The Great Divide in 1881-83. The schism did not resolve the question for the German Baptist Brethren, and queries about dress were fielded at Annual Meeting almost every year.

A resolution passed by Annual Meeting in 1898 did not adopt more new rules. Instead, it called for stricter adherence to previous rulings. This did not sit well with many members who believed the issue of dress was sapping the strength of the denomination. Others believed dress should be determined by occupation, local custom, local environment, and family customs. Many felt dress should not be made a test of membership.

Three queries concerning dress appeared on the agenda for Annual Meeting in 1909. A study committee was appointed. The committee's report issued in 1910 presented historical and biblical reasons for retaining the rules, but did not provide suggestions for reconciling differences within the membership. Instead of adopting the report, delegates passed a motion naming a new study committee.

The report of the new committee was presented in 1911. In essence, it said that while prescribed dress was ideal, it should not be made a test of membership. Members who dressed simply were to be accepted in the fellowship, while those who dressed in worldly fashions were to be disciplined. In effect, simplicity and modesty were the new standards, not conformity.

One of the lengthier debates in Brethren history followed, but the committee's report was eventually adopted. Several attempts were made in subsequent years to change the 1911 action, but none had any significant effect.

As with many other changes, the style of dress for Brethren in Indiana did not change overnight. Many older members continued to wear the traditional garb for the rest of their lives. Change also tended to be slower in rural areas than in urban.

One of the last vestiges of the traditional dress was the prayer covering for women. The majority of women were still wearing prayer coverings well into the 1950s, especially at love feast and communion. The use of the prayer covering now varies widely from congregation to congregation. In some Indiana churches, the majority of women wear a prayer covering during worship services; at others, the prayer covering has become an interesting relic from the past.

Politics

Another sign of change in the Brethren has been an increasing involvement in political affairs. The original Dunkard settlers in Indiana had as little to do with politics as possible. Even being seen in the vicinity of a political rally was grounds for a visit from the ministers and deacons.

While a few Brethren had begun to be politically active in the late 1800s, World War I served as the catalyst for pushing the Brethren as a whole into the political arena.

When the United States entered World War I, a military draft was instituted. Brethren who held to the traditional values of peace and nonviolence were suddenly the object of severe persecution. Those who refused to serve in the military were imprisoned, and those who were inducted into the military were often the object of threats and derision if they made their objections known.

A special annual meeting was called Jan. 9, 1918, at Goshen City Church of the Brethren to deal with this problem. The result was a resolution approved by the delegates that became known as the "Goshen statement." It affirmed the traditional Brethren position on peace and military service and was sent to President Woodrow Wilson and other government officials. The delegates also appointed a Central Service Committee to deal with peace concerns and a Committee for Relief and Reconstruction.

Official government reaction to the Goshen statement was swift and harsh. On July 8, 1918, the officers of the special meeting at Goshen and the authors of the Goshen statement were threatened with prosecution for sedition by the War Department under provisions of the Espionage Act of 1917. A delegation met with Frederick P. Keppel, an assistant to Secretary of War Newton W. Baker, but they were unable to reach a compromise. After a great deal of prayer and consideration, the members of the Central Service Committee agreed to withdraw the Goshen statement from circulation and affirmed their loyalty to the U.S. government.

This experience led the Brethren to join other historic peace churches in lobbying the government for recognition of their religious objection to military service. By the time the draft was instituted again for World War II, there was official recognition for conscientious objector status. While not freed from government service, those who were conscientious objectors were allowed to serve in civilian capacities not connected with the military. Many young men from Indiana participated in Civilian Public Service camps and other forms of service such as being hospital orderlies during the 1940s.

Political involvement became even more evident during the 1960s. While a few Brethren had been candidates for local and state offices during the first 60 years of the 1900s, the decade of the 1960s brought a new kind of political action—demonstrating for and against specific causes.

One of the first issues to surface was voting and housing rights for Afro-Americans. This was followed in quick succession by peace activism during the Vietnam War, equal rights for women, abortion (both pro and con), the environment, and other causes. Many Indiana Brethren, particularly young people, participated in demonstrations, letter-writing campaigns and other forms of political action. Like the rest of the denomination, many Indiana Brethren have also been uncomfortable with such overt involvement.

It is typical of late 20th century Brethren that there is no universal agreement on any of these issues. Although the Brethren have historically been a peace church, surveys show a large block of the membership does not support that position. Many Brethren served in the military in Vietnam while others were on picket lines protesting against the war. The same difference of opinion is true for such emotionally charged issues as equal rights, the death penalty, and abortion.

It is perhaps one measure of how much the Brethren have changed in the last century that such diversity of opinion within the membership is tolerated and accepted as the norm. A person's position on such issues is no longer held as a test of membership.

10

Institutions

Following The Great Divide of 1881-83, many who remained with the German Baptist Brethren were interested in reaching out in new ways, much as had been advocated by the Progressives before the schism. This resulted in a variety of new activities including homes for orphans and the elderly, educational institutions, and camping programs, among others. One of the first and most active of these areas was higher education.

Higher education had been the subject of much debate throughout the 19th century. The Brethren accepted and even encouraged elementary education (usually through the eighth grade), but many people were suspicious of education beyond that level.

At the same time, the Brethren viewed teaching as an acceptable occupation, even holding it up as a worthy goal for its members. This created a dilemma because it usually required more than eight years of classroom work to become a teacher. The Brethren gradually became more accepting of high schools and attendance through grade 12, so this became less of a problem.

Education beyond this level, however, was consistently criticized through most of the 1850s. Several queries came to Annual Meeting between 1800 and 1858 asking about the propriety of Brethren involvement in colleges and academies. In each case, the delegates said Brethren should not establish such schools and should not be involved with them.

This position was suddenly reversed in 1858 when Annual Meeting declared that as long as these schools were conducted as private commercial ventures and in accordance with gospel principles, there was no reason for opposition.

One reason for this reversal may have been the increasing involvement of Brethren as educators. As the public school system developed, requirements for teachers became more stringent and demanded additional training. Brethren educators were inclined to meet these new standards regardless of the position of Annual Meeting, and few Brethren were willing to challenge the actions of these teachers because teaching was looked upon as a noble calling.

After the Annual Meeting action in 1858, there was increasing agitation by the Progressives for Brethren to become involved in higher education. It became one of the major issues in the 1881-83 split.

Although there were many nuances to the arguments for and against higher education, both sides of the argument were grounded in a fact they both agreed upon: increasing numbers of young Brethren were attending colleges, and many of them were leaving the Brethren way of life.

To those opposed to Brethren involvement in higher education, it was clear the reason these young people were leaving was because their education was causing them to question their beliefs. Therefore, higher education was the root of the problem and had to be eliminated.

Those promoting higher education drew a far different conclusion. They pointed out that young Brethren seeking higher education had to go to colleges and academies often sponsored by other church denominations, such as Methodists and Baptists. It was under this influence that many were leaving their traditional faith. Therefore, the answer was to provide Brethren-sponsored and influenced colleges which would not only help to keep Brethren young people in the fold; they could also be used as an evangelistic tool to espouse Brethren beliefs to students from other faith traditions.

A few of those who believed in higher education decided to take matters into their own hands and organized the first colleges and academies.

Salem College

The first college established by Brethren was located in Indiana. Although short-lived, it paved the way for the successful colleges which followed it.

A number of Hoosiers were among the most active Dunkards in their support of higher education. A meeting was held at the Antioch Church in Andrews, Ind., Feb. 10, 1870, to consider the idea of establishing a college or high school in the state. A formal resolution was passed at this meeting calling for the establishment of a college and calling for support from Annual Meeting.

The resolution came before the Middle Indiana District meeting where it met stiff opposition. After intense debate, it was agreed to pass the resolution on to Standing Committee.

At Annual Meeting, delegates reaffirmed the action of 1858 which, in effect, neither supported nor hindered the effort.

While this maneuvering was taking place, the Northern Indiana District took the process a step farther on May 28, 1870, when district meeting accepted a proposal from the town of Bourbon. Bourbon had been the site of a previous failed effort by another denomination at establishing a college. The town had taken possession of the grounds and buildings when the college operation ceased.

Bourbon officials offered to donate the grounds and buildings to the Dunkards if they would "establish a first class institution of learning and continue it in Bourbon."

Delegates to district meeting accepted the offer with very little dissent. An agreement between the Bourbon citizens' committee and officers of district meeting was drawn up which called for a college to be developed like the school at Oberlin, Ohio, except for the theological department. If, at some future time, the property was no longer used for a college, it would revert to the town.

The effort to establish the new school was quickly organized with a goal of establishing the first classes before the end of 1870, and it was decided the name of the new school would be Salem College. The first board of trustees included Jesse Calvert, Milford, president; J.B. Shively, Inwood, treasurer, Keylon Heckman, Bourbon, secretary, Paul Kurtz, Goshen, librarian; Joseph Harden, Goshen; and David Shively, Bourbon. They hired Oliver W. Miller, principal of the former Vienna Academy (a failed attempt at a Brethren academy in Pennsylvania), as the new president and recruited a small group of professors and teachers.

The organizers were keenly aware of the controversial nature of their actions. In an effort to head off some of the criticism, they announced in the first school catalog that the intent of the college was to supply "the means of acquiring an advanced education under the influence and tuition of members of our own fraternity." They also said Salem College would be "managed entirely by Brethren; having for its object mental and moral excellence instead of external display."

They also listed 17 laws and regulations governing student conduct. One regulation required students to sign a good conduct code. Another stated, "Indecent and profane language, rude and boisterous conduct, tippling; frequenting taverns, inns, beer houses, places of mere idle amusements and resorts of bad company, gambling, betting, games of chance, smoking tobacco within the college enclosure, or carrying concealed firearms or deadly weapons, and every other species of vulgar and immoral conduct are absolutely forbidden, and will subject the offender to punishment."

Students were not allowed to have general meetings together unless approved by a faculty member; no one from outside the college could address students without faculty permission; and secret societies and organizations were strictly forbidden.

Salem College received considerable support from both Indiana and Ohio, and the organizers met their goal when eight students began classes on Dec. 14, 1870. Twenty-two had enrolled by the end of the term.

A dedication service was held during the first term with the dedication address given by Barnabas C. Hobbs, the state superintendent of public instruction.

The second term began March 20, 1871, with 20 students, and there were 87 (89 by some accounts) enrolled by the end of the term. The fall term opened with 75 students and increased during the year to about 125. The future looked bright and there was great hope.

This early optimism quickly vanished, however, in the midst of a number of problems. Oliver Miller and the board of trustees clashed over several policy issues. A number of Brethren and a sizeable group of citizens from the Bourbon area felt the college should have been located at Warsaw, about 12 miles east.

In addition, a catalog was produced and distributed by a group of "friends of the institution" which was widely viewed as inflammatory. It described Salem College as being equal to any institution of its kind in the United States and Europe.

Miller resigned in the summer of 1871 to establish another school at Warsaw to be called Pleasant Hill College. This effort failed, however, and Miller returned to Salem College one year later.

The establishment of Salem College only served to intensify the debate over higher education. Within months of its opening, a query was forwarded to Annual Meeting in 1871 asking whether or not Salem College was being operated under the authority of the church.

Annual Meeting responded that it did not consider Salem College to be a church school, nor was it conducted by the general brotherhood. The statement acknowledged that the college was under the control of members of the church and was being supported by other members, but the denomination itself was not financing it in any way.

Intense debates over the college raged in church journals of the day. Many objected to the college being dedicated in the name of the

German Baptist Brethren without first getting the consent of the church. Several districts, including the influential Middle Pennsylvania District, passed resolutions protesting the use of the name Brethren with the college without obtaining permission to do so.

The college continued to operate successfully in the 1871-72 school year, but the 1872-73 year was financially disastrous as student enrollment nosedived. The trustees were forced to close the college in 1873, just four years after it was founded.

Many people blamed the closing of the college on active opposition of a number of Brethren which, they said, kept students away. Whatever the reasons, the failure of the school was a financial disaster for a number of individuals who had been major supporters of the effort. Paul Kurtz, for example, was financially ruined and worked for many years to pay off the debts that were left behind. Elder Jacob Shively, who had been a leader at the Yellow River (Mount Pleasant) church since its beginning, was so embarrassed by the failure of the college that he moved to the Union Church west of Plymouth. A special committee appointed by Annual Meeting helped to settle the debts, and the three-year contract between the church and the community of Bourbon was upheld.

For those deeply involved with Salem College, it must have been a bitter experience. History shows that the effort was not lacking; the project was simply ahead of its time, and the church, as a whole, was not yet ready to support a college.

History also shows the effort was not in vain. Salem College was the pioneer attempt to establish a Brethren college, and it helped focus the debate over higher education. The lessons learned from the Salem College failure were put to good use in subsequent efforts which were far more successful.

Manchester College

The dream of a Brethren college did not die with the failure of Salem College. A number of individuals and groups continued to push the idea. Several parallel streams of activity must be traced to a culminating point in 1895.

L.T. Holsinger from Ladoga conducted a survey which showed there were more than 100 young people from Indiana Brethren homes who were attending state and private colleges. He took the issue to the Southern Indiana District Conference in 1892, and the conference appointed a committee to consider the problem.

The committee met in Ladoga where they found the community willing to turn over an old school building to the Brethren and ready to back the effort with substantial gifts.

The committee brought a petition to Annual Meeting in 1893 asking permission to establish an institution of higher learning at Ladoga if they could raise $40,000. The committee then canvassed the area to raise the money, but they were only able to obtain pledges for $23,000.

During this same period, the United Brethren had established a college at Roanoke, but the facilities were not adequate and the denomination approved moving the location of the school. When this became known, competition arose between the communities of Elkhart, Churubusco, Columbia City, Kendallville, and North Manchester who all wanted the school. Only North Manchester was able to raise the required amount of money, so the United Brethren agreed to locate the school there.

A new building was begun in the summer of 1889 and the first classes were held in November. For five years, the United Brethren struggled to operate the school, but endowments did not materialize as expected and the effort was given up five years later.

Meanwhile, Prof. Emanuel S. Young had become interested in starting a Brethren college. Annual Conference authorized a committee to locate a place for the new school. Committee members included Prof. Young, Simon S. Young of Mt. Morris, Ill.; Levi T. Holsinger, Ladoga; Levi H. Eby, Summerville, Kan.; and David Hollinger, Pittsburg, Ohio.

Ladoga, Muncie, Nappanee, and North Manchester made bids for the school. In the spring of 1895, the locating committee met with a group from North Manchester. The town agreed to deed the college property (which included 10 acres of land and one major building) and $5,000 in cash to the Brethren if the Brethren also raised $5,000 and invested it in the college. Prof. Young was particularly in favor of the North Manchester site, so the committee quickly raised the needed $5,000 and assumed ownership of the land and building. Articles of incorporation for Manchester College were filed with the state in May.

Emanuel Young was named the first president of the college and was a member of the board of trustees. Other board members included Levi T. Holsinger, Simon S. Young, Gorman B. Heeter, David Hollinger, Levi H. Eby, and George L. Shoemaker. Simon Young (Emanuel's brother) was also appointed business manager of the college. Construction of a new building closely resembling the original built by the United Brethren was begun in the fall of 1895.

The first classes opened Sept. 11, 1895. The faculty for the 207 students included Emanuel Young, president, biblical literature; H.W. Ward, Latin and Greek; A.B. Ulery, natural science; E.M. Crouch, mathematics and English; W.R. Oyler, commercial; N.J. Beachley, stenography and penmanship; Marguerite Bixler, voice and piano; and M.R. Myers, elocution.

In addition, the faculty at Manchester taught 10-day Bible institutes in many churches throughout the state. Over 1,000 students were enrolled in these popular courses.

Over the next four years, money problems began to mount. All financial obligations for the school were the responsibility of private individuals, and the church took no responsibility. Emanuel Young resigned as president following the 1898-99 school year. H.P. Albaugh served as president for only one year. He was succeeded by L.D. Ikenberry who acted as chairman of faculty, not as president, during the 1900-01 school year.

By 1901, the situation at Manchester was critical. The college was $27,000 in debt and there seemed to be no forward progress. There was serious doubt the college could survive.

It was at this point that Elder I.D. Parker came on the scene. He had been on the faculty of Salem College and served as president of the board at Ashland College, Ashland, Ohio, during a very dark period of time. He had traveled across the country raising funds for the General Mission Board. Many felt he was the man who could save Manchester.

Elder Parker, Otho Winger (while still a student), and others launched a heroic effort which included several strategies. Although the trustees had already pledged a great deal of money to the school, they agreed to give even more.

Elder Parker traveled to district conferences in Indiana, Illinois, and Ohio to convince the delegates to take over the college if it could be turned over free of debt. Districts who agreed to this arrangement included Northwestern Ohio, Southern Illinois, Northern Indiana, Middle Indiana, and Southern Ohio.

Elder Parker then personally pledged $500 and convinced many others to do the same. The result was that on May 6, 1902, the college was debt-free when it was turned over to a board of trustees elected by the participating church districts. The new board included I.D. Parker, Frank Fisher, Daniel Snell, S.F. Sanger, L.A. Bookwalter, J.B. Light, H.J. McClure, and Jacob Wyne.

Prof. E.M. Crouch, who had been one of the original faculty members, was chosen president in 1901 and continued in that capacity under the new arrangement. The college was leased to a board of instructors who were to have direct responsibility of the operation of the school.

A number of critical improvements were made over the next few years including the construction of a men's dormitory and an improved library. Perhaps the most critical step forward was the gaining of full accreditation from the state on April 9, 1909. This status gave the school real legitimacy in the eyes of many potential students and faculty members. Also during this period, the Southern Illinois District withdrew from participation and the Southern Indiana District was added.

By 1910, the lease arrangement proved to be unsatisfactory. The solution was to turn over direct control to the board of trustees elected by the participating district conferences. Otho Winger, then vice president of Manchester, presented the plan to the district conferences. Many delegates were cool to the idea because it put the districts at more direct financial risk. Some of these objections were overcome by including a provision in faculty contracts which said the contracts would become void if not paid within 30 days.

Edward C. Bixler was hired as the new president in 1910. He was the first man to head the college who had obtained a doctorate degree. He held the position for only one year.

In January 1911, a new era for the college began with the election of Otho Winger as president. He was only 33 years old at the time.

Winger began his teaching career in a one-room school in Grant County where many of his students were Indian children. He attended Manchester from 1898 to 1902, then was a student at Indiana University at several times from 1902 to 1907 earning both bachelor's and master's degrees. During this same period he also served as high school principal at Sweetser, Ind., and superintendent of schools at Hope, Ind.

Winger brought a new energy and enthusiasm to the Manchester campus. In 1911, he led an effort to raise money largely among the faculty and students which resulted in the construction of a new gymnasium. Students did most of the work on the project.

In the years following, several more new buildings were constructed and additional land was purchased. In 1920, an administration building was built which linked the original college building (Bumgardner Hall) and the second building on the campus (the old Bible school building). A combination gymnasium and auditorium building was erected in 1926.

Much of the construction that occurred during this period was made possible by L.D. Eikenberry who served as treasurer and business manager from 1901 to 1943. He also had experience in construction and personally drew up the plans for many of the buildings that were erected on the campus. His knowledge of architecture and practical ability to deal with contractors saved the college untold amounts of money.

Until 1912, Manchester had never graduated more than two students a year. Under Winger's leadership, that total quickly began to grow until there were 21 graduates in 1915, 31 in 1920, 66 in 1925, and 154 in 1930. Enrollment during this period increased from 24 in 1910-11 to 611 in 1930-31.

One of the keys to the success of the college during this period was Winger's effort to improve the academic program. A major component of this work was recruiting able faculty members. One of his methods was to contact former Manchester students who had not completed their college degrees but were teaching in high schools. He persuaded a number of them to join the Manchester faculty and finish their college degrees at the same time. Many of these people later became active leaders at the college, including Vernon F. Schwalm who would succeed Winger as president. The curriculum was expanded and departments were added.

In 1932, two major events occurred which helped assure the survival of the college. Up to that time, Manchester had been accredited only by the State of Indiana. Winger led an effort which led to partial accreditation by the North Central Association of Colleges. Full accreditation followed rapidly and gave the school wider recognition as a legitimate academic institution.

Also in 1932, Mt. Morris College in Illinois merged with Manchester. Mt. Morris had experienced great difficulty throughout the 1920s, and a series of presidents had attempted to solve the problems with no great success. The final blow came in 1931 when a major fire destroyed the gymnasium.

An agreement to merge with Manchester was reached the following year. All records were transferred to Manchester and the assets were divided equally between Manchester and McPherson College, McPherson, Kan.

Another major historical year for Manchester was 1941. Otho Winger resigned as president that year due to ill health. During his 30-year tenure, he had taken a small, foundling college with four buildings and 24 students and built it into an accredited academic institution with a faculty of 40 and an enrollment of over 1,000. Even more than that, Winger was so highly regarded as a churchman that he was largely responsible for changing the negative attitudes many Brethren held toward higher education.

Vernon F. Schwalm succeeded Winger as president of Manchester. Born and raised on a farm southeast of South Bend, he was one of the faculty members Winger had recruited from the high school teaching ranks and had been at Manchester 16 years as a teacher and dean. He was serving as president of McPherson College when called to become president at Manchester.

Schwalm became president just as the United States became involved in World War II. The draft had drastic effects on enrollment which plummeted from an average of about 650 to a low of only 320 in the spring of 1944. During the war years, there were about 300 women on campus while the number of men enrolled in classes fell to only about 75.

Like most other colleges, Manchester experienced a major influx of students immediately following the war. Enrollment in 1946 soared to 865, including 539 men.

As a counterpoint to the war years, Manchester established a pioneering peace studies program in 1948. It was the first program of its kind anywhere in the United States and allowed students to graduate with a major in peace studies.

At the conclusion of World War II, the ranks of the faculty had diminished as well as the number of students. With increased enrollment, Schwalm faced the task of rebuilding the faculty.

At first, he tried to recruit leading Brethren educators, but they seldom stayed more than a year or two before taking advantage of other opportunities. So Schwalm copied Winger's actions of recruiting educators from the high school ranks and then encouraging them to further their own education while on the faculty, much as he himself had done. This proved to be a successful strategy and led to a number of faculty members obtaining their doctorates while on the staff at Manchester. In fact, there were more faculty members who had earned doctorates when Schwalm retired in 1956 than at any other time in the school's history.

The late 1940s and early 1950s also saw a great deal of construction on the campus. A new men's dormitory was built in 1947 and named for Dr. Calvin Ulrey, a trustee and generous donor. The Winger Memorial Building was completed in 1953, and a new women's dormitory, East Hall, was finished in 1956. Plans for the construction of a new science building were well under way at the time of Schwalm's retirement in 1956.

During his term as president, Vernon Schwalm brought many changes in the way the college operated: higher academic standards for the faculty, rigorous financial management, and an improved physical plant. His influence brought a more professional attitude toward higher education than Manchester had ever before experienced.

Schwalm's successor, A. Blair Helman, grew up in the coal mining towns of Pennsylvania. He received a bachelor's degree from McPherson College, McPherson, Kan., in 1946, and a master's degree in history from the University of Kansas in 1947. Helman was ordained in 1942 and served as a pastor in Newton, Ottawa, and Wichita, Kan. He also taught history at the university level in Kansas.

Helman was serving as chairman of the board of McPherson College at the time of his election as president at Manchester. The transition to a new president was a calm one. As Helman later described it, "After lunch, Schwalm went home, and I went to the office." At age 35, he was one of the youngest college presidents in the United States, much like Otho Winger had been.

Helman immediately set about building on the foundation left by Vernon Schwalm. This included improving the financial base and continuing the ongoing building program. Under his guidance, the science building planned during Schwalm's term was completed. By 1961, a new dormitory for men was constructed, additional dormitory space for women, a new maintenance building, and the Petersime chapel. A new student union was completed in 1964, and a new library was constructed. During his first 10 years as president, Helman oversaw the construction of seven new buildings and building additions and the addition of nearly 40 acres to the campus.

It was a time of dramatic growth. The operating budget increased from $753,000 to $2.3 million, and enrollment increased from 930 to 1,500 in 1970.

The 1960s became a turbulent era with conflicts over issues created by the Vietnam War and social change. A particularly tense episode was the appearance of Martin Luther King Jr. at a convocation in 1968. The North Manchester community was particularly unhappy. Security included FBI agents, state police, and buses filled with troops. During King's speech, plainclothes officers were located throughout the audience and at every door and window. King was assassinated only two months later.

There were a number of active protests against the war on campus, and large numbers of Manchester students traveled to Washington, D.C., to participate in peace marches.

President Helman insisted on rational dialogue in the midst of this turmoil. His leadership maintained good relationships with supporting churches, alumni, and the community at a time when many other colleges were struggling.

There was also significant expansion of the academic program during these years, and the first master's degree program came into being.

A new financial campaign in the 1970s raised funds for the construction of Cordier Auditorium and a significant increase in the endowment fund of $5 million. A second phase of this program raised funds for a new physical education center constructed in the late 1980s.

Helman announced plans to retire in 1986 following a 30-year tenure as president. The board launched a search which led to the selection of William P. Robinson. This selection was notable for the fact that he became the first president from outside the Church of the Brethren and who had no prior connection to Manchester College. He is

a man of strong religious faith, however, who has repeatedly emphasized the importance of the college's connection with the Church of the
Brethren.

Robinson has become noted for his excellent relationship with
students. He has also focused on increasing the number and quality of
students at the college, and there has been a renewed emphasis on the
spiritual life.

Manchester College has had a tremendous impact on the Church
of the Brethren well beyond Indiana's borders. Many of its graduates
have gone on to become leaders in the church and other fields.
Hundreds of graduates have had distinguished careers in education,
medicine, public service, and pastoral roles.

For many, Manchester was the place where both their professional
and spiritual lives were nurtured to prepare them to face the world. It is
a role Manchester College continues to fill in the name of the church.

Camp Mack

Interest in summer camping programs for youth began increasing during
the early 1920s. C.H. Shamberger, national youth secretary, arranged for
youth camps to be held at Winona Lake near Warsaw during the summers of 1921 and 1922. Another summer camp was held at Ludlow Falls
in southern Ohio in 1923, and two camps were held in 1924 at Camp
Nelson Dodd near Mansfield, Ohio, and at Oakwood Park on Lake
Wawasee near Syracuse, Ind.

Lawrence W. Shultz attended all of these camps as an instructor
and had done a study at Northwestern University on the value of
summer camps and conferences for youth.

The idea of building a separate camp for Brethren youth was raised
at both of the summer camps held in 1924. Shultz was asked to lead a
committee whose job was to establish such a camp. Other members
included Manly Deeter, John Eberly, Russell C. Wenger, and Moyne
Landis.

Also attending the 1924 camps was John W. Lear, an instructor at
Bethany Biblical Seminary. After attending the camps, he spent a week at
Lake Waubee near Milford, Ind., in a cabin owned by Jacob B. Neff. He
told Neff that he thought the site would be perfect for a Brethren youth
camp. Neff immediately wrote to Shultz offering his farm land as a site
for the new camp.

After touring several sites, the committee unanimously agreed
Neff's property on Lake Waubee was the perfect choice. In October
1924, both the Middle Indiana and Northern Indiana district conferences
gave their approval to the purchase of six acres of land on the eastern
shore of Lake Waubee from Jacob and Chloe Neff. The following

November, an additional 40 acres were purchased from the Syracuse Cement Company.

On Thanksgiving Day 1924, a group of volunteers began clearing brush from the site. It was decided the new camp would be named Camp Alexander Mack and that future buildings and other significant sites would be given names of significance in Brethren history.

Plans were immediately laid for the first camp to be held in the summer of 1925. This resulted in a rush of activity in the spring. The first donation received was from the Pine Creek Church. The money was used to build a cabin to house volunteer workers. In the following months, 12 cabins, Sarah Major Hall, and W.R. Deeter Cabin were constructed.

A dedication service was held July 4, 1925. Deeter Cabin was the only major building completed and only the foundation for Sarah Major Hall had been built. The dedication address was delivered by Otho Winger in a pouring rain as people huddled in the cabin and under a tent. L.W. Shultz later remembered that Winger spoke while water filled his shoes.

The first youth camp opened only three weeks later on July 27. By that time Sarah Major Hall had been framed in and was used as a dining hall, kitchen, and classrooms. Doors and windows had not yet been set in place when the first campers arrived.

Over the next 20 years, a series of major improvements were made as the camp and the camping program expanded. The next major building to be added was Becker Lodge, named for Peter Becker, the Brethren pioneer who led the first group of Dunkards from Europe to America. Much of the material for the construction of the original part of the lodge came from two disorganized churches—Pleasant Chapel, located just northeast of the camp, and Solomon's Creek, located near Benton. Both buildings were dismantled and stored in Sarah Major Hall until construction on Becker Lodge began. Most of the actual construction work occurred in 1934 after the camp received a substantial loan from D.W. Kurtz. There was a severe drought that year which increased the number of volunteers available to work on the project. Over 50 men were working at the site on a single day. The lodge was finally completed in 1936.

During the same period of time, Quinter-Miller Auditorium was being built (named for James Quinter and R.H. Miller Sr.). Men from the Northern Indiana District challenged their counterparts from Middle Indiana to build the big auditorium in 1933. It was designed to hold 2,000 people and took eight years to complete with most of the construction limited to the summer months. Field stone from the surrounding area was brought in to form the outside walls, and stained glass

windows were donated by John Worthman from Fort Wayne. The
windows were built into the walls at both ends of the hall. Northern
Indiana District Conference has met in the auditorium most years since
the building's completion in the spring of 1941.

Ulrich House was built over a six-year period from 1943-48 with
primarily volunteer labor, and Shultz Chapel (named for L.W. Shultz) was
built in 1948. John Worthman again donated stained glass windows for
this building. John Miller, the head carpenter for the chapel project, was
the first to be married in the chapel when he wed Lorna Sellers there.

A unique contribution to the camp was a set of murals depicting
Brethren history, sponsored by the Youth Camps. Medford D. Neher,
who was serving as pastor at North Poplar Ridge Church, Defiance,
Ohio, completed the paintings between 1945 and 1949. They were hung
in Quinter-Miller Auditorium and dedicated June 5, 1949.

L.W. Shultz completed a remarkable tenure of 30 years as director
of the camp in 1956. Raymond Hoover succeeded him and served until
1973. Arden Ball then became camp director in 1974.

While the camp has always been host to groups other than
Brethren, in recent years a new emphasis has been placed on year-round
use of the campground and facilities. Wampler Retreat Center was
completed in the early 1980s as an all-weather meeting site for small
groups. Becker Lodge was completely remodeled over several years in
the late 1980s and early 1990s and now serves as a conference center
with overnight guest accommodations and complete meal facilities.

The Indiana Camp Board, which oversees the operation of the
camp under the direction of the two districts in Indiana, has proposed a
long-range development plan for the campground, including the acquisition of additional acreage. This plan was still under consideration by the
Northern Indiana and South/Central districts in 1992.

Caring For Their Own

While Brethren were looking outward in home and foreign missions,
they did not lose sight of the needs close to home. Many were concerned about those unable to care for themselves at opposite ends of
the age scale: orphans and the indigent elderly who often ended up in
county asylums and poor farms.

Perhaps the more widely known such effort in Indiana was the
Mexico Home, predecessor to Timbercrest, but the first such facility was
actually built in the Southern Indiana District a few years earlier. It was
known officially as the Aged Persons Home and Orphans Asylum of the
Southern District of Indiana.

The move to establish a home for the elderly and orphans came as
query to the Southern District Conference in 1881. "Will not this district

meeting take some steps to erect an asylum for our poor members and orphan children?"

The answer was, "We will."

A committee of six men was appointed whose duty it was to travel throughout the district soliciting funds for the project and drawing up suitable plans. They included Elder Heil Hamilton, Elder John Caylor, Elder Daniel Bowman, Elder Jacob Rife, John W. Metzger, and William Hershberger.

The following year, it was reported $3,376.85 had been raised for the project. District delegates voted to proceed while continuing to raise funds until at least $4,000 had been raised.

The first building was erected in 1884 on a site three miles north and two miles west of Sulpher Springs in Henry County, Ind. Upper Fall Creek was the closest congregation. A separate building for orphans was constructed a few years later.

Bylaws for the home (variously referred to as the APH&OA or OPH&OA) were presented and approved at the 1886 district meeting. The duties of the superintendent were detailed as were admission procedures for the elderly and for orphans.

In 1887 the home had four residents, and district meeting passed two additions to the bylaws. Some congregations were beginning to send only those among their number who were very ill and required extensive care. A new rule was adopted that the home congregations of such people were responsible for the extra expense required for such care.

There was also a case in which a resident (referred to as an "inmate") had been allowed to visit the home congregation. While on the visit, this person made complaints about the treatment they were receiving. This resulted in a committee from the home congregation being sent to the superintendent to investigate the charges.

Although the investigation resulted in a vindication of the superintendent, district delegates believed that such investigations were improper. So they passed a rule that said any subsequent complaints were to be brought to the board of trustees for further action, not directly to the superintendent.

The home was also in the business of taking care of orphans and was quite successful in placing many of these children with new families. In 1890, it was reported that four children were living at the orphanage. An additional six children had been received and all six were placed in homes.

By 1889, the ownership of the home had become an issue. The original plan had been for the 15 congregations who contributed to the development of the home in 1882 to hold stock in the home in proportion to their contributions. Instead, the project was developed and ownership was held by the district.

A query to the 1889 district meeting challenged this method of ownership and suggested the district should relinquish control, turning it over to a joint-stock company owned by the congregations. It was suggested this method of ownership would put the home on a more solid basis financially. The query was tabled, but this transfer of ownership occurred a few years later. The ownership was then transferred back to the district about 1917.

Finances plagued the operation of the home from early on. A farm was established as a method of providing self-supporting income, but the operation was still largely reliant on contributions from churches and individuals. By 1891, it was reported the superintendent was owed two years back salary. The population at the home until about 1908 was fewer than 10 elderly people and from 10 to 15 children.

A series of improvements were made in the early 1900s, including new farm buildings and general maintenance, but by 1919, district meeting was told donations had been far too small to move ahead with planned improvements to the heating system, water supply, and electric wiring. Only about $2,200 had been raised, less than half of what was needed. The district approved a proportional assessment to each church to raise the funds.

In 1920, it was reported there were six elderly people and one boy living at the home. No further children could be cared for until more repairs were made, but there was no money available. The repairs were made the following year, and in 1921 it was reported there was room for 20 children.

The census reached a record in 1923 when there were 33 children and 14 elderly being cared for. A number of improvements were completed in the next few years resulting in a report in 1924 that the district had one of the most modern and best equipped institutions in the brotherhood.

In 1926, the census peaked with 36 children and 22 elderly people, and it was the most prosperous year the home had ever enjoyed. The Great Depression loomed just ahead, however, and the optimism quickly faded. By 1930, district delegates voted to discontinue caring for children and the census began to dwindle in ensuing years.

In 1934, it was reported the home had been operating at a loss for eight years and the farm operation had been losing money for four years. In addition, donations had nearly ceased and indebtedness was growing at an alarming rate.

The 1935 district meeting agreed to the sale of the home and farm. A public sale was held Nov. 7, 1935, and all of the houses and equipment used in the operation of the farm were sold. The 148-acre farm acreage was sold to Charles Kennedy in 1936. The indebtedness was paid off a few years later, and the district voted to keep intact an endowment fund of nearly $11,000.

Discussions about the possibility of joining in the operation of the Mexico home began in 1944. A specific proposal was considered at the 1950 district meeting. The proposal suggested the Southern Indiana District turn over $20,700 to the general fund of the Mexico Home. This represented the capital left over from the operation of the home which was closed in 1936.

In addition, the district would share the operating expenses on an increasing scale, beginning at 8 percent the first year and increasing to one-third by the seventh year.

Many Southern Indiana delegates objected to paying for one-third of the operating cost. While it was true the district represented a third of the state, only one-sixth of the membership was within its boundaries.

The proposal was sent to a committee which came up with a revised proposal. Of the more than $20,000 held by the Southern Indiana District, $5,500 in an endowment fund would remain under direct district control. The remainder would be given to the Mexico Home operating fund.

Operating expenses would be increased on a sliding scale of 8 percent the first year, 12 percent the second year, 16 percent the third year, and 20 percent the fourth year and every year after that. The remaining 80 percent was split between the Northern and Middle Indiana districts.

This proposal was adopted by a large majority.

The Mexico Welfare and Orphans Home

The Mexico Home was largely the creation of three people: Levi P. Miller and Frank and Lillie Fisher.

Levi Miller was a wealthy and generous member of the Mexico congregation. In April 1889, Miller asked the Middle Indiana District Conference held at the Salamonie Church for permission to build "an old folks and orphans home" at his own expense. The district conference gladly accepted this generous offer.

Miller immediately selected a board of trustees to govern the operation of the home. They included Elder Noah Fisher from the Mexico Church, Elder Daniel Shively from Pipe Creek, John Snowberger from Lower Deer Creek, Daniel Horning from Manchester, and James Himelick of Mexico. The board quickly established an organization, the facility was constructed, and a dedication service was held on Sept. 15, 1889.

Frank Fisher was hired as the first superintendent. He was a young preacher, teacher, and farmer from White County when called to the task after answering an ad in *Gospel Messenger*. He and his wife, Lillie, moved and quickly took up their duties.

As the first residents moved in, the Fishers made a quick discovery —older people and young children did not mix well. Fisher talked to Miller about his problem. Miller's solution was that another, separate building needed to be built for the children.

Miller made an offer to build a second building, again at his expense, if the district would agree to pay for the operating expenses of the facility. His proposal was made at the 1892 district conference held at the Roann Church.

Although there was tremendous appreciation for Brother Miller's generous offer, the delegates were very concerned about their ability to finance such an operation. The debate lasted most of the day until the session was adjourned for the evening meal.

Fisher was extremely discouraged and told Miller he was convinced the project would be voted down on the grounds of support. Miller, who was determined to see the project through, told Fisher to return to the conference and tell them he would build, furnish, and support the orphans' home without any expense to the district.

As soon as the meeting resumed, Fisher laid out Miller's even more generous offer, and it was accepted, although still with some reluctance.

The second building was erected, but very few children came to live there. So Frank Fisher made a bold move—he went to several surrounding counties and made a proposition. If county officials would send their orphan children to his home, they would be housed at Mexico for three months; if they had not been adopted at the end of the three months, the Mexico Home would keep them at the home's expense.

When they found out about it, the Mexico Home trustees were less than pleased. Some criticized Fisher for making the offer. Children soon began arriving, however, and the Mexico Home was very successful in finding adoptive families. Within a year, the Mexico Home was the third largest orphanage in Indiana.

Large numbers of idle children soon presented new problems, however, and Fisher realized he had to find something for them to do. Once again, he consulted the home's patron, Levi Miller.

Miller approached the 1899 district conference at Bachelor Run with a new proposal. He said he had given $1,000 to each of his own children, and he proposed to give another $1,000 to the district to purchase 15 acres of land adjacent to the orphans' home for the purpose of agricultural training.

The offer was accepted, and Fisher launched into farming with the children with his usual boundless energy and enthusiasm. Other contributions and money from a growing endowment fund were used to purchase an additional 90 acres.

Frank and Lillie Fisher directly operated the home for 14 years and for many years after that were directly connected to the operation as business managers and by serving on the board. Many young children reached adulthood considering Frank and Lillie Fisher as their parents.

The operation of the home grew steadily through the early 1900s. By the mid-1930s, there were 75 children and 60 older residents living there. They were closely connected to the nearby Mexico Church, and it was a common sight to see a line of youngsters marching to the church on Sunday morning and back again after morning services.

State rules governing orphanages became very stringent in the early 1940s. The new rules would have required spending a great deal of money to upgrade the aging facilities at Mexico, so the orphanage was closed Dec. 10, 1942.

The Mexico Home continued to be a sanctuary for older residents. It came under the joint control of all three districts in Indiana in 1951, described earlier in this chapter.

The Mexico Home trustees had been searching for a new superintendent for some time when they finally located Orville and Lois Sherman in 1959. The Shermans agreed to a one-year term of service, but it was over 18 years before their tenure finally ended.

Timbercrest

Stiffening state regulations and aging facilities again forced the districts to make some hard choices in the 1960s. A long-range planning committee selected a 20-acre site near North Manchester for the construction of a new retirement facility. This land was purchased in 1961, and an architect was hired. The name Timbercrest was selected.

The biggest hurdle was finding money to build the new facility. Initial cost estimates of $900,000 mushroomed as time passed to nearly $1.5 million. By the time bids were opened on March 15, 1966, the lowest combination of bids was for more than $1.8 million.

By trimming certain aspects of the project, the cost was brought down to less than $1.4 million. The board also approved selling notes to finance construction. The combination of these two actions led to a ground-breaking ceremony Oct. 12, 1966.

Construction of the original building took nearly two years. A public open house was held Feb. 25, 1968, with more than 2,000 people in attendance. Residents of the Mexico Home were moved to their new quarters at Timbercrest March 12, 1968, in the middle of a snow storm.

The central unit was finally completed in September, and Raymond Peters spoke at dedication ceremonies Sept. 22, 1968. Two additional wings were added in 1969 and 1970.

Orville and Lois Sherman retired at the end of 1978 after more than 18 years as administrators. David Lawrenz, who became assistant administrator in 1974, was named administrator and continues in that role today.

In the early 1970s, the board became aware that many people were interested in living at Timbercrest outside the central unit. This led to the construction of a number of independent duplexes beginning in 1974. As interest in these units grew, an additional 30 acres of land were purchased, and more units were constructed through 1984.

Construction of another wing for the central unit was completed in 1985.

Phase II of the long-range plan for Timbercrest began in 1987 with construction of a new health care facility and more residential units. Also added was a residential unit for assisted care which helps people operate at a maximum level of independence.

A centennial celebration was held in June 1989 observing the 100th anniversary of the founding of the original Mexico Home. Former Indiana Gov. Otis R. Bowen was a special guest at that event.

Timbercrest continues to grow and change to meet the needs of its residents. Planning is currently under way for further expansion of independent living units.

11

Hoosiers Meeting The World

The Church of the Brethren in Indiana has been richly blessed with an abundance of talented leaders who were willing to answer God's call. A few have served in ways that not only strengthened the church in Indiana but have had a large influence on the whole denomination and even beyond to the entire world. The lives of a few of the outstanding examples are outlined on the pages that follow.

Eldon Burke

Eldon Ray Burke was born June 14, 1898, in Marshall County near Walkerton, Ind. He went to Manchester College, graduating in 1922, and studied at the University of Chicago. While teaching in public schools near Plymouth, he met Cecile Davis whom he married in 1924.

Burke taught at Ohio Northern University and also served as a pastor, then served on the faculty at Shimer College in Illinois. He then served on the faculty at Ball State Teachers College (now Ball State University) in Muncie, Ind., from 1937 to 1943.

In 1943, the Burkes responded to a call from the church, and Eldon went to work for the Brethren Service Committee to open the relief center at New Windsor, Md. While performing this task, he was named administrator for the Council of Relief Agencies Licensed for Operation in Germany (CRALOG) following the fall of Germany at the end of World War II in 1945. Burke was headquartered in Bremen, Germany, through 1951. During that time, his agency handled over 100,000 tons of relief

Eldon Burke

Brethren Historical Library and Archives

supplies valued at more than $60 million. The food shipped into Germany through CRALOG literally meant the difference between life and death for thousands of people.

Following his work in Germany, Burke went to Poland, then to Iraq with the International Volunteer Service.

Burke returned to the U.S. in 1956 and joined the faculty at Manchester College. He remained part of the faculty until his retirement in 1970.

In 1975, Burke was honored by the German Federal Republic for his relief efforts with CRALOG 30 years earlier. He was also given an honorary degree by Manchester College in 1977.

Homer and Marguerite Burke

Homer and Marguerite Burke were both Indiana natives who pioneered mission work in Nigeria and Puerto Rico.

Homer was born in 1896 near Plymouth and studied medicine at Northwestern University. Marguerite was born near Middlebury in 1898. She contracted tuberculosis during nurse's training while in her early 20s. Because of this, no doctor would consider her for foreign service, which had been her dream.

Following their marriage, the Burkes applied to join the infant mission effort being started by the Brethren in Nigeria. They were accepted, including Marguerite in spite of her health problem.

The Burkes first arrived in Nigeria in 1924 and began their work by establishing a local health service. Beginning by supplying simple first aid, they gradually gained the trust of the Nigerians and developed a small hospital.

Although their emphasis was on providing medical care, the Burkes never forgot their evangelistic calling. It was Homer who extended the first evangelistic call in 1927 that brought forward the first converts to the Nigerian church.

Marguerite was a full partner in the mission work. She made important contributions to the medical treatment being provided, but also became well known for her identification with the Nigerian people,

Brethren Historical Library and Archives

Marguerite Burke   *Homer Burke*

quickly learning the language and accepting local customs. This was a great help in establishing the Burkes as trustworthy among the local population.

The Burkes stayed in Nigeria for 14 years before coming home in 1938. Homer established a medical practice in Bremen, Ind., and practiced medicine there until 1946. Then they accepted a call to work at the Castaner Hospital in Puerto Rico until 1961. Marguerite's quick ability to adopt local languages and customs again served them well.

The Burkes returned to the U.S. for a short time in 1961 with the intention of retiring, but they once again answered the call for help. This time they returned to Nigeria in 1962 where they would stay until 1974. While individual health care was still an important part of their work, much of their emphasis during this second period of service was on public health programs: innoculations, baby clinics, and health instruction.

The Burkes finally retired to Indiana in 1974. Marguerite died in 1978 and Homer died in 1983.

Andrew Cordier

Although born in Ohio in 1901, Andrew Wellington Cordier spent a large portion of his professional life in Indiana, was ordained in Indiana, married a native Hoosier, and is buried in North Manchester.

Cordier spent his childhood near Canton, Ohio, where he was part

*Andrew Cordier is shown at far right during a session at the United
Nations. With him are U Thant, center, and Dag Hammarskjöld
(Brethren Historical Library and Archives)*

of the East Nimishillen Church. He decided to attend Manchester
College after hearing Otho Winger preach. After earning a degree at
Manchester in 1922, he enrolled at the University of Chicago where he
earned a master's degree in 1923 and a doctorate in 1926.

He became part of the Manchester College faculty in 1925 while
still finishing his doctorate degree. He taught and chaired the Department of History and Political Science until 1944. He married Dorothy
Butterbaugh of North Manchester in 1924 and was ordained as an elder
in the Manchester congregation in 1938.

During his years at Manchester, Cordier traveled extensively
throughout Europe, the Middle East, and Paraguay. He was particularly
influenced by his observations in the Sudetenland and Danzig in Europe,
and by the aftermath of the Chaco War in Paraguay.

Cordier developed a wide reputation as a forceful speaker in
dozens of engagements throughout the Midwest and the rest of the
country. He actively opposed isolationism and spoke for an international
perspective leading to the peaceful resolution of conflict.

As his reputation grew, he become ever more in demand and was
drawn into the political arena. He served as a speech writer for Alf
Landon during Landon's 1936 campaign for U.S. president. He also

served as campaign manager when his colleague, Manchester Prof. J. Raymond Schutz, ran for a seat in the U.S. House of Representatives.

Cordier's national and international contacts grew even larger when he was named the first chairman of the Brethren Service Committee from 1941 to 1945. In 1942, he traveled to Puerto Rico to look at possibilities for a Brethren project there. This trip eventually led to the establishment of the Castener Hospital.

In May 1944, Cordier was granted a one-year leave of absence from his teaching duties at Manchester. The following October, he was appointed to a position as an adviser on international security to the U.S. State Department and resigned his post at Manchester. It was in this role with the State Department that he served on the U.S. delegation to the United Nations Conference in San Francisco. He was then sent to London in 1945 where he was instrumental in developing the United Nations charter. It was later said he could recite the entire charter from memory.

From 1946 to 1962, Cordier served as executive assistant to the U.N. Secretary-General and as under-secretary in charge of the General Assembly. This essentially made him the "right-hand man" to Trygve Lie, Dag Hammarskjold, and U Thant during their terms as secretary-general and put him at the center of the international stage. He was instrumental in getting Dean Rusk and Yakov Malik to talk together following the Korean War when relations between the U.S. and U.S.S.R. were at a low ebb. He spent weeks convincing Egypt's President Nassar to accept a Cordier-devised formula which eased the Suez Canal Crisis in 1956. Following the death of Hammerskjold in a plane crash (which Cordier always believed was not an accident), Cordier practically ran the United Nations until U Thant was appointed.

Cordier resigned his United Nations post in 1962 shortly after U Thant's appointment to become dean of the Graduate School of International Affairs at Columbia University in New York. In the late 1960s, Columbia became a center for student unrest over the Vietnam War and other social protests. Protests turned violent and students took over and occupied buildings. When Grayson Kirk announced his resignation as president of Columbia, the board turned to Andrew Cordier.

At the age of 67, Cordier became acting president of Columbia University at the most troubled point in the institution's history. Within weeks, the violence of the protests had subsided, and Cordier was able to return stability to the campus.

From the start, Cordier made it plain he was not interested in being Columbia's president on a permanent basis, and in 1970 he returned to his position as dean. His professional career was topped with a nomination for the Nobel Peace Prize in 1973.

Following the death of his wife in 1972, Cordier began working on a book based on memoirs of his days at the United Nations. He was still writing that book when he died July 11, 1975. Andrew and Dorothy Cordier are buried at North Manchester near Manchester College where Cordier Auditorium serves as a reminder of the life of this great church-man.

John Eberly

The success of thousands of student exchanges between the U.S. and other countries can be directly traced to one man—Indiana native John Eberly.

Eberly was born near North Webster, Ind., in 1904. His parents saw no need for any of their 13 children to have much education, so John literally ran away from home to attend and graduate from high school. With help from the North Webster Church of the Brethren, Otho Winger, and high school teachers Glen and Viola Whitehead, he graduated from Manchester College in 1929 and earned a master's degree from Indiana University in 1932.

While serving as president of the Northern Indiana Youth Cabinet, he met Ollie Heaston who was president of the Middle Indiana Youth Cabinet. They were married in 1925.

Eberly taught school and served as a pastor in Indiana from 1927 to 1948. He was one of the principle founders of Camp Mack, along with L.W. Shultz and others.

Eberly accepted an assignment in Italy in 1948 with the Brethren Service Commission. One of his duties was to distribute breeding stock being shipped to Europe by Heifer Project.

He pioneered the Brethren Student Exchange program in 1949-50. Two groups of teen-agers from Germany were brought to the U.S. to live with farm families and attend local high schools. Fifty were chosen from refugee camps and another 40 from a rural youth group in southern Germany.

This first effort was so successful that 400 students were approved for the program in 1950. The Farm Bureau and the National Grange joined as sponsors along with American Field Service and Kiwanis International. Students from Austria and a few other countries were included during this second year.

At the same time, Eberly capitalized on a suggestion from Thurl Metzger, then a Heifer Project representative in Europe, that Polish agriculture students be involved in an exchange program with the U.S. Ten students were involved in the first exchange in 1948, but the program was stalled because of East-West political tensions.

Eberly returned to the United States in 1950 to become director of the Brethren Service/Church World Service Center at New Windsor, Md. One of his primary responsibilities was to continue as adminstrator of the student exchange program. In 1957, the program received interdenominational support and became known as the International Christian Youth Exchange. The program continues to operate today with hundreds of students exchanged each year between the U.S. and dozens of other countries.

The Polish Agricultural Exchange program was restarted in 1958, 10 years after its suspension. Eberly succeeded in negotiations with the Polish government which resulted in a number of fruit and vegetable specialists being assigned to locations in Ohio and Washington. Another 20 came the following year. Over the years, several hundred Polish agriculture experts have participated in the program.

Eberly became the Church of the Brethren representative in Washington, D.C., in 1964 where he regularly testified before Senate and House committees on behalf of the church. He also wrote extensively in *Messenger* about legislative activity affecting the church, particularly the military draft. During this time he also served as a leader with the National Inter-religious Board of Conscientious Objectors and was a part-time pastor and district moderator.

In 1966, Eberly received the Distinguished Service Cross, First Class, of the Federal Republic of Germany for his extraordinary service to the German people. At about the same time, returning German exchange students formed the John Eberly Society which promoted and encouraged the ICYE program.

Eberly retired to Indiana in 1970 and remained there until his death in Fort Wayne Oct. 13, 1985. Just a year earlier, he had received an honorary doctorate of divinity degree from Manchester College.

Kermit Eby

One of the most prolific writers ever produced by the Brethren was Kermit Eby.

Eby was born on a farm southwest of South Bend in 1903. He graduated from Manchester College in 1927 and attended the University of Chicago. He was employed as a school teacher for a number of years in Indiana and Michigan.

Eby traveled to the Orient in 1933 as a member of a Quaker mission. He became executive secretary of the Chicago Teachers Union from 1937 to 1942, then became the assistant director of education and research for the Congress of Industrial Organizations (CIO) in Washington, D.C. He visited Japanese-American internment camps in the U.S. in 1942 for the Church of the Brethren, then went to Japan in 1945 as a member of the U.S. Commission for the Reorganization of Education.

Kermit Eby

Brethren Historical Library and Archives

Eby accepted a position on the faculty at the University of Chicago in 1950. He served as a professor of social sciences until his death from cancer Aug. 10, 1962.

Although he authored more than 100 articles for a wide variety of magazines and periodicals, he is probably best known for the uniquely Brethren point of view expressed in his books. In *The God in You* (1954), *Paradoxes of Democracy* (1956), *For Brethren Only* (1958), and *Protests of an Ex-Organization Man* (1961), he wrote eloquently about his Indiana Brethren upbringing and heritage and how they had shaped his life and beliefs.

Thurl Metzger

While Dan West supplied the idea for Heifer Project International, Thurl Metzger supplied the hands that made it a worldwide success.

Metzger was born near Sidney, Ind., a tiny community in Kosciusko County a few miles north of North Manchester. He taught school at Atwood and Kewanna from 1938 to 1942. He graduated from Manchester College in 1941 and married Ruth Landis the same year.

Drafted into the army in 1942, Metzger registered as a conscientious objector and was sent to a camp at Walhalla, Mich. He later went to work in an agricultural unit at the University of Minnesota.

Unable to find a teaching job after the war because of his conscientious objector stance, Metzger began working with Heifer Project and became the organization's representative in Europe. Ben Bushong retired as executive director of Heifer Project in 1951, and Dan West asked Metzger to take over the job.

Metzger immediately launched a campaign to increase support for HPI and guided its incorporation as an independent, nonprofit corporation in 1953. From an office at North Manchester, he successfully guided HPI during years of tremendous growth. Metzger traveled extensively from the very beginning. By 1958, he had already made six trips to Europe, three to Latin America, and one to the Far East.

He also wrote extensively, and his stories were often published in

Messenger. He wrote of his dismay that cheese, butter, and grain were piling up in warehouses in the U.S. while much of the world was still hungry. He appealed for more understanding of the problems in Latin America and urged Brethren to share food to build peace as a positive way to demonstrate the will of God. "A majority of the people in the world are hungry, diseased, illiterate, exploited and restless," he wrote. "We did not pay much attention to them; in fact, we did not know much about them ... until we discovered that they were becoming militant."

HPI's impact under Metzger's direction has been felt around the world. In the late 1970s, the Korean Minister of Agriculture stated that over half the chickens in his country were offspring from HPI chickens sent after the Korean War. The Korean dairy industry was largely rebuilt from dairy cattle supplied by HPI.

In the 1960s and 1970s, HPI became more involved in the breeding of animals for specific climates. In India, for example, bulls from the U.S. were bred with native Indian dairy cattle. The resulting crossbred cows produced four times as much milk as the native cattle. Within five years, the original six bulls had more than 30,000 offspring. Continued work in this area created what was termed a "white revolution" in the country and milk quickly ceased to become a scarce commodity.

Another HPI effort crossed Brahman cattle with Angus to produce a breed called Brangus. The result was a better meat-producing cow that could withstand tropical climates.

Although HPI is perhaps best known for its work with cattle, Metzger guided the organization as it branched into many other areas as well. Animals shipped to needy areas have included chickens, goats, swine, rabbits, and even bees.

HPI was directly affiliated with the Peace Corps in several countries during the 1960s and has been closely allied with agriculture ministries in many countries. More than 100 countries around the world have benefited from HPI's programs.

A major change occurred in 1971 when a beef-stock corporation donated a herd of 2,000 cattle to HPI. This enabled the organization to establish a 1,200-acre ranch near Little Rock, Ark., and the national office was moved from North Manchester to Little Rock in 1972. HPI now operates five regional offices across the U.S., including one in Goshen, Ind.

Metzger finally retired in 1981 after guiding HPI for 30 years. He still travels occasionally to promote HPI, but after a lifetime of international work now prefers to limit his trips within the boundaries of the United States. During a farewell address at his retirement, Metzger said, "The road to development is very long, it is filled with frustrations, and it is, in fact, more of a pilgrimage than a plan ... A sense of destiny requires that we have a firm belief that this is what God wants us to do ... and that we are willing to take risks, with God as our final evaluator."

Lawrence W. Shultz

Although Lawrence W. Shultz is most often connected with the development of Camp Mack, in later years he led groups of Brethren on tours that acquainted them with the European homes of their ancestors and brought them into contact with the Holy Land described in the New Testament.

Schultz was born Oct. 24, 1892, in Huntington County, Ind. He married Cora Winger June 1, 1915. He was baptized in the Salamonie congregation in 1900, elected to the ministry in 1910, and became an elder in 1919.

He was a school teacher in Huntington County and began studying at Manchester College while still working as a public school teacher. He received a degree from Manchester in 1914 and later earned a master's degree from Northwestern University in 1924. He was a high school principal before joining the faculty at Manchester College in 1924 as a teacher and librarian.

Lawrence and Cora Shultz

Brethren Historical Library and Archives

Shultz was instrumental in the development of Camp Alexander Mack (described in detail in Chapter 10, *Institutions*), and he and his wife, Cora, were managers at the camp for over 30 years.

He was active on a number of boards and committees for the Middle Indiana District from 1923 to 1946 and also served on the denomination's Board of Christian Education from 1923 to 1946 and the Brethren Service Committee from 1939 to 1946. He accompanied several relief shipments to Europe.

Shultz was active in book publishing writing seven books himself, assisting with six more, and helping to reprint many more which had been lost for some time. His topics covered Brethren history, genealogy, and Indian lore.

One of his principal interests was leading Brethren tour groups from 1949 to 1970. He led at least 25 groups on tours to Europe, the

Holy Land, and to points of Brethren interest in the U.S. and Canada. Several hundred people participated in these tours to more than 30 countries which brought many of them in close contact with their Brethren heritage for the first time.

Shultz was a resident of Indiana his entire life and died in the Hoosier state May 22, 1982.

Dan West

One of the giants who strode large across the Church of the Brethren in the 20th century was Dan West. Kermit Eby, one of his good friends, once wrote of him, "Dan West is a modern mystic, yet, like all his Brethren forebears, practical."

Born in Preble County, Ohio, in 1893, he graduated from Manchester College in 1917 and spent most of his adult life on farms near Goshen, Ind., with his wife, Lucille, and their five children.

As a young man, West was inducted into the U.S. Army in 1918 with the understanding that he would be assigned to noncombatant duties. When he was assigned to a machine gun batallion, he refused to serve and expected to go to prison for his stance. Instead, he was discharged from the army.

West studied at Columbia University, Harvard University, Ohio State University, and Chicago University. He obtained a master's degree at Cornell University in 1920. He then taught high school at several schools in Ohio. He was actively involved in youth work and summer camps during his summer vacations. During the years 1927 to 1930, he spent most of the summer months providing leadership to summer camping programs with other leaders such as Chauncey Shamberger, Perry Rohrer, and Alvin Brightbill.

West served on the denomination's Board of Christian Education from 1928 to 1930, then accepted an appointment as director of youth work in 1930. He met and married Lucille Sherck in 1932 and, although he was a member of the national staff, he chose to live on a farm near Goshen, Ind., rather than at Elgin, Ill., saying he preferred to remain close to the "grass roots" of the church. He was a member of the Elkhart Valley Church for many years.

He was active in peace education throughout these years. He was one of the organizers of "20,000 Dunkers for Peace" in 1932 which sought commitments from those who agreed not to engage in war. He encouraged young people to participate in work camps and peace caravans.

A turning point in West's life came in 1937 when he went to Spain for five months where he worked with a relief campaign aiding the victims of both sides in the Spanish Civil War. He wrote a number of letters and articles which were printed in Brethren publications that opened the eyes of many to the need for better relief organizations.

The idea that eventually became Heifer Project International began to take shape while West was in Spain. He often stood handing out powdered milk and water to long lines of mothers and children. While he knew the supplies he was distributing were saving lives, he also knew these same people would be back the next day. The eyes of these people—especially the children— haunted him, and he became determined to find a way to break the cycle of handouts and hunger.

Upon his return from Spain

Brethren Historical Library and Archives

Dan West is shown speaking at a Heifer Project International dedication service for a shipment of heifers bound for South America.

in 1938, West began proposing the idea of shipping dairy cows to areas in need to restock the devastated farms so a steady supply of milk could once again become available. In addition, the recipient of the animal would agree to give the first female offspring to someone else in need. Many of his neighbors in Elkhart County took up the idea and a volunteer group formed Heifers for Relief.

The first official church recognition of the program came in May 1942 at a meeting of the Northern Indiana District Men's Rally at the Middlebury Church of the Brethren. The Brethren Service Committee adopted it as an official service project the following June.

The idea behind Heifer Project was so elegantly simple that it appealed to many, and soon hundreds of animals were being donated. Because ships were not available during World War II, the first animals were sent to Puerto Rico, Mexico and the southern U.S. beginning in 1944. Thousands of cattle and horses were then shipped to Europe at the close of World War II. The United Nations Relief and Rehabilitation Administration supplied the ships, and hundreds of young Brethren men volunteered to take care of the animals during the voyages as sea-going cowboys on these "cattle boats."

During the 1950s and 1960s, Heifer project expanded rapidly, and it become an inter-denominational effort. Literally millions of animals have been sent to places where they are desperately needed. Today,

Heifer Project International ships thousands of animals each year to more than 100 countries around the world. But the heart of the effort remains Dan West's simple idea of giving aid in a way that will help the most.

While he is probably best known for Heifer Project, West served the denomination in a variety of roles working for the Board of Christian Education, Brethren Service Commission, and the Chrisitian Education Commission. He was very active throughout these years in supporting peace education, service projects, and human relations sessions. He retired in 1959.

West became the first lay person to be elected moderator of Annual Conference in 1965. Delegates to the 1966 conference still remember his use of a towel of service instead of a gavel to conduct the business sessions.

West contracted amytrophic lateral sclerosis in 1968. He was honored at the 25th anniversary celebration of Heifer Project in 1969, but could not speak because the disease had affected his voice. He died Jan. 7, 1970.

Otho Winger

One of the finest leaders ever produced by Indiana was Otho Winger. Winger was born Oct. 23, 1877, near Somerset in Grant County. He was baptized at the age of 10, and sometime during his early teen-age years decided he wanted to attend Mt. Morris College in Illinois. However, his father, John, was severely injured in a farm accident. After spending several weeks in a hospital, John returned home but never fully regained his health. It fell to Otho to help look after the family.

Although he had never taken high school courses, Winger took and passed the examination for a teacher's license in 1895. He then won a job as a teacher at the Indian Village school. During this time, he was elected deacon at the Cart Creek Church, then licensed to the ministry in 1897.

Winger enrolled at Manchester College in the fall of 1898 and plunged into his studies. It was at a time when the college was in a very precarious position financially. In 1901, Elder I.D. Parker was called in to help rescue the school from financial disaster. Otho Winger agreed to help and, with Parker in the lead, spent the winter months helping to raise $30,000. This money got the school out of debt and was to prove crucial to its survival.

While at Manchester, he met Ida Miller who was a teacher of typing and shorthand. They were married July 24, 1902.

It was also in 1902 that Winger decided to continue his studies at Indiana University. After one year as a student, he took a position as principal of the high school at Sweetser to earn more money for school. He returned to IU in 1905 and received a bachelor's degree.

He was appointed superintendent of schools at Hope, Ind., in the fall of 1905, but also continued studying at IU, eventually earning a master's degree in 1907.

Winger accepted an offer to teach history and education at Manchester College in the fall of 1907. It was the beginning of an association that would last for the next 34 years.

After just three years on the faculty, Winger was named vice president of the college in 1910, then was elected president in 1911. Although he accepted the post, he made it clear that he had not sought it. In his book, *Memories of Manchester,* Winger wrote, "I was not ambitious for any such

Brebren Historical Library and Archives

Otho Winger, president of Manchester College for 30 years, is shown at right with David N. Howe, president of the school when it was operated by the United Brethren.

job. I came to Manchester hoping to get a few years of college teaching and get a little money so I could go on to the university and take my doctor's degree, and teach history in some college and spend some time writing books.

"I shall never forget the night the trustees called me in and said that I had been elected president of the college. I frankly told them that I didn't think they had selected me because I was best fitted for the presidency, but because they thought I was about as well-fitted to break my neck trying as anyone else they knew."

At the time he became president, Manchester's future was anything but assured. There were fewer than 100 students, and it was not really a college in the true sense of the word. It was better described as an academy or Bible school. Most of the students had not graduated from high school before coming there and only a few were doing true college-level work.

All that changed during Winger's 30-year tenure as president. He worked very hard to upgrade the education level of the faculty and to improve the academic program of the school. He traveled widely to recruit top-notch Brethren students and garnered financial support which put the school on a stable foundation.

One of the proudest moments of Winger's life was the winning of accreditation by the North Central Association of Colleges in 1932. It was the seal of approval which made Manchester a legitimate academic institution and helped assure the school's future.

When Winger reluctantly retired in 1941 due to ill health, Manchester's enrollment had grown to an enrollment of over 1,000 students, and seven major buildings had been added to the campus.

Although Winger's name has most often been associated with Manchester College, he also worked tirelessly for the Church of the Brethren. Ordained as an elder in 1910, he was devoted to the church of his youth. He was an officer of the Middle Indiana District nine times, including six terms as moderator. He was also reading clerk of Annual Conference three times and was elected moderator six times including 1921, 1923, 1925, 1928, 1931, and 1934.

Winger was particularly active during a period in the 1920s which eventually led to the schism which created the Dunkard Brethren. He spent many hours late at night writing lengthy letters by the dozen to dissenting church leaders, particularly in the East, in an effort to keep them part of the church. His diaries contain notations showing he wrote as many as 20 to 30 letters in a single evening, often staying up until 2 a.m. Many of these letters were written on a manual typewriter and still exist in the archives at Manchester College.

By 1926, matters were coming to a head. Winger was convinced the large group in eastern and southern Pennsylvania with whom he had been corresponding did not want to leave the church, but there was another conservative block that was preparing to leave and wanted the Pennsylvania group with them. Winger himself estimated this could have involved as many as 14,000 people, which would have made it a much larger schism than the three-way split of 1881-83.

Queries had been submitted by the Pennsylvania group which Winger knew could not pass. He also knew that if they didn't pass, the group was likely to leave. On Monday evening before the opening of Annual Conference, he penned a substitute motion which he believed would be accepted by both the conference delegates and the Pennsylvanians. He was right. The motion passed, and the Pennsylvania group remained with the Church of the Brethren. Fewer than a thousand members actually left to form the Dunkard Brethren, and the group continues today with a membership of about 1,100.

While his correspondence with church leaders was particularly heavy during these years, he wrote literally thousands of letters to many people on nearly every topic imaginable. He was a highly visible man, and people from all across the brotherhood wrote to him for advice on everything from church doctrine to how to handle a difficult child.

In addition to his Annual Conference duties, Winger was also a member of the General Education Board from 1911 to 1915 and from about 1920 to 1941, and the General Mission Board from 1912 to 1943, including a 16-year tenure as chairman.

In his biography of Winger, Vernon Scwhalm noted that most of those who were affiliated with him at Manchester were unaware of how much work Winger did for the church in the area of missions. In addition to his work on the mission board, he corresponded personally with many people actively at work on the mission field. He and his wife made a round-the-world tour in 1928 visiting Brethren mission fields. He wrote detailed reports of the trip in Brethren periodicals and in a book, *Letters From Foreign Lands* (1928).

Winger was also a historian. His *History of the Church of the Brethren in Indiana* (1917) was a landmark, and it was said that he knew more about the history of the Church of the Brethren in Indiana than any other man alive. He contributed frequently to the pages of *Gospel Messenger* and authored at least eight books.

Winger had enjoyed robust health all his life, but this gift began to fail him in the late 1930s. With great reluctance in the spring of 1940, he announced his intention to retire as president of Manchester College the following year.

Ida Winger died Jan. 29, 1944. Otho's health continued to decline until his death Aug. 13, 1946.

Vernon Schwalm, Winger's successor as president of Manchester College, delivered the funeral sermon. In that sermon he said, "In the gallery of great men in our room of memory we will give him a place and say—and continue to say—whenever we speak of him, 'Here was a good man.'"

12

Mother Churches, Founding Families

From a tiny band of settlers in Union County, the Dunkards spread through Indiana like wildfire, taking their unique brand of the Christian faith with them wherever they went.

Early church growth followed a pattern. The first churches were founded by early bands of settlers. As more people came into an area, the original church territory was split and new congregations were formed.

Part of the rapid growth was due to simple demographics. Indiana was one of the fastest growing states in the United States from about the 1820s through the 1840s. Much of this growth was due to immigration, and that was true for the Dunkards. The bulk of the early settlers came from Ohio, Pennsylvania, and Virginia. At one time, it is estimated that one of every seven people in Indiana was a Dunkard.

Once they had arrived, settlers tended to have very large families. Eight to 12 children was the norm, and very large families of 15 to 20 children were not uncommon. Most of these children were raised in the church and stayed with it their entire lives.

There was also a zeal for spreading the gospel. A number of special men spent a good portion of their lives on horseback, traveling to scattered Dunkard settlers where they held services for anyone who wanted to attend. Their efforts led many people of non-Brethren background to the decision to be baptized. Most of these "circuit" preachers were attached to one of the original congregations in Indiana.

These original churches are often referred to as "mother churches," and the name is appropriate. Most of the more than 100 active congregations in Indiana today can trace their lineage to one of these mother churches.

Otho Winger in his *History of the Church of the Brethren in Indiana* identified 21 congregations as mother churches. He included

Four Mile (1809);
Nettle Creek (1820);
Raccoon, later Ladoga, (1826);
North Fork, later Pyrmont, (1829);
Bachelor Run (1830);
Elkhart, later West Goshen, (1830);
Portage (1831);
Mexico (1838);
Eel River and Manchester (1838);
Turkey Creek (1838);
Mississinewa (1841);
Salamonie (1845);
South Bend (District), later North Liberty, (1846);
Yellow River (1848);
Somerset (1848);
Rock Run (1850);
Blue River (1852);
Cedar Creek (1853);
Pine Creek (1854);
White (1858);
and Walnut Level (1867).

Depending on how you define a mother church, Winger's list may be too large or too small. For example, if you define a mother church as a church formed independently by a new group of settlers without assistance from another Indiana church, then Nettle Creek must come off the list. Nettle Creek was organized through the efforts of ministers from Four Mile.

One of the best examples of a mother church is the old Elkhart (West Goshen) Church. Elder Daniel Cripe was one of the first settlers on the Elkhart Prairie near Goshen in 1829 and formally organized a new congregation in 1830. From that beginning came Turkey Creek (1838), Rock Run (1850), Yellow Creek (1856), Baugo (1868), and Little Pine (1950). A multitude of congregations then sprang from these daughters until the entire family tree rooted in West Goshen contains the names of 28 congregations, most of which are still active.

This pattern was repeated in varying degrees throughout the state and was one of the secrets for the great success of the Indiana church.

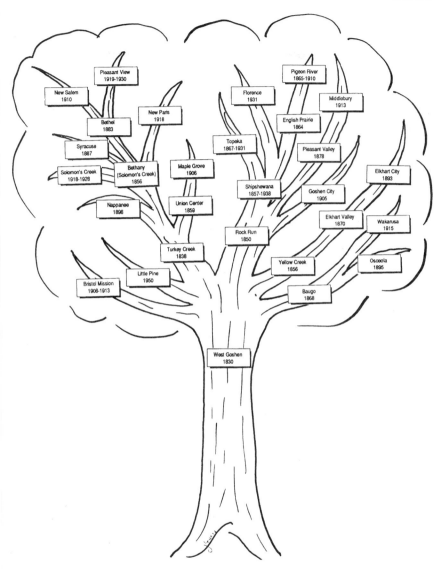

One of the best examples of a mother church is the old Elkbart (West Goshen) Church. Elder Daniel Cripe was one of the first settlers on the Elkbart Prairie near Goshen in 1829 and formally organized a new congregation in 1830. From that beginning came Turkey Creek (1838), Rock Run (1850), Yellow Creek (1856), Baugo (1868), and Little Pine (1950). A multitude of congregations then sprang from these daughters until the entire family tree rooted in West Goshen contains the names of 28 congregations, most of which are still active.

(Illustration by Jane Bowers)

Founding Families

The growth of the early church in Indiana is really the story of people—people of strong faith who believed in the importance of spreading the gospel as they understood it.

At first glance, it might seem more appropriate to label this chapter *Founding Fathers* since most of the early church leaders were men. But behind almost every major Indiana church leader was a family just as dedicated to the work of the church as the person usually given most of the recognition. We will attempt to paint brief portraits of some of the leading pioneer families in the Indiana church.

Bechtelheimer

Samuel Bechtelheimer Sr. was born in Franklin County, W.Va. He and his wife first moved to Clermont County, Ohio, then to Henry County, Ind., in 1827 where they were pioneer members of the Buck Creek congregation. Of their 10 children, two sons, David and Samuel Jr., became elders.

David Bechtelheimer was born in Ohio in 1821. He married Mary Stump in 1841 and moved to Kosciusko County in 1842 when it was still a wilderness and full of Indians. It is said they had only $5 in cash when they arrived. They settled in an area that at the time was within the territory of the Mexico Church.

David was called to the ministry in 1849. He became an elder in 1856 and was placed in charge of the Beaverdam Church. He was widely known for placing the interests of the church before his business and even, at times, his family. He was a carpenter by trade and one time lost an entire week's wages to preach at funerals, for which he didn't receive a penny.

The Beaverdam Church lost many members in the denominational split with the Progressives in 1882. David moved his family to Nebraska where his wife died in 1891. He returned to Indiana, remarried, and became active in the Upper Deer Creek congregation. He was the presiding elder at Lower Deer Creek when he died in 1896.

Samuel Jr. was called to the ministry in 1857 at Monticello. He was active for a time at Upper Deer Creek and was elected elder at Lower Deer Creek. He was the presiding elder at Lower Deer Creek when he died in 1894.

Berkey

Elder Jacob Berkey was born in Somerset County, Pa., and moved to Indiana in 1848. He and Sarah (Lint) Berkey were the parents of eight children, five born in Pennsylvania and three born in Indiana. The Berkeys settled in Elkhart County on a quarter section of land located across the road from the present site of the Rock Run Church east of Goshen.

When they arrived in Elkhart County, the closest congregation was Elkhart (West Goshen). The Berkeys soon began to actively organize a new congregation closer to their home.

Rock Run was organized in 1850, and Jacob Berkey was elected to the ministry the same day. He was soon ordained and placed in charge of the congregation.

Elder Berkey became widely known for his preaching, both in German and English. He spent many days traveling throughout northeast Indiana and southwestern Michigan which resulted in the organization of a number of new congregations.

Jacob Berkey was described as a man without fear who was not afraid to confront sin. He was strongly opposed to the use of tobacco and whiskey and was one of the earliest Dunkard temperance lecturers. He was often considered progressive in his thinking, advocating the single mode of washing feet at love feast and the formation of Sunday schools. One of the first protracted (revival) meetings was held at Rock Run under his leadership.

Elder Berkey served on a number of special Annual Conference committees. The Annual Conference of 1868 was held in his barn

His wife, Sarah Berkey, was well known for her hard work in keeping the Berkey household intact while her husband was often traveling for the church. She was largely responsible for the home and the farm while her husband was gone for days at a time.

The story is told that when the Rock Run congregation began talking about building a meeting house, some of the members objected on the grounds that they would have to wait to eat their noon meal until they had traveled all the way back home instead of having a fellowship meal. Elder Berkey reportedly volunteered to feed anyone in his home who felt this was a problem. There is no record that Sister Sarah raised any objection to this offer.

In fact, the Berkeys became widely known for their great hospitality. It is said that dozens, even hundreds of visiting Dunkards were fed and housed in their home.

About 1879, Jacob and Sarah moved to northeast Texas where he was instrumental in establishing several congregations. In the spring of 1881, he was called to conduct an anointing service. His route required him to cross a rain-swollen stream near Gainsville. A man on the other side warned him not to cross, but Elder Berkey waded into the water on horseback and was swept away. His body was recovered the following day. The judge and lawyers of the county, who had been impressed by his preaching, paid for his burial outfit. Sarah lived until Oct. 26, 1888.

One of their sons, Isaac, was 7 years old when the family moved to Indiana. He married Cornelia Andrews from New York. They lived on a farm across the road from the Rock Run Church adjacent to his father's farm.

Isaac was called to the ministry in 1885 and became superintendent of the Sunday school at Rock Run about the same time. He was ordained in 1891 and was placed in charge of the church on the same day, just like his father. He served as presiding elder for 20 years, and he served on Standing Committee at Annual Conference four times. Isaac died in 1921 just a few months after the death of Cornelia. They were the parents of five sons.

Bowman

Benjamin Bowman was born in Montgomery County, Ohio, and moved to the area of the Nettle Creek congregation soon after it was organized in 1820. He was well known for his ability as a preacher, both in German and English, and was elected presiding elder at Nettle Creek in 1830. He served on Standing Committee and several special Annual Conference committees. Late in his life, Elder Bowman moved to the Mississinewa congregation where he died in 1856.

Four of Benjamin's sons became Dunkard ministers. John Bowman was elected at Nettle Creek. He moved to Huntington County where he became the first elder of the Antioch (Andrews) congregation. Daniel Bowman became presiding elder at Nettle Creek in 1863. David Bowman was elected to the ministry late in life and was known as "Squire" Bowman because he was a justice of the peace. Jacob Bowman was also elected to the ministry and was known as an able preacher.

A number of Bowman grandsons and great-grandsons followed their ancestors into the ministry.

Caylor

Elias Caylor was born May 22, 1805, near Dayton, Ohio, to John and Salome (Kinsey) Caylor. Tradition holds that Elias was the first white child born west of the Miami River.

Elias married Sarah Umberger in December 1825, and they moved to the Nettle Creek territory in 1837. In 1842 they moved into the Upper Fall Creek congregation where he was elected deacon in 1843 and to the ministry in 1844. As a minister, he frequently traveled through the Indiana wilderness preaching to scattered Dunkards.

Elias and Sarah moved to Hamilton County in 1849 where he helped organize the scattered Brethren into the Stony Creek Church. He became an elder in 1857 and continued his travels on horseback preaching to scattered Dunkard families.

His son, David S. Caylor, was a physician who was elected to the ministry in 1864. Although he had great skill as a physician, his primary interest was the ministry, so much so that it is said he neglected his business and personal affairs to do the work of the church. He was a recognized leader in the Middle Indiana District and served as presiding elder at the Somerset church for many years. He died in 1903.

Several descendants of Elias Caylor were also involved in ministry in Indiana. They included John H., a brother, who was active at Stony Creek; and Abraham Caylor Jr., a nephew.

Cripe

Daniel Cripe was a true pioneer in every sense of the word. He was living in Montgomery County, Ohio, when he was first called to the ministry in the Wolf Creek congregation. He was one of the first settlers in northern Indiana when he came to Elkhart County in 1829 with his brother, Jacob, and two other families.

Daniel settled on a half section of land southeast of Goshen and erected a rude log cabin for shelter. He and his fellow settlers then built a crude plow, and he was selected to be the first to use it because he was the oldest. According to tradition, he was the first white settler to turn a furrow in the Elkhart Prairie.

He returned to Ohio in the spring of 1830 to convince others to move to the new land with him. Among those who followed him into Indiana were some of his children and their families.

As soon as this larger group arrived, Elder Cripe began preaching, largely in German, and a church was officially organized with Cripe as the presiding elder. It was originally called Elkhart, later renamed West Goshen. The first love feast was hosted in 1831 by Elder Cripe who donated the only ewe lamb he had for the meal. This was a considerable sacrifice at a time when livestock was a scarce and valuable commodity.

Elder Cripe was a tremendous force in the fledgling church in northern Indiana for many years, and much of the credit for the success of the churches in Elkhart County and surrounding areas can be laid to his initial efforts. He died Dec. 10, 1859, at age 87. Originally buried in a small cemetery at the south edge of Goshen, the remains of Elder Cripe and his wife, Magdelena, were moved in 1961 to the West Goshen Cemetery where their graves are marked with the original headstones and a newer memorial marker.

Deeter

William R. Deeter was born in Miami County, Ohio, in 1840 and became a teacher at the age of 18. He married Sarah Sipes in 1860. They moved to Delaware County, Ind., in 1866, settling on a farm south of Eaton. They relocated to a farm five miles north of Muncie in 1871, and it was in that year that he was called to the ministry in the Mississinewa Church. He was ordained as an elder in 1874.

In 1881, the Deeters moved to a farm three miles south of Milford and became part of the Solomon's Creek (Bethany) Church. It was at a time when the members at Solomon's Creek were talking about organizing a new church. The result in 1884 was Bethel. Elder Deeter became part of that congregation when it was organized and served as presiding elder for nearly 30 years.

He was also very active on a national basis serving on Standing Committee of Annual Conference many times and as moderator in 1898 at Naperville, Ill. He served as moderator of the Northern Indiana District for a number of years.

One of William Deeter's three sons, Manly Deeter, also became a church leader. He was born in Ohio in 1865 and came to Indiana with his parents. He married Ida Hoover in 1884, and they were baptized by his father.

Manly was called to the ministry in the Bethel Church in 1897 and became an elder in 1901. He served as moderator of the Northern Indiana District five times and as reading clerk three times, twice while his father was moderator. He also served on Standing Committee of Annual Conference several times. He was the presiding elder at Bethel for 16 years and presiding elder at New Salem for the first 15 years of its existence. He was a trustee of Manchester College from 1909 to 1915 and was very successful at raising funds for the college.

Following the death of his wife in 1939, Manley pursued mission work in Michigan's Upper Peninsula and in Kentucky.

Eiler

Samuel Eiler was born in Quebec, Canada, in 1791. His father, a German immigrant, had fled to Canada to escape persecution during the

Revolutionary War due to his beliefs about peace. The family moved to the Dayton, Ohio, area, and it was here that Samuel married Susannah Snyder in 1811.

Soon after their marriage, Samuel and Susannah settled on land near Hagerstown. It was on this land that the original Nettle Creek Church was built.

Because of the Eilers' hospitality and the proximity of their home to the church, the Eiler home became well known as a lodging place for traveling Dunkards. The Eiler homestead was the chief lodging place for Annual Conference in 1864.

At his death June 12, 1875, Samuel Eiler had served as a deacon at Nettle Creek for more than 50 years.

Fisher (Frank and Lillie)

Frank Fisher was born near Camden in 1856. His grandfather, Davis Fisher, was the first minister of the Monticello Church.

Elder Fisher's father, Benjamin, died when Frank was only 11 years old, and he became chiefly responsible for his family's support. In spite of this, he saved enough money to attend Monticello High School and became a teacher.

He married Lillie Reiff in 1881, and he was called to the ministry in the Monticello church in 1882. Frank and Lillie were called to take charge of the Old Folks' and Orphans' Home at Mexico in 1889 and remained there for 13 years. Many of the orphans who were cared for during this period fondly remembered them as Papa and Mama Fisher for the rest of their lives.

Frank Fisher was ordained as an elder in 1898 and served as presiding elder of the Mexico Church until 1921. He was also presiding elder at Huntington City, Pipe Creek, and Manchester for periods of time.

He served as moderator of the Middle Indiana District a number of times and was moderator of Annual Conference at Seattle, Wash., in 1914. He died in 1943.

Fisher (Peter)

Peter and Elizabeth Fisher were among the earliest settlers in the area around Mexico. Peter was born in Virginia in 1792. He married Elizabeth Brower, and they moved to Preble County, Ohio, in 1828. In 1836, they moved to Miami County, Ind., and settled on land about one mile north of Mexico. The Fishers were among the founders of the Mexico Church where he served many years as a deacon until his death in 1879.

The Fishers were the parents of 10 children, including seven sons and three daughters. Three of the sons (Isaac, Jacob, and Noah) were called to the ministry.

Isaac was called at Mexico in 1858 and became an elder in 1867. He served as presiding elder of the Mexico Church for many years jointly with his brother-in-law, Jacob Barnhart, whose wife was one of the Fisher daughters. Isaac Fisher served on Standing Committee of Annual Conference in 1885, and died in 1890 just as he was opening a meeting at the new Mexico meeting house.

Noah Fisher became a deacon in the Mexico Church. He was then called to the ministry in 1870 and became an elder in 1885. In addition to Mexico, he was also active in the Huntington City and Andrews churches.

Jacob Fisher served as a deacon, minister, and elder, all at Mexico.

Gump

Jeremiah Gump and his brother, Jacob, were pioneer preachers in northeastern Indiana.

Jeremiah was the better known and was the more active of the two men. He was born May 7, 1829, in Miami County, Ohio, and he married Sarah Shultz of Huntingdon, Pa., in 1850. They moved to Allen County, Ind., in 1853 when the area was still a wilderness.

Elder George W. Studebaker from Delaware County began to preach in the area and baptized the Gumps June 21, 1854. Jeremiah and his brother, Jacob, were both called to the ministry in the fall of 1854. They were also advanced together in 1857 and ordained as elders in 1862.

Elder Jeremiah Gump preached all through the northeast corner of the state, and most of the congregations in this area can trace their beginnings to him. He served as presiding elder of several congregations, was active in the district, and was elected to Standing Committee of Annual Conference. He was a large man, described as weighing over 200 pounds. He was energetic, enjoyed good health, and loved children, having 10 of his own.

His wife, Sarah, faithfully supported his work in the church and ran the family farm in his absence. Elder Gump often gave her much of the credit for his success. They had been married 62 years when he died Nov. 18, 1912.

Elder Jacob Gump was not as widely known as Jeremiah, but he served more than 40 years in the ministry. When the original Cedar Creek congregation was divided into four parts in 1870, he became presiding elder over three of them.

Jeremiah's son, Jesse, also became an elder. He was called to the ministry in 1898 and became an elder in 1905.

Hamilton

Hiel Hamilton was born in New York May 4, 1811, to Baptist parents. They moved to Fayette County, Ind., where his mother died when he was 12 years old. He was sent to live with friends in Union County where he remained for six years.

He married Nancy Kingery in 1830, and they joined the Four Mile congregation in 1831. Elder Hamilton was elected to the ministry in 1845 at Four Mile, and he moved to Howard County in 1846 in an area that was then within the Bachelor Run territory. It was here that he became well known for his backwoods preaching. Even though he had very little formal education, Hamilton was recognized as the best preacher in the area. He was active in the Southern Indiana District and served as moderator for many years. He became part of the Howard congregation when it was organized in 1852, and became the presiding elder in 1856.

His wife, Nancy, died in 1880. He then married Mary Crull in 1881 and moved to her home in Flora. He died in 1897.

Elder Hamilton's grandson, Dr. O.G. Brubaker, served as a medical missionary in China.

Hardman

David Hardman was an exception among the early Dunkard preachers in Indiana—he was well educated. In fact he taught school for a number of years and possessed his own library.

Elder Hardman was born in 1797 and was part of the Nettle Creek Church most of his life along with his wife, Susannah. He was widely known for his excellent use of language in preaching and his good judgment. He served on a number of special committees for Annual Conference.

It was on a trip to Annual Conference in 1863 in Pennsylvania that he contracted a cold which led to his death of pneumonia. His funeral was one of the largest held at Nettle Creek to that time.

Hoover

George Hoover was born Sept. 26, 1814, in Rockingham County, Va. He married Catherine Reiff, and they were the parents of seven children. They moved to Henry County, Ind., in 1835 settling two miles north of Sulphur Springs.

The Hoovers were baptized by the Dunkards, and George was called to the ministry in the early 1840s. He became the first preacher in the Upper Fall Creek Church where he labored for nearly 50 years.

Elder Hoover devoted nearly all his time to church work, leaving the work of the family farm to his wife and sons. He was most often traveling on foot and on horseback paying pastoral calls on families, conducting marriages and funerals, and preaching. He was known as an emotional preacher, often moving entire congregations to tears.

He was a strong advocate of peace, particularly during the Civil War, which caused him many problems. It is said he had many enemies, some of whom even made attempts on his life. Precautions were often taken when he was making trips that he was not waylaid somewhere along his path. One of his associates was actually shot and killed as he sat by the fireside with his family.

He refused to be intimidated, however, and traveled widely throughout northern and middle Indiana. He was chosen as the moderator for the state conference held in 1866 when Indiana was divided into three districts.

Age began to slow him down in the late 1800s, and he died Dec. 11, 1889. His wife died Feb. 9, 1900.

Elder Hoover's son, David F. Hoover, was also called to the ministry and became an associate with his father in the Upper Fall Creek Church. He became presiding elder at Upper Fall Creek after the death of his father. He was active in the district and served as reading clerk at the 1905 Annual Conference.

Huff

Abram and Sophia (Trowel) Huff were never ministers, but they were critical parts in the formation of the early Indiana church.

Sophia was born in Stark County, Ohio, in 1820 and was married to Abram Nov. 1, 1841. They were both baptized by the Dunkards shortly after their marriage and were soon called to be deacons.

The Huffs moved to a farm in Noble County, Ind., in 1848 and became part of a group which led to the organization of the Springfield congregation in 1850. All of the public services and meetings of the congregation were held either in their home or in their barn until a brick church was built in 1874. For one of the first love feasts before the Huffs had built a barn, they erected a special building constructed with lumber cut by their own sawmill. Over the years, the Huffs hosted nearly every elder of prominence in northern and middle Indiana.

Abram Huff died about 1892, and Sophia died in 1911. They were the parents of three sons and seven daughters, and a grandson, Elder Adam Ebey, served as a missionary in India.

Knisley

John Knisley was born in Montgomery County, Ohio, and moved to Elkhart County, Ind., when he was very young. He married Margaret Bainter in 1837, and they had four daughters.

He served 12 years as a deacon, then was called to the ministry in 1857 and became an elder in 1861. The family had moved to Union County by this time, and he was placed in charge of the Union Church where he served until advanced age forced him to slow down.

During his life, he traveled widely throughout Indiana and a number of other states on preaching missions. He served on Standing Committee of Annual Conference and was a frequent contributor to church periodicals. He was known to support many progressive causes.

His final days were spent in the Pine Creek Church, and he died Feb. 12, 1892.

Kurtz

Paul H. Kurtz was born in Stark County, Ohio, in 1828. He was the son of Elder Henry Kurtz who became the first editor of *The Gospel Visitor.* He moved to Elkhart County, Ind., in 1850 and raised a family of nine children on a farm west of Goshen. He was called to be a deacon and served in that capacity for 45 years

Kurtz was a man of vision who was one of the early supporters of the idea of higher education. He was among those who founded the first college for Brethren. Salem College opened its doors near Bourbon in Marshall County in 1870, but the early effort was not successful and the college closed in 1873. Many observers later blamed the failure on Brethren antipathy toward higher education at the time. Kurtz labored for many years to help pay off the debt left from the failed effort.

Lawshe

Isaac Lawshe was born in New Jersey Nov. 17, 1803, and married Nancy Rockefeller in 1825. It is believed he was elected to the ministry sometime in the 1830s in New Jersey. The Lawshes moved west to Ohio, then on to Indiana where they lived in Union County for a time and were members of the Four Mile Church. They were accepted as part of the Mississinewa congregation in 1850. It was here that he became an active missionary, traveling widely throughout the middle part of the state. A daughter, Mrs. Rhoda Anderson, later recalled, "I can well remember how he used to travel all over the swamps and wilds of Wabash and surrounding counties on his little pony to carry the gospel to the pioneers, and would come home almost worn out, covered with mud, and sometimes with feet frozen. He suffered very much, and I am sure his reward is great."

Elder Lawshe was widely respected for his preaching and debating ability. He was a major force in the evangelistic work that took place at the 1852 Annual Conference at Baintertown, the first held in Indiana.

The Lawshes were the parents of 12 children. They lived near

Somerset for about 10 years, then moved near Pierceton. Elder Lawshe was killed by a team of runaway horses Jan. 21, 1865.

Leatherman

John Leatherman was born in Maryland in 1776. Some of his ancestors were among those who came to the New World in the group with Alexander Mack.

When he was young, Leatherman moved to Tuscarawas County, Ohio, where he lived for 30 years. It was here that he was called to the ministry and made an elder. He moved to Elkhart County, Ind., in 1836 where he quickly became attached to the small band of Dunkard settlers who had come to the area five years before.

"Old Brother Johnny Leatherman," as he was known, began organizing the settlers who were in the southern part of the Elkhart (West Goshen) territory. It was under his guidance that the Turkey Creek congregation was officially organized in 1838.

Elder Leatherman was not a spellbinding speaker, but he was loved by those who knew him and was widely respected throughout Indiana and the denomination. He served twice on Standing Committee of Annual Conference.

He was the father of eight children. His wife died in 1850, and he died a few years later.

Leedy

Joseph Leedy was born in Augusta County, Md., Feb. 1, 1815. He moved with his parents to Preble County, Ohio, where he married Lydia Witter. He was called to the ministry in 1850 by the Preble congregation.

In 1853 the Leedy family moved to Huntington County, Ind., about one mile south of what became the town of Andrews. Here they prospered, and the homestead they carved out of the wilderness soon became a thriving farm.

Elder Leedy was a visionary with a community spirit. His home and later his barn were always open for church meetings. He was joined by his brother, John, and together they laid out the town of Andrews. They built a school house which was also used for church services. The Andrews congregation rapidly grew into one of the leading congregations in the state under their leadership.

While John's activities centered primarily on Andrews, Joseph traveled widely across Indiana preaching and witnessing. He believed in protracted meetings at a time when many in the church were opposed. Though he had only a limited education, he believed in the value of higher education and advocated that position in the church. He was a leader in the district from the time it was organized and served on

Standing Committee of Annual Conference. He was a member of the first Mission Board of the General Conference, serving from 1880 to 1884.

Joseph and Lydia Leedy retired from their farm in 1888 and moved to Huntington. In 1896 they went to live with their son, John, in Andrews. Lydia died Feb. 18, 1897, and Joseph died Jan. 13, 1903.

Long

Peter Long was a boy when his parents moved from Somerset County, Pa., to Holmes County, Ohio. Here he grew to adulthood and married Sarah Kaub. He was called to the ministry about 1860.

In 1863, the Long family moved with eight others to LaGrange County, Ind. Long was instrumental in building the English Prairie Church, donating land for both a meeting house and a cemetery. He was ordained as an elder in 1878 and was presiding elder at English Prairie for 30 years. He was active in the district and served on Standing Committee of Annual Conference one year. He died April 20, 1908.

Metzger

John Metzger was born Dec. 20, 1807, in Blair County, Pa. His family moved to Dayton, Ohio, when he was 12, and it was there he married Hannah Ulrey in 1828. Both of them were baptized soon after their marriage.

John and Hannah moved to Tippecanoe County, Ind., in 1834 where they were among the early settlers. They were early members of what is now the Pyrmont Church.

Metzger was called to the ministry in 1835, and he preached his first sermon in a sawmill to an audience of six people. He quickly became an active and effective preacher. It was said that he was threatened several times by angry men whose wives had been drawn into the church by "Uncle" John's preaching.

He was ordained an elder in 1843. When the Wild Cat congregation was divided, Elder Metzger was placed in charge of the southern half, known as Middle Fork (Rossville). He preached over a wide area in Indiana and served on Standing Committee of Annual Conference six times while living in the Hoosier state.

Elder Metzger moved to Cerro Gordo, Ill., in 1861 where he continued his activity in building up the church. He built at his own expense a meeting house in Cerro Gordo.

His first wife, Hannah, died in 1887, and in 1889 he married Parmelia Wolfe, a widowed daughter-in-law of Elder George Wolfe. They moved to Lordsburg (Laverne), Calif., in 1890 where he remained active in the church. His final public address was given at a district meeting in California in March 1896. He then traveled back to Cerro Gordo, Ill., where he died May 25, 1896. At his death, he had served on Standing Committee 18 times and had traveled thousands of miles on behalf of the church.

His son, John W. Metzger, was called to the ministry in the Middle Fork Church where he also served as presiding elder for many years. He, too, moved to Lordsburg (Laverne), Calif., where he died a few years after his father.

Miller (Jacob)

One of the most remarkable pioneer preachers in the history of the church was Elder Jacob Miller. Although he never lived in Indiana, he was responsible for organizing the first congregation in the state, and no Indiana history would be complete without him.

Miller was born in Franklin County, Pa., in 1735 to German immigrant parents. He was baptized by the Dunkards, called to the ministry, and married while still living in Pennsylvania.

He moved to Franklin County, Va., in 1765, which made him the first Dunkard minister in southern Virginia. He and his wife raised a family of nine sons and three daughters while living there.

Elder Miller became friends with an Englishman, William Smith, who was eventually called to the ministry. Miller and Smith often walked together 10 or 12 miles to lead worship services. Elder Miller would preach in German, and Elder Smith would follow in English. Their efforts laid the foundation for the church in southern Virginia.

In 1800 Elder Miller moved to an area near Dayton, Ohio, on the west side of the Miami River. He was among the first Dunkard ministers to move into Ohio, and may have been the first elder to preach in the state. The area was still a wilderness inhabited by many Indians when he arrived. It is said he visited the Indians often to sing and pray with them and quickly gained their respect and their promise of protection. They called him "the Good man" and "the Great Spirit sent from the East."

Although he was already 65 years old when he moved to Ohio as a pioneer settler, he vigorously pursued evangelism in Montgomery, Darke, and Preble counties in Ohio. These three counties later figured prominently in the movement of the church into Indiana as descendants of the settlers in this area moved farther west.

Elder Miller was aware of the early Dunkard settlers along the Four Mile just across the border from Ohio when they moved there in about 1804. Some of these early settlers included his children. Even though he would have been about 70 years old, he was the first to visit them on preaching missions, which gives him recognition as the first Dunkard elder to preach in Indiana.

In 1809, Elder Miller and John Hart came to the Four Mile and organized what has traditionally been recognized as the first Dunkard congregation in Indiana. It was known as the Four Mile Church and is considered the mother church for the entire state.

Elder Miller died at his Ohio home in 1816 after giving more than 50 years of his life to the ministry. He was buried in a cemetery near the Lower Miami Church. This cemetery was neglected for over 50 years and was cultivated for 20 years before Elder Miller's grave was rediscovered and marked on July 5, 1916, the centennial of his death.

Many of Jacob Miller's descendants became important figures in the Church of the Brethren. One son, Aaron, was born in 1785 in Franklin County, Va., and moved with his parents to Ohio in 1800. He married Elizabeth Hardman, and they had a family of 11 children. The family moved to Wayne County, Ind., in 1818 where they were among the first members of the Nettle Creek Church. He was called to the ministry prior to 1820. In 1829, Aaron and his family moved to St. Joseph County near South Bend. Aaron's son, David Jr., was called to the ministry in the Portage Prairie Church and became an important church leader there.

Another of Jacob Sr.'s sons, David Miller Sr., was also a pioneer leader at Portage Prairie and is often confused with his nephew, David Jr. David Sr. was born in Virginia and came to Ohio with the family in 1800. He was elected to the ministry in Ohio and settled near Hagerstown about 1817. He became the first minister and presiding elder of the Nettle Creek Church. David Sr. and his family moved to St. Joseph County in 1830 where he became the first presiding elder of the Portage Prairie congregation. He died at the age of 52.

When Elder Jacob Miller Sr. died in 1816, he was the father of 12 children and the grandfather of nearly 100. Literally thousands of Millers, some still part of the Church of the Brethren and some not, can trace their lineage to this pioneer Dunkard preacher.

Miller (Jacob Jr. and James)

Jacob Miller Jr. was a grandson of Elder Jacob Miller Sr. He was born March 6, 1812, in Preble County, Ohio, the oldest child in a family of 16 children born to Abraham and Nancy (Huston) Miller. He was still a boy when the family moved to Franklin County, Ind. He married Sarah Backus in 1831, and he worked as a butcher in Cincinnati for a time. In 1833, the young couple moved to German Township in St. Joseph County, Ind., just north of South Bend. They were financially successful and raised a family of 12 children.

The Portage Prairie congregation was organized the same year Jacob Jr. moved into the area, and he was called to the ministry the following year. He was 22 years old, which was remarkably young for such a calling at the time. He quickly became recognized as a gifted leader throughout the denomination.

His brother, James, also moved into the area and was a minister at Portage Prairie. While Jacob Jr. was actively involved in district and national affairs, James concentrated on the home church. The two brothers were instrumental in the effort which led to the construction of a brick meeting house for Portage Prairie in 1851. It was the first church house built in northern Indiana, and one of the earliest in the entire state.

Jacob Jr. served on Standing Committee of Annual Conference eight times, and was a member of many special committees. He and Elder D.B. Sturgis were sent to visit the churches in California and Oregon to help them organize. He was known as an effective preacher, an active reader, and had a large library of his own.

A short time before his death, he expressed the belief that he would be called away suddenly. This occurred suddenly and unexpectedly Sunday evening, Sept. 24, 1871. His funeral was one of the largest ever held to that time.

His brother, James, continued to actively preach at Portage Prairie until his death in 1893. He was said to have baptized more than 2,000 people during his lifetime.

Miller (John)

John Miller was born Dec. 15, 1787, in Pennsylvania. He moved to Montgomery County, Ohio, where he was called to the ministry in the Wolf Creek Church. He was among the first settlers in Elkhart County, Ind., when he moved there in 1835 on the Elkhart Prairie southeast of Goshen. He became an active associate of Elder Daniel Cripe in the Elkhart (West Goshen) Church, then was a leader in the Yellow Creek Church until his death in 1856. Several of his sons and grandsons became leaders at Yellow Creek and Union Center.

Miller (Levi)

Levi Miller was born in Augusta County, Va., Feb. 23, 1817, then moved to Preble County, Ohio, in 1833 with his parents. He married Ursula Eikenberry in 1840, and they moved to Miami County, Ind., two years later.

The Millers, like most of the early settlers, were not wealthy people when they arrived. In order to pay for some of his first land, Miller rode a horse back to Preble County, Ohio, sold the animal, then walked back to his home in Indiana. He was extremely successful, however, and at his death owned 1,000 acres of land and was a major bank stockholder.

In 1889, Miller built the Old Folks' Home at Mexico and gave it to the Middle Indiana District. Three years later, he built the orphans' home nearby and also gave it to the church. He died Dec. 21, 1902.

Miller (Robert Henry)

Robert Henry Miller was one of the great church leaders during the time of its greatest turmoil.

Born June 7, 1825, in Shelby County, Ky., the family moved to Montgomery County, Ind., when he was only 7. He was educated in a log cabin school, then attended academy classes and taught for two terms. He established a reputation as a debater, studied law at home, gave temperance speeches, and took part in political campaigns.

He married Sarah C. Harshbarger in 1846. She was the daughter of a Dunkard deacon. Although raised a Baptist and early interested in the Methodists, he and his wife were baptized by the Dunkards in 1858. He was called to the ministry a few months later.

From 1860 to 1880, Robert was an active preacher, debater, and writer. He was one of the greatest expounders of Brethren doctrine in his day and summed up his beliefs in a book, *The Doctrines of the Brethren Defended*. He engaged in no fewer than nine major debates and contributed to all the major church publications. He served on Standing Committee of Annual conference 12 times, was moderator once, and reading clerk twice.

Robert and Sarah had eight children, but two died in infancy and two more as young adults. Sarah died of pneumonia in 1880 only two months after one of her daughters had died and shortly after her husband had failed financially.

After the death of his wife, Elder Miller accepted an invitation to become president of Ashland College, Ashland, Ohio. While there he married Emma Norris, and they had five children. He resigned Dec. 31, 1881, because the college trustees favored the Progressive movement in the church, and Elder Miller opposed it.

He moved to North Manchester in 1882 where he became their minister. He is often given credit for holding that congregation together during the Old Order and Progressive schisms. He retired in 1890.

Elder Miller was invited to give a series of doctrinal sermons at Mount Morris College in January 1892. He was stricken with pneumonia while there and died the following March. His funeral was one of the first in the new brick church that is now West Manchester.

Moss

William Moss was the first presiding elder of the Mexico Church. He was a big man, weighing over 200 pounds, described as sociable, friendly, and honest. He was highly respected, and many in his community urged him to run for the state legislature.

Born in 1784, he was one of the early members of the Four Mile Church in Union County. He then moved into the Mexico territory as one of the early settlers. He turned the virgin land into a prosperous farm. He was widely known for using his abundance to help others, often selling grain to the poor and letting them pay for it as they could. He spent many days on horseback in the company of a deacon visiting the far-flung members of the original Mexico Church.

When he died Feb. 3, 1857, at the age of 73, he had seen three of his sons called to the ministry: Abraham, William Jr., and Philip.

Abraham Moss remained in Union County where he served the church for over 25 years. He served once on Standing Committee of Annual Conference and several special committees. It is likely he would have been an even larger name in the church, but his life was cut short by typhoid fever.

William Moss Jr. was called to the ministry in the Mexico Church about 1850. He later served as a minister at Bachelor Run, then moved to Greene, Iowa, where he died.

Philip also served as a minister at Mexico.

Murray

Samuel Murray was one of the great pioneer preachers in Indiana. He was born April 1, 1806, in Huntingdon County, Pa. In 1812, his family traveled by wagon to Pittsburgh, down the Ohio River by flat-bottom boat to Cincinnati, then by wagon to the area around Dayton, Ohio. His father died in 1818 when Samuel was only 12. He learned milling and carpentry to help support his family.

Samuel married Phoebe Hart in 1833, and both were baptized by the Dunkards soon after their marriage. She died in 1835 leaving two small children. Two years later, he married a widow, Sarah Myers, with whom he had seven sons and six daughters.

Samuel was called to the ministry in Ohio and moved to Miami County, Ind., seven miles southwest of Peru in 1851. He was a primary organizer of the Pipe Creek Church and became presiding elder in 1857.

Elder Murray's second wife, Sarah, died in 1863. In 1864, he married Catherine Studebaker, and he moved into the Antioch (Andrews) Church where she lived. They had one daughter before Catherine died.

Elder Murray then moved into the Salamonie territory. Within a few years, the membership at Salamonie had increased fourfold and it had become one of the strongest churches in the state. Much of the credit for this increase was given to Samuel Murray.

Wherever he lived, he spent a great deal of time traveling on horseback to preach to the widely scattered Dunkards. Late in his life, he wrote an autobiography which gives some of the best accounts of the life of the early pioneer preachers.

Elder Murray married Leah Eshelman in 1881, then retired from active ministry after he was 80 years old, although he still preached from time to time. His final years were spent with his son in Indianapolis. Preparations had been made for him to preach a sermon on his 100th birthday, but he died the day before that event on March 31, 1906.

Neher

Samuel Neher was born in Clarke County, Ohio, and was called to the ministry in 1863 in Allen County, Ohio. He moved to Wells County, Ind., in 1873 and became very active in missionary work which had just started there and in Adams County. He was the presiding elder for 30 years at Walnut Level, and also served at Pleasant Dale, Blue Creek, and Hickory Grove. He traveled everywhere on horseback to keep his appointments. He died in 1906.

A son, David, and a grandson, Oscar, were both called to the ministry.

Rife

Jacob Rife was born in Wayne County, Ind., Oct. 17, 1826, and his father died when he was only 3. He successfully coped with the hardships of pioneer life but knew its sorrows well. His favorite brother died in a cholera epidemic in 1849, and Jacob buried him with his own hands.

Jacob married Esther Stanley Oct. 15, 1846, and they joined the church in 1851. They had seven children, only three of whom survived to adulthood.

Jacob was called to the ministry in 1851 and was ordained as an elder in 1869. Although he had only a fair education, he was a naturally gifted speaker. It was said he preached at more than 900 funerals during his life. For more than 30 years he traveled an average of more than 3,000 miles a year on behalf of the church. He was active in the Southern Indiana District serving as moderator many times and on Standing Committee of Annual Conference a number of times. He died May 2, 1903, and Esther died in 1915 at the age of 79.

Rinehart

Abraham Rinehart was born July 6, 1823, in Preble County, Ohio. He moved to Cass County, Ind., in 1847 where he joined the Upper Deer Creek Church in 1861. He was called to the ministry in 1863 and became an elder in 1870, serving as presiding elder at Upper Deer Creek for 10 years.

He moved to the Pipe Creek Church in 1881. He was an active missionary traveling widely to preach to scattered Brethren. He died Nov. 30, 1916, at the age of 93.

Rothenberger

George Philip Rothenberger was born in Germany about 1800. He was raised in the Lutheran church, but disliked its cold formality and moved to Zurich, Switzerland. He became a noted preacher in the German Reform church preaching against infant baptism, military service, and civil oaths, and for trine immersion baptism for adults.

In 1839, he met Elder Henry Kurtz who had returned from the United States to visit Europe. Kurtz did some preaching, and one of those who requested baptism was George Rothenberger.

Rothenberger encountered severe persecution following his baptism, and once was beaten and left for dead. He kept up a correspondence with Kurtz and immigrated to the United States in 1841. He first settled in Stark County, Ohio, then moved to Carroll County, Ind., in 1845 and to Kosciusko County in 1851. He became the leader of the effort which established the Tippecanoe Church and was serving as its presiding elder when he died Oct. 30, 1882. His son, Daniel, succeeded him as presiding elder.

Rupel

David Rupel was born in Somerset County, Pa., in 1811. He moved to St. Joseph County, Ind., in 1830 and married Sarah Melling in 1836. They had six children and joined the church in 1852. He was called to the ministry in 1853.

David and Sarah built a large house specially constructed so double doors between rooms could be opened to accommodate church services. He was ordained in 1856 and named presiding elder of Pine Creek.

Later, David donated land on which a new meeting house was built. He announced that everyone was invited to his home after Sunday meetings for lunch. It was typical that 50 to 75 teams of horses and from 100 to 200 people were fed at these gatherings.

David Rupel served as presiding elder at Pine Creek for 34 years, and it became the largest church in northern Indiana during this time. He died Jan. 24, 1894. Several of his descendants were church leaders.

Shively (Daniel)

Daniel Shively was born in Stark County, Ohio, May 31, 1827. He moved to Elkhart County, Ind., married Esther Whitehead Jan. 22, 1852, and they joined the church.

Daniel was chosen to be a deacon when the Solomon's Creek (Bethany) Church was organized in 1856, and he was called to the ministry in 1858. He was largely in charge of the congregation for a number of years until he was formally made an elder in 1878. He died in Goshen at the age of 79 and was buried in a small cemetery at Baintertown near the spot where the 1852 Annual Conference was held.

Shively (Daniel P.)

Born in Montgomery County, Ohio, Nov. 24, 1841, Daniel P. Shively came to Miami County, Ind., in 1852. He was elected deacon at Pipe Creek in 1871, called to the ministry in 1873, and became an elder in 1889. He married Harriet Little in 1864.

He was active in the Middle Indiana District serving as moderator five times and clerk four times. He also served on Standing Committee of Annual Conference in 1893. He was highly regarded and known as "Uncle Dan" to many people.

At the time of his death in 1900, he had served as presiding elder at Pipe Creek for 10 years and had also served in that capacity for three other churches.

Shively (Jacob B.)

Jacob B. Shively was born in Stark County, Ohio, July 23, 1820. He married Anna Bortz July 4, 1841, and they moved to Marshall County, Ind., in 1845. They were the parents of 12 children and suffered through a great tragedy in 1864 when a scarlet fever epidemic killed seven of their children in one week.

Jacob was called to the ministry in 1851 and elected elder within a few years. He was widely known for his travels to scattered Brethren regardless of the weather.

Jacob became the chief promoter of Salem College, the first college owned by the German Baptist Brethren. When the college failed, it cost him his home, but he was never heard to complain about it.

He moved into the Union congregation and became the first elder of the Salem Church when it was organized. He died Jan. 5, 1899.

Shoemaker

David Shoemaker served as a soldier in the War of 1812 and also served as an officer in the state militia in Ohio before he was converted and baptized by the Dunkards. He was called to the ministry and became an elder, serving in the Sandy Church in Ohio for several years.

In 1850, Elder Shoemaker moved to Huntington County, Ind., settling on land just north of the town. He was the first minister and elder of the Clear Creek Church, and was instrumental in organizing Sugar Creek. He died Dec. 9, 1855, at the age of 66.

Snell

Jacob S. Snell was born in Preble County, Ohio, Oct. 16, 1836. He came with his parents to Indiana in 1844 and married Clara Bowman in 1860. They were the parents of 12 children.

Jacob joined the church in 1868 and helped organize the Spring Creek congregation. He was called to the ministry in 1871 and became an elder in 1887, serving as presiding elder at Spring Creek for 11 years. He often served as a Middle District officer and twice was elected to Standing Committee of Annual Conference. He died Feb. 4, 1899.

Jacob's brother, Daniel, was born in 1838. He married Mary Jane Heckman in 1861. He had assisted his brother for several years by the time he was called to the ministry in 1885. He became an elder in 1898 and was placed in charge of Spring Creek at the death of his brother. He served in this capacity for 10 years.

Daniel served twice on Standing Committee of Annual Conference and was a trustee of Manchester College for several years. Failing eyesight forced him to give up much of his church work a few years before his death.

Studebaker

Studebaker is a famous Indiana name, both inside and outside the church. This first sketch will deal with the famous wagon makers and auto builders.

Peter, Clement, and Henry Studebaker were three brothers who arrived from Germany with other Dunkards in Philadelphia in 1736. A descendant, John, first lived in Pennsylvania. He met his wife, Rebecca Mohler, at a Dunkard meeting.

John built a Conestoga wagon to move his family to Ohio in 1836 where he operated a blacksmith shop near Ashland. A Dunkard congregation met in their home.

Several years later, he used the same Conestoga wagon to move his family to South Bend, Ind. This wagon is still on display at the Studebaker museum in South Bend.

Two of his sons, later joined by three others, began to build wagons in South Bend, and by 1878 they were considered the leading wagon builders in the country. The company later went on to manufacture automobiles and racing cars.

The huge success of the Studebaker brothers caused a rift between them and their church. The final straw may have been their building of wagons for the U.S. Army. A delegation of Dunkard deacons from Pennsylvania was sent to South Bend to admonish them for this activity and for their "high" style of living. Of the five brothers, only Henry resigned from the business and returned to farming. He could not sanction building wagons for the U.S. Army which were then used in efforts to suppress the Mormons, to whom the Studebakers had also sold wagons.

Still, their Dunkard heritage never left them. The brothers lived by their father's motto, "Always give a little bit more than you promise." John Mohler Studebaker, who remained active in the business until shortly before his death in 1915, kept a painting of his boyhood home above the mantle in his office and a picture of his father on his desk.

Studebaker

Another branch of the Studebaker family played a much more prominent role in the church. Jacob Studebaker lived in Pennsylvania. Shortly after his death, his wife and four sons moved to Ohio. Among Jacob's descendants were John U. Studebaker and George W. Studebaker, first cousins who devoted much of their lives to building the Indiana church.

John U. Studebaker was born in Ohio in 1816 and moved to Delaware County in 1837. He and his wife joined the church the same year. He was called to the ministry in 1849 and became an elder in 1859. He was presiding elder at Mississinewa for many years, and he died in 1901.

George W. Studebaker was the more widely known of the two cousins. He was born in Pennsylvania in 1818, moved to Ohio, then came to Delaware County, Ind., in 1833. He was chosen to be a deacon in 1841, and the older Dunkards gave him permission to exhort, although he had to remain seated. He was called to the ministry in 1842 and became an elder in 1850.

George was famous for memorizing long passages of scripture and was a familiar sight to many as he rode his white horse among the scattered churches. He was married four times and had a total of nine children. In 1882 he moved to Fredonia County, Kan., where he remained active in the church until his death in 1905.

Studebaker (Jacob)

Jacob Studebaker (not the same Jacob listed above) was born in Montgomery County, Ohio, in 1793. He was among the first settlers to move to Elkhart County, Ind., settling on the Elkhart River northeast of Goshen. He became a builder and helped erect the first public building in Goshen.

Jacob served as presiding elder for a time at Rock Run and was well known for his poetry. He died in 1878.

Stutsman

Daniel B. Stutsman was born in Montgomery County, Ohio, and married Elizabeth Bashor in 1829. They settled in Elkhart County, Ind., in 1832. He served as a deacon, minister, and presiding elder in the Elkhart (West Goshen) congregation. He was nearly blind for the last few years prior to his death Aug. 9, 1887.

Swihart

Jonathon Swihart was one of the first Dunkard ministers to come to Wabash County. He and his wife, Elizabeth, came from Stark County, Ohio, in the early 1840s settling two miles north of Roann. The territory was still the home of many Indians at the time, and Jonathon was well known among them as a peacemaker. Jonathon died in 1849, but he left behind seven sons, six of whom became preachers.

Aaron, the oldest, was a pioneer in the Walnut Church. He was elected deacon in 1858, minister in 1863, and elder in 1891. He died from a concussion caused by an accidental discharge of a gun while visiting his son in Brethren, Mich., in 1903.

David was called to the ministry in the Roann Church in 1873. He was an able preacher and was active in the Sunday school program. He became an elder in 1901 and was soon named presiding elder at Roann. He died in 1905.

George was called to the ministry in the Blue River Church in 1876. He later moved to Wawaka and finally settled west of Goshen where he served as presiding elder at West Goshen for several years. He died in 1916.

Jacob was called to the ministry at Blue River in 1884. He later moved to Missouri where he died.

Samuel and Clarence Swihart went with the Progressives and became ministers in the Brethren Church.

Teeter

Lewis W. Teeter was born in Wayne County in 1845. He married Nancy Ellen Bowman.

He served as a deacon for a number of years after he joined the church in 1868. He was called to the ministry in 1876 and became an elder in 1885 at the age of 40. He was made presiding elder at Nettle Creek, a position he held for 32 years.

Elder Teeter preached more than 4,000 sermons and conducted more than 400 funerals during his life. He was district moderator 13 times, served on Standing Committee of Annual Conference 12 times, and was moderator of Annual Conference once. He was a member of the

General Mission Board and served as a trustee at Manchester College. He spent 10 years writing a commentary of the Bible, helped edit Sunday school quarterlies, and frequently contributed to church publications. He died Oct. 28, 1927.

Tracy

One of the best preachers in the early church was James Tracy. Little is known about his origins, but he was nationally prominent by 1842. Owen Opperman wrote that he came to northern Indiana about 1852.

Tracy was of Irish descent and had a powerful voice. He was fond of using illustrations from nature during his sermons.

Tracy began his Indiana work in the South Bend area, but preached throughout northern Indiana. His only failing was in making financial ends meet, but this was largely explained by his devotion to the church. He was a skilled carpenter, but often turned down work so he could fulfill church commitments. He was known to have walked for several miles to preach at a funeral after being refused transportation by other Brethren who were too busy to take him.

When the Rock Run Church was organized, they asked Tracy to move among them. This he did, but he was with them only a short time. He became ill and died April 30, 1857, at the age of 57.

Wenger

Christian Wenger was born in Lebanon County, Pa., Dec. 10, 1814. He moved to St. Joseph County, Ind., in 1834 and in 1838 married Esther Studebaker.

Wenger spent most of his life on a farm near South Bend. He was called to the ministry in the St. Joseph congregation and later was made an elder. He was presiding elder for several congregations in the area, and served on a number of special committees appointed by Annual Conference.

Whitehead

Although they were not ministers, the Whitehead family in northern Indiana was a remarkable clan which became instrumental in expanding the church.

About 1837, six Whitehead brothers and three sisters moved from Montgomery County, Ohio, to Elkhart County west of New Paris. The family included brothers Samuel, Peter, Adam, Valentine, John, and Lewis, with sisters Esther Stutzman, Mary Conrad, and Margaret Lentz.

The area they settled was still part of the original Elkhart (West Goshen) territory. John Leatherman was active in the area at the time, and the Whiteheads soon became part of the Turkey Creek district which he organized in 1838.

The Turkey Creek group decided to build a church in 1854. Peter Whitehead and another brother donated land for the church. A third brother donated timber, and John Whitehead donated land across the road for a burial ground. The church which was built is now known as Maple Grove and was the second church building in northern Indiana. For many years it was known informally as the Whitehead Church. Many of the original Whitehead settlers are buried in the cemetery across the road.

Whiteneck

John Whiteneck was born near Roanoke, Va., in 1802. He moved to Union County, Ind., in 1825 and married Lucy Kingery in 1828. He was called to the ministry in the Four Mile congregation and later was made an elder.

In 1847 he moved to Wabash County where he built a farm of several hundred acres on the banks of the Mississinewa River. He was instrumental in organizing the Somerset congregation about 1850 and was presiding elder until his death in 1868.

Elder Whiteneck was known as a powerful figure in the pulpit, and his life was an example to others. He once refused to sell some of his corn at a very good price because some poor members of the church needed it, and he sold it to them at a much lower price.

Whitmer

Whitmer is a name associated with the founding of the South Bend (North Liberty) Church. Abraham Whitmer was born in Lancaster County, Pa., and moved to Montgomery County, Ohio, when he was 16. At age 23, he married Catherine Bowman, daughter of Elder Jacob Bowman of the South Bend Church. Abraham and Catherine moved to St. Joseph County, Ind., in 1831 where he was called to the ministry and ordained.

When the South Bend and Portage churches were divided, Abraham became presiding elder of South Bend. He spent 30 years preaching throughout the territory until his death of typhoid fever in 1872 at the age of 66.

Daniel Whitmer, one of Abraham's 11 sons and daughters, succeeded his father. Daniel was born April 21, 1842, and was elected to the ministry in 1861. He became an elder in 1879. Except for two years in North Dakota where he founded the Williston Church, Daniel spent all of his 90 years on the farm where he was born. He served 33 years as presiding elder of the North Liberty Church.

Daniel's son, Merrill Whitmer, was born in 1873. He was called to the ministry in 1892 and advanced to elder in 1904. This was during a seven-year period he spent in North Dakota. He moved to North Manchester so his sons could attend college, then moved back to the Whitmer homestead in St. Joseph County where he spent the remainder of his life. He served for a time as presiding elder at North Liberty and was also a member at Pine Creek.

Wysong

Daniel Wysong was born Sept. 28, 1842, in Montgomery County, Ohio, and moved with his family to Elkhart County, Ind., when he was only 3. He taught school for several years, and married Mary Miller in 1862. They settled on a farm east of Nappanee.

Daniel was called to the ministry at Turkey Creek in 1874 and served for more than 40 years. He was widely known for his successful evangelistic meetings at which literally hundreds of people were brought into the church. He became an elder in 1898 and served as presiding elder at Turkey Creek from 1898 to 1906. He was a member of Standing Committee of Annual Conference in 1910, and served as presiding elder at Nappanee for a number of years until his death in 1924.

Daniel's brother, Henry Wysong, was born Feb. 6, 1853, and became a teacher and farmer. He married Lovina Miller in 1875, and they settled on a farm near the Turkey Creek Church east of Nappanee. He was elected to the ministry in 1898 and became an elder in 1904. He served on the district mission board and ministerial board before his death in 1935.

Book II:
The Congregational
Stories

Agape
11610 Lima Road
Fort Wayne, IN 46818
Membership: 98

The Agape Church of the Brethren was formed in 1968 by a small group which had been part of the Pleasant Hill congregation. They felt the need to move to a more populous area.

A meeting house was constructed on Carroll Road about four miles northwest of Fort Wayne in Allen County. The facility served the congregation until 1979 when a group of about 30 launched a new building project on S.R. 3 about a mile from the original building. Ground was broken on Palm Sunday, April 4, 1982. The first service in the new building was held Dec. 16, 1982, and a dedication service was held March 20, 1983. Current Sunday morning worship attendance is now about 150.

An annual event for the church has been the School for Christian Growth which is conducted as a series of meetings during one week in June. Special evening learning sessions for children called "Family Focus" are also held at six-week intervals throughout the year.

A mark of the young congregation's growing maturity was the ordination of Thomas Wagner March 18, 1990. He went on to become a pastor in Muskegon, Mich.

Akron

208 S. Maple
P.O. Box 296
Akron, IN 46910
Membership: 71

Akron has the unique heritage of having been affiliated with both the
Church of the Brethren and the Brethren Church. Although it is now
exclusively affiliated with the Church of the Brethren, it is the only
congregation in Indiana to have held this dual affiliation.

The congregation was organized sometime between 1885 and
1890. The original church building was located southeast of Akron
across the road from the New Highland School, a country schoolhouse,
and the church was known as New Highland Brethren Church. The
church was originally an independent organization, but the decision was
made to affiliate with the Brethren Church about 1914.

About 15 years later, the Highland congregation learned of a larger
and better church building in the town of Akron which was being
abandoned by another denomination. The in-town location was preferred by many of the members who lived in Akron, so the country
church was abandoned in 1930, and the congregation changed its name
to Akron.

About the same time this move was made, the Akron congregation came into contact with a group of Church of the Brethren members who were meeting in the area but had no church buiding of their own. The two groups began worshipping together, and it was agreed in 1932 that these families could become associate members of the church. This led to a decision on Nov. 11, 1934, to become a cooperative member of both the Brethren Church and the Church of the Brethren.

A system of alternating pastors from the two denominations was developed, and church finances were split evenly to support both denominations. About 1957, the congregation began to reconsider support for two demoninational programs. This led to a decision June 10, 1965, to affiliate exclusively with the Church of the Brethren.

The original church building has been remodeled several times including 1948-49 and 1958. A basement was added along with a kitchen, classrooms, and a new entrance. A home next to the church was purchased for a parsonage in 1947.

Another renovation project was completed in 1992 which included new carpeting in several areas and a new ceiling in the fellowship hall and kitchen. A new sound system was also installed along with a new organ. A dedication service and organ recital were held March 29, 1992.

Anderson
741 S.R. 9 N.
Anderson, IN 46012
Membership: 223

The Anderson Church traces its beginnings to the Annual Conference of 1893 held in neighboring Muncie. The General Mission Board was told at that meeting that several Brethren families were living in Anderson. The board sent Ella Raffensperger to organize a Sunday school as the beginning of a mission point under the direction of the Lower Fall Creek congregation. She organized the first service on June 22, 1893, in an upstairs room at Ninth and Jackson streets. Six months later, services were moved to another rented building on the ground floor at the southeast corner of Main and 21st streets.

The country was in the midst of a major economic crisis in 1894 when the small group decided they wanted a building of their own rather than paying rent each month. After a brief search, the ideal location seemed to be two lots at the corner of McKinley and 22nd streets which were for sale at $60 apiece. Many of the members were unemployed and none had that kind of money, so Fred Fesler, J.S. Alldredge, and Henry Rodecap were sent out to solicit funds from businessmen in the town. During two half days of visits, they were able to raise the necessary $120, including contributions from some with a reputation for never giving to church causes. The success of the fund drive was attributed to the reputation of the Brethren for taking care of their poor and their simple approach to life.

The next step was to construct a building. Many of the materials were donated, including timber from wooded lands owned by Noah Shock, Henry Larcher, and Fred Fesler. Labor was also donated, and work on the project was directed by Elder John R. Wellington. A dedication service was held in October 1894.

Additions were made in 1911 and 1915, and a completely new, brick structure replaced the original meeting house in 1930. It was remodeled in 1959 which included the addition of an educational wing.

The congregation hosted Annual Conference in Anderson in 1932 and again in 1939. Both conferences were held on the college grounds of the Church of God.

The church grew rapidly during its first 50 years and became one of the largest congregations in the state by the late 1940s. The way has not been entirely smooth, however. There was serious disagreement when the congregation changed from free ministry to a paid staff about 1940. Another major upheaval came during 1983-84 when a number of members left.

Major change was initiated by a fire which was discovered in the early morning hours on Sept. 8, 1972. A new roof was being installed on the educational wing, and it is believed a cigarette dropped in the roofing material started the blaze. The fire burned into a crawl space above the sanctuary and destroyed the main church building, although the educational wing sustained only smoke and water damage.

Services were temporarily moved to Anderson North Side Middle School while repairs were made to the educational building. Services were then resumed in the basement of this building until a decision could be made on rebuilding the church.

The members eventually decided to construct a new church at a new location, and Irvan Krull was named chairman of the building committee. The committee purchased six acres of land from an estate on the west side of S.R. 109, and construction was begun at this site in 1973 by Shepherd Construction Co. A setback was suffered during a windstorm which blew down trusses over the chapel and collapsed the walls. Fortunately, the $30,000 in damage was covered by insurance.

In spite of this difficulty, the congregation moved into the new facility in October 1974. The educational building on McKinley Street was sold to Liberty Christian School.

Andrews
262 E. McKeever
Andrews, IN 46702
Membership: 22

Although Elder William Moss preached in the area around Andrews (formerly known as Antioch) as early as 1838, it wasn't until 1853 and the arrival of Joseph Leedy that regular services began to be organized. Leedy was the first resident minister. He began by holding services in his cabin, then his barn, and, finally, in a new school in Antioch. His brother, Elder John Leedy, soon moved from Ohio and helped with the work. A third brother, Abraham, joined them several years later.

The church was officially organized as Antioch in 1855. A church building was constructed in Antioch in 1860. It was unusual for its day because it was located in a town and had a church bell. The meeting in 1866 which led to districts being formed in Indiana was held in this church. Because it was such a strong church, there was even serious consideration given to founding a Brethren college here.

The 20-year period beginning about 1881 was a very difficult time at Antioch. The deaths of the Leedys (John, 1881; Abraham, 1898; and

Joseph, 1903) left the church without its traditional leadership. In addition, it was caught in much of the division which occurred in the denomination between the Old Orders, Progressives, and Conservatives. Several members who had been elected to the ministry from Antioch left the denomination as divisions occurred in the early 1880s.

Elder Noah Fisher and a small core of faithful members continued the work, however, and the congregation remained intact.

An expansion project was begun in 1954 which created a basement under the original building. The new space provided classrooms, a new kitchen, and a fellowship hall. The project was completed in 1955.

The sanctuary of the church was remodeled and modernized in 1976.

Antioch
Bethel Pike and 500 W.
Muncie, IN 47304
Membership: 30

Antioch Church of the Brethren began life in 1860 as the Killbuck German Baptist Brethren Church. There were 10 charter members when the congregation was organized in the western part of Delaware County west of Muncie.

Sometime during the 1870s, a union house was constructed about eight miles west of Muncie along Jackson Pike, although the exact location is unknown. Three denominations (Methodist, German Baptist Brethren, and Christian Newlights) shared the building which was known as Pleasant Run. The Summitville Church was also part of the original Killbuck territory. It was organized separately in 1880.

In 1890, the Killbuck congregation built a new meeting house five miles northwest of Muncie which was known as Antioch. The Pleasant Run building was later abandoned.

Long-time Antioch member Cletis R. Bowers, writing in 1980, recalled stories from twice-a-year communion services held by the

Killbuck congregation. The two-day affairs often drew a number of curious observers to see these Dunkards and their "soup suppers." A few hecklers occasionally caused a disturbance, so the Brethren hired a young Methodist man to keep the peace. His name was John Sherman Alldredge, and on April 18, 1890, he married a Brethren girl named Leathy Lucinda Wellington. He later was elected to the ministry by the Brethren. Alldredge eventually entered politics and served in the Indiana House of Representatives and Senate from 1916 to 1932.

When the name of the denomination was changed to Church of the Brethen in 1908, the Killbuck congregation accepted the name, although it was not changed in Delaware County records until 1946 when the members voted to drop the name Killbuck and adopted Antioch.

A major construction project was launched in the 1950s when a basement was built south of the existing building. The structure was then moved over the basement which is the building's present location.

Antioch showed steady growth through most of its history. The original 10 members multiplied to 40 by 1882, and the membership had grown to 120 in 1950. However, the congregation was divided in 1959 in a dispute over the charismatic movement, and membership declined. By 1980, there were only 21 members.

Arcadia

26812 S.R. 19
Arcadia, IN 46030
Membership: 92

The early history of the Arcadia Church of the Brethren often focuses on the lives of two men: Elder Joseph McCarty and Elder Elias Caylor.

Elder McCarty was born in Ohio in 1817 and married Mary Surface in that state. He moved to Indiana in 1850 by blazing a trail through the dense Hoosier woodlands into the northern part of Hamilton County. He built a home on property located about six miles west and one mile north of what is now Arcadia, and it was here that he reared a family of of 12 children and three orphans. He erected a grist mill on the banks of a stream flowing through the property and also worked as a carpenter.

Several members of the Four Mile Church, the first organized congregation in Indiana, had moved northwest from Union County into Hamilton County in the years before Elder McCarty arrived. In addition to the work of establishing a new home and business, Elder McCarty soon began a traveling ministry, preaching and holding communion services for these scattered Dunkards throughout the county.

Elder Caylor also moved to Hamilton County about 1849 from Henry County, settling on a farm east of Noblesville. He was born in 1805, the 16th child in his family and said to be the first white child to be born west of the Miami River. He was instrumental in organizing the Stoney Creek Church (now Beech Grove) in 1850 which at the time included all of Hamilton County. He and Elder McCarty often traveled together preaching throughout Hamilton County and as far west as Montgomery County.

Elder Caylor moved to a farm near Arcadia about 1855, supposedly after some unknown internal difficulties at Stoney Creek. This resulted in the formal organization of a new church in the north half of Hamilton County in 1856 which was known as Cicero. The name was later changed to Arcadia. Caylor was the first presiding elder and McCarty was the minister.

Arcadia was the second church of any kind to be organized in the area, following a Lutheran congregation by only four years. The members met in homes, schools, and barns. The last communion service held in a barn was at a farm owned by Andrew Eller, great-grandfather of several current church members.

In 1865, the church purchased one acre of land from Elder Caylor for $60. A white frame meeting house was erected in 1866 and a cemetery was begun on land adjacent to the church.

Elder Caylor was a farmer and also operated a harness shop in Arcadia. He later returned to the Noblesville area where he died in 1889 at the age of 84. Elder McCarty remained as the presiding elder at Arcadia until his death about 1876.

The first Sunday school was organized in 1893 with Elias Smeltzer as president. The program was expanded to 12 months a year (evergreen) in 1899.

I.B. Wilke became the first paid minister to serve the church. He served as pastor and elder from 1923 to 1931.

The original white frame building was remodeled in 1908 and underwent a series of improvements in subsequent years, but it remained basically the same and served the congregation for 109 years. Finally, the members voted in May 1975 to erect a new church building.

Ground was broken May 25, 1975, and construction of a new church began just a few feet east of the old building. The first worship service in the new church was the dedication held in November 1975. The old, white frame church was razed a short time later. The congregation celebrated the burning of the mortgage on Sept. 18, 1983.

Bachelor Run
Route 1
Bringhurst, IN 46913
Carroll C.R.s 200S. and 350E.
Membership: 75

The Bachelor Run congregation came into being with the 1838 division of Deer Creek. This division came about because of a disagreement between Peter Replogle and Peter Eyman over several points of doctrine. (See the Lower Deer Creek history for additional detail.) Eyman was placed in charge of the Bachelor Run territory which included most of Carroll County and extended into White and Howard counties. The remainder of the territory was renamed Lower Deer Creek, and Replogle was named presiding elder.

The difficulties between Eyman and the rest of the brotherhood continued until he and several of his followers were finally disfellowshipped in 1848. They formed a new organization called the

New Dunkers, later the Church of God, which was centered primarily in the area of White County.

The Bachelor Run congregation continued to grow without Eyman, and the first meeting house was constructed in 1854 near the southeast part of Flora. A second meeting house, known as the country house, was built in 1856 five miles southeast of Flora on the Little Bachelor Run Creek.

A major event in the life of the church occurred in 1858 when Bachelor Run hosted Annual Conference.

Bachelor Run lost several members when the Howard County Church was organized in 1852 and again when the Monticello Church was organized in 1865.

The first Sunday school program was established in 1866.

The membership totaled 350 in 1880, but a third of the congregation left the following year when the Old Order division occurred. Included in the 126 who left were three ministers and three deacons. Another group was lost in 1882 in the split with the Progressives.

In spite of these setbacks, the congregation remained active. The country house was remodeled in 1882 and the town house was renovated in 1884. The country house was remodeled again in 1910.

In 1911, the town house was organized as a separate congregation. It was renamed Flora, and the country house retained the name Bachelor Run.

The Bachelor Run building was destroyed in a fire May 27, 1944. A new church was built at the same site and was dedicated Oct. 19, 1947. The congregation of fewer than 200 members at the time had managed to pay the $42,000 cost of the new building by the time it was dedicated.

Baugo

64066 C.R. 1,
Wakarusa, IN 46573
Membership: 111

Baugo Church of the Brethren, located in western Elkhart County, was organized in 1868. A number of Brethren families living in Elkhart and St. Joseph counties were among the first members and Joel Shively was their minister. Weekly meetings were held in homes and barns throughout the area for the first 10 years.

The first church building was constructed in 1878 about three miles northwest of Wakarusa. The northern half of the congregation was split off into a new congregation in 1893 with the purchase of a Methodist church at the east edge of Osceola. This became the Osceola Church

of the Brethren.

A meeting house had been built in Wakarusa in 1895, and in 1915, Wakarusa and Baugo were reorganized into two separate congregations. In 1918, the original Baugo meeting house was razed. A basement was then dug on the same site and a new church building constructed. The Baugo Church was served by the free ministry until 1948.

A special centennial celebration was held in 1968, and a major renovation and addition project was completed in 1971 which added classrooms and a narthex. The congregation sponsored a family of Laotian refugees in 1983, assisting them in beginning a new life in this country.

Beacon Heights

2810 Beacon St.
Fort Wayne, IN 46805
Membership: 328

A presentation by Charles E. Zunkel, General Brotherhood Ministry and Home Missions Secretary, in 1952 was the catalyst for the founding of the Beacon Heights Church of the Brethren in Fort Wayne. Zunkel spoke on Jan. 20, 1952, in Fort Wayne about how new churches were being started throughout the country. Some members of the Fort Wayne Church of the Brethren had been talking about the need for a new church in the city, and when people were invited to stay and talk to Zunkel about home missions, a group of 50 stayed. A site selection committee was formed, and just six weeks later an option was taken on a 5.25-acre tract of land on Beacon Street.

The Beacon Heights Church was officially organized in August, and the first worship service was held Sept. 7, 1952, at the Fort Wayne

YMCA. Don Hursh was hired as the first pastor July 1, 1953. A parsonage was built and dedicated Nov. 15, 1953. Worship services and Sunday school classes were held in the basement of the parsonage until the educational unit for the new church (located across the street) was completed and dedicated May 29, 1955.

Ground was broken for the sanctuary and additional classrooms Sept. 11, 1960. Dedication for this new facility was held Oct. 8, 1961. Over 1,000 hours of labor had been donated by the members.

The need for more space was felt by 1977. A project was designed which remodeled the existing building, added classrooms, and provided a new parking area and entrance. Dedication was held Sept. 21, 1980.

In nearly 40 years of existence, Beacon Heights has grown from 33 members to over 300. Nettie Senger, one of the charter members, was a missionary in China from 1916 to 1939. She gave her collection of old and rare Bibles to the church, including the first Bible printed in the colonies by Dunkard Brethren forbearers in 1743. The Nettie Senger Bible Collection was given to Bethany Seminary in 1975.

A major event in the life of the congregation came in 1985 when Guy Wampler Jr., then pastor at Beacon Heights, was elected moderator-elect of Annual Conference.

Beacon Heights has had a pulpit exchange and fellowship activities with Shiloh Baptist Church, a black congregation in Fort Wayne, for over 25 years. The congregation has also sponsored Latin American refugees.

The congregation been involved in community projects from the beginning. Kevin Keller, a member of the church, served as the volunteer director for flood relief during major floods in the city during the mid-1980s. In 1988, Beacon Heights was given the Ecumenical Service Award by the Associated Churches of Fort Wayne and Allen County for its work in the community. Among the projects cited when the award was presented were support for Associated Church outreach programs; being active in refugee work; being instrumental in the relocation of a free health and dental clinic; serving as a nutrition site for the elderly; participation in an offender restoration program; and declaring itself a sanctuary for Salvadoran refugees.

Beech Grove
7767 S.R. 13S
Pendleton, IN 46064
Membership: 100

Beech Grove traces its heritage to the old Stoney Creek church organized in 1850 by Elder Elias Caylor. Stony Creek had very large boundaries, but most of the membership was located in Hamilton County.

A new church was formed in 1860 in the northern part of Hamilton County which was known as Cicero. This was followed in 1878 by another new congregation in the eastern part of Hamilton County and the western part of Madison County that was called Beech Grove. There were 50 charter members. There was also a third congregation formed called Noblesville, but it did not survive.

Elder Elias Caylor was part of the original Beech Grove group, but there were problems and he moved to the Cicero church which was later named Arcadia.

Sometime before 1900, the southern part of the Beech Grove Church was organized as a separate group called Sugar Creek. This church only existed for a few years before it was disorganized and the members transferred to Beech Grove. The original Stony Creek Church also did not survive, which makes Arcadia and Beech Grove the only survivors from this active group north of Indianapolis.

Bethany

P.O. Box 52
New Paris, IN 46553
3 miles south, 1 mile east of New Paris on U.S. 6
Membership: 114

The Bethany Church has a unique heritage as being part of some of the largest historical events of the church in Indiana, in addition to being the mother church for several congregations.

The church was officially organized as Solomon's Creek at a meeting on Oct. 19, 1856, in the home of David Coy one mile north of Syracuse. The territory included Jackson and Benton townships in Elkhart County and much of northern Kosciusko County. Elders Henry Neff and John Leatherman of the Turkey Creek Church were instrumental in the founding of Solomon's Creek, and the first ministers were Frederick P. Loehr and Martin Weybright.

For the first eight years, worship services were held in homes, barns, and schools. They were an energetic group and acted as hosts for what is believed the first district meeting held in northern Indiana in 1857.

In 1864, the Brethren throughout northern Indiana united to build for Solomon's Creek one of the largest churches in the district. It was near the end of the Civil War, and many Brethren men were paying commutation taxes to avoid the military draft. This made it difficult to raise funds, but the task was accomplished. The new building was located on U.S. 6 south of New Paris. Martin Weybright lived to see construction of the new church begun, but died before the first worship service was held there.

In 1882, the relatively young congregation served as host for one of the largest and most famous of all Annual Conferences at Arnold's Grove, about one mile west of the church. It was at this conference, where attendance estimates have ranged as high as 10,000-15,000 people, that the split occurred between Progressives and Conservatives which led to the formation of a new denomination now known as the Brethren Church. A few Solomon's Creek members left with the Progressives, but membership was not seriously affected.

The Solomon's Creek congregation was extremely active in helping to form new congregations prior to 1920. Some were successful and some were abandoned. Some of the mission points which succeeded were Syracuse begun in 1887, New Salem in 1897, Bethel in 1905, and New Paris in 1917.

The name Bethany was adopted in 1912. Credit for the name is given to Amsa Clem who was elected to the ministry in 1899 and ordained in 1908. He served as presiding elder at Bethany for many years.

The church building was remodeled in 1901, and a more extensive renovation was conducted from 1947-49. This project added a basement, classrooms, and living quarters for the pastor. A new brick sanctuary was built onto the original frame building in 1968.

A series of special events was held in 1981 in observance of the congregation's 125th anniversary. The celebration culminated on Oct. 18 with Dr. William Eberly as the featured speaker.

Bethel

Box 396
Milford, IN 46542
Corner East and Catherine streets
Membership: 73

The beginnings of the Bethel congregation can be traced to 1881 when Elder William R. Deeter moved from Delaware County to Kosciusko County. The area at that time was within the boundaries of the Solomon's Creek district and included two churches, Bethany and Pleasant View. There were about 100 Brethren living in northeast Kosciusko County and, with the coming of Elder Deeter, a movement was made to divide the Solomon's Creek District. The southern part of the district was broken off in 1884 and was named Bethel. It included Pleasant View Chapel

Elder Deeter organized services which were held for a number of years in a school house at Milford. Another church called New Salem

was built in 1897 southeast of Milford within the Bethel District. It became a separate congregation in 1911.

The Bethel group in Milford organized a Sunday school in the late 1890s which was housed in the second floor of a business building. Brother and Sister L.M. Neher moved to Milford in 1902 from North Manchester. They helped organize regular preaching services. Services in the Milford building had to be discontinued in December 1903 because the building was declared unsafe. The congregation had previously talked about building their own church, so losing their meeting place became a catalyst for action. A building fund was established in 1904, and a new church was soon being constructed at East and Catherine streets. Much of the labor was donated by the members, and free timber came from a woods owned by James Arnold. The dedication service was held Nov. 12, 1905.

There was no baptistry in the original church building. Members were taken to a nearby lake or some other church for the service. A new baptistry was added in 1908.

Pleasant View Chapel, which had continued to be affiliated with Bethel, was finally broken off as a separate organization in 1915.

The church was served by the free ministry until a paid pastoral program was begun in 1925. Communion services were held in the sanctuary until a remodeling program in 1945 provided enough space for the service to be held in the basement.

Although the original church building is still in use, the Bethel congregation has supported a series of additions and renovations over the years. Dedication of a new education wing was held Sept. 15, 1968. A combined 70th anniversary celebration and dedication of a remodeled sanctuary was observed Oct. 5, 1975. A special 75th anniversary celebration was held in 1980.

Bethel Center

1770 S.R. 26W.
Hartford City, IN 47348
Membership: 48

Brethren services were held at irregular intervals in the area around
Hartford City through much of the 1800s. Most of the preaching was
done by ministers from Mississinewa.

   The key to the organization of a permanent church was a trip
made to Mississinewa in 1885 by Levi Winklebleck and his mother. Both
were baptized, and Winklebleck immediately began active efforts to
organize a church nearer their home close to Hartford City.

   A series of revival meetings conducted in 1886 by Elder Joseph
Spitzer dramatically increased the number of people interested, and
Bethel Center was officially organized on July 1, 1886, in a one-room
school. There were 30 charter members. The first communion was held
in a tent.

   Winklebleck and Samuel Wilson were elected deacons. The
following year, Winklebleck and John Rodgers were called to the
ministry. Winklebleck was then ordained and placed in charge of the
church.

   The first church building was constructed about two miles west of
Hartford City on an acre of land donated by Deming Frint. The building

was dedicated by Elder Spitzer at a special service Jan. 25, 1887. The congregation grew rapidly and soon included 175 members.

A second church building was constructed in Hartford City in 1895. The congregation was divided soon after this. The group in the city was known as Hartford or Hartford City, while the country group retained the name Bethel Center.

Levi Winklebleck moved to California in 1908, and attendance at both Bethel Center and Hartford City dropped off dramatically over the next few years. Both churches were placed under the control of the Middle Indiana Mission Board in 1916. The two congregations were combined at the Bethel Center location, and the Hartford City location was abandoned.

Bethel Center rebuilt itself over the next few years and again became a viable congregation. The 50th anniversary was celebrated in September 1936 with a special all-day program. George Studebaker was the guest speaker.

In 1947 a basement was dug, and the church building was moved from its original site to the place where it is now located. The project experienced a near-disaster one night when concrete forms gave way and the sides of the new basement walls caved in. Members spent most of the night shoveling out the wet cement and starting over.

A 24-acre farm was purchased in 1955. Members of the church donated their time to farm the land, and the house became the Bethel Center parsonage.

New restrooms were installed in 1962 to replace outhouses which had served for 75 years. A major renovation program was undertaken in 1966 which improved both the interior and exterior. Fred Miller, pastor at the time, used pieces from some of the old joists to make a cross which still hangs over the baptistry at the back of the pulpit.

Bethel Center became one of the first churches in the state to hire a female pastor when Phyllis Carter was called in 1968. She served until 1972. During that time, the church organizational structure was changed and the first church board was elected.

Members had dreamed about building a fellowship hall for a number of years. That dream became a reality Nov. 13, 1981, when an addition to the church was completed. The first major event held in the facility was the congregation's annual turkey supper at which 200 people were served. The new facility included a new kitchen, the fellowship hall, new restrooms, a pastor's study, a nursery, and a large entryway. A nursery school program was housed in the fellowship hall for a few years.

Bethel Center celebrated its centennial during a three-day observance Sept. 19-21, 1986.

Blissville

6250 Spruce Trail
Plymouth, IN 46542
Membership: 123

Blissville was organized as a separate congregation in 1912, but the origins of the church begin much earlier as part of the Pine Creek Church.

Pine Creek was growing rapidly and the members constructed several meeting houses in the territory. The original Blissville meeting house was built sometime in the early 1870s followed in 1877 by the Center House and a few years later by the Oregon House.

In 1912, members of the southern half of the Pine Creek district asked to form a separate organization. The request was granted and this group, which included the Center House, the Blissville House, and the Oregon House, became known as the Blissville Church. The Center House was organized as a separate congregation in 1917, and services were discontinued at the Oregon House in 1925.

John Markley was recognized as the leading force in the congregation during its early years and served as presiding elder for all but two years from 1912 to 1935.

A major remodeling project was undertaken in 1952 which added a full basement, kitchen, baptistry, and restrooms. The auditorium and classrooms were also renovated.

A parsonage was constructed in 1963. This house was sold in 1980.

The church building was again extensively remodeled in 1981.

Blue River

3040 E. 700 N.
Columbia City, IN 46725
Membership: 267

A migration from Montgomery County, Ohio, was largely responsible for the founding of the Blue River congregation. Twenty-one members were part of the original group when it was organized in 1852. Some of the early family names included Zeigler, Hyre, Olinger, Rogers, Shoup, Kinzie, and Zumbrun. Joseph Zeigler and Wesley Hire were elected to the ministry soon after the church was organized, and Christian Kinzie was the first deacon.

For the first 20 years of the congregation's history, worship services were held in homes and barns of members. The first church building was constructed in 1872 about seven miles west of Churubusco in Whitley County.

A committee was appointed in 1903 to consider building a new church. The merits of remodeling the existing building or constructing a new church were debated for some time, but a decision to build new was finally made in 1907. Land was purchased near the 1872 building and a new church was completed and dedicated in 1909.

The congregation moved from the free ministry to a supported pastorate in 1921. Samuel J. Burger was the first pastor to be hired under this system and served until 1923. The church was without a regular pastor for over a year until L.U. Kreider was called in 1925. Kreider served as pastor and elder for the next 23 years (until 1948). He provided key leadership and is still given credit for much of the success of the congregation.

The need for additional space was again felt in 1944 and a committee was appointed to raise funds. A remodeling program was approved in 1952, and ground was broken in 1954. The remodeled church was dedicated on May 1, 1955.

A major event in the life of Blue River occurred in 1961 when a decision was made to support a new church in Columbia City. Fifty-six members of the Blue River congregation left to become part of the new church.

Even with this large block of members moving out, the Blue River congregation continued to grow throughout the 1960s. An additional two acres of land adjacent to the church was purchased in 1974. The congregation decided in 1975 to construct a completely new building in two phases, and a groundbreaking ceremony was held on July 27. Construction was begun a few months later, and a service to lay the cornerstone was held March 28, 1976. Guy E. Wampler Jr. was the speaker at a dedication service for the new building May 15, 1977.

Bremen

403 S. Montgomery St.
Bremen, IN 46506
Membership: 217

The Civil War had only been over for a year when the Bremen Church of the Brethren was organized in 1866. The new church was carved out of the northern part of territory which had been served by what was known as the Yellow River Church. The Bremen Church counted 55 people among its original members.

The first church building was located southeast of Bremen at the corner of what is now S.R. 331 and C.R. 3. This building was torn down in 1913, and a new church was built within the Bremen city limits at the corner of Sherman and Montgomery streets. David Kauffman donated the land for the building which continues to be the congregation's home.

Several remodeling projects have been undertaken since that time. The most extensive was completed and dedicated Oct. 10, 1954. A new parsonage was built and dedicated Oct. 18, 1964.

The 100th anniversary of the congregation was celebrated Oct. 9, 1966.

Throughout its history, the Bremen church has been actively involved in outreach programs. Several of its members participated in sending shiploads of cattle to Europe following World War II, and a number of members have participated in Brethren Volunteer Service terms.

Missionaries from the congregation have included Dr. Homer and Marguerite Burke and Bob and Mary Louise Swank.

Buck Creek
Route 1
Mooreland, IN 47360
2.5 miles southeast of Mount Pleasant
Membership: 46

A group of Brethren in the northern part of the Nettle Creek territory began meeting with Elder John Bowman of Hagerstown in the early 1840s. These early meetings were held in the homes and barns of those who were part of the fellowship.

The congregation was officially organized in 1845, and the first communion service was held in the home of Jacob Houser Sept. 17, 1846. He was the first member of the congregation to be elected a minister in 1852.

The church building was built in 1867 two miles west of Blountsville. It was originally a two-gable building constructed on a low rock foundation. A remodeling project in 1898 included raising the original building and digging out a basement underneath. Another remodeling project in 1922 added an annex on the south side of the building. A rededication service was held Nov. 5, 1922, with Evangelist S.J. Smith as the featured speaker. The day is recorded as one of the greatest days in the history of the congregation with several hundred in attendance.

The first Sunday school was organized in 1872, and was originally held only in the spring and summer. It was expanded to a year-round program within a few years.

Early in the life of the congregation (about 1880), a major migration to Kansas reduced the number of members by about a third. Included were some of the leading families, deacons, a minister, and the presiding elder. It was a difficult time for Buck Creek, but the migration resulted in the formation of the Osage Church in southeastern Kansas.

The congregation celebrated the centennial of the church building Oct. 8, 1967.

Buffalo

S.R.s 39 and 16
Buffalo, IN 47925
Membership: 58

Emigration of Brethren families from Ohio was in large measure the spark that led to the founding of the Buffalo Church, originally known as Beaver Creek.

A number of Brethren families emigrated from Ohio and settled in Pulaski County near Winamac in the early 1860s, including a minister, Abraham Miller. But it was not until 1873 that the foundation of a new church was laid. Daniel Freeman, a minister from Ohio, moved to the area in 1873 and was ordained. In the same year, several members of the Pike Creek Church met with Elder Freeman and decided to organize a new congregation to be called Beaver Creek. Some of those from Pike Creek included John Snoeberger, Joseph Amick, Andrew Culp, J.B. Royer, and J.A. Warren.

The first meeting house was built in 1889. Elder Freeman did most

of the preaching, assisted by Jeremiah Hahn. Brother Hahn was handicapped by ill health and asked the district mission board for assistance about the turn of the century. The mission board responded and took over the church until 1941.

In the late 1920s, the need was felt for a better church building and a better location. This led to the purchase of a former Presbyterian church building in Buffalo. The district approved changing the name from Beaver Creek to Buffalo in 1932.

A major remodeling was completed in 1942, and the church was rededicated. This was shortly after the congregation took full responsibility for its own support in 1941.

A series of major improvements to the building were made from 1950 to 1990. The congregation celebrated 50 years of serving from the present location in 1980.

Buffalo's location on the banks of the Tippecanoe River places it in the midst of a major summer vacation area. This factor has shaped much of its ministry over the years, including special services to the vacationers, even though this does not add to the total membership of the congregation. The congregation has for a number of years set aside 10 percent of the total church income to support mission programs. A visitation team from the church also makes regular stops at two local health care centers. Cooperative services with a neighboring congregation are held each year during Holy Week.

Burnettsville

P.O. Box 38
North Main Street
Burnettsville, Ind. 47926
Membership: 51

Brethren from Pennsylvania and Ohio began settling in the Burnettsville area soon after the Civil War. These early families attended services at Monticello, at least a two-hour trip by wagon.

By the mid-1870s, Brethren in Burnettsville were talking about holding worship services closer to their homes. This was accomplished in 1878 or 1879. These services were at first held in homes, then in a local Baptist church.

The Burnettsville group operated as a branch of the Monticello congregation until it was organized separately as Burnetts Creek in 1889. The first church building was constructed in 1890. Like most Brethren churches of the time, it had separate entrances for men and women. Russell Reiff, writing a history of the church in 1989, reported one member recalled that "male saints were to sit in front on the preacher's right and the male sinners behind them, the female saints on the other side in front and the female sinners behind them."

The young congregation was among the very first churches in Indiana to begin paying the pastor. George Heeter was hired on a part-time basis in 1899 and was paid $200 a year. Burnettsville was heavily criticized by some of its neighbors at the time for having to hire someone to preach to them.

The church launched into a major remodeling project in 1924. A basement was dug under the building, and the entire structure was modernized. Otho Winger was the speaker at dedication services July 26, 1926.

The remodeling project was completed with a $7,000 debt. The members were able to keep up interest payments, but paying on the principle was a problem. Finally, the congregation organized an auction at which donated items were sold along with apple butter and cider made by the members. This auction was held each autumn for several years until the loan was paid off.

Burnettsville reached a membership peak in the 1920s. This was drastically reduced during the Great Depression of the 1930s, but the church continued to be active in its community.

Another major remodeling project was completed in 1971 when the arrangement of the sanctuary was changed. The entrance to the church was relocated, the pulpit was moved to the west end of the building, and new pews were installed.

The 100th anniversary of the congregation was celebrated in 1989.

Camp Creek
7486 N. S.R. 19
Etna Green, IN 46524
Membership: 123

Elder David Shively was the recognized leader of a group of people who formed the Camp Creek congregation. It was organized in 1879 from the eastern part of the old Yellow River (now Mount Pleasant) territory.

The first ministers included Elder Shively's son, George Shively, plus Aaron Mow and Peter Hammon. The members met in homes and barns for the first year until a new meeting house was constructed in 1880 five miles north of Etna Green. The first Sunday school was organized in 1883 by Aaron Mow.

Owen L. Harley became the first paid minister in 1917. The church also adopted in 1916 a system of assessing dues to each family to fund the operation of the church. This system continued until 1944 when a unified budget was put in place.

The original Camp Creek church building has been enlarged and remodeled several times during its existence. The most recent renovation occurred during 1982-83.

Cedar Creek
5952 C.R. 07
Garrett, IN 46738
Membership: 95

Brothers Jeremiah and Jacob Gump were among a group of settlers who came from Miami County, Ohio, to Allen, Dekalb, and Noble counties in Indiana in 1853. Elder George Studebaker made preaching trips into the area and baptized the Gumps and several of their neighbors.

Both Gump brothers were called to the ministry in the fall of 1853 at a meeting held in the loft of a cabin owned by Samuel Shadows. The cabin was located just south of Avilla, and those in attendance reached the loft by climbing up a ladder and entering through a small window opening. Elders James Tracy, Jacob Berkey, and John Miller were present for this ministerial election.

The Cedar Creek church was organized in 1855 and grew quickly under the leadership of the Gumps and Elder Studebaker. Jeremiah Gump became a well known evangelist and preached throughout the northeast corner of the state, while Jacob was active in attending to the needs of the home church.

Cedar Creek grew to 125 members by 1873, but they were scattered over a wide area. It was decided to divide the territory. Pleasant Hill was organized in the west, Cedar Lake in the north, Little St. Joe in the east and the remainder stayed with Cedar Creek. Elder Jacob Gump was placed in charge of Cedar Lake, Little St. Joe and Cedar Creek, and Elder Jeremiah was given charge of Pleasant Hill, which was near his home.

The Little St. Joe congregation never grew beyond a few members, and it was disorganized in 1914. The members were placed with Cedar Creek or a congregation at Hicksville, Ohio.

For 30 years, the members of Cedar Creek met in the homes and barns of its members. Land for a meeting house was purchased in 1875, and the first church building was finally constructed in 1885. Major additions were made in 1927 and 1956-57.

Cedar Lake

2939 C.R. 15
Auburn, IN 46706
Membership: 125

Cedar Lake Church came into existence with the division of the Cedar Creek territory. The northern part of the territory was split off in 1873, and Cedar Lake was organized as a separate congregation in this region in 1874. Jacob Gump was the presiding elder, and James Barton was called as the first minister. He later was ordained an elder and served as presiding elder until his death in 1902.

There were 42 charter members of the congregation. They built a house of worship in 1876 northeast of Garrett, which still serves as the basic structure.

The first Sunday school program was organized in 1912. A long interest in missions led to the congregation's partial sponsorship of Velma Ober who served in China.

The building has undergone a series of improvements over the

years beginning with a major remodeling in 1942 which also included a rededication service. Other improvement projects occurred in 1951-52, 1961, and 1966. An addition was built onto the original building in 1973-74 that included new classrooms and new entrances for the sanctuary and narthex. A dedication was held during the congregation's centennial celebrations Sept. 14-15 and 21-22, 1974. Dr. Donald Durnbaugh and Dr. Dale Brown were the speakers.

Two special programs sponsored by the congregation are the Scamper School, a preschool program, and an annual Harvest Festival for the entire community. Both programs were started in 1973.

Christ Our Shepherd

857 S.R. 135 N.
Greenwood, IN 46142
Membership: 92

Christ Our Shepherd Church of the Brethren in Greenwood is one of the newest congregations in Indiana.

The new group began meeting in October 1986 as a mission point under the sponsorship of the South/Central District. Northview Church of the Brethren in Indianapolis has also been involved in the effort. Wendell Bohrer was the primary organizer and has been serving as pastor since its inception. The first meetings were held in his garage. On the first Sunday of March 1987, the group moved the meetings to the Wilson-St. Pierre Funeral Home.

A milestone was reached in 1990 with the construction of the first phase of a planned three-phase building program. The first service in the new building was held Sept. 9, 1990.

A steering committee served as the governing body for the group until Jan. 1, 1991, when the first church board was elected. Ron Yoder

was elected the first board chair and Pat Wood the first recording secretary.

Christ Our Shepherd has approximately 92 members and is actively moving toward a goal of 100 members to attain Fellowship status.

Columbia City

112 N. Washington St.
Columbia City, IN 46725
Membership: 39

The present church at Columbia City is the result of the second group to form a Church of the Brethren congregation in the city.

The first Brethren families settled in the Columbia City area in the 1860s. They were members of the Blue River Church, but most lived 10 to 12 miles from the meeting house built in 1872, and travel was often difficult.

Daniel Brown, a deacon at Blue River, was instrumental in helping several families organize a new congregation. Elder Jeremiah Gump was the first presiding elder when the church was formed in 1875. A meeting house was built one mile west of Columbia City.

The Columbia City congregation met with varying degrees of success for the next 50 years but suffered from a lack of consistent leadership. There were never more than 40 members at any time. Eventually the church building was sold, and the congregation met in rented facilities for a short time. The District Mission Board took charge in 1927, and the church was disorganized. Members transferred to other Brethren churches in the area.

The second attempt to establish a Columbia City church began in 1960, and once again most of those involved were from Blue River. A survey to assess interest was conducted in May 1960, and in July it was

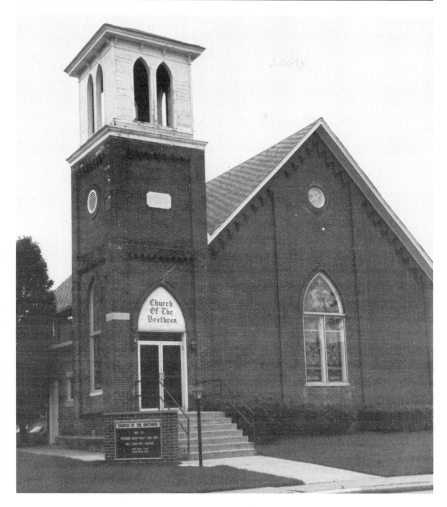

decided to lease a building at Washington and Jackson streets which was previously home to the Columbia City Church of God.

The first congregational business meeting was held Jan. 9, 1961, and Moyne Landes was secured as pastor. The first worship service was held May 7, 1961, and Columbia City was officially recognized by district conference the following August. The congregation approved the purchase of the building from the Church of God Dec. 7, 1961.

Columbia City quickly became a strong part of the Northern Indiana District and was a stable home for its members. In 1972, the church entered the most difficult period of its history. James Linton was hired as pastor and, at first, the church showed renewed vigor and growth. By 1975, however, differences arose between the members and the pastor over several issues including support of the denomination and its institutions.This eventually led to Linton's resignation in late 1975. He formed the Columbia City Independent Brethren Church (unaffiliated with any denomination), and about 20 members left the Columbia City Church of the Brethren with him.

The church quickly recovered and became active in its community once more.The interior of the building was remodeled in 1980, and an exterior refurbishing project was begun the following year.A new entryway and sign were added in 1983, and the kitchen was remodeled in 1986.

The 25th anniversary of the Columbia City Church was observed during special services May 4, 1986.

Communion Fellowship
114 S. Sixth St.
Goshen, IN 46526
Meets at Peddlers Village, C.R. 28
Membership: 120

Communion Fellowship is one of the newest churches in Indiana, and is one of very few with dual denominational affiliation.

The group began in 1977 with informal weekly meetings. Doug Fike, who had grown up in the Church of the Brethren in Puerto Rico, provided initial leadership. Others attending were primarily students from Church of the Brethren and Mennonite backgrounds.

Communion Fellowship emerged in 1983 after several years as a student group on the Goshen College campus. In the fall of 1984, it was accepted by both the Church of the Brethren and the Mennonite Church.

Since moving off the Goshen College campus in 1983, Communion Fellowship has met in a variety of settings including homes, Bethany

Christian High School, and, finally, at the Peddlers Village Auction Barn at the west edge of Goshen since 1988.

Team leadership is a hallmark for Communion Fellowship. Congregational leadership is given by a team of elders, a team of deacons, and overseers. Small groups have been an integral part of the fellowship since the beginning. Each cell has a leader, and a special team oversees the cell group program.

Mission is also a major emphasis. Six missionary teams are currently serving in China, Thailand, India, and Puerto Rico. The church also sent four people in 1987 to Lancaster, Pa., to assist in establishing a new church in that city. The result was the formation of Acts Covenant Fellowship which has become a thriving congregation reaching out to the unchurched in Lancaster.

Crest Manor

1342 E. Berkshire Drive
South Bend, IN 46614
Membership: 141

Crest Manor Church of the Brethren is the descendant of the first South Bend church which was organized in the early 1840s. The original territory included all of southern and eastern St. Joseph County. Elders Abraham Whitmer, Jacob Bowman, and George Shively were the resident preachers for meetings which were held primarily in homes and barns.

Sometime in the 1860s, the territory was divided. An area which included approximately the western half of the original retained the name South Bend, and the remainder was called St. Joseph.

The first church building in South Bend was erected in 1877 at the corner of Miami Street and Indiana Avenue. It was located on farm land donated by Martin Wenger and was known as the Wenger Church. Martin Wenger was one of the early leaders of the church and is believed to have emigrated from Ohio. His great-granddaughter, Jeanette Tolle, is still a member at Crest Manor.

H.W. Krieghbaum, a son-in-law of Martin Wenger, was called to the ministry in 1882. He was the first superintendent of the Sunday school program when it was organized in 1878. He was ordained and later became presiding elder until his death in 1912. Although the date is unclear, the name of the church was changed during this period to First Church of the Brethren of South Bend.

The church building was remodeled in 1900 and again a few years later. It was completely replaced in 1922 with a new brick building.

First South Bend was for many years one of the larger churches in the Northern Indiana District. Three men who served as moderator of Annual conference since 1950 have also served as pastors at First South Bend including Harper Will, Paul Robinson, and Charles Zunkel.

By the early 1960s, discussions about building a new church had been going on for some time. The decision was finally made to relocate in the Crest Manor subdivision on the city's south side. The first service in the new building was held in July 1963, and it continues to serve as home to the congregation.

Crest Manor has consistently been involved in its community. It was one of three churches which established the Broadway Christian Parish in 1961, and a nursery school program was launched in 1965. More recently, the congregation has sponsored two families from Southeast Asia, and a Samaritan Counseling Center was opened at the church in 1989.

A major celebration was held in 1977 for the centennial of the building of the first church.

Eel River

Route 2, Box 194-A
Silver Lake, IN 46982
Membership: 113

Eel River was one of the very early churches in Indiana and is the mother church for several congregations.

Joseph Harter came to Indiana from Montgomery County, Ohio, in September 1836. He settled on the Eel River where the town of North Manchester is now located. His son, Eli Harter, was the second person to erect a cabin in North Manchester, and Eli's daughter, Phoebe, was the first white child born in the area. Joseph Harter eventually erected a grist mill and became a major landowner in the North Manchester area.

The Harters, who were Dunkards, were soon joined by others from southern Ohio including Daniel Swank, Isaac and David Ulrey, Samuel Ulrey, Jacob Cripe, Jacob Swihart, and Jacob Metzger.

This small group of Brethren was soon listening to preaching by visiting elders including William Moss from Mexico and Daniel Cripe, John Miller, and John Leatherman from Elkhart County.

Eel River was officially organized in 1838 with Joseph Harter as the first minister. The territory covered a large area with North Manchester located approximately in the center.

The congregation was divided in 1852. The northern part retained the name Eel River and the southern section was called Manchester. David Ulrey, who was ordained in 1850, was named the presiding elder of Eel River.

Eel River developed three separate meeting houses. The first, known as the Middle House, was built about 1860 on three acres of land which had been donated by Joseph Ulrey Sr. in 1844. The second was built in 1868 about three miles east and a half mile south. It was known as the East House. The third house, or West House, was built two miles east of Silver Lake.

Following the death of David Ulrey in 1866, Elders Jacob Metzger and Jacob Cripe were given oversight of the congregation. Cripe died in 1875, and Metzger led a large group of people into the Old Order movement in the schism of 1881.

In spite of this setback, Eel River continued to attract new members and grow. Two Sunday school programs were started: the first at the East House in 1890, and the second at the Middle House in 1893. The original Middle House building was replaced in 1897 by a new brick church building.

The three houses of Eel River were separated into independent congregations in 1913. The Middle House retained the name Eel River, the East House was named Plunge Creek Chapel (now Liberty Mills), and the West House was called West Eel River

Baptisms were held in a creek at the rear of the church building. In 1916, a baptistry was built in the church basement. Water was heated in large kettles to fill the new baptistry, which made baptism a much more comfortable experience for new members.

Eel River completely renovated the old brick church building in 1950. Also in 1950, the congregation purchased an 80-acre farm. The house was used as a parsonage; the land was farmed by members of the congregation who used the revenue to support the programs of Eel River

A new program to minister to students at nearby Manchester College was launched in 1970. This led to a very strong young adult program which benefitted the entire church.

Eel River joined West Eel River in a yoked pastoral arrangement in 1977. This arrangement served both churches for nine years when it was again decided to seek separate pastoral leadership. Eel River then hired Jane Flora in 1987 as the congregation's first woman pastor.

Eel River sponsored a weekend of activities to celebrate the 150th anniversary of the congregation Sept. 16-18, 1988. A special invitation was sent to churches in the area which trace their lineage to the original Eel River Church, including several congregations now affiliated with the Brethren Church, Old German Baptist Brethren, and Fellowship of Grace Brethren.

Elkhart City

248 W. Wolf Ave.
Elkhart, IN 46516
Membership: 283

The Elkhart City Church grew out of the Elkhart Valley congregation. Several Elkhart Valley members lived in Elkhart and it is believed home meetings began taking place in the city about 1890. Property was purchased Sept. 2, 1892, at 1618 S. Sixth St. in the Oak Park Addition, and a church building was erected and dedicated there in 1893. At this time, the congregation was known as the Oak Park German Baptist Brethren.

At a council meeting on June 30, 1897, it was decided to formally organize the new group as a separate church. This was accomplished

with an election on July 27, 1897, and the name of the congregation was changed to Elkhart City Church of the Brethren.

Elder Isaac Parker had come to the church in 1893 and was instrumental in its early growth. Sixty new members joined the congregation during his first year. With this record of leadership in mind, the congregation chose him to be the first pastor.

The church building was remodeled in 1902, and an addition was built in 1917. The building was again remodeled in 1923. This project included the construction of a baptistry which replaced the practice of holding baptismal services in the Elkhart River, even in the dead of winter when ice had to be cut from the river.

Elkhart City continued to grow rapidly. The congregation anticipated future needs by purchasing property at the corner of Wolf and Benham in 1928. A parsonage was built at that location in 1930.

After several years of planning, ground was broken at Benham and Wolf for a new church on July 15, 1949. The new facility was dedicated June 25, 1950.

A Sunday school program has been part of Elkhart City from the beginning. The need for more classroom space led to the construction of an education wing which was dedicated Nov. 17, 1963. This was followed a year later with the opening of a preschool program on Sept. 14, 1964. The program now includes four classes of preschool youngsters and serves as a major outreach program since most of the children are from families who are not members of the church.

Members of Elkhart City have been very active throughout its history in supporting church and community service projects.

Elkhart Valley
24955 C.R. 24 E.
Elkhart, IN 46517
Membership: 118

The earliest beginnings of the Elkhart Valley congregation can be traced to 1845 when Sebastian Frame moved from Montgomery County, Ohio, to Elkhart County in the area of what is now Dunlap. The territory at that time was in the northwest part of the Elkhart congregation (now West Goshen). It was later divided and was part of the Yellow Creek Church territory at the time a movement for a new congregation began to take shape in the early 1860s. The Frame family had by then been joined by Daniel Bigler from Gettysburg, Ohio, and George, Henry, and David Puterbaugh from Miami County, Ohio.

Construction of the first church building was begun in 1865 and completed in 1866. When the entrance was altered in 1903, a shingle dated 1865 was found wedged behind a door jamb. The new church was located near C.R.s 11 and 24, about two miles southeast of Elkhart.

Sebastian Frame had died by the time Elkhart Valley became a separate congregation in 1870, but his son, Gabriel, was the first member elected to the ministry that year along with Amsey Puterbaugh. A few members left the congregation with the 1882 split of the Progressives, but it did not affect membership greatly.

One of the biggest events in the life of Elkhart Valley was acting as the mother church when the Elkhart City congregation was formed in 1893. Elkhart Valley shepherded the new congregation until it became a separate organization in 1897.

Another point of pride for Elkhart Valley is that it was for 10 years the home congregation for Dan West and his family, founder of Heifer Project International. Dan West was the guest speaker at the congregation's centennial celebration Sept. 11, 1966, and a memorial in his honor is located at the church.

A major renovation and addition project was completed in 1955-56. The sanctuary was reversed and a balcony added. A two-story addition was built on the back of the building providing new classrooms and office space.

Church membership rose to a peak of more than 250 while John McCormick was pastor during the 1950s and early 1960s. However, a major division occurred about 1973 and attendance dropped to as low as 60 at one point. The congregation has since recovered and membership now stands at 118.

English Prairie
Route 2, Box 579
Howe, IN 46746
Membership: 48

Two men, Peter Long and Jacob Berkey, figure prominently in the founding of the English Prairie Church.

Peter Long was born in Pennsylvania and moved to Holmes County, Ohio, as a boy. He was married there and elected to the ministry about 1860. In 1863, he and eight other families settled in LaGrange County, Indiana.

Elder Jacob Berkey had settled farther west in eastern Elkhart County in 1848. He is generally acknowledged as the primary leader of the Rock Run congregation beginning with its founding in 1850. He was quickly advanced to elder and spent many days on trips to preach in eastern Elkhart County, LaGrange County, and southern Michigan.

Elder Berkey learned of the new Brethren settlement in LaGrange County soon after the newcomers arrived and helped Peter Long establish a new church. Originally known as Fawn River, the new church was formally organized in 1864, just one year after the settlers arrived. The name was later changed to English Prairie.

The congregation met in the homes of members, and love feasts were held in barns. A notice published in *Christian Family Companion*, a church publication from Tyrone, Pa., on Sept. 14, 1869, invited members to attend the love feast to be held in Peter Long's barn. Long was ordained as an elder in 1878 and given charge of the church. He remained the presiding elder until his death in 1908.

A church building was constructed at the present site in 1873. As might be expected, it was built on land donated by Peter Long. A Sunday school program was organized in the early 1880s, perhaps 1883.

English Prairie was very active in promoting services in several nearby communities in the late 1800s and early 1900s. One of the most active sites was known as Oak Grove, located in the area south of Bronson, Mich. An attempt was made to purchase a building owned by the Oak Grove Mennonite Church, but by 1904 those plans had fallen through. A building committee was appointed in 1906 and funds were raised. A small frame meeting house was constructed, and the first love feast in the new building was held in the fall of 1907. The fledgling group continued to meet into the early 1920s, but attendance declined to very small numbers and the building was sold in 1924.

Attention eventually focused primarily at English Prairie where the congregation was active in both foreign and home missions. The first vacation Bible school was held in 1936. A parsonage located just across the road from the church was purchased in 1945 when Raymond Risden was hired as the first paid minister.

The 125th anniversary of the congregation was observed at a special service on Oct. 8, 1989.

A number of improvements have been made to the English Prairie Church building over the years. While it looks much different today, the original 1873 framework still supports the work of the congregation.

Flora

410 S. Center St.
Flora, IN 46929
Membership: 245

Establishing a founding date for the Flora Church of the Brethren is not a

simple matter. The congregation can trace its beginning to a small group of Brethren in Carroll County in 1828 that was at that time known as the Deer Creek Church. Flora members, however, prefer to date their beginning as 1838 when the Deer Creek congregation was divided and the Bachelor Run congregation was formed.

Meetings of the Bachelor Run group were held in homes and barns until the first church building was erected in 1854 just southeast of Flora at a place known as Pike's Peak. A second church building was erected in 1856 five miles southeast of Flora on Little Bachelor Run Creek. The church near Flora was called the Lower House and the building on Bachelor Run was known as the Upper House. The Bachelor Run congregation worshipped together on alternate Sundays at each house. The original Lower House was a wood frame building. It was remodeled in 1884, then replaced by a brick structure which was dedicated March 31, 1903

By 1911, the Bachelor Run congregation was large enough that the decision was made to divide the territory into two separate congregations. The final vote for division came at a council meeting Dec. 14, 1911. Immediately after the vote, members of the Lower House met and adopted the name Flora Church of the Brethren.

Art glass windows were installed and dedicated in 1941, and a major renovation program was begun the same year. The interior of the building was renovated in 1970, and the basement was renovated in 1983.

Church membership suffered considerably during the divisions of the 1880s. Beginning with a membership of about 350, 126 were disfellowshipped in 1881 when the Old Order Brethren left the denomination. Included in that number were several ministers and deacons. The following year, another group of unknown size left when the split with the Progressives occurred. In spite of these heavy blows, the congregation managed to regain its membership of about 350 within a few years.

The Flora Church has been a major supporter of Heifer Project International from the program's beginning and still contributes to the purchase of livestock.

A centennial observance was held in 1938. One of the biggest recent events for the congregation was a homecoming celebration Nov. 6, 1988, which was an observance of the church's 150th anniversary.

Florence
17975 Centreville-Constantine Road
Constantine, MI 49042
Membership: 52

The Florence Church has the distinction of being the only church outside the boundaries of Indiana which is part of an Indiana district. Although there were at one time several churches along the Indiana-Michigan border which were daughters of Indiana congregations,

Florence is the only one that remains.

The Florence congregation grew out of the Shipshewana Church, which was disorganized in 1938. Frank and Lillian Reed were members of the Shipshewana Church who lived near Centreville, Mich., located about 18 miles from Shipshewana. They and other neighbors were interested in having services closer to their homes. Sometime after 1925, George Sherck, then pastor of the Shipshewana Church, asked the district mission board to investigate the possibilities of holding services near Centreville. It was decided the board would send a minister every other Sunday, and E.C. Swihart of Elkhart agreed to do the preaching.

Permission was gained to use a former German Reformed church building on the Centreville-Constantine Road for the meetings. The first Sunday school was organized in this building May 12, 1927.

J.E. Jarboe held two weeks of evangelistic meetings for the group in March 1929, and 35 new members were added to the fellowship. This new, larger group asked George Sherck to become their minister. He resigned at Shipshewana in September 1929, and purchased a farm near the little Michigan church.

The Florence Church of the Brethren was officially organized as a separate group in May 1931.

In 1940, the Florence congregation attempted to purchase the building they had been using. Instead, they were given a life lease on the building for $4 because the deed for the property had been made to the people of Florence Township for religious purposes only. The little church building, which was originally constructed in 1876, was then remodeled and classrooms were added. Additions were also made in 1964 and 1974.

Four Mile
Route 3
Liberty, IN 47353
Membership: 46

Four Mile was the first congregation organized in Indiana and has sent many people on who founded new congregations in Indiana and other states. It can truly be called the mother church for the entire state.

Some of the first Dunkard activity in the region came in 1803 when James and Samuel Huston (brothers) and Joseph Kingery settled on the Ohio side of the state line in Preble County. Their land bordered on the Little Four Mile Creek.

Land on the Indiana side of the Greenville Treaty line was surveyed and opened for settlement in 1805. Among the first to settle along the Four Mile that year in what is now Union County, Ind., were John and

Polly (McClure) Miller. John was a son of Elder Jacob Miller. He became known as Potter John because he built a kiln and made bricks from the clay on his land. It was also to distinguish him from another John Miller in the area (possibly a cousin) who was known as Col. John due to his past service in the militia.

Others soon began moving into the area including Tobias and Sarah (Henderson) Miller, Abraham and Nancy (Huston) Miller, Daniel and Elizabeth (Shideler) Miller, and Aaron and Elizabeth (Hardman) Miller.

Another settlement began forming about seven miles north on the headwaters of the Little Four Mile, also known as the Upper Four Mile. These settlers included Philip and Anna (Miller) Lybrook, William and Elizabeth (Lybrook) Moss, and Jacob and Barbara (Lybrook) Kingery.

This was the beginning of a steady stream of Dunkard settlers into the area. Most of them came from Franklin County, Va., although some also came from Ohio and Pennsylvania. As the names of the original settlers listed above suggests, many were members of the same families. Some of the family names included Witter, Kingery, Moss, Eikenberry, Landis, Shideler, Ridenour, Rife, Moyer, Brower, Rinehart, Toney, Fosher and Fiant.

Elder Jacob Miller was the presiding elder of the Bear Creek congregation in Ohio. A number of his children were among those who settled on the Four Mile, and he came periodically to visit and to preach. In 1809, he and Elder John Hart came from Ohio and formally organized a new church which took the name Four Mile. It was the first Dunkard congregation in Indiana. John Moyer and Daniel Miller were chosen for the ministry, and Christopher Witter and Joseph Kingery were chosen as the first deacons.

The membership of Four Mile increased rapidly as settlers continued to pour in. Most of the early services were held in the area known as the Lower Four Mile, but travel was often difficult for those living around the Upper Four Mile. It required a journey on foot or horseback of about seven miles through dense forest. In 1813, it was decided to split the congregation into two groups. Moyer and Miller lived in the southern portion and became responsible for the Lower Four Mile group. Baltzer Lybrook lived in the north. He was called to the ministry and was given responsibility for the Upper Four Mile.

Peace treaties with the Indians soon began opening up the interior of the state for settlement. A number of families who originally had settled in the Four Mile territory began moving farther west and north. Aaron and David Miller moved north and became the first ministers of the Nettle Creek Church. A number of families moved into the Raccoon Creek (later Ladoga) area. Potter John Miller followed several of his children there in about 1823. Several families moved to the Ladoga area, then moved on to Iowa where they helped start new churches. A mass migration in the 1830s, perhaps spurred by a terrible cholera epidemic in 1832, took Four Mile families into St. Joseph, Miami, Carroll, Huntington, Wabash, Grant, and Hamilton counties where new churches were formed.

In spite of these migrations, the Four Mile continued to be a thriving Dunkard community because those who left were quickly replaced by others coming in fron the East. The first church building in Indiana was erected by the Lower Four Mile group during the 1840s. It was a 40-foot by 50-foot wooden structure located about two miles north of College Corner, Ohio, along the Four Mile. It was used until 1873.

One of the keys to the success of the Lower Four Mile during this period was the leadership provided by Elder Daniel Miller, one of the original ministers. But he left in 1854 with about 20 members in a mass migration to Iowa. The group included Brethren from Ladoga and Carroll County, many of whom originally were members at Four Mile. This migration weakened Lower Four Mile considerably, and they soon asked to rejoin Upper Four Mile. From then on, the church was known simply as Four Mile.

A new meeting house was built in the Upper Four Mile area in 1857 on land donated by John and Elizabeth Moss. The original building had a large fireplace in the north end where food for communion services was prepared in large kettles. This building was lifted and a basement dug underneath it in 1895. The fireplace was removed and a large brick stove was built in the basement.

The church was remodeled again in 1913 when the original double entry doors were replaced by a single vestibule. The pulpit was moved from the south end to the north end and Sunday school rooms were added.

The scattered membership led to the construction of several houses of worship. The original Lower Four Mile building was demolished in 1873. It was replaced in 1875 by a new building near Cottage Grove. It was eventually sold in 1929.

Another building was constructed in 1868 northeast of Connersville in Fayette County. It was known as the Whitewater House. In 1913, the group meeting at this location organized as a separate congregation known as New Bethel. The congregation was active for a time but soon began to decline, and New Bethel was disorganized in 1933.

Another church building was purchased in West Florence, Ohio, in 1886. Services were held there until 1908 when the building was sold.

For a period of time in the late 1800s, Four Mile operated four separate church buildings (Four Mile, Whitewater, Cottage Grove, and West Florence). Services were alternated between the four sites with each site active once every fourth Sunday.

Four Mile adopted a paid ministry in 1919 with the hiring of A.P. Musselman. Four church members purchased a house in Kitchel for the parsonage. The church assumed payments in 1926, and it became the property of the congregation.

Four Mile retained a thriving membership through most of the first half of the 20th century. Like many rural churches, however, the congregation has lost members as many of its youth have moved on to find jobs in larger communities. In 1968, Four Mile joined Richmond in a yoked parish arrangement. Victor Bendsen was the first pastor to serve both congregations. The yoked pastorate continues to serve both churches today under the leadership of Clyde Hilton.

Goshen City

203 N. Fifth St.
Goshen, IN 46526
Membership: 514

The town of Goshen was located in the center of a hotbed of Brethren activity in Elkhart County, but nearly all of the meetings and organizing were in rural areas. As more people began to live in towns rather than on farms, the Brethren began to shift their attention to urban areas.

This happened in Goshen in the 1890s. Among the first to preach in Goshen were Hiram Forney, Levi Hoke, and Isaac Berkey. Elder Forney held evangelistic meetings in Goshen in a tent in 1895 which led to organized prayer meetings in the homes of A.D. Miller, D.R. Yoder, M.C. Schrock, A.J. Miller, and Henry B. Hess.

Since Goshen was formally part of the Rock Run territory, these early meetings fell under their authority. The Goshen group quickly outgrew home meetings, and a hall was rented. A decision was made in 1898 to buy or build a church in Goshen. After considering several possibilities, a lot was purchased at the corner of Fifth and Clinton streets and a brick church building was erected in 1899. Goshen City Church of the Brethren was officially organized as a separate congregation in 1905. The membership at that time totaled 180.

An active Sunday school program was part of the new church from the beginning, and the music program has a long tradition with active adult, children's, and bell choirs.

By the time the 50th anniversary of the original building was celebrated in 1949, the Sunday school program was bursting at the seams. The members began talking about an expansion project and a building fund was established in the early 1950s.

The decision was made to remain at the Fifth and Clinton site, but its downtown location made expansion difficult. A new L-shaped church building was designed and built around the old 1899 building. Construction began in 1957 and was completed in 1959. The original building was then demolished. It remains one of the largest churches in the state.

Goshen City has long been active in outreach programs. A major event was a joint project between the church and the Association for the Disabled of Elkhart County (ADEC) to develop a group home for mentally handicapped adults. The church purchased the home of a member, and ADEC operated a program there to help their clients learn to live independently. It was the first program of its kind in the state and has since led to major restructuring of the programs offered for the mentally handicapped in Indiana. The home was eventually sold to ADEC in the mid-1980s, but the church has remained an active supporter of programs for the handicapped.

The congregation supported a series of remodeling projects in the 1980s. The entry was enclosed in 1980, and a major remodeling of the large sanctuary and chapel was completed in 1984-85. A new drive-up entry on the east side of the building and an elevator were built in 1990.

The elevator project led to the start of an adult day care program in 1991 which is open to the community. The program provides care during the day for elderly adults and is aimed at helping them stay at home with their families rather than having to move to a nursing home. The charge for the service is based on family income.

Another major event in the life of the congregation was the election of Pastor Phyllis Carter as moderator-elect of Annual Conference in 1990. She served as Annual Conference moderator in 1992 while continuing her full-time pastorate at Goshen City. She was the second woman to hold the moderator's post in the history of the denomination.

Guernsey

Route 4, Box 600
Monticello, IN 47960
Membership: 61

The Guernsey Church has an independent history of only 25 years, but the congregation has been active for more than 100 years.

The first Brethren settlers came from Pennsylvania into the White County area around Monticello in the early 1830s. The area at that time was part of the Bachelor Run Church.

The Brethren population in White County continued to grow. This led to the formal organization of the Monticello Church in 1859. Although there was no meeting house, the congregation established preaching points throughout the territory. By 1887, seven different points were listed including Pike Creek, Burnetts Creek, Paton, Oak Grove, Palestine, Winamac, Bowman School House, and Guernsey. Burnetts Creek (now Burnettsville) was organized as a separate congregation in 1898. Pike Creek and Guernsey continued operating as two meeting houses of the Monticello Church, but the other four preaching points were discontinued.

Brethren had been holding a union Sunday school in the Gopher School House (about one-half mile north of the present Guernsey

Church) since the 1860s. The Monticello Church later acquired a quarter interest in a Methodist meeting house across the road from the school. Brethren services were held there on Sunday afternoons while the Methodists met on Sunday mornings.

A.R. Bridge and David Dilling were instrumental in establishing the Guernsey Church, and both served as free ministers. Members of the Joseph Kellenberger family also played a major role.

Mr. and Mrs. Frank Pettit donated a corner plot of ground about six miles northwest of Monticello in 1913. The first church building was constructed there and dedicated on Dec. 21, 1913, with Grover Wine of North Manchester as the featured speaker. David Dilling spoke briefly noting that only $40 remained to be paid on the building. A collection at the service yielded $138. It was the last service Dilling ever attended. He became ill a few days later and died Jan. 2, 1914.

The church was extensively remodeled in 1939. The project included digging a basement under the building and constructing a new front entrance at the southwest corner. The project was undertaken at the end of the Great Depression, and money was still scarce. Much of the labor was donated, but a considerable sum of money was still needed. To help raise funds, each family in the church planted an acre of corn and donated the proceeds from the yield to the building project. Donations ranged from $18 to $21 per acre. The women of the church also served lunch each Monday at the Monticello Community Sale.

A major day in the life of the church was the dedication service held Aug. 25, 1940. J. Oscar Winger gave the dedication address, and

Pike Creek members dismissed services for the day to join in the celebration with Guernsey.

Guernsey continued to grow throughout the 1940s, especially the children's department of the Sunday school program. Mrs. Jessie Lantz is given much of the credit for the growth of this program.

The need to enlarge the church was being felt again as early as 1947, but that need was put on hold in favor of building a parsonage in a joint project with Pike Creek. The new home was built just west of the Pike Creek meeting house and was completed in July 1948. A mortgage burning ceremony was held in 1951.

Guernsey turned its attention to its own needs again in 1954 with another remodeling project that added seven classrooms, a balcony, and a baptistry. The "God's Acre" plan was used once more, and other fundraisers were held. New pews, a pulpit, and an altar were added a short time later.

A new wing was added to the church building in 1964 which gave Guernsey the luxury of indoor rest rooms for the first time. A larger kitchen was added in the basement, and three large classrooms were built on the first and second floors.

A major decision in 1967 led to the formation of Guernsey as an independent congregation with its own church board. Pike Creek also became independent which marked the end of the Monticello Church.

However, both congregations voted to retain a yoked pastorate, an arrangement which has continued to the present day. The two congregations jointly maintain the parsonage near Pike Creek, and many activities are shared by the two churches. A tradition is an annual Easter Sunrise Service sponsored by the two youth groups.

Attendance at Guernsey peaked in the 1960s at about 75. Attendance has since declined and now averages about 25.

Hickory Grove

Route 1, Box 118-B
Dunkirk, IN 47336
Membership: 56

Hickory Grove claims an independent history dating to 1882, but the congregation traces its origins to an even earlier date.

Several families living in Jay County traveled the 12 to 15 miles by horseback or wagon every Sunday they could to Walnut Level located near Petroleum. But the trip was long and arduous, especially in bad weather. Wilson Hutchinson, a member of Walnut Level, moved to the Jay County area in 1872 and organized a new fellowship in the Sugar Grove school on the Corwin homestead. It was located about one-half

mile southeast of the present site of the church.

The congregation was officially separated from Walnut Level in 1882 and was known as Camden Church of the Brethren, named for a small town nearby. A new church building was constructed in 1886 near the current site at the intersection of S.R.s 1 and 26.

There was a period of decline in the 1890s, but the membership began to increase again in the early 1900s. A Sunday school program was started in 1907. A basement was dug under the church building in 1913 adding needed classroom space.

There was another Camden, Ind., located in southern Indiana and, in 1914, the Camden in Jay County changed its name to Pennville. This made the name and location of the church confusing. So, a query was approved by district conference in February 1914 to change the name of the church to Hickory Grove. The name was chosen because of the many hickory trees surrounding the church.

A storm badly damaged the church on June 30, 1929, but repairs had been made by October. An extensive renovation was completed in 1944 with a rededication service held July 23.

The first parsonage was purchased in Pennville in 1956. This was replaced in 1976 with a new parsonage built on land donated by a member near the church.

The members took a major step forward with the construction of a brand new church building in 1980. The new building is located immediately behind the original 1886 building but set farther back from the highway intersection. A contractor was hired to erect a shell, and members and friends donated many hours to complete the work. Construction was started in 1979 and the congregation moved into the building in February 1980. Dedication services were held at a special homecoming celebration in October.

Howard

C.R.s 1516 N., 1150 W.
Kokomo, IN 46901
Membership: 22

The Howard Church of the Brethren congregation has the unique distinction of worshipping in the same building for more than 125 years, although the meeting house is now in its third different location.

The first Brethren settlers in Howard County came from Union County where they had been members of the Four Mile Church. Hiel Hamilton was ordained Dec. 1, 1845, and ministered on horseback to settlers in the Howard County area.

Howard County Church was officially organized in 1852. Its territory was originally part of the Bachelor Run territory and included all of Howard County and parts of Clinton and Tipton counties. Hamilton was elected presiding elder in 1856.

The first meeting house was built in 1865 south of Wildcat Creek about two miles south of where the church now stands 11 miles west of Kokomo. This location was difficult for some of those living north of the creek to reach, especially during periods of heavy rain and in the spring when winter snows melted.

The 1881 division with the Old Order Brethren had a major impact on the Howard Church. Membership at that time was 160 and about a third left in the split. This included two ministers and two of three deacons. Some of these members returned to the congregation in 1918.

In 1886, the congregation decided a new location was needed for the meeting house. Daniel Bock had been elected presiding elder that year and donated land north of Wildcat Creek. Instead of building a new meeting house, the original building was moved. It was taken apart in three sections, each section was moved by horse and wagon two miles north, which is also the present site, and then put back together on top of a stone foundation.

Although the denomination changed its name in 1908, it wasn't until 1914 that the Howard Church adopted the new moniker. The German Baptist Howard County Church became the Howard Church of the Brethren.

A renovation project in the late 1940s added classrooms and an entry at the west end of the building which made the sanctuary a little smaller. A gas furnace was also installed which took the place of two wood stoves which had been the only source of heat to that time.

An extensive renovation project was undertaken in 1967 which included moving the building a third time. A basement was dug about 100 feet north. The church building was raised in one piece from the rock foundation and moved in place over the new basement. Even though the renovation project changed the look of the interior, the main frame remained the same, including the original hand-hewn beams which measure a foot square. The crossbeams are 40 feet long and the beams running the length of the building measure 60 feet.

The membership of the Howard Church decreased through most of the 1900s, but has recently seen some growth. The church participated in the Education for Shared Ministry Program from 1983-86. Martha Cory was ordained in 1986 and has been serving as pastor since that time.

Huntington

306 E. Washington St.
Huntington, IN 46750
Membership: 160

Several members of the Church of the Brethren were living in Huntington in 1891, but the nearest church was Clear Creek, located several miles outside the city. Travel was difficult and Mrs. Nancy Kitch, affectionately known to many as Grandma Kitch, was one of the first to ask that services be held in town. Elder Dorsey Hodgden of the Clear Creek church and representatives of the nearby Markle, Huntington County, and Salamonie congregations organized meetings once a month in the old courthouse.

Elder Noah Fisher came to Huntington in the fall of 1893 and held

a series of successful meetings which led to new members, and a Sunday school was organized. This growth made it evident that a church in Huntington was needed.

Although the Huntington city group was considered part of the Clear Creek church, all four churches named above met and agreed to support the construction of a new church in town. The new building was erected on the corner of Washington and Guilford streets in 1894 for $8,000. The lot included a house north of the church which served as a parsonage until 1946 when it was rededicated as a parish house and used for Sunday school classrooms. Huntington City was organized as a separate church at a council meeting in 1899.

From 1901 to 1906, the church was without a resident pastor and was supported by the District Mission Board. Much of the credit for keeping the church alive during these years is given to a handful of Sunday school leaders including Jonathan Sprinkle, Isaac Brumbaugh, Cora Emley, and Effie Tuttle. Their efforts were helped considerably when David Neher, a minister from Michigan, moved to Huntington.

The church building was remodeled in 1909 when a balcony was added, and a basement was dug under the church in 1914. The present parsonage east of the church was purchased sometime between 1928 and 1931. By 1935, Huntington City boasted a membership of 312 and had grown to over 400 by 1950.

The original parsonage building was razed in 1958 to make way for a major addition to the church building. This new facility included space for classrooms and a new church office.

A major sanctuary renovation program began in 1966. The project removed the balcony and the seating in the sanctuary was reversed.

Iglesia Evangelica Emanual

404 S. Walnut St.
South Bend, IN 46619
Currently meeting in homes
Membership: 10

Iglesia Evangelica Emanuel has the unique distinction of being the only Hispanic congregation in Indiana. It is also affiliated with three denominations: Church of the Brethren, Mennonite Church, and General Conference Mennonite Church.

Brethren and Mennonites became interested in forming a ministry to the Hispanic community in the South Bend area in the early 1980s. In 1983, Fabricio Guzman became pastor of South Bend City Church of the Brethren, and the Brethren did some early demographic studies. Guzman then came into contact with Sam Hernandez of the General Board of the Mennonite Church who was exploring similar possibilities.

A meeting of leaders from the three denominations was held in Wakarusa in April 1984. Brethren attending were Guzman, Ronald Finney, and Rene Calderon. As a result of that meeting, three students in the Hispanic Leadership Training program at Goshen College were selected to serve in a summer program. Felipe Cantu, Gilberto Gaytan, and Amparo Geuvara were supervised by Guzman, and the three denominations pledged their support.

For 10 weeks during the summer of 1984, the three students made contacts in the South Bend Hispanic community and conducted Bible study sessions. They were successful in generating interest, and the first combined meeting was held at a health clinic on the corner of Western and Walnut streets that autumn. The students continued to meet with the South Bend group during the school year with Cantu as team leader.

In May 1985, Cantu graduated from Goshen College and accepted a pastorate in Illinois. A pastoral search was initiated, and Gaytan was chosen to be the first pastor and to give leadership to a church planting effort. The group at that time was known as Templo Evangelico Emanuel.

Gaytan and his wife, Gloria, were successful in helping the fledgling congregation grow. Because of this growth, they approached the South Bend City Church in December to see if they could rent their building. The South Bend City Church was formally closed as an active congregation in January 1986, and the Northern Indiana District began leasing the building to Iglesia.

The formal beginning of the congregation occurred on March 16, 1986, when the church was officially chartered. On the same day, the name of the church was changed to Iglesia Anabautista Emanuel, and

Gaytan was ordained. All three sponsoring denominations participated in the service.

Gaytan served as pastor until August 1990. He was replaced by Jacob Tijerina who was installed in January 1991. The name of the church was changed again to Iglesia Evangelica Emanual.

Also in 1990, the congregation decided to move to be closer to the center of the Hispanic community in South Bend. Services are held in rented facilities at 404 S. Walnut St. The old South Bend City Church building at 802 W. Van Buren St. was sold by the district to an independent congregation. The sale was approved at the September 1991 District Conference.

Tijerina resigned in the spring of 1992, and the congregation moved to a house church model and is served by free ministers.

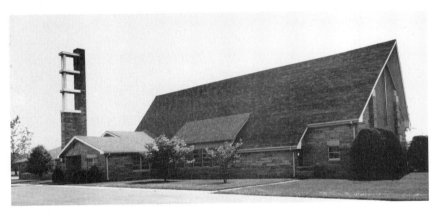

Kokomo

311 W. Lincoln Road
Kokomo, IN 46902
Membership: 237

Kokomo Church of the Brethren was one of the early churches to benefit from the migration from the country to the city, although it took nearly 20 years from the time interest in a church was first expressed until it became reality.

Elder Daniel Bock and his wife and Sister Silas Deardorf were among the first Brethren to move to Kokomo, which was located on the boundary between the Howard and Greentown (later Plevna) congregations. Elder Bock first lived in the eastern part of Kokomo and held membership in the Greentown congregation. Other members of the two rural congregations also began moving to Kokomo to retire from their farms or seeking jobs in the city.

Elder Peter Houk from the Howard congregation became interested in the group of Brethren who lived in Kokomo. He helped organize the first services in 1906 which were held in the home of Granville McClaines. Services were later moved to the Kokomo city hall.

Leslie E. Ockerman, a minister from Ohio, moved to Kokomo in 1912 and began preaching regularly. He was ordained April 23, 1915, and was placed in Kokomo as pastor by the District Mission Board. The Kokomo congregation obtained permission to solicit funds from other congregations in the state to build a new church, and a building was erected at 917 S. Market St. during the summer of 1916. A dedication service was held Nov. 5 that year.

For the next 50 years, the Kokomo congregation grew steadily until it was decided a new church was needed. The solution was the construction of a church building on Lincoln Road which was dedicated in 1960. However, the building was to serve as a home for the congregation for only five years. A tornado ripped through the city in 1965 destroying the church.

Quickly recovering from their shock, the members arranged to hold services at the Courtland Avenue Friends Church while plans were laid to rebuild. A new structure soon rose from the wreckage at the Lincoln Road site with help from congregations throughout the state and the entire denomination. It was dedicated in 1966 and remains home for the Kokomo congregation.

Lafayette

1107 S. 18th St.
Lafayette, IN 47905
Membership: 81

Members of the Fairview, Rossville, and Pyrmont churches living in Lafayette began talking about the need for a new church in the 1940s. Gasoline rationing during World War II prevented them from attending services at the country churches every week.

A survey of Brethren families living in Lafayette was conducted to determine if there was interest in forming a new congregation. This led to a meeting in March 1946 at Columbian Park chaired by Robert Sink. Enough interest was shown to begin regular services, and the first service was held the same month at University Presbyterian Center, West Lafayette. Harold Michael, a student at Bethany Seminary, led the service. At a business meeting following the first service, it was decided to hold bi-weekly worship services at the YWCA on Sixth Street.

An organizational meeting was held at the home of George and LaVona Hildreth on Sept. 14, 1946. Thirty-one people agreed to become

charter members of the new congregation.

Services were moved to the Seventh Day Adventist Church, Eighth and Union streets, on Dec. 8, 1948. It was here that the first new members were baptized and the first love feast was held.

A building fund was soon started, and land was purchased May 10, 1949. Membership had increased to 75 when ground for the first church building was broken on April 20, 1952. Financial support from the district and denomination and much volunteer labor boosted the local efforts. The first service in the new building was held Feb. 22, 1953, and it was dedicated July 12, 1953, with Charles Zunkel as the speaker.

The first love feast in the new building was held in the autumn of 1953, but the kitchen had not yet been completed so a traditional fellowship meal could not be served. The menu for that first communion included ham salad sandwiches and peaches.

A parsonage was purchased in 1954 at 1409 S. 22nd St. from Donald Blue, then the mayor of Lafayette. This debt was paid off in 1967.

Heavy rains in April 1964 backed up sewers and caused a flood of 46 inches of water in the basement of the church. Many church records were destroyed.

An educational unit had been part of the original plan for the church building. Construction of this wing began in the spring of 1965 and was completed the following autumn.

The 25th anniversary of the congregation was celebrated on Oct. 17, 1971, and a 40th anniversary observance was held in 1986.

Students attending Purdue University have always been an important part of the life of the Lafayette Church. A garage owned by Gale Felix at Sylvia and Salisbury streets was remodeled for the use of students in 1956. In 1957, the districts in Indiana purchased a house at 214 Marstellar St. and converted it to accommodate 30 men. It was used as a cooperative under the name Stellar Brothers, but it was discontinued after a few years, sold to the university, and later torn down.

Ralph McFadden and then Chuck Boyer served on a part-time basis to work with Brethren and other students at the university. This work led to the formation of United Campus Ministries Association with three other denominations. The group later combined with two other denominations to form University Church.

Lafayette Church members became involved with refugee resettlement in 1955 with the arrival of the Richard Billep family from Germany. The family later moved to the Chicago area.

In 1981, the Minh Van Nguyen family arrived from Vietnam. Lafayette and University Church sponsored the family until they moved to Washington, D.C.

A number of outside groups have used the church building for their activities including Boy Scouts, Camp Fire, other youth groups, and aerobics classes.

Members of the church also helped found Mediation Services of Tippecanoe County and have been active in the local Habitat for Humanity organization. Recently, several members have been active in planning the Sunrise Child Care Center for infants of teen-age mothers.

LaPorte

414 Hawthorne St.
LaPorte, IN 46350
Membership: 72

The LaPorte Church of the Brethren was originally part of the Portage Church territory. It covered a large area which included the northwest part of St. Joseph County and all of LaPorte County in Indiana, plus Cass and Berrien counties in Michigan.

Elder Jacob Miller of Portage Prairie preached at the first service in LaPorte County in 1853. The group gathered in a barn owned by Jacob Heckman. The first love feast was held in 1859 in a barn owned by Jacob Replogle. This was followed by the organization of a Sunday school program in 1864 with meetings held at the home of Mr. and Mrs. William Merchant.

The LaPorte Church was officially organized in 1869 by Elders Jacob, James, and David Miller. It included all of LaPorte County, and Isaac Miller was the first resident elder.

The first meeting house was located five miles north of LaPorte and was known as the Rossburg House. It was purchased from the Christian Church in 1873 and was used until 1923 when it was sold for $223.

A second building was constructed in Waterford in 1895 on land donated by Jasper Cross. This meeting house was only used for a few years and was sold in 1920 for $1,000.

A small group of LaPorte members began meeting at the home of a member on Kenwood Street near the site of the present church. This group spearheaded the construction of a small mission building on Weller Avenue about two blocks east of the present building in 1916. It was later sold for $1,200.

All of the money from the sale of the three buildings was pooled into a common building fund. This resulted in the purchase of property and construction of a new church at 414 Hawthorne St. in 1923. It was dedicated March 2, 1924, with Otho Winger as the dedicatory speaker.

Pastoral leadership for LaPorte was supplied by the district from 1920 to 1931. A great deal of effort was given by the LaPorte group to the founding of a new congregation in Michigan City during this time. The evangelism effort weakened LaPorte, but a few dedicated families successfully labored to keep their congregation active.

The church building was damaged by a fire in 1952. The congregation repaired and improved the building with the addition of a new heating system and kitchen. Services were held at the LaPorte YMCA building while construction was in progress.

A new parsonage was constructed next to the church in 1959, and additional land south of the parsonage was purchased in 1960.

In 1964, the congregation was named the beneficiary of a large bequest in the will of Agnes Merchant, a long-time LaPorte member. The money was used to purchase additional property north of the church building and to help fund construction of a new sanctuary in 1972. It was connected to the old building by a new entry area, and the old sanctuary was turned into a fellowship hall. A dedication service was held Oct. 8, 1972, and the mortgage was burned Feb. 8, 1981.

Liberty Mills

P.O. Box 101
Liberty Mills, IN 46946
Membership: 185

Liberty Mills Church of the Brethren began life in 1913 as the East House of the Eel River church. It was formed by a group of people from the eastern part of the territory served by the Eel River Church.

The first meetings were held in a school, but a church building was soon erected and the congregation became known as the Plunge Creek Chapel. The congregation had grown to 100 members when fire destroyed the original church building on April 12, 1927. Meetings were held in the Haines School building until a former Methodist church building was purchased. The name was changed to Liberty Mills Church of the Brethren in 1929.

Major renovation was completed in 1944, and a house two blocks from the church was purchased in 1949. It was occupied by Howard Kreider, the first full-time pastor. The parsonage was sold in 1968.

A unique part of the church's history includes the purchase of a 170-acre farm in 1955. The Men's Work organization farmed the property and donated more than 40 heifers to the Prentiss Institute through

Heifer Project International. A portion of the farm property was sold in 1963, and the remainder was sold in 1966.

An extensive remodeling and addition program was begun in 1955 and Dr. Paul Robinson, president of Bethany Seminary, spoke at the dedication service July 22, 1956.

The congregation celebrated its 50th anniversary with special services Dec. 8, 1963. T. Wayne Reiman of Manchester College was the special speaker.

The first vacation Bible school was held in 1923 and has been held each year since then except for two years during World War II and one year when there was a great deal of illness.

In spite of the fact that minutes from the business meetings from 1913 to 1959 have been lost, a history of the congregation was published in 1988.

Lincolnshire

6404 S. Calhoun St.
Fort Wayne, IN 46807
Membership: 326

Lincolnshire Church of the Brethren was one of the first churches in Indiana to be formed as a result of the movement of people from the farm to the city.

Mr. and Mrs. Jacob Ahner moved to Fort Wayne in 1889 followed in 1890 by Mr. and Mrs. Frank Colclesser. Both couples had attended Clear Creek Church of the Brethren located just north of Huntington. Since there was no Church of the Brethren in Fort Wayne, they began attending a Free Methodist Church. But they missed their association with the Brethren and decided they would either start a mission point or return to Clear Creek.

The families found other former Brethren in the city and began holding prayer meetings in homes which quickly expanded to include preaching by Brother Ahner and others. Since Fort Wayne was located on what was then the dividing line between the Northern Indiana and Middle Indiana districts, the mission boards of both districts provided financial support to pay for rented halls.

The Fort Wayne Church of the Brethren was officially organized Feb. 14, 1897, with 14 charter members including Mr. and Mrs. Jacob Ahner, Mr. and Mrs. Milton Fisher, Mr. and Mrs. Frank Colclesser, Mr. and Mrs. Walter Langstaff, Mr. and Mrs. Henry Baker, Mr. and Mrs. Lonnie Fisher, Mr. and Mrs. James Hughes, John Blocher, Amos Eby, William Finney, Daniel Keim, and Mary Mertz.

The fellowship continued to grow and a permanent church building was constructed in 1901 on the corner of Smith and Green streets on property purchased by the denomination's General Mission Board. A large group of 45 members was added to the Fort Wayne congregation the same year when Flat Rock Church of the Brethren, located in southern Allen County, was disorganized. Responsibility of the Fort Wayne church was transferred to the Northern Indiana District in 1906.

The next few years were a time of struggle for the congregation and membership dwindled to just a few people. The doors of the church were actually closed for a time in 1913, and consideration was given to selling the property. However, regular services were resumed in 1919.

A turning point came in 1925 with the hiring of Wilbur Bantz as the first full-time pastor. The congregation grew rapidly during his tenure, and the church was remodeled and a parsonage built.

By 1954, with a membership of over 400, it was decided that a new and larger church building was needed. Property was purchased at 6400 S. Calhoun St. in 1955, and a parsonage was built on part of the property in 1956. The old church building was sold in 1957, and ground was broken for the new church in 1958. The first service was held in the new building Feb. 15, 1959, and the congregation was renamed Lincolnshire Church of the Brethren.

The congregation has sponsored a number of refugees since the end of World War II including people from Poland, Germany, Latvia, Indonesia, Uganda, and Iraq. The church has also been actively involved in the community with a number of projects including a nursery school program started in 1960.

The 75th anniversary of the congregation was celebrated in 1972, and members are looking forward to the centennial observance in 1997.

Little Pine

57061 C.R. 19
Goshen, IN 46526
Membership: 41

Little Pine has functioned as an independent congregation since 1950, but activity affiliated with the church can be traced back more than 125 years.

    The work began in the 1860s primarily as a Sunday school program under the direction of the West Goshen Church (then known as the Elkhart Church). An acre of land on the east side of C.R. 19 was purchased in 1866 from Jacob and Mary Sigerfoos. A small, white frame building was constructed which was known as the Pine Creek House or the North Congregation.

    An additional two acres was purchased in 1882 to establish the Pine Creek Cemetery.

    A number of improvements were made to the building during the first half of the 20th century. The original double entrance was replaced with a single entry, and a vestibule with cloak rooms was added. A partial basement was dug prior to 1920 and central heat was installed.

Pine Creek remained under the supervision of the West Goshen congregation until it was officially organized as a separate church in 1950 with 28 charter members. The pulpit continued to be filled by the free ministry until 1961 when Ralph Hoffman became the first minister to be paid on a part-time basis.

The congregation decided in 1956 the old frame building was no longer adequate, so plans for a remodeling project were begun. However, land adjacent to the building needed for additional parking could not be secured.

In March 1957, the church was able to purchase 2.5 acres across the road from the original building, and it was decided to construct a new church on that land. Ground was broken Nov. 30, 1958, and the first services in the new brick building were held Dec. 13, 1959. A dedication service was held May 29, 1960. The original church building was finally sold in 1978.

A significant event in the life of the congregation occurred on Palm Sunday 1965 when a series of tornadoes ripped through the area. Several families from Little Pine suffered losses, and the entire church pitched in to offer assistance. Just 18 months later, the church celebrated a centennial and homecoming on Oct. 9, 1966.

Additional land next to the church was obtained in 1976 and a new parsonage was constructed.

In September 1983, Little Pine entered the Education for Shared Ministry program with Thomas J. Clark as the minister-in-training. Porter Bechtel Jr., Janet Ryman, Jessie Zimmerman, and Anna M. Clark also participated as lay persons-in-training.

Clark became the pastor at Little Pine Jan. 1, 1987, on a part-time basis and was ordained June 6, 1987. He continues to serve as pastor of the congregation.

Locust Grove

Route 1, Box 392
Cambridge City, IN 47327
Membership: 80

Locust Grove has functioned as an independent congregation since 1954, but the church can trace its history to almost 100 years earlier than that date.

The members of Nettle Creek, the second-oldest congregation in Indiana, decided in the late 1850s to build several meeting houses in

addition to the central house. This decision led to the construction of a new church building in 1859. It was located about three miles southwest of the original Nettle Creek building in a thick stand of locust trees, so it was naturally called Locust Grove. The original 32-foot by 32-foot building was enlarged in 1906 to provide more space for Sunday school classrooms.

For 95 years, Locust Grove operated as part of the Nettle Creek Church served by one elder and one general council. It became an independent congregation when a reorganization plan was approved April 2, 1954.

A 1957 renovation program modernized the building, and a new piano and organ were installed. Another major building program was begun in 1960. The entire building was raised, and a basement was built under it. This new space housed a kitchen, a large meeting room, nursery, rest rooms, and classrooms. The exterior was also improved.

Locust Grove was served by part-time pastors for many years. The church took a major step forward in 1987 when Mark Baliles was hired as the first full-time pastor.

Logansport

2405 Shadowlawn Drive
Logansport, IN 46947
Membership: 102

Elder Allen A. Oberlin and family moved to Logansport in 1895. He opened a Sunday school and preached in Logansport and in Adamsboro,

six miles to the east. Adamsboro had been organized from a portion of the old Mexico territory, but had become very weak at the time.

The Oberlin family left after a year, and the Brethren effort died out until 1900 when A.G. Crosswhite held a series of evangelistic meetings and baptized seven people. The Middle Indiana Mission Board then supported a regular preaching program, and a successful Sunday school was organized. Josephine Hanna and Dossie Webb were instrumental in the mission work along with Isaac Moss, a deacon, and L.P. Kurtz, also later elected a deacon.

The Logansport Church was officially organized in 1906. The Adamsboro Church was considered part of it until it closed in 1913.

The Oberlin family moved back to Logansport in 1907 and brought fresh life to the effort. Charles R. Oberlin, a son, was elected to the ministry in 1907 and assisted his father. After a two-year absence from 1908 to 1910, the Oberlins returned to Logansport and Charles was ordained in 1912. Allen died in 1916, but Charles continued the work and was also successful in evangelism efforts in other churches.

The Logansport congregation had been meeting in a rented hall. A building fund was started in 1916, and funds were raised in Logansport and throughout the Middle Indiana District for a new church building. The first building was erected at East Market and 17th streets in 1919.

A major event in the congregation's life came on Palm Sunday, 1945, when Lyle C. Albright announced he was leaving as pastor to go to Nigeria as a missionary. The church and the entire community joined the effort to raise funds for equipment the Albrights needed in Nigeria.

Another major transition occurred in 1969 with the decision to build a new church in a new location. The congregation worshipped at the Logansport YWCA for a year while the new church was under construction at 2405 Shadowlawn Drive. It was completed in 1970.

Loon Creek

734 W. 100 S.
Huntington, IN 46750
Membership: 58

Loon Creek was officially organized in 1912, but its history actually dates to meetings in the area being held as early as 1850. At that time, it was part of the Salamonie territory. Meetings were held in homes and a school.

The first church building was erected in 1884-85 along S.R. 5 five miles southeast of Huntington on land donated by Aaron Bowman. Meetings were held here regularly, although the church remained part of the Salamonie territory until 1912.

At the time of the official organization in 1912, Loon Creek already had about 100 members. A landmark event for the congregation was the ordination of D.W. Paul in 1913. He became elder and remained in that leadership position for the next 33 years.

The church was remodeled in 1917-18, and a new parsonage was constructed in 1948. A major addition to the church was built in 1958, and another addition and remodeling project was completed in 1967.

The 50th anniversary of the church building was celebrated in 1935, and the 100th anniversary occurred in 1985.

Descendants of the congregation's founders are still members at Loon Creek including Wilbur Bowman, grandson of Aaron Bowman, and Glen Paul, grandson of D.W. Paul.

Lower Deer Creek

Route 1, Box 226-A
Camden, IN 46917
Membership: 56

The Lower Deer Creek Church owes its existence to a few Brethren families who moved into the Carroll County area near Camden along Deer Creek in 1828. Among them was Peter Eyman, a minister, and Samuel Wise, a deacon. This small group began holding meetings, often in a barn located east of Delphi owned by Peter Replogle. Replogle was elected to the ministry in 1829. It is believed the group was formally organized as a congregation called Deer Creek about 1830.

Disagreements arose between Eyman and Replogle over how to conduct communion and other matters of church doctrine. Unable to settle their differences, the church territory was divided in 1838. The dividing line was very irregular in an attempt to satisfy individual members who wanted to follow either Replogle or Eyman. Replogle stayed with the Deer Creek congregation, while Eyman led a new group on Bachelor Run, located near what is now Flora.

The division did not dampen the disagreement. A special general conference was held at the home of John Koontz, northwest of Camden, Sept. 24 and 25, 1848, and one of the items on the agenda was the continuing dispute between Replogle and Eyman. Both sides were found to be in error and were counseled to forgive and realign themselves with the work of the church. Eyman and some of his followers were unwilling to accept this counsel, however, and in a special meeting in a barn owned by John Flora, Eyman and others were disfellowshipped. Some later returned, but Eyman and a number of his followers, including a number from the Deer Creek group, formed the New Dunkers, later known as the Church of God.

In spite of this difficulty, Deer Creek continued to grow. The first church building was erected in 1852, which still serves as the basis for the existing church.

The membership declined briefly in 1854 with the organization of the Upper Deer Creek Church from part of what was the original Deer Creek territory.

In 1881, a large group of members, including much of the leadership of ministers and deacons, left the church as part of the Old Order split in the denomination. They built a new church building less than two miles away, and the original congregation was renamed Lower Deer Creek.

Division came again the following year with the Progressive split in the denomination in 1882. More members left, but Lower Deer Creek continued to grow in spite of the defections. A Sunday school program was begun in 1888.

The church was first remodeled in 1887, and new roof was put on in 1917. Candles used for lighting were replaced by kerosene lamps which were replaced by brass lamps and, finally, electricity was installed in 1937. The largest remodeling job was begun in 1946 and finally completed in 1949. The church was raised up and a basement dug underneath the building which allowed space for new classrooms.

The first musical instrument, a pump organ, was given to the church in 1928. It was replaced with a piano in 1932, and an electric organ was purchased in 1955.

A parsonage was constructed near the church in 1966, and periodic improvements to the church building were made throughout the 1960s and 1970s. This included new pews in 1976. The basement was renovated in 1988.

One of the traditions of Lower Deer Creek has been the annual Birthday Sunday Dinner, which was begun in 1937. The event has been held every year since and, in 1991, it was voted to change the name to the Lower Deer Creek Homecoming.

Descendants of the original settlers have been members of Lower Deer Creek throughout its history. Some of them today include Kenneth Cripe, Robert Scholl, Claude Wise, Helen Cree, and Doris Maxwell. In

May 1991, Kandice Cripe was baptized in the church at age 9. She is the great-great-great-great-granddaughter of Peter Replogle.

Manchester

Sixth and Walnut
Manchester, IN 46962
Membership: 730

A division of the Eel River Church of the Brethren in 1852 marks the beginning of the Manchester Church of the Brethren. After meeting in homes for a few years, it was decided in 1856 that a church building was needed. Jacob Heeter offered to donate land and timber and other members volunteered their labor. In a short time, a log church measuring 30 feet by 40 feet was erected at the site three miles southeast of North Manchester.

New members were being added at a rapid pace, and most of these new people lived north and west of the town. The log meeting house was located too far away from them for easy travel, and it was quickly becoming too small. A large frame building was erected in 1858 two miles west of North Manchester at the site of what is now the West Manchester Church of the Brethren.

New members continued to be added, and many of them were residents of the town of North Manchester. It became apparent that a meeting house within the city itself was needed. Property on North Walnut Street was purchased and a new brick building was erected in

1881. Elder R.H. Miller Sr., then president of Ashland College, preached at the dedication service. One year later, he was called by the Manchester congregation to be elder and pastor.

For the next 10 years, Elder Miller was a leading force in the congregation. The 1880s were years of division between Progressives and Conservatives in the denomination. The Manchester congregation was almost evenly divided in its loyalties to these competing factions, and a split could easily have occurred. Elder Miller is given much of the credit for holding these factions together and for leading the congregation into a position of great influence throughout the denomination.

A measure of that influence is evident by the large number of denominational meetings that were held in or near North Manchester. Annual Conference met in a large frame meeting house west of the town in 1878 with more than 15,000 in attendance, and again in 1888 within the town limits. Thousands also attended annual conference at the same location in 1900. The Manchester congregation played a large part in annual conferences held at Manchester College in 1929 and 1949.

Because there were two buildings in the Manchester district, services alternated between the city church and the "west house." The two churches separated in 1911 and became independent congregations. The west church was called the North Manchester Church and later changed its name to West Manchester. The city church was known simply as Manchester, and later became known as the Walnut Street Church.

The original Manchester building erected in 1881 became too small, especially with the addition of a Sunday school. It was replaced in 1907 with a much larger brick building. An addition was made to the east side in 1925. A major renovation of the sanctuary was completed in 1950, and it was decided at that time to change the name of the church from Walnut Street to Manchester. This was in part due to the fact that the entrance of the building was changed from Walnut Street to the Sixth Street side. Another major renovation and addition project was successfully completed in 1982.

Maple Grove

21381 C.R. 46
New Paris, IN 46553
Membership: 109

Maple Grove Church of the Brethren carries the unique distinction of having the oldest church building still in use in the Northern Indiana District.

The original church was known widely as the Whitehead Church,

and for good reason. About 1837, six Whitehead brothers and three sisters moved to the area west of New Paris from Montgomery County, Ohio. The family included brothers Samuel, Peter, Adam, Valentine, John, and Lewis, with sisters Esther Stutzman, Mary Conrad, and Margaret Lentz. The area at that time was all part of the Elkhart (now West Goshen) territory. In 1838, the territory was divided, and the part settled by the Whiteheads became part of the Turkey Creek district.

The Turkey Creek group decided to build a church in 1854. Peter Whitehead and another brother donated land for the church, a third brother donated timber, and John Whitehead donated land across the road from the church for a burial ground. Many of the original Whitehead family members are buried in this cemetery. The church which was built on the site was the second in northern Indiana.

The congregation divided in 1859, and the original meeting house became part of the Union Center district. A new brick building was constructed northeast of Nappanee in 1866. Although it was officially the Union Center Church, it was known widely as the Brick Church because it was one of the first churches to be built with brick.

Services continued to be held in the original building southwest of New Paris, and most people of the time referred to it as the Whitehead Church. A Sunday school program was organized in 1870. Finally in 1906, it was organized as a separate congregation and was named Maple Grove.

The original church building was raised on jacks in 1944 and a basement dug underneath it to make room for Sunday school classrooms and a kitchen. It was rededicated in 1947.

The congregation celebrated its 100th anniversary in 1954.

The sanctuary was renovated in 1956, and a groundbreaking ceremony for a new educational wing was held in 1960. The two-story addition was completed and dedicated in 1962.

A new sanctuary was built with volunteer labor at the east end of the building and dedicated in 1979 on the church's 125th anniversary.

Marion

2302 S. Geneva Ave.
Marion, IN 46953
Membership: 145

Shortly after the turn of the century, Marion became home for a number of members of the Church of the Brethren. They began calling for services in the city.

The closest congregation was Landessville (now disorganized) and Elder J.W. Norris, the pastor at Landessville, agreed to begin holding services in Marion. The first meetings were held in the Canton Glass factory in West Marion in 1911.

Norris and Elder Daniel Snell held revival meetings that year which led to the formal organization of the West Marion congregation on Dec. 18, 1911, with 60 charter members.

The congregation grew rapidly and the Mission Board of the Middle Indiana District purchased property at West Second Street and Forrest Avenue in 1912. A building was constructed at the site in 1913.

Fire destroyed the church Feb. 9, 1936. The congregation accepted an offer from Central Christian Church to use their building while a new church was built. Central Christian had no pastor at the time, so West Marion filled the pulpit for both congregations temporarily.

A new church was built at the same site and dedicated Oct. 17, 1937. L.W. Shultz was the featured speaker.

The name of the church was changed from West Marion to Marion Church of the Brethren June 5, 1951. The decision had much to do with the fact that the church at Landess (which was sometimes referred to as the Marion Church) had been disorganized in 1929.

The church at Second and Forrest was remodeled and a rededication service was held in June 1957.

The congregation relocated to a new building at 26th and Geneva avenues in 1970. The first service at the new location was held March 1, 1970. An educational wing was added in 1979. A special service was held May 20, 1979, for the laying of a cornerstone, and the building was dedicated June 17, 1979.

The roof of the church was damaged in a storm in the spring of 1991. A disaster group from the South/Central District helped Marion members put on a new roof June 1, 1991.

Markle

520 W. Logan
Markle, IN 46770
Membership: 93

The Markle Church was known as Eight Mile when it was organized in 1852 from the eastern part of the Salamonie territory. Samuel Murray was the first elder for the group which met in homes and barns throughout the area and grew to include about 100 members. The first church building was erected in 1877 on the farm of Robert Smutts, located about four miles north of Markle.

Eight Mile was one of the churches in Indiana which suffered the most in the 1882 split with the Progressives. A great many of the members, including much of the leadership, sided with the Progressives (Ashland Brethren). They joined the new denomination which was formed and took over the Eight Mile Church building. However, they were unsuccessful in this location and abandoned the building which was later torn down.

The members who remained with the Conservatives continued to meet and gradually recovered from the split. In 1887, a church building in Markle was purchased from the Free Will Baptists. The name was changed from Eight Mile to Markle in 1902.

Relocation of the church was necessary in 1955 because of the construction of a new highway bridge over the Wabash River. The church building was sitting in the middle of the planned improvement at the south end of the new bridge.

Trustees negotiated with the state and settled for a $54,600 cash payment. This money and a loan from Manchester College was used to pay for a new church building located in a woods at the west edge of Markle on property purchased from Lillian Earhart. Many hours of volunteer labor went into the $125,000 project.

A new parsonage was constructed in 1966.

Mexico

P.O. Box 296
Mexico, IN 46958
Membership: 362

Peter and Elizabeth Fisher and Nathaniel and Frances Clingenpeel were the first Brethren settlers in Miami County when they settled an area west of what is now Mexico, Ind., in the fall of 1836. They came from Preble County, Ohio, where Brother Fisher had served as a deacon.

A larger contingent from the Upper Twin Creek congregation in Preble County joined the Fishers and Clingenpeels the following year. They included Jacob Brouwer (a minister), deacons Jacob Flora and John Brower, Jonathon Fisher, Michael Fouts, Henry Brower, Daniel Albaugh, Peter Sayger and Susannah Dillman.

Irregular services were held in the homes and barns of the Brethren until 1838 when Elder William and Mary Moss moved to the area from Union County, Indiana. He saw to it that regular services with preaching were held.

The church was formally organized in 1839, and the first communion services was held in a barn owned by John Fisher in 1840. About the
same time, several members who were doing well financially built new
homes. They were specifically designed with removable partitions so
that two or more rooms could be joined to accommodate church
meetings. Annual two-day communion services were held in barns,
nearly always in October. Baptism services were held in the nearby Eel
River.

The congregation took a major step forward in 1861 with the
construction of a new brick church building. It was used until 1892
when it was replaced by a larger frame building that was used for over
80 years.

The original territory of the Mexico Church covered a wide area
which included parts of Miami, Cass, Fulton, and Wabash counties. As
the territory was developed, a number of groups sprang up and were
supported as mission points by the Mexico Church. Churches in this
category which are still active include Roann and Peru. Several other
churches were active for a time, and then abandoned. They include
Wolleytown (also known as the Old Macedonian Church), which was
disorganized between 1893 and 1898; Courter, which was closed in
1923; Beaver Dam, which closed in 1913; Adamsboro (also known as
Mount Calvary), which was disorganized by 1910; Mud Lake, which
closed in 1906; and Kewanna.

The Mexico church was long associated with the Mexico Home.
The home was the brainchild of Levi Miller, a member of the Mexico
Church who wanted to build a facility to care for the elderly. He obtained approval from the district and the home was opened Dec. 15,
1889. He followed this with the construction of a second building in
1892 which was devoted to the care and placement of orphans. The
orphanage closed in 1942, but the Mexico Home continued to operate
until 1968 when it was replaced by the Timbercrest retirement community at North Manchester.

While it was in operation, the orphans at the home walked to the
Mexico Church every Sunday to attend services. Many of the elderly
residents who were physically able also attended these services. In later
years, a loudspeaker system was installed at the home so the residents
could listen to the services without having to go outside.

A primary activity of the church was the support of Lillian Grisso
who served as a missionary in India from 1918 until her retirement in
1959. Involvement in missions has continued with the support of a
number of people working in Nigeria, India, and Ecuador, as well as a
$17,000 loan to the Kentucky Mountain Housing Project in 1986.

The old 1892 building had been remodeled a number of times over
the years, including the addition of a basement. A committee formed in

1962 recommended construction of a new church building rather than remodeling the old one. Discussions were also held about the possibility of sharing a new building with a Methodist group, but the congregation voted against the idea. A proposal to build a separate new church building was then defeated in 1968.

It took until 1975, but the idea for a new church located on the west side of U.S. 31 was finally approved. Ground was broken in 1976, and the dedication service for the new building was held Jan. 23, 1977. The 1892 building was torn down. Repayment of a 15-year mortgage was completed in less than six years, and a special ceremony was held Dec. 12, 1982, to mark the occasion.

The sesquicentennial of the congregation was marked by a series of special events during 1989. It included a historical service patterned after those held 150 years ago, and the baptism of several members in the Eel River. A booklet containing an extensive history of the congregation was also published.

The Mexico congregation has enjoyed a steady increase in membership since 1959. The current membership is over 350.

Michigan City
2308 E. Michigan Blvd.
Michigan City, IN 46360
Membership: 49

The founding of the Michigan City congregation was the culmination of the dream of Elder Eli Roose who was the pastor at LaPorte. The LaPorte Church sponsored a mission in Michigan City beginning with the construction of a church in 1927. Elder Roose served both congregations for the next five years. A special emphasis of the new church was a Sunday school program for neighborhood children. The first communion service was held in 1930.

Michigan City was officially recognized as a separate organization with 10 charter members just a short time before Elder Roose died in 1932. His funeral was the first to be held at the church.

The church continued under the direction of the district mission board until 1954 when it became self-supporting. Pastoral leadership was supplied by students from Bethany Seminary until 1942 when David Schecter became the first full-time minister. The first parsonage was purchased in 1944.

The church basement was remodeled in 1945, and a major remodeling and addition program was completed in 1965. The mortgage for that project was paid in just 10 months.

Michigan City and LaPorte joined in a yoked parish project in 1970.

The shared pastoral arrangement continued until 1989.

The Michigan City Church served as host for Head Start classes for 10 years and has served as a neighborhood center. The congregation has also been involved in service to inmates at the Michigan City State Prison and Westville Correctional Facility.

Middlebury

206 S. Mill St.
P.O. Box 67
Middlebury, IN 46540
Membership: 188

The Middlebury Church of the Brethren traces its roots to the nearby Pleasant Valley church. Plans for a church located in Middlebury had been discussed for several years. Sunday evening services were held in an auditorium in Middlebury during the summer of 1909.

Concrete plans for a new church were laid at a council meeting April 1, 1911, when it was officially agreed to build a new church building in the southeast part of Middlebury on land donated by A. Haines. He also acted as building foreman and directed the work of both volunteer and paid workers.

The dedication service for the new building was held Nov. 5, 1911, with the Rev. I.B. Trout, Lanark, Ill., as the featured speaker. This was followed by two weeks of revival meetings.

The Middlebury and Pleasant Valley congregations operated as one administrative unit until the Middlebury congregation was officially organized at a council meeting on May 2, 1913. The dividing line between the two congregations was established as the township line between Middlebury and York townships in Elkhart County.

Free ministers served the church until 1923. Part-time ministers provided leadership until 1933 when the first full-time pastor was hired.

One of the proudest moments for the church came in 1942 when the congregation hosted the Northern Indiana District Men's Rally. It was at this meeting that Dan West's idea for Heifer Project International was officially adopted. Middlebury has actively supported the organization ever since and hosted a 25th anniversary celebration in 1969. During the 1980s, the church adopted an annual two-day weekend observance to honor Dan West and Heifer Project. The equivalent of at least one heifer is donated each year.

The 50th anniversary of the church was observed Nov. 5, 1961.

A new parsonage was constructed in 1970, and a major church addition was completed in 1978. The sanctuary was remodeled in 1986 in time for the congregation's 75th anniversary, which was coupled with a "Dan West Day" observance.

A major event in the life of the congregation was the death of member Orpha Nussbaum in 1988. At age 112, she was not only the oldest member of the congregation, but she was also listed by the Guinness Book of World Records as the oldest living person in the world at the time of her death.

The congregation has been consistently active in community outreach programs. Middlebury members support a ministry to the Faith Mission in Elkhart, and the Wee Care Nursery School program was begun in the church fellowship hall in 1982. The church also supports several programs specifically geared to children and young people of all ages.

Mount Pleasant

5699 C.R. 10
Bourbon, IN 46504
Membership: 99

Mount Pleasant was known as Yellow River when it was organized in 1848. The territory included the eastern half of Marshall County. There were 21 founding members of the congregation, and Jacob Shively was the first minister.

    Yellow River grew rapidly in its early years and became the mother church to Walnut (organized in 1864), Bremen (organized in 1866), and Camp Creek (organized in 1879). These new congregations reduced the Yellow River membership by about 130.

    Elder Shively was one of the primary backers of Salem College during its years of operation from 1870 to 1873. The college operated at Bourbon until its financial failure. He was deeply embarrassed by this turn of events and left Yellow River to become part of the Union Church where he served as elder until 1878.

    Yellow River built its first meeting house in 1880 when there was a membership of 100. This building was remodeled in 1920, and the name Mount Pleasant was adopted in 1926. The renovated building had only been in use nine years when it was destroyed in a disastrous fire in November 1929. Reconstruction began almost immediately, and a new building was erected and in use just five months later in April 1930. A major addition and remodeling project was undertaken in 1958-59, and the new limestone structure was dedicated in August 1959.

Muncie

1714 W. Royale Drive
Muncie, IN 47304
Membership: 62

The Muncie Church owes its existence to the sponsorship of four surrounding churches and the hard work of Elder George Studebaker and his wife, Mollie.

A group of German Baptist Brethren members living in Muncie made a request for services in their community. A meeting was held Sept. 28, 1897, to consider this request. Attending were representatives from Mississinewa (now Union Grove), Killbuck (now Antioch), Upper Fall Creek, and Buck Creek.

Delegates to this meeting agreed to support initial efforts in Muncie, and the Studebakers were asked to begin the work. They were given $200, a house, a barn, and fuel. The understanding was that Elder Studebaker would use the first six months to try organizing a new congregation. If successful, his term would be extended to one year.

Elder Studebaker began by holding a series of three extended meetings just outside Muncie beginning Oct. 1, 1897. Regular meetings were then held in a building at 310 S. High St. Permission was given to organize a Sunday school program. Much of this work was done by Mollie, and the first Sunday school classes were held the second Sunday of June 1898.

A church building and adjoining parsonage were purchased for $1,900 and dedicated June 5, 1898. This building was located at the corner of Jackson and Council streets. There were 27 charter members when the church was officially organized June 30, 1898, and they held their first council meeting July 14. The four adjoining churches withdrew their support at this time, and the district mission board took over sponsorship of the infant congregation.

Elder Studebaker remained as pastor and presiding elder until 1906 when he moved to North Manchester. He continued as presiding elder through 1907. A series of short-term pastorates then followed until Elder Studebaker returned in 1911 and remained as pastor until 1932.

Remodeling projects were completed in 1930, 1936, and 1945, including repairs from a fire which damaged the building. The 50th anniversary of the church was observed Oct. 10, 1948.

By 1960, the Muncie congregation recognized the need for a new church facility. Land was purchased at 1714 W. Royale Drive in 1961, and construction of the new building began in 1964. The first service was held July 5, 1965, followed by a dedication service on Aug. 17. Dale Brubaker was serving as pastor at the time the new church project began, but Floyd Brenneman had been called by the time it was finished and he served as the dedication speaker. The mortgage was burned in 1977.

A new parsonage located just east of the church was purchased in 1990.

Nappanee
301 Mack Drive
Nappanee, IN 46550
Membership: 176

Members of the Turkey Creek Church were responsible for organizing the first Brethren services in Nappanee as early as 1877, only two years after the town was officially platted. The decision to build a meeting house was made in 1883, and the new structure on East Market Street was dedicated May 24, 1884. Nappanee was organized as a separate congregation in July 1898 with 148 charter members. J.C. Murray was elected the first presiding elder.

The first Sunday school program was organized in 1887 in cooperation with a United Brethren Church group. Meetings were held during the afternoons. Two years later, the program was taken over by the Brethren.

A major remodeling program was carried out in 1917. A basement was dug under the building, a furnace for central heat was installed, a foyer was added, and a balcony was constructed to provide room for Sunday school classes. A few years later, the basement was enlarged which allowed the construction of a new kitchen.

A 50th anniversary celebration was held in 1948, and the membership had grown to about 250 by the early 1950s. The church was literally bursting at the seams, and a mobile home was added to provide temporary classroom space. A small amount of property was available at the rear of the church on East Market, but it was separated by an alley which the town did not want to close.

A new parsonage was constructed in 1954 at what was then the east edge of the town. An additional 4.2 acres of land was purchased adjacent to the parsonage on Feb. 21, 1955, with an eye toward building a new church at the site.

That dream became reality with a groundbreaking ceremony March 15, 1959. The cornerstone was laid Sept. 27, 1959, and the first service in the new building was held March 13, 1960. The old church building on East Market Street was sold to the Roman Catholic Church.

The membership at Nappanee continued to grow steadily and had reached about 375 by the time the 75th anniversary was celebrated in 1973. The church entered a period of decline, however, in the late 1970s, and membership now stands at less than 200.

Nettle Creek

5761 N. Brick Church Road
Hagerstown, IN 47346
Membership: 101

Nettle Creek was the second church organized in Indiana. Ministers from the Four Mile congregation began preaching in the northwest part of Wayne County, and a small group of members was formed west of Hagerstown. Elder David Miller from the Four Mile congregation came to the area and organized the members into a congregation in 1820. He was later assisted by his brother, Daniel.

For more than 20 years, meetings were held in homes, barns, and groves throughout the Hagerstown area. Because travel was often difficult, the meetings were moved to make it possible for more members to attend. The area covered ranged from Cambridge City in the south to fives miles north of Hagerstown.

The church membership steadily increased, but there were problems. Private distilleries in the area were common, and several of the owners were Nettle Creek members. The church, referring to an Annual Conference decision from 1781, tried to convince these members to abandon the business. Some did, but others did not and left the church or were disfellowshipped.

The need for a church building became evident as the membership increased. The decision to build was made in 1844, and construction of a building 50-feet by 90-feet was completed in 1845 southwest of Hagerstown. The entire congregation met regularly in this building until it was decided to build several chapels about equally distant from the main church to make it easier for the members to attend. This decision led to the construction of White Branch in 1858 about four miles northwest of Hagerstown, and Locust Grove in 1859 about three miles southwest. Olive Branch was located in a building purchased from the Methodists.

Services at the chapels were held on the first and third Sundays and at the central Nettle Creek building on the second and fourth Sundays. Nettle Creek also held services in a fifth building called Maple Grove Chapel for a number of years on fifth Sundays.

David Miller served as elder at Nettle Creek until 1833 when he and his brother moved to northern Indiana. They were followed by several capable men including L. W. Teeter, who served from 1885 to

1923, and O.D. Werking, who served from 1923 to 1954, a remarkable period of 69 years.

In 1874, a fault was found in the foundation of the central Nettle Creek building. A new brick building was constructed just north of the original site in 1875. The old building was torn down and is now the site of a cemetery. Many of the original Nettle Creek members are buried here.

A Sunday school program was started in 1868, and by 1873 there were three organized Sunday schools in operation.

Services at the Maple Grove Chapel had been abandoned by this time, and Olive Grove was discontinued in 1922. White Branch and Locust Grove continued to be part of the Nettle Creek church until action in 1955 made them separate congregations.

The 1875 building was remodeled beginning in 1928 and underwent a series of improvements through 1940. The changes included new Sunday school classrooms, a baptistry, and a new south entrance which replaced the original separate entrances for men and women.

Ground was broken for a new sanctuary in 1967, and the first services were held in the new building in 1968. The old building was turned into an educational wing.

One of the traditions at Nettle Creek is an Easter sunrise service and breakfast. The youth are in charge of the early worship service and serve a breakfast prepared by a committee.

A major event in the life of the congregation was a sesquicentennial celebration in the fall of 1970. More than 500 people registered during the two-day event.

New Hope
Route 2
Seymour, IN 47274
Membership: 24

New Hope Church of the Brethren is the result of a mission effort by the Church of the Brethren General Mission Board. Brothers Jacob and Sherman Rider obtained permission from the board to do mission work. They went to Jackson County and held revival meetings in a school near Uniontown. Their work led to the organization of the New Hope Church on Feb. 3, 1891.

Two of the early leaders in the congregation were James Spall and W.L. Ross, who donated timber and stone for the construction of a new building on land donated by Jim Gagel near Seymour. Both Ross and Spall had been part of a German Baptist Brethren congregation near Retreat before becoming involved with New Hope. Both men were

eventually called to the ministry about 1900.

New Hope was placed under the supervision of the district mission board about 1916 and became able to support itself and a pastor by 1949.

A tornado damaged the church beyond repair in the mid-1940s, but regular meetings were still conducted in a variety of sites. Additional land was purchased back of the old church in 1948, and an existing building which had been used as a chapel was purchased. It was moved to the New Hope site and renovated with volunteer labor. The old building was razed. A dedication service for the new church building was held Sept. 12, 1948.

A new parsonage was constructed in the mid-1960s on land adjacent to the church. An addition to the front of the church in the 1970s added a new entrance, a classroom and rest rooms.

New Paris

Fourth and Division streets
P.O. Box 27
New Paris, IN 46553
Membership: 292

Interest in forming a church in New Paris began before the turn of the century. Some of the first meetings were held from 1886 to 1889 in an

old Methodist building until the building became too dilapidated to use. Sometime after 1900, a Sunday school program was organized at the high school (now the elementary school).

The New Paris group was operating under the authority of the Bethany Church. At a revival meeting held in the fall of 1915, a plea was made to form a building fund. Bethany approved construction of a new church and work was begun in the spring of 1916. Most of the masonry work was completed and rafters had been set in place when disaster struck in July, and the partially completed structure collapsed. It was eventually determined that the weight of a bell tower was too great to be supported by the hollow tile framework being used in construction.

The site remained a crumbled ruin until the spring of 1917 when new funds were raised and the project was restarted. Volunteers from the Rock Run, Maple Grove, and Bethany churches joined those in New Paris to salvage brick from the ruins, and construction began again. A dedication service for the new building was held in December 1917.

Those attending at New Paris formally petitioned Bethany to be recognized as a separate organization. The petition was approved and the congregation was officially organized at a meeting Sept. 16, 1918. Charles Arnold was elected presiding elder, and there were about 50 charter members.

In September 1919, the church council approved a request for a piano, although the vote came after a great deal of discussion and opposition. The number of members doubled during that first year.

An addition to the original building was constructed in 1935-36 which added classrooms and a kitchen. In 1944, the congregation purchased land immediately north of the church and constructed a cabin which is used for recreational gatherings.

New Paris adopted the supported ministry in 1957 with the hiring of Kenneth Hollinger as pastor. A parsonage was also purchased that year.

The 50th anniversary of the New Paris Church was celebrated in 1968, and plans were laid that year for construction of a new sanctuary. Ground was broken March 2, 1969, and the first service in the new facility was held April 26, 1970. In 1980, the old sanctuary was razed, and a new education wing was built.

Three charter members survive from the original group of 50 who developed the New Paris Church. They include Abe Neff and his wife, Fern (Martin) Neff;, and Hazel Culp.

New Salem

P.O. Box 55
Milford, IN 46542
Membership: 43

The New Salem congregation was officially organized in 1911, but had been part of the Bethel church prior to that time. The church building was constructed south of Milford in 1897 while still a part of Bethel.

John Stout was the first presiding elder of the new congregation, and the ministers included Emeral Jones and Manly Deeter. Raymond Lantis was called as the first salaried pastor in 1920.

A parsonage was purchased in 1942, and a new educational wing was added to the original church building in 1967.

North Liberty

P.O. Box 206
Lafayette and Market streets
North Liberty, IN 46554
Membership: 169

The division of the St. Joseph County territory in 1868 marks the
beginning of the North Liberty Church of the Brethren. The congregation was initially known as the South Bend German Baptist Brethren
Church, and the church was 30 years old before it adopted the name
North Liberty.

Meetings were held in a number of sites including a building
located on the farm of Abraham Whitmer, a family name associated with
North Liberty church leadership for several generations. A second
location was a German Baptist Brethren meeting house located on
Michigan Road south of South Bend. Meetings were at times held in
both locations at the same time, or on alternate Sundays. The congregation often referred to their meeting houses as the East House and West
House. Travel before the turn of the century was not always easy. Most
roads were dirt and a few were not much more than paths. Power was
supplied by horses or simply by walking. Having two meeting sites
made it possible for more people to attend services.

A decision was made in 1870 to construct a new church. This was completed in 1873 and became known as the Oak Grove Church, although it was still considered to be a part of the North Liberty group.

The interest of the congregation began centering on the town of North Liberty by the turn of the century. Services were being held in the Williams and Taylor schools close to North Liberty in 1901. When an Episcopal Church in North Liberty was offered for sale, the congregation took advantage of the opportunity and purchased the building in 1903. It remains the site of the church to the present time.

One of the largest events in North Liberty history was the friendly division of the congregation into two distinct churches. The Oak Grove building had continued to be an active meeting site, and it was finally agreed in 1917 that it should become a separate congregation no longer affiliated with North Liberty. The division was completely friendly and was viewed as a sign of a growing church.

There were 47 charter members of the North Liberty church following the division, and the congregation continued to grow. It is believed there were even more charter members of the Oak Grove congregation, but it did not grow as rapidly. In fact, meetings of the congregation began to dwindle by as early as 1921, and became very irregular by the early 1930s. Regular services were no longer held after 1936 and the congregation was disbanded in 1942. Some local historians believe one of the reasons the Oak Grove congregation did not prosper was that it continued the practice of strict congregational discipline in matters of dress and behavior while the North Liberty congregation followed more moderate guidelines adopted by Annual Conference in 1911.

Whatever the reasons, the North Liberty congregation thrived. Major renovation and additions to the building were successfully completed in 1923 and 1952, and a parsonage was purchased and remodeled in 1947. Another major renovation and addition program was completed in the late 1980s. A Sunday school program begun in 1893 has been an active part of the congregation's ministry. Free ministers gave way to part-time paid pastors about 1917, and full-time pastors have given leadership since the 1940s.

Northview
5555 E. 46th St.
Indianapolis, 46226
Membership: 157

Northview Church of the Brethren has operated under several names during its lifetime in Indianapolis. The origin of the church dates to Thanksgiving Day in 1901 when P.H. Beery, Charity Himes Brubaker, and

Alice Boone organized a public service with the support of the Southern Indiana District Mission Board. This first service was held in a rented hall on the corner of State and Hoyt streets. The first love feast was conducted about a year later with 17 members present.

A Sunday school program was organized in 1903 at 57 Germania Avenue, later known as North Belleview Place. A lot was purchased at this location and construction of a church building was completed in 1905 with a dedication service in November of that year. The church was called First Indianapolis Church of the Brethren. It was an active congregation in serving its community on the west side of the city. At one time, Sunday school enrollment reached 250. On Feb. 5, 1917, it was released by the mission board and became an independent congregation.

The original building was sold to the Indianapolis Park Board in May 1923. This was followed by the purchase of the Grace Presbyterian Church on Jan. 1, 1924. at 3201 N. Capitol Ave. A dedication service was held May 11, 1924.

Because the name "Grace" had been attached to this building for so long, the congregation voted on Dec. 28, 1923, to change its name to Grace Church of the Brethren. The church operated under that name until May 10, 1943, when it was voted to change the name again to First Church of the Brethren.

By 1952, the congregation felt a need to find a new location due to the scattering of the membership and the condition of the church building. A groundbreaking ceremony for a new church was held on a 10-acre plot at 46th Street and Ritter Avenue on Nov. 6, 1955. The name was changed to Northview Church of the Brethren, and the first service in the new building was held on Thanksgiving in 1956, exactly 55 years after the first service in Indianapolis was organized. A parsonage was built at this site in 1956.

A recent project for the church has been assisting the South/Central District in planting a new congregation in Greenwood. The first meetings were held in 1986 and have resulted in the founding of the Christ Our Shepherd Church.

North Webster

P.O. Box 391
North Webster, IN 46555
Membership: 70

North Webster was originally called Tippecanoe by the 35 members who organized the congregation in Kosciusko County in 1852. The first meeting house was built in 1861 about two miles north of the town of North Webster. By 1882, the church reported a membership of 140.

The early 1900s were difficult years, however, and the church gradually lost membership. In 1922 the district mission board stepped in and helped with the purchase of an existing church building on South Main Street in North Webster from the Evangelical Church. The country house was closed, and the name of the congregation was changed to North Webster in 1929.

The church building was renovated in 1967, and by 1980 the membership had increased to nearly 90 and had become self-supporting. In the late 1980s, the congregation adopted a plan to construct a new church building at the west edge of North Webster. It was built with the help of considerable volunteer labor from throughout the Northern Indiana District and became home to the growing congregation in 1991. The previous church building was sold to another congregation.

North Winona

2475 E. C.R. 100 N.
Warsaw, IN 46555
Membership: 249

North Winona was known as Washington when it was organized soon after 1860 under the leadership of such Indiana stalwarts as Jeremiah

Gump, Ephraim Brumbaugh, Norman Workman, and Levi Workman. George Workman was one of the first from Washington to be called to the ministry. The original boundaries of the territory the new congregation fell across both the Northern Indiana and Middle Indiana districts.

During the early years, the congregation met in as many as three separate locations, one of which was called Oak Grove. Jesse Calvert became part of the church in 1877, and was soon ordained and made presiding elder. Under his leadership, a new central meeting house was built at the present location about three miles northeast of Warsaw and dedicated on New Year's Day 1880.

There was a decline in membership about 1900 to the point that disorganization was seriously considered. But assistance from the district and determined work by a core group of members helped the congregation grow once more. The 1880 building was remodeled in 1916, and a dedication address was given by Otho Winger. The name of the congregation was changed from Washington to North Winona in 1919.

A new sanctuary was built and dedicated in 1969. In 1978, the original 1880 building was demolished and a new educational wing built in its place.

North Winona has a long history of fostering leadership for the Indiana church, and in the last few years has become particularly active in reaching out to new people. Worship attendance has more than doubled to more than 400 since the late 1980s.

Osceola
58362 Beech Road
Osceola, IN 46561
Membership: 161

The Osceola Church grew out of the northern part of the Baugo territory in the late 1800s. The church was officially organized in 1895. Elders Joel Shively and Hiram Krieghbaum and ministers Peter Huffman

and Jacob Bowers provided early leadership.

Property for a meeting house was purchased in 1893 on C.R. 20 at the Elkhart-St. Joseph county line. Some records indicate a church building may have been located at this site as early as 1855.

There are no records for the church prior to 1919, but there was an active Sunday school in operation at that time.

Lola M. Grant became a member of the church on Oct. 16, 1920. She recalls being part of a group of 16 who were taken to the Wakarusa Church for baptism because the Osceola Church had no baptistry, only a creek running nearby. She was given a covering to wear after her baptism, a practice which she continues to this day.

Lola recalls the men of the church sitting on one side and women on the other with the children seated in front. The meeting house was heated by two wood stoves, one on each side of the room. A member who had a large woods and four sons furnished the firewood.

In 1935, the meeting house was lifted and a full basement was constructed. This added much space for Sunday school classrooms. A parsonage was purchased in 1939 when the congregation began to pay the minister. It was later remodeled.

Land on Beech Road south of Osceola was purchased in the mid-1960s and a parsonage was constructed at this site in 1966. This was followed in 1969 with the construction of a brand new church building. The original church building was later sold.

The church has experienced several minor divisions through the years. The most recent was in the early 1970s when several people left through their association with the charismatic movement based around the Faith Assembly in Kosciusko County. This same group affected several other Church of the Brethren congregations in the area.

Osceola members have supported a number of local outreach programs including rescue missions in Elkhart and South Bend.

Plans are already being discussed for the observance of the congregation's centennial in 1995.

Peru

134 E. Fifth St.
Peru, IN 46970
Membership: 255

The Peru Church resulted from work done by the Mission Board of the old Middle Indiana District. Elder Silas Fisher and others had been holding meetings in the area for some time when it was decided there was enough interest to organize a congregation and build a church.

The congregation was officially organized on March 16, 1912, with 60 members. The new church building at Fifth and Benton streets was dedicated the following day with a sermon preached by Otho Winger. Elder J.W. Norris led a series of revival meetings immediately after the dedication which increased the membership rolls by 21.

Some of the charter members who were instrumental in getting the new congregation started were George and Ursula Sonafrank, who had moved to Peru from Iowa; Frank and Daisy Peters, originally from Franklin County, Virginia; and Peter Houk, a native of Germany, and his wife. Others included Silas and Fanny Fisher, Mr. and Mrs. John Neff, and Mr. and Mrs. Frank Morris.

The 1930s were very active years for the church with a balcony added in 1932 and a large addition built in 1937.

It was also in 1937 that the Bethany class from the Peru Church began what became known as the Bloomfield Mission, later organized as a separate congregation.

A major event in the life of the Peru Church was the decision to build a new building at 134 E. Fifth St. in 1957. Ground was broken on July 17, 1957, and a dedication service for the new building was held May 17, 1959. Blair Helman, president of Manchester College, was the speaker.

A unique feature of the new building was a bell donated by the C&O Railroad. At the dedication service, a speaker noted, "Its sound has saved many lives before and could save many more by calling them to worship."

Pike Creek

Route 4, Box 600
Monticello, IN 47960
Membership: 123

The original Dunkard settlers who located in the White County area around Monticello came from Mifflin County, Pa., from 1831 to 1835. They were at that time part of the Bachelor Run territory.

The Monticello Church was organized in 1859. It included all of White County plus additional territory to the north and east. Monticello had a very active membership which aggressively established itself in the area. By 1887, a total of eight separate preaching points had been established including Pike Creek, Burnetts Creek, Paton, Oak Grove, Palestine, Winamac, Bowman School House, and Guernsey. Burnetts Creek (now Burnettsville) was organized as a separate congregation in 1898. Pike Creek and Guernsey continued operating as two separate groups of the Monticello Church, but the other four preaching points were discontinued.

The original Pike Creek meeting house was built in 1868 northwest of Monticello. It was completely renovated in 1944. The dedication address was delivered by Vernon F. Schwalm, president of Manchester College.

A parsonage was built in 1948 just west of the church. This was undertaken as a joint project with the Guernsey congregation. A mortgage-burning ceremony was held in 1951.

A major transition occurred in 1967 with a decision to form independent congregations out of Guernsey and Pike Creek. This marked the official end of the Monticello Church.

However, both congregations voted to retain a yoked pastorate, an arrangement which has continued to the present day. The two congregations jointly maintain the parsonage near Pike Creek, and many activities are shared.

Pine Creek

69531 Pine Road
North Liberty, IN 46554
Membership: 98

The area now served by the Pine Creek Church was originally part of a large region called the South Bend territory. It included land from the Michigan border all the way south to Plymouth.

As early as the 1830s, Abraham Whitmer of Sumption Prairie and brothers Jacob and David Miller of Portage Prairie began making regular circuits to hold meetings in homes and schools. While the Millers were involved from time to time, Whitmer was the primary Brethren presence. He was born in Lancaster County, Pa., and moved to Ohio as a young man. He then settled in St. Joseph County in 1831.

Also among those early St. Joseph County settlers were Mr. and Mrs. Jacob Rupel. They were regular attenders at the meetings led by Whitmer, and their son, David, was elected to the ministry in 1852. That same year, Washington Fenson, also a minister, moved into the area.

David Rupel married Sarah Melling in 1836. When they built a house, it was designed with double doors which opened between rooms specifically so the house could accommodate worship services.

Many church meetings were held in that house.

The Pine Creek congregation was officially organized in 1854 with Whitmer as presiding elder and Rupel and Fenson as ministers. David Rupel was ordained an elder in 1856 and became presiding elder of the church.

The work at Pine Creek was highly successful and membership grew so large that no home or school in the area could hold those who wanted to attend. This was true even after the southern part of the Pine Creek territory was separated to form the Union Church. So in 1866, the congregation built two meetings houses: the East House and the West House. The East House (located across the road from the present church) was built large enough to accommodate communion services for the entire congregation.

As membership grew, Pine Creek built a third meeting house in the southern portion of the district. It was known as the Blissville House. This was followed in 1877 by the construction of a fourth church building known as the Center House. Also in 1877, the original brick West House was destroyed by a tornado. It was replaced the same year with a new frame building.

Pine Creek operated in all four locations until June 1912 when members of the southern half of the district asked to form a separate organization. The request was granted and this group, which included the Center House and the Blissville House, became known as the Blissville Church.

When the North Liberty congregation was formed in 1917, many of those who attended services at the West House transferred their membership to the new group. Pine Creek voted to discontinue services at the West House in 1921, and the building was sold in 1925.

A Sunday school program was established in 1881. Its success and

the condition of the church building led to a decision to remodel the
East House in 1914. That project included digging a basement under the
building.

The church council approved hiring the first paid minister in 1931,
and the position was filled by H.A. Claybaugh in 1932. A parsonage was
built on land across the road from the church in 1933. It was replaced
by a new parsonage at the same site in 1961.

The growth of the church, particularly the Sunday school program,
led to another major remodeling project in 1950. A dedication service
was held July 8, 1951.

Pine Creek has long been involved in mission and outreach
activities. Winnie Cripe, a granddaughter of David Rupel, went to China
from Pine Creek which supported her work from 1911 until her death in
1934. Homer and Marguerite Burke, who were members at the Center
House, served in Nigeria and Puerto Rico. Pine Creek has also supported
the hospital project at Castaner, Puerto Rico, from its beginning. Nancy
Herbster, who grew up in the Pine Creek Church, is currently serving as
an optometrist in Nigeria.

The congregation helped 29 displaced persons settle in the area
following World War II and actively supported the foreign student
exchange program. Members have also been involved in prison ministry
for the past 20 years and support local homeless shelters and food
pantries. Many have volunteered labor for Habitat for Humanity projects.

The Men's Work organization was formed in 1945, and the group
purchased a 120-acre farm across the road from the church in 1954. A
park was developed on a portion of the land along the Yellow Bank
Creek, and a shelter house was erected in 1973.

A major event was the construction of a new church building in
1982. Ninety acres of the farm land was sold and the money was
invested while plans for a new church building were made. Ground was
broken on a portion of the remaining 30-acre plot Sept. 5, 1982, and
construction began immediately. The building was nearly closed in when
the financial institution in which the money from the sale of the land
was invested declared bankruptcy. The event could have been a catastro-
phe, but the members immediately responded with interest-free loans
and donations to keep the project on track. Some of the investment
money was eventually recovered and all borrowed money was repaid by
Sept. 21, 1986.

The congregation moved into the new building in November 1983,
and a dedication service was held Sept. 15 and 16, 1984, on the
congregation's 130th anniversary. The old church building was razed in
1985, and the location on the opposite corner from the new building is
marked with a commemorative plaque.

Pipe Creek
Route 4, Box 331-AA
Peru, IN 46970
Membership: 64

The first Church of the Brethren settlers in southern Miami County were
David and Samuel Puterbaugh and their wives. They came from Montgomery County, Ohio, and settled in Pipe Creek Township. Others soon
followed.

These early settlers at first traveled all the way to Mexico to attend
the new congregation organized there in 1839. But travel was difficult,
and the settlers soon began to talk about holding Sunday meetings closer
to home.

These Pipe Creek Township Brethren were holding their own
meetings by the spring of 1851 in homes and barns. Samuel Murray, a
minister in the second degree, moved to the area from Ohio that same
year, and soon had regular services organized. Pipe Creek Church was
officially formed in 1852, and Abraham Moss was named the first elder
in charge.

The first meeting house was built in 1856 a half mile south of
Nead on land donated by Daniel Shively Sr. It was located in a woods in
a small valley and near a spring which furnished fresh water.

The church grew rapidly under Murray's leadership. He was
ordained an elder in 1857 and was given charge of the church. From the
original 16 charter members, the membership rolls grew to 300 by the

time Elder Murray moved on in 1864.

With the rapid increase in membership, the original building soon became too small. A new brick building was constructed in 1871 on two acres of land donated by Hannah Metzger. It was located slightly north and several miles west of the 1856 building. Bricks for the 40-foot by 80-foot building were baked in temporary ovens across the road, and the Rev. Willis Maugans, writing in 1986, said he often turned up brick bats every time he plowed that field in the 1940s and 1950s. The new church was the largest in Miami County at the time it was finished.

The denominational split of 1881 was felt at Pipe Creek when a number of members left to join the newly organized Old Order German Baptists. They built a new church in 1883 about 1.5 miles north of the Pipe Creek Church.

A similar event occurred again in 1928 when 14 members left to join the newly organized Dunkard Brethren because they felt Pipe Creek had become too progressive. They were among those who formed a Dunkard Brethren congregation at the old Stroop School building which was later named Midway.

Depending on the source, a Sunday school program was organized at Pipe Creek in either 1884 or 1887 and has been part of the church ever since.

A series of improvements was made to the Pipe Creek building throughout the late 19th and early 20th centuries. A major change in 1923 created a new seating arrangement, although men and women were still seated on opposite sides. A new furnace replaced two old wood stoves in 1925.

A large addition was constructed in 1954 which added a fellowship hall, kitchen, rest rooms, classrooms, and an enlarged sanctuary. The new facility was dedicated Sept. 18, 1954.

A major event in the life of the church came in 1958 when the 250th anniversary of the denomination was observed. The Pipe Creek and Upper Deer Creek congregations met together at Pipe Creek for love feast, an event that is still fondly remembered by those who were present.

The main church building was remodeled in 1963 with a dedication service held on Aug. 18. Among many improvements, the project included closing off the west entrance which had been maintained from the beginning with the east entrance as separate points of entry for men and women.

Pipe Creek was served by the free ministry throughout its history until 1964 when Robert Hoover was called as the first full-time, paid minister. It was also that year that the members voted to receive new members on their former baptism.

A parsonage was constructed in 1966 on a portion of a 40-acre farm which was purchased by the church. The land was farmed by the men of the church for several years, then rented. The farm and parsonage were sold in 1981.

Pittsburg

Route 2, Box 200-B
Delphi, IN 46923
Membership: 112

Pittsburg Church of the Brethren traces its origins to a small group of people who began meeting in nearby Delphi in 1918. On Thanksgiving Day of that year, Dr. Eli and Maude Blickenstaff invited all the Brethren families in the area to their home. The group then began meeting regularly on Sundays in homes, primarily the Blickenstaff home.

The Delphi group was organized as a preaching point in 1920. J.G. Stinebaugh and Grant F. Wagoner handled most of the preaching and pastoral duties. By 1921, the group had grown to include 58 members including 25 who had been baptized, and there was strong sentiment for finding a permanent church house.

In 1922, the congregation purchased a former Presbyterian church building located on Union Street just two blocks from the courthouse. The congregation used the main floor while the upper floor was rented as a public school. The original debt of $6,000 had been reduced to $2,700 by 1924 with contributions from members, local businessmen, and other congregations in the western part of what was then the

Middle District.

With the coming of the Great Depression, local members were not able to support the church by themselves. The district contributed $1,000 in 1928 and another $640 in 1929.

As the depression deepened, it soon became apparent that the district could not continue to support all of the mission points that had been established. A committee of elders was appointed to study the weaker churches and, at a meeting at the Delphi Church in November 1930, a majority of the church members voted to disorganize. All members were given church letters

Many of the Delphi Church members transferred their memberships to the Lower Deer Creek congregation; some transferred to other denominations. The church building was sold for $845, and the district paid off a remaining bank note of $528.

However, a few members from the Delphi congregation were unwilling to give up their special fellowship. Immediately after the disorganization vote, they began holding Sunday meetings at the home of the William Heiland family. Brother Heiland was working on the railroad when he noticed an abandoned church building on a hill in nearby Pittsburg. The building was a former Methodist Church, but was at the time owned by the Pittsburg Community Building Association. Heiland, Elmer Irelan, and Anna Cripe Cheeseman worked out an agreement with the trustees of the association that they could have exclusive use of the building if they would renovate it and be responsible for maintenance and insurance.

The first service in the building was held Dec. 3, 1930. Very little is known about the congregation during the next eight years. It is believed some baptisms were held, although there was no baptistry in the church building. The first love feast was held April 15, 1938, with equipment borrowed from the Pyrmont Church.

Time had helped diminish the hard feelings remaining from the disorganization of the Delphi Church, and by 1939 the congregation was interested in becoming an official part of the Church of the Brethren. A meeting with Middle District officials was held March 3, 1939. Thirty-two people signed a charter membership list and an additional 14 had signed by the time the congregation's organization was officially approved at the Middle District Conference in October.

Much of the success of the little congregation was due to the work of charter members John and Ruth Laprad. John was a full-time mail carrier, but was licensed to the ministry and served as the pastor until 1966. They remained members until 1970, when John accepted a pastorate at the Lower Deer Creek church.

From the beginning, members of the Pittsburg congregation knew their church building was not adequate. The small building had only one room and no plumbing. Members had to bring fresh water with them. Recognizing the need, a building fund was started in 1940.

With the onset of World War II, however, the church was unable to obtain a permit to buy lumber. Two small poultry houses were moved in to help relieve the demands on the 100-year-old original building.

A second building fund was established in 1945, and it had grown to $6,000 by 1950. A 1.4-acre plot located north of Pittsburg was donated to the church in 1952 by George Brewer. Several more years of planning and fund-raising were required until finally, on June 9, 1957, ground was broken for a new church building located on the land donated by George Brewer plus an additional 2.7 acres purchased from him for $1,500.

On March 23, 1958, 121 people met at the old building for the final time, then marched in a procession up the hill to the new building. The official dedication was held May 25, 1958, with 323 in attendance. A total of $25,000 of the $55,000 construction cost was financed, and the debt was retired in 1962. A parsonage was constructed on the original lot donated by George Brewer in 1967.

The congregation celebrated their 25th year in the church building in 1983, and their 50th year as a congregation in 1989.

Pleasant Chapel

2010 C.R. 8
Ashley, IN 46705
Membership: 98

While the official year of organization for Pleasant Chapel is 1921, its history predates that time by several years.

Members of the Cedar Lake congregation, including J.H. Elson, Daniel Phillips, and others, began holding periodic meetings in the northern part of the Cedar Lake territory in the early 1900s. Many of these meetings were held in homes and, occasionally, at the Neidig School which was located on C.R. 19 about one mile south of the present church building. Those who attended the services became interested in forming their own group.

Working with Elder John Urey and the District Mission Board, a Sunday school organization was developed. The first meeting was held on the first Sunday of January in 1912 in the old Putt school house, located at C.R. 19 and C.R. 4 in DeKalb county. Elder Urey came once a month to preach. Later that year Elder Urey moved to Auburn and, in 1913, the mission board agreed to send preachers to the little group on a regular basis.

Known as Cedar Lake North, the group steadily increased its membership. Successful negotiations were completed with a Mennonite group to hold meetings in their church building. Cooperative services with the Mennonites were held for a short time, but the Mennonite group began to die out, and in 1917, the Brethren purchased the church building. A remodeling project, including the addition of a basement, was completed in 1918.

The question of dividing the Cedar Lake territory was officially raised in 1921. Approval by the Cedar Lake congregation was given on May 5, and the first trustees were elected on May 19. They were S.D. Ober, Carl Thomas, and Ellis McClish. The name Pleasant Chapel was adopted on May 22.

Improvements have been made to the facility over the years. The church building was enlarged and remodeled in a major project during 1949-50. A parsonage was purchased in 1962, and additional land was purchased for the church grounds in 1963. A remodeling project in 1970-71 renovated the basement with a new kitchen, rest rooms, and heating system. New pews were also added to the sanctuary. A shelter house was constructed in 1983.

One of the first preschool programs in the area was started at the church in 1981, and a youth club was started in 1988. Pleasant Chapel has also been actively involved in cooperative ventures with other churches in the area for vacation Bible school and Easter services.

Pleasant Dale

Route 2, Box 331
Decatur, IN 46733
Membership: 297

In the fall of 1844, Mr. and Mrs. Phillip Hartman brought their seven children to the Indiana wilderness from Westmoreland County, Pennsylvania. They were the first Brethren family to settle in Adams County when they settled on the banks of Peterson Creek east of Peterson, Ind.

Phillip Hartman died only a year later, leaving Mrs. Hartman to care for her brood of seven and carve out a wilderness farm at the same time. She was successful and was the only Brethren member in the area for the next 15 years.

Finally in 1860, Mr. and Mrs. Israel Stoneburner moved from Hocking County, Ohio, and established a farm just a mile from the Hartman property. Mrs. Stoneburner was a member of the church, but Israel was not baptized until several years later.

Walnut Level was organized in 1867, and the Adams County group became a part of that organization. Samuel Stump, a minister who lived near Markle, heard of the small Brethren settlement in Adams County in 1868. He traveled to meet them and arranged for monthly meetings. Assisted by John Metzger, who preached in German, the meetings were held in Israel Stoneburner's barn in the summer and in a school house near Peterson in the winter. Within a few months, George Studebaker from Delaware County became the primary preacher.

The group began to grow and, in 1870, Studebaker was invited to debate Christian Stalter of the Brethren in Christ on the Lord's Supper. Studebaker must have handled himself well because eight people were baptized into the German Baptist Brethren group at the close of the debate. A love feast held in late June 1870 was attended by 14 members.

New members were added by baptism and through a Brethren contingent which migrated to the Adams County area from Wayne County, Ohio. The Adams County Brethren organized as a separate church in 1889 with D.M. Byerly as the first minister and Samuel Neher as the first elder. A new church was constructed southwest of Peterson in 1890. Silas Gilbert, speaking at the dedication service, proposed the name Pleasant Dale, and it was adopted by the members.

The active little church continued to grow which led to the need for additional space. A building fund was established in 1954, and a major remodeling and addition project was launched. The old building was extensively remodeled, including enlargement of the sanctuary, and a new building was added which provided classrooms, a kitchen, and other facilities.

A brand new sanctuary was constructed in 1983 on the southeast side of the old church building. A special mortgage-burning ceremony was held on Homecoming Sunday, Sept. 16, 1990.

Programs for children have been a special focus at Pleasant Dale. In 1926, Dulcie Cover, wife of pastor S.L. Cover, organized an interdenominational Bible school. Over 170 children attended that first year. Continued growth of the program created space problems, so older children were moved to the nearby Kirkland School. School consolidation left the program without enough classrooms, so the entire program was moved to the Adams Central School in Monroe. A total of 241 children were enrolled in the program in 1990.

A preschool program was launched in 1979 with Barbara Barger as director. Classes were held every Wednesday morning. The program was expanded to two days a week in 1981, and it was doubled in 1990 with a second set of two-day-a-week classes added.

Pleasant Valley

P.O. Box 1518
C.Rs. 8 and 35
Middlebury, IN 46540
Membership: 57

Pleasant Valley grew out of the Rock Run Church. Jacob Berkey from Rock Run and others did the early preaching in the area which resulted in the construction of a meeting house in 1867. It was located at the present site.

Pleasant Valley was separated from Rock Run as an independent organization in 1878. The first minister was Joseph Hoover, who had been elected at Rock Run.

The congregation grew rapidly and included about 200 members

in 1913 when it was equally divided into two congregations. The northern section retained the name Pleasant Valley while the southern part became the Middlebury Church.

A basement was added to the original church building in 1915, and electricity was installed in 1935.

Pleasant Valley suffered through a major division in 1976 which left it in a much weakened condition. Larry Killingbeck had been called as pastor in the early 1970s. Under his leadership, a large part of the congregation began a movement toward separating from the denomination. This group eventually left along with Killingbeck to form New Life Christian Center nearby.

With help from the district and other sister churches in the area, Pleasant Valley has continued to function as a viable congregation.

Pleasant View

7050 W. 1000 S.
South Whitley, IN 46787
Membership: 82

Pleasant View Church of the Brethren was officially created as a separate congregation Aug. 12, 1913, from the territory of the Sugar Creek

Church. The congregation was located in a building constructed in 1902 five miles south of South Whitley. In its early days, it was often referred to as West Sugar Creek.

David Kreider was one of the early leaders of the young congregation. He came to the area from Darke County, Ohio, in 1855. J.A. Snell was also among the early leaders and served as the third elder of the congregation. J.H. Wright was elected the first elder.

The Reelhorn School, located adjacent to the church building, was purchased in the early 1930s by the Ladies Aid Society. It was remodeled several times over the years and became a fellowship hall.

The need for additional space was felt by 1952, and a committee was formed which planned a project to connect the two separate buildings with an educational unit. Several members donated trees which were felled in November 1953 and taken to a sawmill on July 4, 1954, in a 10-truck caravan. Construction was well under way in January 1955 when a fire nearly destroyed the fellowship hall and damaged the new addition. But the volunteer laborers took up the task and were set back by only about a month. Dedication of the new building was held Aug. 22, 1955.

At the completion of the 1955 project, members were already expressing the desire to remodel the sanctuary. Plans were finalized in 1964 and construction began in January 1965. The project moved the rostrum and pulpit from the south end of the building to the north end in addition to a complete renovation of the building. Most of the labor was again volunteered, and a dedication service was held May 15, 1966.

Plymouth

1130 N. Michigan St.
Plymouth, IN 46563
Membership: 223

The Plymouth Church came to life rapidly in 1916 at the request of a number of people living in Plymouth including N.O. and Pearl Troyer, Ira and Julia Mock, Edith Mock, Edith Troyer, and Frederick Marsh.

Permission was granted by the Northern Indiana District to hold a Sunday school for a three-month period. It was placed under the authority of the Union Church, and N.O. Troyer was put in charge. Thirty-nine people attended the first meeting on the first Sunday in January 1916.

On Feb. 28, the Plymouth group asked that preaching services be held twice a month. The Union Church agreed to supply a preacher once a month and the Mission Board took the second Sunday. These first meetings were held in a building known as the Dr. E.R. Wood Hall in the 100 block of North Michigan Street.

On March 25, the Plymouth group was back with another request, this time to become a separate congregation. The request was granted, and the Plymouth Church was officially born with 29 charter members. John F. Appleman of the Union Church was elected the first elder. The Plymouth group secured their own pastor with financial help from the mission board when Rev. Eli Heestand was hired in September 1916.

The new congregation purchased a home at Garro and Water streets on May 18, 1918, and remodeled it so it was suitable for church services. It was used for two years, then sold and moved. The new church building was constructed on the same site. Services were held in the Gem Theater until the new church building was dedicated in September 1921. Many local businessmen supported the effort, and the building was completely paid for at the time of the dedication. It was remodeled and enlarged in 1937.

The congregation continued to grow and was soon bulging at the seams. A building fund was established in 1945, and a new site on North Michigan Street at Baker Street was acquired in 1947. Fund-raising began in earnest and took a variety of forms, including a special effort which raised $33,000 in 30 days. The women of the church opened a Thrift Shop in downtown Plymouth which operated for eight years. The $9,000 raised in the shop during those years helped support the build-ing fund and organ fund. It was also used to purchase new hymnals, a PA system, and choir robes.

The decision to move ahead with construction was made Jan. 12, 1951, and ground was broken the following March 4. By Sept. 6, an additional $20,000 was needed to continue construction. This special need was presented at a Sunday morning service and a pledge board was placed before the congregation. Individuals went forward and placed their names on the board until the money was pledged.

The new church building was not without its critics. It was designed by an Episcopalian and was considered by some Brethren throughout the state as too fancy and too expensive. Some members of the Plymouth congregation also questioned the decision to purchase several lots across the street from the building site. Present members are now grateful for this foresight which has provided the church with adequate parking areas.

Plymouth was one of the earliest congregations in Indiana to employ two staff people. This began in the summer of 1954 when Ruth Graham was hired as Christian education and parish worker for the summer months. The church was so pleased with her work that she was employed full time in 1955 as director of Christian education. Plymouth has functioned with two full-time staff members ever since.

Sunday school has always been a vital part of the Plymouth Church. Sunday school attendance was even higher than worship attendance for a period of time about 1970. The times of worship and Sunday school were switched to have worship first so that fewer people would leave, and worship attendance is now larger than Sunday school.

Plymouth has supported many projects that have had profound effects on its community and beyond. The congregation supported **Wilbur and Joyce McFadden as missionaries to Indonesia in the 1950s and 1960s. They have also supported a number of refugee settlement programs and foreign student exchanges.**

A community day care center was opened at the church Sept. 14, 1970. During the next nine years, a number of Plymouth Church members served as part of the staff along with six Brethren Volunteer Service volunteers. The program was moved into a new building in 1979, but Plymouth Church members continue to be an active part of it.

Part of a large estate was willed to the church in 1966, and a portion of the money was used to establish an endowment fund which has supported students planning to enter pastoral ministry or other church-related work.

The 75th anniversary of the congregation was celebrated Sept. 28-29, 1991. The two-day celebration was attended by all former pastors who were still living.

Portland

977 Chicago Ave.
Portland, IN 47371
Membership: 31

The Portland (formerly Bear Creek) congregation owes its existence to the persistence of three sisters who wanted preaching services in their area of Indiana. Amanda Garber, Margaret Andrews, and Annie Petry, whose husbands were not yet members of the church, succeeded in getting a number of ministers to hold services in the Portland area.

The scattered membership organized into what was then called the Bear Creek Church. The membership became deeply divided between the Old Orders and Conservatives. This resulted in a large group leaving with the Old Orders in the 1881 schism, and they formed the Blue Creek congregation in the northern part of the Bear Creek territory.

Amanda Garber's husband, Henry P. Garber, joined the church and was soon called to the ministry. He and his wife became leaders of the Bear Creek Church until their deaths, Henry in 1901 and Amanda in 1908.

Bear Creek obtained a half acre of land in 1889 at the southeast edge of Portland, and a one-room meeting house was built and dedicated in 1891. It has been renovated several times and still serves the congregation, now known as Portland.

Membership at Portland has fluctuated widely over the years from about 100 down to only three, and at one time it was placed under the direction of the District Mission Board. Loyal members have continued to worship together, and today Portland is still a small but active church.

Prince of Peace
53105 N. Ironwood
South Bend, IN 46635
Membership: 112

The Prince of Peace congregation is the direct result of a decision by the district to establish a new church in South Bend.

On Dec. 6, 1958, the Northern Indiana District purchased a nine-acre site on the north side of the city. Construction of a parsonage was begun in August 1959 and was completed in January 1960.

Robert Swank served as the first minister, and he held the first services in the basement of the parsonage. The initial meeting of interested families was held at the home of George and Freda Rupley in January 1960, and the first Sunday school classes were held the following April.

Ground was broken for a new church building in March 1961. The first service in the new building was held in the basement the following October, and the sanctuary was completed in February 1962. Prince of

Peace became a chartered congregation on Palm Sunday, April 15, 1962, and the new building was dedicated on June 10.

From the original 36 charter members, Prince of Peace has grown slowly over the past 30 years to its present size.

Pyrmont

Route 4, Box 226
(S.R. 550 eight miles south of Delphi)
Delphi, IN 46923
Membership: 114

The Pyrmont congregation began with the migration of 16 people from Montgomery County, Ohio, in 1828. In that year, David Ulrey and members of his family came by wagon and settled along the North Fork of the Wild Cat Creek in Carroll and Tippecanoe counties about two miles southwest of the present site of Pyrmont. Eleven of the 16 settlers were Dunkards including David Ulrey (a deacon) and his wife; John Shively and his wife; David Ulrey Jr.; Leonard Ulrey; Christian Replogle and his wife; Joseph Replogle; and Samuel Ulrey and his wife.

The little band of Dunkards met as often as possible, and Samuel Ulrey was elected deacon in 1829. The first real preaching did not occur until 1830 when Elder Jacob Brower and a Brother Garber came from Ohio to visit the North Fork settlers. Samuel Ulrey and John Shively were called to the ministry while Brower and Garber were there.

The first communion service was held in 1831 in a barn which had just been erected by David Ulrey.

More settlers were arriving, and the congregation was formally organized in 1832 as North Fork with 16 charter members. Meetings were held every two weeks in homes and barns or outside in pleasant groves during good weather.

New Dunkard settlers were drawn to the area and the church grew rapidly. The territory was divided in 1845 along a boundary later known as the Lafayette and Burlington Road. Elder John Metzger was placed in charge of the new territory known as Middle Fork which was located entirely in Clinton County. Elder John Shively was placed in charge of the North Fork territory which covered parts of Carroll, Clinton, and Tippecanoe counties.

The first North Fork meeting house was erected in 1852 on land donated by Jacob Wagoner in the village of Pyrmont The 40-foot by 60-foot structure was built of the heavy native timbers from the surrounding land. A communion service was held to open the building instead of a formal dedication service.

The Civil War years were difficult for a number of North Fork members. Since Dunkards opposed going to war, many men had to pay as much as $500 to gain an exemption from the draft.

The first Sunday school program was organized in 1866 and was held in a school at Pyrmont.

A second territorial division occurred in 1872 along the county line between Tippecanoe and Carroll counties. The west division in Tippecanoe County was named Fairview and the east portion in Carroll and Clinton counties retained the name North Fork. Members were allowed to choose which congregation they preferred to be part of regardless of where they lived. Elder John Shively was placed in charge of the new Fairview congregation while Elders Isaac Cripe and Jacob Wagoner were placed in charge of North Fork.

In 1877, a brick meeting house was constructed three miles east of Pyrmont near Owasco to make it easier for those in the eastern portion of the North Fork district to attend regularly. This building served for about 30 years before it was abandoned.

North Fork lost a number of members in the Old Order denominational division of 1881. Some sources list the loss of 28 members while others place the number as high as 90. Among those who left were Joseph Wagoner, a minister, and Abraham Wagoner and Daniel Metzger, deacons. Only one member was lost the following year in the split with the Progressives.

Elders L.T. Holsinger and E.M. Cobb came to North Fork in 1899. They provided the impetus for the construction of a new meeting house. Elder Holsinger presided at a council meeting June 13, 1899, at which a ways and means committee was appointed. This committee reported raising more than $3,000 at another meeting Aug. 3 plus an equivalent amount in labor. A building committee was appointed, and the next several months were spent gathering materials and transporting them to the site.

In the midst of this activity, the congregation voted on March 10, 1900, to change their name from North Fork to Pyrmont German Baptist Brethren.

The last service in the old church was held March 11, 1900, and the following day the building was torn down. A new masonry building was erected on the same site. It was dedicated Nov. 18, 1900, with Elder D.L. Miller of Mount Morris, Ill., as the speaker. It is recorded that more than 900 people were present for the dedication.

Following the lead of the denomination, the congregation again changed its name in 1908 to Pyrmont Church of the Brethren.

Two Pyrmont natives, A. Raymond Cottrell and Rosa Wagoner Kaylor, served as missionaries in India. Rosa Kaylor died there in 1913 and was the first missionary wife to die on the mission field.

The brick church had served for only 25 years when it was destroyed by fire on Sunday, Dec. 27, 1925. A large crowd gathered as flames swept through the structure leaving only a pile of ashes. The cause was traced to a faulty chimney flue. There was no insurance to cover the loss of the building and contents.

In spite of this setback, the congregation immediately laid plans to build a new meeting house while they worshipped in a nearby school. Construction began in the early spring of 1926 on the same site as the previous church. The new building was completed in November at a cost of $11,400. Otho Winger was the speaker at a dedication service on Nov. 14, 1926.

The centennial of the formation of Pyrmont was celebrated on Sept. 18, 1932, with a harvest meeting, homecoming, and centennial observance all rolled into one. A large crowd gathered to hear Edward Frantz of Elgin, Ill.

The first recorded payment for pastoral services came in 1931 when home ministers were paid $3 per sermon. The first musical instrument, a piano, was purchased in 1935.

From 1938 to 1955, Pyrmont shared a yoked pastorate with Rossville, the ancestor of the old Middle Fork group, but has maintained an independent pastorate since that time.

At the Dec. 5, 1950, council meeting, John W. Root made a gift of $10,000 toward the purchase of the Solomon Ulrey farm. The farm was purchased by Pyrmont Feb. 23, 1951, for $32,500, and a loan was paid off in 1962. The farm was sold in 1965.

A parsonage was built in 1955 just east of the Pyrmont Church building at a cost of $13,215. The Rev. Ralph Petry and family were the first to occupy the new home.

The Fairview congregation disbanded on Aug. 25, 1968, and 15 members from that congregation were accepted at Pyrmont in March 1969.

The youth of Pyrmont began participating in the annual Feast of the Hunters Moon at Fort Ouiatenon, Lafayette, in 1972. Each year since then, they have served buffalo stew and French marble cakes with the proceeds used to pay their expenses to National Youth Conference.

The sesquicentennial of Pyrmont was celebrated Aug. 15, 1982. The day began with an old-fashioned breakfast and morning worship services. A basket dinner was held at noon followed by reminiscing and a hymn sing. Guest speakers for the day included Dr. Carroll Petry, district minister; Patricia Helman, North Manchester; and Dr. John Wagoner, Anderson.

Richmond

20 N.W. 15th St.
Richmond, IN 47374
Membership: 36

The development of a church at Richmond occurred over a period of several years. The need for a congregation had been felt for some time when a meeting was called in the fall of 1925 at the home of Mr. and Mrs. William Hieger. As a result, church services were held in homes for about three months with Luther Petry doing most of the preaching.

A room was secured in the Colonial Building in Richmond. Services were held there, and the first Sunday school program was organized even though the group lacked a minister.

After a few months, a school building was rented at West Fifth and School streets, and the first service was held April 26, 1926. Sister Pearl Jackson from Losantville, Ind., agreed to fill the pulpit of the fledgling congregation in June 1926. She was called to other duties about a year later, and the Richmond group was once again without ministerial leadership.

After a few months, Martin Hoover was chosen to provide leadership, and it was during his tenure that the Richmond Church was officially organized. An organizational meeting was held Oct. 19, 1927, and the organization was completed on Nov. 9 when 31 charter members were received. A building fund was also established at this meeting, and a total of $12.25 was raised

Services lapsed for a time in 1928, but Elder Oscar D. Werking of the Hagerstown Brick Church and the Southern Indiana Mission Board worked hard to re-establish the new congregation. N.E. Baker was secured as the first resident pastor the church had ever had. He was able to bring the group back to life, and plans for a building program were laid out.

Ground for a new building was broken in October 1930 on land purchased by the mission board. Baker left in April 1931, but the congregation continued with the project. Money was raised in small amounts, and members of the congregation worked hard on evenings and weekends to construct the new building. The church was completed 13 months later, and a dedication service was held Nov. 11, 1931.

Walter J. Heisey was chosen as pastor July 5, 1932, and it was during his tenure that the congregation purchased tables and other items needed to hold communion services.

The first long-term pastorate began in January 1935 with the placement of E.O. Norris. He remained with the church for the next 15 years and is given much of the credit for helping the congregation to become self-supporting.

A major addition and renovation program was completed in 1951. Three additional classrooms were added at the west end of the building, and a new kitchen was installed. A dedication service was held Dec. 9, 1951.

A yoked parish was established with the Four Mile Church in 1968 in which the two churches share a pastor. That relationship continues as a strong one.

The 50th anniversary of the church was observed Nov. 27, 1977.

Roann

S. Chippewa St.
P.O. Box 257
Roann, IN 46974
Membership: 218

The Roann Church was originally part of the Mexico congregation. When it was formally organized in 1855, it was known as the Squirrel Creek Church, named for a small stream which flowed into the Eel River. About 90 members were part of the original congregation.

Meeting in homes and barns, the congregation began laying plans to construct a church building. Those plans had to be put on hold for a few years during the Civil War because the members were contributing heavily to pay the assessment for those who were drafted. The first house of worship was finally constructed in 1864 and was located just across the river from Roann.

In 1882, the congregation voted to change the name of the church to Roann.

It was also in 1882 that a number of members left in the split with the Progressives. Membership was also affected during the late 19th century and early 20th century by emigration to the West. This movement included some of the congregational leaders.

The original church building (which burned to the ground several years later) was sold about 1920, and a vacant Presbyterian Church at the south edge of Roann was purchased and remodeled. A dedication service at the new location was held Sept. 25, 1921. A parsonage was purchased in 1950.

Membership at Roann has fluctuated widely over the years. At one time, there were 250 members at the old Squirrel Creek Church. The number dropped to as low as 50 in the 1950s, but has since rebounded to over 200.

The congregation launched a major improvement project in 1987 with the construction of a new building across the street from the building purchased in 1920. Both buildings are currently in use. The 1987 project was the first phase of a planned three-phase building program at the site.

Rock Run

64985 C.R. 33
Goshen, IN 46526
Membership: 92

The name Jacob Berkey looms large in the early history of the Rock Run Church. Berkey was born in Somerset County, Pennsylvania. He moved his family to Ohio, then to Elkhart County, Indiana, in 1848, where he purchased a quarter section of land east of Goshen.

The area was then part of the Elkhart territory which, at that time, covered most of the northern half of Elkhart County. Because the territory was so large, it was often difficult for members to attend Sunday services. Support began to build for a separate organization east of the Elkhart Prairie, and Jacob Berkey was one of the leaders of the movement.

Rock Run was formally established in 1850 and originally included a large part of the east half of Elkhart County. Jacob Studebaker, one of the first ministers elected in Elkhart County, was named elder and

Berkey was elected to the ministry. He was soon elevated to elder.

James Tracy also served as an able minister with Berkey during these early years. However, he died of typhoid fever in 1857.

The new congregation grew rapidly, and soon there were more members attending services regularly than could comfortably fit in any of the homes or barns available. Berkey called a meeting on Jan. 21, 1859, at Union Chapel Church, located northeast of the present church. Some members objected to a church building, and one of their complaints was that people would not attend if dinner were not served. Elder Berkey silenced those complaints by issuing a standing invitation for dinner at his home to anyone who could not go home for dinner.

A committee of three men was appointed to lead the effort to construct a church building. They purchased a plot of land from Elder Berkey and erected a small frame building.

Rock Run rapidly established itself as influential among the Brethren. Annual Conference was held in Elder Berkey's barn in 1868. The location was just across the road from the present church.

Elder Berkey was a forward-thinking man. He promoted the idea of Sunday schools long before they became popularly supported. When he wanted to organize a Sunday school program in the early 1860s, there was a great deal of objection. So, he arranged to join a program organized by a Methodist group at a nearby school. When the Sunday school was moved to the church in 1868, his son, Isaac Berkey, was named the first superintendent. It was not easily accepted, however, and many of the older members refused to enter the building while Sunday school was in session. When the first Sunday school conference in northern Indiana was held in 1876 at the Wawaka Church, Jacob Berkey was the chairman and Isaac was secretary.

Evangelism was also high among Elder Berkey's priorities. He traveled throughout the area as far east as Fort Wayne preaching in German and English and was instrumental in developing congregations at English Prairie, Topeka, and Pleasant Valley. He was also among the first to organize and promote evangelistic meetings. It is believed the first protracted evangelism meetings in northern Indiana were held at Rock Run in the early 1860s. Many members were added during these meetings.

By 1875, the congregation had outgrown their first building. The old building was sold to Jacob Berkey, and a larger frame structure was constructed at the same site. Seventy-nine people contributed, but it was not enough to meet the $3,000 building cost. To raise the remainder, a tax on real estate was levied on each member.

The congregation moved services to the Union Chapel Church while the new building was being erected. An inexperienced carpenter had been hired, and the frame collapsed before it was completed. A new carpenter was hired in 1876, and the new church was completed that year.

Jacob Berkey moved to Texas about 1876. He was on his way to anoint a sister when his horse rolled over in a rain-swollen stream and he drowned in 1882.

The work at Rock Run continued, however, and led to the formation of the Goshen City congregation in 1905 from a mission point founded by Rock Run. A mission point was also established in Millersburg in 1885, but it was not successful.

Ervin Weaver was hired as the first paid pastor in 1923. The Isaac Berkey home and farm was purchased in 1925 as a parsonage. It was eventually replaced with a new home in 1957.

Fire destroyed the Rock Run building on June 3, 1928. Services were moved to nearby schools until a new brick building was completed the following Dec. 2.

A special program for youth was established in 1924. It included basketball teams for boys and girls for a number of years.

The men of the church were early supporters of Heifer Project established by Dan West at the end of World War II.

The Rock Run Credit Union was organized in 1943. It served the financial needs of members until it was disbanded in 1968.

The centennial of the congregation was observed in 1950 with Kenneth Morse, then editor of Gospel Messenger, as the guest speaker.

A major remodeling project was undertaken in 1969 which included the addition of a new front entry. It was dedicated July 26, 1970.

The 125th anniversary was observed in 1975 with a series of special services on the four Sundays of October.

Rossville

P.O. Box B
 Plank and Ramsey streets
Rossville, IN 46065
Membership: 182

When John Metzger moved his family by covered wagon from Montgomery County, Ohio, in 1834, he settled near the Middle Fork of Wildcat Creek in the area of Carroll and Tippecanoe counties. They found a group of Brethren already there and immediately joined them.

This group was officially organized in 1832 as the North Fork congregation in what was known as the Wildcat territory. David Ulrey had moved his family to the area from Ohio in 1828 and worship

services were soon begun as more families settled.

The North Fork group was quick to recognize John Metzger's talents and elected him deacon the same year he settled. He was then called to the ministry in 1835 and ordained to eldership in 1843.

Elder Metzger became known as a powerful preacher and was active throughout these years providing strong leadership for the southern half of the Wildcat district. By 1845, the membership had grown to the point that it was decided to divide the district. Elder John Shively was placed in charge of the northern half of the district which was then known as North Fork, now known as Pyrmont. Elder Metzger was placed in charge of the southern half, then known as Middle Fork, later as Pleasant View, and finally as Rossville.

The original meeting house was built shortly after the congregation was organized. It was located on the Metzger farm about five miles southwest of Rossville and was known as the Middle Fork Church. A cemetery was started shortly after the church was built about one-half mile east of the church building. The cemetery was officially named Pleasant View in 1888 and remains in use today.

In 1865, the growing congregation built a second meeting house on the Harrison Grochenour farm located four miles southeast of Rossville. Originally known as the Upper Church, it was renamed New Hope on Feb. 2, 1892. Although exact records are not available, the church was closed in 1905 or 1906 and the building later razed.

A third meeting house was erected in late 1873 in Edna Mills, four miles west of Rossville.

During the years when the Middle Fork congregation had three meeting houses, services were held in all three locations one Sunday and only at Middle Fork on the next Sunday. Evening services were held at all three locations nearly every week. Love feasts and quarterly council meetings were held at the Middle Fork Church.

After the 1882 split between the Progressives (Brethren Church) and the Conservatives (Church of the Brethren), the Edna Mills meeting house was used on alternate Sundays by the two groups until the late 1800s. This sharing of the building created some unique problems. For example, the Progressives purchased an organ and used it during their worship services. The next week when it was the turn of the Conservatives to use the house, the organ was unceremoniously shoved into a closet.

At a special council meeting on Feb. 2, 1886, Middle Fork members decided to dismantle their original meeting house and build a new one on the same site. The old building was demolished by July 27, 1886, and construction on the new building began. The first worship service in the new building was held on Oct. 24, 1886. John Flory from Virginia preached at the dedication service and remained there until a love feast on Nov. 6, 1886. The name was officially changed from Middle Fork to Pleasant View at a meeting on Nov. 16, 1886.

Although the New Hope group died out, the Edna Mills contingent remained vital, and there was talk of constructing a new building as early as 1894. The group decided against that step on March 7, 1903, however, and decided to stop meeting in that location because the building was in such poor repair. It was donated to the township trustee on Sept. 5, 1903, and the land was given back to Hannah Mellinger, the original owner. The building was eventually sold to Sam Roth. He and his family operated a general store from that location until 1978, and the building is still standing today.

With only the Pleasant View building now available for use, the members voted on March 3, 1906, to build a new church in Rossville. D.D. Hufford was hired as architect and contractor, and the new building was dedicated on Dec. 23, 1906. William Lampin, Polo, Ill., conducted a series of revival meetings soon after the dedication which resulted in 35 new members. The new site was known as the Rossville German Baptist Brethren Church. Although Church of the Brethren was adopted as the denominational name by Annual Conference in 1908, the Rossville Church did not accept the change until Dec. 9, 1914.

Services continued to be held at the old Pleasant View Church after Rossville was built, but it was finally closed on March 15, 1915. It was opened only one more time on June 15, 1925, for the funeral of Elder John E. Metzger. He had at one time served as writing clerk for all three of the churches since before 1885, and his last request was to have his funeral at Pleasant View.

With the closure of Pleasant View, the members concentrated their attention on Rossville. A Ladies Aid Society was organized in 1907, the first youth group was organized in 1915, and electricity was added in 1916. The youth purchased a piano in the late 1920s.

Minerva Metzger was sent from the church to the China mission field where she served from 1910 to 1940. She returned home due to the war and died just prior to the Pearl Harbor attack in 1941.

The church continued to grow which resulted in talk of expansion by 1953. A plan for renovation was adopted on May 25, 1957, and ground was broken on Sept. 7, 1958. Walter Hufford and his sons, Richard and Robert, son and grandsons of the original architect and contractor, were hired as contractors. Dr. Vernon Schwalm, president of Manchester College, spoke at the dedication service on July 12, 1959.

In 1980, a gift from the estate of the Krebheil family provided the church with $27,000 and a collection of German Bibles and other rare books. The money was put into a trust fund, and the books were given to Manchester College. A rare Holland Bible, about 400 years old, and a very rare original copy of Martyr's Mirror are now protected and on display at the college.

Rossville experienced a major increase in membership and attendance during the late 1980s. A bequest of nearly $400,000 from the estate of Viola Baker was used to construct a larger parking area, install air conditioning, and purchase new kitchen and sound equipment. Nearly $90,000 of the bequest was given to various Christian missions and projects.

Salamonie

2662 W. 600 S.
Warren, IN 46792
Membership: 209

The first Brethren families began moving into southern Huntington County in 1836 when Daniel Hardman moved his family to a farm located north of Lancaster, then known as River Post Office. Although he moved back to Wayne County within a few years, a number of other Brethren families had moved into the area during that time.

These families began meeting irregularly in the late 1830s. One of the first services occurred when Solomon Shideler was visited by his cousin, Benjamin Bowman, a minister from Wayne County.

The Salamonie congregation (originally spelled Salimony) was formally organized in 1845 with 18 charter members. It originally included all of the southern half of Huntington County and part of Wells County. As the population of the area increased, portions of the territory

were split off to form new congregations including Markle in 1852, Antioch in 1855, and Prairie Creek in 1861.

All of this activity occurred before there was a church building. The meetings were held in homes and barns and, during good weather, in orchards and groves.

Salamonie was one of the first congregations in Indiana to form a Sunday school program, even before it had a church building. The first Sunday school was held in 1866 at the Stringtown School during the spring and summer months.

The first church building was erected in 1868 near the Salamonie River in the town of Lancaster. Much of the timber was donated by members and many of the main beams were hand-hewn on the church grounds. It measured 60-feet by 80-feet and included one large room. There were two entrances, one for men and one for women, with a platform for the ministers located between the doors. Two wood stoves at opposite ends of the room provided heat. The members frequently referred to the building as the Lancaster House.

The Sunday school program moved to the new church in 1869, but it did not stay there long. It was again moved to area schools including the Zook School and the Reams School. It was moved back to the church by the mid-1890s and became a year-round program sometime prior to 1905.

By 1881, the congregation was considering the construction of a second meeting house in the eastern portion of its territory. This led to the building of the Loon Creek Church in 1884. The first council meeting was held at Loon Creek in 1886. From then on, the council meetings were regularly rotated between Salamonie and Loon Creek.

The decade beginning in 1910 ushered in a number of changes for the Salamonie congregation. First, Loon Creek was organized as an independent congregation in 1912. Then the Salamonie council approved the hiring of the first pastor in 1914. This action was followed by the hiring of Elder J.W. Norris in 1916.

A major remodeling program was undertaken in 1918. A balcony was constructed, rooms for children in the Sunday school program were added on a new second floor, a baptistry was built behind the pulpit, and a new central heating plant was installed. The project was completed in time to host the Middle District Conference in 1919.

The first parsonage property was purchased in 1923, and a piano was introduced for worship services in 1924. A youth group was established in the 1930s along with a vacation Bible school program.

Another remodeling project in 1940-41 added a new entrance to the church building and a chime tower. A new parsonage was purchased in 1943. The centennial of the congregation was observed in 1945 with special services.

In 1946, an old Methodist Church located across the road from Salamonie was deeded to the congregation. It was turned into a recreation hall for young people and was used about 20 years.

The first Christmas Eve service was organized in 1955 and has become an annual tradition. The sponsorship of a Boy Scout Troop was begun in 1957, and a Cub Scout group was added a few years later.

Major change occurred in 1962 with the news that the church property was located in the flood area of the planned Salamonie Reservoir. After looking at a number of alternatives, the church council voted on March 22, 1964, to relocate the church and parsonage. A site was secured one mile away on S.R. 124, and construction plans were accepted in May 1965. A groundbreaking ceremony was held Oct. 10, 1965.

The last service in the old building began Aug. 7, 1966. The members then drove to the new building for the first service in the new sanctuary. It was dedicated Sept. 25, 1966.

The Salamonie congregation has long been active in supporting ministries outside its own doors. The first recorded offering specifically for missions was taken in 1877. A missionary committee was elected in 1919 and was active for many years. The church began supporting Dr. John and Esther Hamer in Africa in 1958, then Donald Fancher in Indonesia and, more recently, Rae Mason after the Hamers returned to the U.S. in 1969.

The Salamonie congregation has supported a number of displaced families and operated a support program for migrant workers in the community.

The 125th anniversary of the congregation was observed with a series of special services all through 1970. Homecoming celebrations were started on the last Sunday in September. One service included a walk to a nearby barn erected in 1856 which was the site of early Salamonie worship services. The barn was razed in 1990.

Southside Fellowship

3003 Benham Ave.
Elkhart, IN 46517
Membership: 119

Southside Fellowship, Elkhart, is a young congregation with a distinctive history. It is one of very few congregations in Indiana which maintains denominational affiliations with the Church of the Brethren, General Conference Mennonite Church, and Mennonite Church.

Southside traces its beginnings to Belmont Mennonite Church, Elkhart. In 1965, Belmont was bursting at the seams, and a small group met in August to discuss the idea of forming a new congregation as an alternative to building a larger church. A steering committee was formed which included Galen Miller, Delbert Detwiler, Henry Hochstetler, John Stalter, and David Lehman. The first Sunday morning worship service was held Nov. 14, 1965, at Concord West Side Elementary School.

The little group continued to meet on Sundays at the school and in homes on Wednesday evenings until 1968, which became a watershed year. Most of the members agreed they needed to find another place for their worship services. Some wanted to build a multi-purpose building and a building fund was actually started. It was eventually voted, however, to hold services at the Associated Mennonite Biblical Seminaries Chapel, which at that time was not being used on Sunday mornings. It has been the home for Southside ever since.

It was also in 1968 that the first full-time pastor was chosen. The possibility of sharing professional staff with Hively Avenue Mennonite Church had been explored, but the members of Southside felt they needed their own, full-time pastor. Earl Sears was chosen as pastor/ teacher and officially began his duties in January 1969, moving to Elkhart from Illinois. He remained in the position until 1988.

Professional leadership is now provided by Pam Dintaman and Willard Roth, who were installed as co-pastors Feb. 4, 1990.

South Whitley
P.O. Box 454
107 Mulberry St.
South Whitley, IN 46787
Membership: 60

A meeting in 1913 led to the formation of the South Whitley Church of the Brethren. Residents of South Whitley were attending several rural churches including Sugar Creek, Pleasant View, and Spring Creek. But the city residents decided to hold meetings of their own.

A home was purchased in 1916 and construction of a new church building on that site was begun in 1922 and completed in December 1923. Otho Winger, president of Manchester College, spoke at the dedication service.

A major renovation program was carried out from 1926 to 1928 which added a balcony and additional space for Sunday school classrooms. The coming of the Great Depression the following year put the congregation in great financial difficulty, and there was serious consideration given to disorganizing the church in 1931. However, the members continued to support their church, and they were able to become self-supporting within a few years.

A new major renovation program was successfully completed in 1953 and improvements were again made in 1983.

Spring Creek
Route 2
Pierceton, IN 46562
Membership: 132

Originally part of the Eel River territory, approval for creating the Spring Creek Church began at a meeting at the Eel River Church Feb. 17, 1870. The new organization was finalized at a meeting March 26, 1870, in the home of Levi Fox.

The first church building was constructed in 1871 about 2.5 miles northeast of Sidney in Kosciusko County. Additions and repairs were made in 1900 and 1907. Fire destroyed the building in February 1917, but a new church was erected on the same site and a dedication service was held Nov. 11, 1917. Extensive improvements were made in 1950.

Spring Creek lost a few members in the division of 1882, but the losses may have been kept to a minimum because of the progressive programs that were sponsored by the congregation. It is believed Spring Creek began one of the first Bible school programs in Indiana and had an active Sunday school program by at least 1876, which would also make it one of the early ones in the state.

Many of the early church leaders came from the area around Greene County, Ohio, and early family names include Snell, Mishler, Swartz, Newcomer, Hardman, and Reiff.

Spring Creek owns a farm which has been home to several of its pastors. A tradition for several years has been the making of apple butter in the fall as a church project.

Sugar Creek
Tunker, IN
6 miles southeast of South Whitley
Membership: 24

A group of settlers in Whitley County officially organized the Sugar Creek Church in 1850. David Shoemaker was the first elder of the group which met in homes for the first 17 years. A highlight of the early years was a love feast held in a barn owned by Jacob Metz in 1861 at which 12 new members were baptized.

Ira Calvert was the elder when the decision was made to construct a brick meeting house in 1867. The church was located in a settlement known as Dunkard's Corner, named for the many Dunkers who lived in the area. The village, located about six miles southeast of South Whitley, later became known as Tunker.

Sunday school was introduced in the Sugar Creek Church about

1895, and a Ladies Aid program was introduced in 1911.

A second meeting house was built five miles south of South Whitley in 1902. It was then known as West Sugar Creek, but officially became independent in 1913 and was renamed Pleasant View.

The church building was redecorated in 1946 and a rededication service was held the last Sunday of June. Most of the roof was torn off during a storm in 1948, but the damage was quickly repaired. Another remodeling program was completed in 1960 which added Sunday school classrooms and a social room.

Heritage Day was observed Sept. 14, 1975, in celebration of Sugar Creek's 125th anniversary.

Syracuse
304 W. Main St.
Syracuse, IN 46567
Membership: 82

Syracuse was originally part of the Solomon's Creek (now Bethany) congregation. The original church building was constructed in 1887.

Syracuse became an independent congregation in 1907 with John W. Kitson, Abraham L. Neff, and John C. Stout as the first ministers.

Otho Warstler was called to the ministry and provided strong leadership along with John S. Neff and William Jones. The small congregation did well until sometime during the 1920s when membership began to dwindle and there was talk of disorganization.

In 1930, the District Mission Board stepped in. They called J. Edwin Jarboe to hold a series of revival meetings at the church. He met with great success and continued as the pastor for seven years. His tenure helped revive the congregation.

The church building was improved by adding a full basement and a balcony. An addition was made at the rear of the church building in 1947 which was originally used as a church parsonage.

A major remodeling project was completed in 1970.

Turkey Creek
72906 C.R. 13
Nappanee, IN 46550
Membership: 91

Turkey Creek Church of the Brethren has the distinction of being one of the oldest congregations in the state. It was the third church to be established in the Northern Indiana District when it was organized in 1838. The historic church building, located at Gravelton four miles east of Nappanee, dates from 1878.

Elder John Leatherman is credited with organizing the Turkey Creek District in the southern half of Elkhart County and the northern half of Kosciusko County. Born in Maryland in 1776, he moved to Tuscarawas County, Ohio, as a young man and remained there for 30 years. It was there that he was ordained. He moved to Elkhart County, Indiana, in 1836 and became part of the church in the Elkhart District (now West Goshen) before organizing the Turkey Creek District in 1838. Sunday meetings were held in the homes and barns of members and, occasionally, in school buildings. The first meetings were held at the home of Jacob Brumbaugh

The first meeting house was built in 1854 at the site of what is now Maple Grove Church of the Brethren. Turkey Creek was the local church sponsor of Annual Conference in 1852 when it was held at Baintertown between Goshen and New Paris. The Union Center territory was created in 1859 out of the northwest portion of the Turkey

Creek District. The 1854 building, known as the Whitehead Church, was included in the Union Center territory, so Turkey Creek members again began meeting in homes.

The present Turkey Creek building was constructed in 1878 and, although many improvements and additions have been made over the years, the main building would still be quite recognizable to the original builders. Indoor rest rooms were installed in 1952. A major renovation was completed in 1978, the centennial year for the building, which added an office, nursery, vestibule, and two all-purpose rooms.

The Turkey Creek congregation was instrumental in the growth of the church in northern Indiana from the 1850s to about 1918. At least nine congregations can trace their origins to Turkey Creek. They include Union Center, Maple Grove, Bethany (originally Solomon's Creek), North Winona, Bethel, Nappanee, Syracuse, New Salem, and New Paris.

The Turkey Creek congregation was also a sponsor for Annual Conference in 1882 held at Arnold's Grove, located southeast of the intersection of U.S. 6 and Ind. 15 north of Milford. It was at this conference that a major denominational division occurred which led to the formation of what is now the (Ashland) Brethren. About a fourth of the Turkey Creek membership left with the Progressives when the split occurred, but most of them or their descendants rejoined Turkey Creek in later years. Peter Stuckman, who was serving as minister at the time of the split, is given much of the credit for holding the congregation together during a trying time. The church was also ably served for 40 years (1913-1953) by Leroy Fisher in the free ministry.

A milestone was observed in 1988 when the Turkey Creek congregation celebrated their 150th anniversary, an achievement very few congregations in Indiana can match.

Union

10483 S.R. 17
Plymouth, IN 46563
Membership: 62

Union Church is an example of a congregation that wouldn't give up.

The church was originally organized in 1858 by a group of 40 people in Marshall County who took turns hosting meetings in their homes and barns. It included part of what had been the Pine Creek territory. Abraham Whitmer is credited with being the first preacher along with John Knisley, John Hoover, and Marvin Hamilton.

The first meeting house was built in 1871 four miles west and one mile south of Plymouth. Elder John Knisley's wife, Margaret, died prior to the completion of the interior of the new building. Her funeral was

the first service held in the church. Elder Knisley originally moved to the Elkhart area from Ohio, then moved to Marshall County. He is considered one of the primary motivating forces in the early church.

The congregation grew rapidly and established a mission point just across the county line in Starke County. A building had been constructed there by 1881, and Salem was organized as a separate congregation in 1895. It was disorganized, and the last council meeting held June 30, 1955.

A second new congregation was established in Plymouth in 1916 under the sponsorship of the Union Church. About half the Union membership joined the Plymouth Church when the new urban church was organized.

There was also a major loss of members in the 1890s when a number of families emigrated to the North Dakota area.

The 1920s brought a rapid decline in membership. Most of the members were farmers, and they began moving in large numbers to Plymouth and South Bend. The decline was so great that the congregation was disbanded in 1929.

The empty church building became the responsibility of the Plymouth Church trustees. It was well maintained and was used for occasional gatherings such as reunions and special services. In 1946, the Plymouth trustees, in consultation with the district, decided to sell the property, and an auction was scheduled. The night before the auction was to be held, a group of people who wanted to keep the building and reopen it as a church came to the trustees with their request. This last-minute appeal presented a real quandary. The auction had been widely advertised, and it was too late to call it off.

The plan that was agreed upon split the land and the building so that they would be sold separately. Most bidders were interested in the land, not the building. The building was auctioned first and sold to the group who wanted to reopen it as a church. This made the land worth very little to the other bidders since they would have to negotiate with the owners of the building who did not want to move it. The Union group was then able to purchase the land at a very good price.

Since that time the main building has remained intact, but a number of improvements have been made including a new entry, kitchen, balcony classrooms, a small social room, and rest rooms. Ground was broken in 1990 for a new fellowship and classroom building, and it was completed in 1992.

Special observances were held in 1958 on the 100th anniversary of the founding of the congregation, and again in 1971 for the centennial of the church building. The building has been designated a historical site in Marshall County.

Union Center
70535 C.R. 11, Route 1
Nappanee, IN 46550
Membership: 406

The Union Center Church was organized in 1859 by splitting off the northwest portion of the original Turkey Creek District. It included what at that time was known as the Whitehead Church, now known as Maple Grove, which is located southwest of New Paris. Meetings of the new congregation were held in several locations including the Whitehead Church and homes and schools in the area.

Henry Neff Sr. was the first elder of the congregation. He died Nov. 29, 1868, at the church just a few minutes after preaching a sermon.

A new church building was constructed in 1866 northeast of Nappanee on land donated by Levi Cripe. It was a large building and was unusual because it was built of bricks which were made at the construction site. It was one of the first brick churches in the area and was referred to for many years as the Brick Church. A diary kept by Levi Ulery indicates the congregation was meeting in the new church as early as April 1866.

A Sunday school was organized in 1879 and was very active from the beginning. At one time, Union Center was holding Sunday school in four locations, including at two schools.

The Union Center congregation supported regular services at both the Brick Church and the Whitehead Church from 1866 on. In 1906, a request was made to divide the territory and make Maple Grove (Whitehead) a separate congregation. The church council approved the request. Part of the division included giving one-third of the communion dishes to Maple Grove.

The attention of the congregation now focused on the Union Center site. A number of new groups were organized including a Ladies Aid Society in 1918 and a youth organization about 1930. Music became a major part of church life with a number of quartets, trios, and octets formed on an informal basis beginning in the 1920s. These groups have sung both at Union Center and at many other churches in the area. A piano was added in 1930 and the youth purchased the first organ in 1956.

The church was served by the free ministry until 1945 when Arthur Keim was hired as the first full-time pastor. A parsonage was built for the pastoral family in 1948-49.

A number of minor improvements to the building were made over the years, including moving the main entrance and the seating arrangement, but the Brick Church remained basically the same for about 90 years.

After two years of planning, the congregation voted on April 26, 1955, to move ahead with a major remodeling and addition project. A fund-raising drive was launched in January 1956 and final plans were adopted April 29, 1957.

A ground-breaking service was held Nov. 3, 1957. Following a week of evangelism meetings, the church was closed and the congregation met at the nearby Union Center School for a year. The first service in the newly remodeled building was held Nov. 2, 1958, in the Fellowship Hall. Services were held there until Feb. 1, 1959, when the first service was held in the remodeled sanctuary. It was doubly meaningful because it was also the 100th anniversary year of the formation of Union Center. The new facility was dedicated May 3, 1959, with Paul Robinson, president of Bethany Biblical Seminary, as the guest speaker.

Farm acreage adjacent to the church became available in 1960. The land was purchased by 10 members of the congregation and held in trust until the church was able to purchase it in 1967. A softball field has been developed on a portion of the land, and it is used by church and community groups in the area.

A library was started in 1970, and the church hired the first full-time associate pastor in 1979. The congregation sponsored the resettlement of a Vietnamese family in 1979 and a Cambodian family in 1980.

The 125th anniversary of the congregation was observed with special meetings Sept. 8-9, 1984.

Union Center is once again entering a major building project which will add considerable space to the building. Construction was begun in the spring of 1992.

Union Grove

900 N. and 100 W.
Muncie, IN
Membership: 67

Union Grove is one of the oldest congregations in Indiana, although it was originally known as Mississinewa.

Several Brethren families from Miami and Darke counties in Ohio moved to Delaware County in Indiana about 1838. Elder Isaac Karns visited the group that year and encouraged them to hold social and religious meetings. They did this on their own until the spring of 1841 when John Younce, a minister, moved to the area from Miami County, Ohio. The church was officially organized that same year and was known as the Mississinewa German Baptist Brethren Church.

It was from this fellowship that one of the influential families in the church in Indiana sprang—the Studebakers. George W. Studebaker was called to the ministry in 1842, followed by David and John S. Studebaker in 1843, and John Studebaker in 1847. The Studebakers were well known for missionary work travelling on horseback throughout middle and northern Indiana. John S. Studebaker moved to Cass County, Indiana, in 1846 and was instrumental in starting the Upper Deer Creek Church. George W. Studebaker moved to Fredonia, Kan., in 1882 and was active in starting a church there. David Studebaker moved to Miami County, Ohio, in 1855. John U. Studebaker, the last to be called to the ministry, served Mississinewa for over 50 years until his death in 1901.

Meetings were held in homes and barns. Three barns, in particular, were frequent sites for communion services. A barn owned by John U. Studebaker was located one mile south of Eaton on S.R. 3. It was dismantled in the winter of 1990 and taken to Lafayette where it was rebuilt into a log cabin house. Another barn owned by the family of Joseph Snider still stands five miles southwest of Eaton and is being used by Snider's descendants. A third barn located just west of the Snider farm was destroyed by a tornado in late 1947.

The first church building was constructed in 1857. It was located just west of Eaton along the Mississinewa River. It was later torn down and the property was sold to a gravel company.

The Mississinewa congregation branched out and began holding services in Shideler, Royerton, Hartford City, Matthews, and Union Grove. The Union Grove group was the most active and a church building was erected for them in 1885 three miles southwest of the original Mississinewa building. A Sunday school program was started in 1886.

Because the original building on the Mississinewa River had been abandoned and the congregation was meeting in the building constructed for the Union Grove group, the name was changed to Union Grove in 1933. The building was remodeled and a rededication service was held June 23, 1946.

The building has undergone a series of improvements since that time. An addition was constructed to the front of the church in 1957, the interior was paneled and new pews installed in 1964, and the members built a new fellowship hall and classrooms at the rear of the building in 1968.

Although Union Grove has experienced some difficult times in its history, the dedication of a few families has helped make it a source of spiritual growth in its community. A witness to that fact was the celebration of the church's 100th anniversary in its current location on Oct. 20, 1985.

Upper Fall Creek
Route 2, Box 274
Middletown, Ind. 47356
Membership: 46

The Upper Fall Creek Church grew out of the Nettle Creek congregation. Ministers from Nettle Creek traveled to the areas around Buck Creek and Upper Fall Creek near Middletown throughout the 1830s and early 1840s. This led to the formation of the Upper Fall Creek Church in 1845 with 25 charter members. George Hoover was elected the first minister of the new congregation and served for nearly 50 years.

A major part of the congregation's life was the Orphans and Old Folks Home. The Southern Indiana District began a campaign to raise funds for the home in 1881. The first building was erected in 1884 three miles north and two miles west of Sulphur Springs. A separate orphanage was constructed a few years later. Ownership was initially held by the district. The ownership was later transferred to congregations who originally contributed to the project in proportion to their contributions. Ownership was again transferred back to the district in 1917.

Because Upper Fall Creek was the nearest church, many of the residents of the home attended services there. The congregation was also involved in many programs at the home.

The home was closed in 1935-36 when there were only two residents remaining. The buildings and farm equipment were sold at a public sale in November 1935, and the farm was sold in 1936. In 1951, the district conference voted to join the other districts in Indiana in support of the Mexico Home.

The first church building for Upper Fall Creek was built in 1852 about two miles west of Middletown. A new brick church was built in Middletown in 1882.

The church was served by the free ministry until 1928 when ministers began to be paid for each sermon. Full-time pastoral support began in 1946.

A major renovation program was begun shortly after the congregation's centennial was observed Nov. 11, 1945. The project was completed in 1946.

A new parsonage was constructed in 1950.

A series of improvements to the church building have followed including a new front entry in 1957; remodeling of the basement in 1964; interior renovation in 1970; and new siding on the outside plus new carpet and pews in 1979.

Wabash

645 Bond St.
Wabash, IN 46992
Membership: 117

The first recorded meeting about the formation of the Wabash (City) Church was held in the home of Thomas Circle on July 3, 1913. Attending that meeting were Charles Circle, Henry Bolinger, Dorsey Brubaker, and Arthur Dillman. Those present laid plans for a series of revival meetings which were held in a tent on Walnut Street between Wabash and Huntington streets Sept. 7-28, 1913. D.M. Byerly and J.W. Norris led these services during which 13 were baptized and four were "reclaimed."

There were 29 charter members listed on Nov. 20, 1913. The little church had no building, but met regularly in rented quarters for the next seven years. The first meeting place was the Masonic Temple, then in a room on East Canal Street, and finally in a room above Case's Bakery at the corner of Hill and Wabash streets. The first Sunday school program was organized Dec. 17, 1913.

William Detrick, a licensed minister, moved to Wabash in 1914 to take a job as a teacher at Wabash High School. He immediately took an interest in the new church and became the first pastor in 1916.

A building at 375 Ohio St. was purchased in 1920, and the first service was held there on Easter Sunday, March 7, 1920. A series of revival meetings was held at the new location from April 4 to May 2 which increased the membership by 20. Some remodeling was completed in 1932, and a major renovation project was undertaken in 1937 followed by a rededication service.

A parsonage at 576 N. East St. was purchased in 1941 and remodeled in 1947. Property adjacent to the church and parsonage was purchased in 1948 and was used as a parish house.

The church was under control of the district mission board from its inception in 1913 until 1944 when it was officially organized as a separate congregation.

In the fall of 1954, the church embarked on its first every-member enlistment campaign called "Advance With Christ." It resulted in a significant growth in church membership and financial support. The annual campaign was changed in 1961 so that it was conducted before the annual budget was set. This move created a pattern for following years.

Land for a new parsonage was purchased at 1284 Falls Ave. on Feb. 1, 1956. Groundbreaking ceremonies were held March 17, 1957, and the new home was completed Nov. 19. The Rev. and Mrs. Carroll Petry were the first pastoral family to occupy the parsonage.

Land for a new church building was purchased at 645 Bond St., also on Feb. 1, 1956. Ground was broken on the first Sunday in July 1958. Most of the construction was completed with volunteer labor from the congregation. Even the work of issuing and selling bonds to finance the project was volunteered. The cornerstone was laid Nov. 23, 1958, and the first service in an incomplete building was held May 17, 1959. Work continued for several more months, and a formal dedication service was held Oct. 16, 1960.

A major event in the life of the congregation was the commissioning of the Rev. Carroll and Margie Petry for service as missionaries to Nigeria. They were commissioned in June 1963 and served a seven-year term.

Wakarusa

Spring and Union streets
Wakarusa, IN 46573
Membership: 53

The history of the Wakarusa Church is connected to the Baugo Church. Baugo originally covered portions of eastern St. Joseph County and western Elkhart County, including Wakarusa, when it was formed in 1868.

Because a number of Baugo members lived in or near Wakarusa, Baugo sponsored the construction of a church in Wakarusa in 1895. The two buildings were informally known as the Country House and the Town House, and about 150 people attended services at each location. A Sunday school program was formed by Baugo in the same year, so there has always been Sunday school at the Wakarusa location.

After 20 years, the Wakarusa group petitioned to become a separate organization. This was accomplished at a meeting Dec. 22, 1915, and Christian Metzler was elected the first elder.

The Wakarusa building has changed very little since it was first constructed. Renovation projects from 1965-68 remodeled the basement and entryway and a new heating system was installed, but the building would still be very familiar to the founders.

Walnut

5975 19th Road
Argos, IN 46501
Membership: 111

Walnut Church of the Brethren was officially organized in 1864 in southeastern Marshall County. The original 35 members met in homes and later used the Forest School, located one mile north of the present church building. Aaron Hoffman was elected minister and Henry Deardorff was elected soon after. Both men served until their deaths and are buried in Walnut Cemetery next to the church.

Because the school was not large enough to accommodate communion services, communion was held in five large barns in the community, although regular Sunday services continued to be held at the school.

A major step forward was taken in 1882 when the congregation purchased four acres of land at the site of the present church building for $200. A white frame building was erected. It included separate entrances: one for men and boys to enter and one for women and girls.

In the spring of 1913, the original church building was moved and a new masonry church building was constructed. Electric lights were added in 1928.

The congregation was served by free ministers until 1922. At that time, Hayward Claybaugh was hired on a part-time basis and the congregation has been served by salaried pastors ever since.

Fire destroyed the church on Jan. 2, 1944, and plans were immediately laid to rebuild. While construction progressed, the congregation met in a school building one mile west of the church site. The first worship services in the new building were held in January 1945, and dedication services were held March 18, 1945. It is this building that continues to serve the congregation.

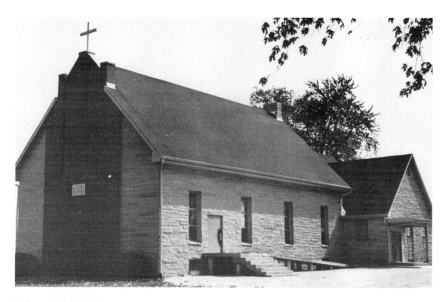

West Eel River

P.O. Box 306
Silver Lake, IN 46982
Membership: 93

The history of the West Eel River Church is tied to the Eel River congregation prior to 1913. A frame building was constructed about 1868 a short distance east of the current location and was known as the West House of the Eel River congregation. The group meeting here pioneered the Sunday school idea by opening a program in 1891.

A new masonry building was begun in 1909 located two miles east of Silver Lake. It was dedicated in June 1910.

A meeting to organize the congregation as a separate church was held June 21, 1913, with Samuel Lockrone presiding. The name West Eel River was chosen, and Hugh Miller was the first pastor. Early elders were George Swihart and T.D. Butterbaugh.

A project to add space for Sunday school rooms was begun in 1959, and the dedication service for this facility was held Nov. 20, 1960. A later renovation project reversed the direction of the sanctuary.

West Goshen

1200 Berkey Ave.
Goshen, IN 46526
Membership: 246

The West Goshen Church is a mother church in the truest sense of the term. It was founded by some of the earliest settlers in northern Indiana, and 28 congregations can trace their lineage to this congregation.

Elder Daniel Cripe was one of the first settlers on the Elkhart Prairie south and west of what became Goshen when he moved there from Montgomery County, Ohio, in 1829. Making the move with him were Jacob Cripe, Christ Stouder, and John Pipenger. Owen Opperman, writing in 1897, described Elder Cripe as, "...a man of medium height, was broad shouldered and well muscled; his face was smooth shaven and his complexion was light. Being of kindly disposition, he made friends and commanded the love and respect for all who knew him."

Cripe and his fellow settlers arrived in the spring of 1829 and quickly erected rude log cabins for shelter. They also constructed a wooden plow so crops could be raised to see them through the coming winter. It was decided the oldest should be the first one to use the plow, so Elder Cripe, according to tradition, became the first white man to plow a furrow on the Elkhart Prairie.

Elder Cripe traveled to Montgomery County, Ohio, early in 1830 and convinced several others to return with him to Elkhart County. This included his son, Samuel Cripe, Martin Weybright, Jacob Studebaker, and John Cripe, Elder Cripe's nephew. Later that spring, John Cripe's daughter, Roseanna, was born. She was the first child born among the Brethren in northern Indiana.

With about 16 Brethren scattered throughout the area, Elder Cripe gathered them together in 1830 and delivered the first sermon to a Brethren group in northern Indiana. He also formally organized the Elkhart Church that year and was elected presiding elder and minister. Charter members of the organization included Elder Cripe and his wife, Magdelena; John Miller; Martin Weybright; Samuel Cripe; John Cripe; Elizabeth Stutsman; Mr. and Mrs. John Woolsey; and Jacob Cripe. The original territory included all of Elkhart County.

The first love feast was held in late summer 1830. No beef was available in the wilderness, so Elder Cripe donated a ewe lamb, the only one he had. About 20 people participated at Elder Cripe's home and some declared it was the most enjoyable they had ever attended.

As more settlers arrived, the demands of ministry became greater. Elder Cripe declared he needed help, so Jacob Studebaker and Martin Weybright were elected to the ministry. They were the first ministers ordained in northern Indiana.

The original Elkhart Church territory began to be divided as new congregations were formed. Turkey Creek became the first in 1838 in southern Elkhart County; Rock Run was organized in the eastern portion of the county in 1850; and Yellow Creek was organized in the west in 1856.

The year 1859 was a landmark year for the congregation. This was the year that Elder Cripe died at the age of 87. He and Magdelena were originally buried in Dierdorf Cemetery at the eastern edge of the Elkhart Prairie. Their remains were moved in 1961 to the West Goshen Cemetery next to the church where the spot is marked with their original headstones and a large, new marker.

It was also in 1859 that the first meeting house for the Elkhart Church was erected. The land was purchased from Jacob and Catherine Cripe for $1. Little is known about the original meeting house erected at this site, and there are no known photos. It has been described as a one-room, white frame building with a large double door in front and a single door in the rear. There is also some indication that there was a second building on the site for a time. It was referred to as the dwelling house and was evidently used for a kitchen and for overnight lodging of guests.

Two acres of land for a cemetery were purchased in 1863. The property was located adjacent to the church and was purchased from the Cripes for $100. This was the start of what has since become the

West Goshen Cemetery. It was deeded to the City of Goshen in 1975.

Even though a meeting house had been built, love feast and communion services continued to be held in the barns of members of the congregation well into the 1880s. It is believed the first love feast to be held at the church was in May 1883.

The Old Order division in 1881 resulted in the loss of a few members, but many later returned. The division with the Progressives (Ashland Brethren) in 1882 also resulted in the loss of a few members, but most remained with the original Elkhart German Baptist Church.

In 1885, the congregation decided to build a new, larger meeting house. The new church was built of brick and became a source of some minor controversy over an incident involving the windows.

Valentine Berkey was appointed to secure materials for the project. He wanted arched, cathedral-type windows and doors for the new building, but also knew the congregation would never approve them. He had the frames built in two sections: the lower section was of the standard rectangular shape and the top section was arched. These top sections were kept out of sight as construction progressed. When the bricks reached the tops of the rectangular sections, the arched tops were installed and bricked in place before anyone could voice an objection. Thus, the new church became the first German Baptist Church in Indiana to have cathedral-type windows and doors.

The dedication service for the new building was held in October 1886. A newspaper account of the time reported 800 people attended brought there by 285 teams of horses. About 200 people had to stand outside the church building during the service.

The old church building was sold for $40, moved to another site and turned into a private home.

A Sunday school program was established in the new building in 1890.

An acetylene gas lighting system was installed in early 1902. The system caused an explosion on the evening of April 1, 1906, which was heard four miles away. Three members of the church were injured but later recovered. A small addition at the south end of the building, however, was blown to pieces. Electric lights were installed in the church the following September.

In 1915, the name of the church was changed from Elkhart to West Goshen. The Elkhart City Church was organized in 1897, and there had been confusion ever since.

The 100th anniversary of the congregation was celebrated Nov. 27, 1930, with Otho Winger as the featured speaker. The first snowstorm of the season hit the same day which prevented many from attending.

West Goshen had always been served by the free ministry, but in

1943 the council voted to pay ministers $3 per sermon and $300 a year to the presiding elder. The final step toward a full-time pastor was discussed for several years before David Berkebile was finally hired March 13, 1949.

Another project which had been discussed for about three years was the construction of a building to be used by church groups for social activities. Construction was finally approved March 30, 1948, and the resulting building became known as the church cabin.

A two-story education wing was constructed at the rear of the church building in 1955 and dedicated March 18, 1956. This was followed in 1965 by a remodeling project for the sanctuary. A dedication service was held June 13, 1965.

The congregation experienced severe difficulties during the mid-1970s which led to the loss of a number of members. Most of the controversy centered around the charismatic movement, primarily through a group known as the Faith Assembly (also known as the Glory Barn) in Kosciusko County, which affected several Brethren congregations in the area. Following the resignation of Curtiss Weddle as pastor in 1975, Lester Fike served as an interim pastor. He is given much credit for helping the congregation re-establish its footing. Charles F. Stouder was then hired as the next full-time pastor.

The 150th anniversary of the congregation was celebrated in 1980. A major part of this observance was the publication of a detailed history of the church written by Dean Henry.

West Goshen has long been involved in outreach projects and has been one of the strongest supporters of district and denominational programs. The church has supported the resettlement of at least seven refugee families from Europe and Asia since the 1950s.

One of the best known people to come from West Goshen was Anna Warstler. The church supported her through three tours on the mission field in India from 1931 to 1955. She then worked in the Elgin, Ill., offices for 14 years until her retirement. She was honored at a special service at West Goshen in 1970.

West Manchester

P.O. Box 66
North Manchester, IN 46962
Membership: 81

West Manchester traces its lineage to the old Eel River Church through the Manchester congregation.

The original Eel River Church was founded in 1838 and covered a large territory around North Manchester which has since been divided

into several congregations. The first division in 1852 resulted in the
establishment of the Manchester congregation. This group built a log
meeting house three miles east of North Manchester in 1852. It was
replaced in 1858 by a larger building which was constructed on the
present site of the West Manchester Church. It was here that Annual
Conference was held in 1878 with an estimated 15,000 to 20,000 people
in attendance. Sarah Major, the first woman preacher in the Church of
the Brethren, was one of the primary speakers. Her appearance attracted a great deal of attention in the area from non-Brethren as well as
Brethren.

A few members were lost when the Old Order German Baptist
Brethren split from the denomination in 1881, and a few more left the
following year in the split with the Progressives (Ashland Brethren).

The old frame building was replaced in 1891 with a larger brick
building which still forms the basis for the present West Manchester
meeting house. It was dedicated in August 1891. Elder R.H. Miller, who
was one of the primary backers of the new building, lived just long
enough to see his dream completed. His death on March 8, 1892,
resulted in one of the first funerals to be held in the new building.

The official division with Manchester occurred in 1911. The
Manchester congregation had constructed a second building in the town
of Manchester in 1881. The group that remained with that church
adopted the name Manchester while the country group originally

adopted the name North Manchester. The name was changed soon after to West Manchester to help eliminate confusion with the name of the town. Otho Winger was chosen as the first elder at an organizational meeting in September 1911.

A major remodeling program renovated the old building and added new space in 1953-54. Vernon F. Schwalm was the speaker at a dedication service held April 25, 1954. A district conference was hosted at the newly renovated building in 1956.

White Branch

Route 2
Hagerstown, IN 47346
Membership: 75

For most of its long history, the White Branch Church was part of the Nettle Creek Church. Nettle Creek covered a wide-ranging territory around Hagerstown from the time it was formed in 1820. The first church building was constructed southwest of Hagerstown in 1844. It was a good location, but travel for those in outlying areas was often difficult in the spring and winter months.

By the early 1850s, there was strong sentiment for Nettle Creek to establish other points of worship to make it easier for some of the members to attend services. One of those points was White Branch.

Land was purchased five miles northwest of Hagerstown from John and Nancy Clapper along White Branch, a tributary of Nettle Creek. Part of the purchase agreement gave the church the right to use spring water from a spring located on the Clapper family property. A small chapel was constructed on this land in 1858.

Services were held on the first and third Sundays of each month. The members were expected to attend services on the second and fourth Sundays at Nettle Creek, which was known locally as the Brick House. All council meetings and love feasts were held at the Brick House.

The first Sunday school program was organized in 1873, but the Nettle Creek Council ruled that Sunday school on the second and fourth Sundays could only be held at 3 p.m. so that all members would be free to come to the Brick House for morning services. For many years, Sunday school was held only from April 1 to about Sept. 30 because of cold winters and bad roads. About the turn of the century, the program was changed to an "evergreen" Sunday school with classes held all year.

Revival meetings became an early tradition. The meetings were usually held during the winter months because that was when farmers were not so busy and because no special meetings were held at the Brick House during that time. The meetings were often as much social events as religious gatherings, and the small church was usually filled to the bursting point.

Daniel Bowman was named the first elder in charge of White Branch. He was also the first Sunday school superintendent and was primarily responsible for pulpit duties. Carl Hilbert was named to share preaching duties with Elder Bowman in 1918. Brother Hilbert took over most of the preaching in 1939 when Bowman resigned. Hilbert continued in his largely free pastoral role until 1954.

Present members of White Branch often view their forbearers as "progressive" and a group which continually pushed the boundaries with the church council at Nettle Creek. One example is Sunday school. After 48 years of abiding by the "afternoon rule" on the second and fourth Sundays, they asked in 1921 for permission to hold Sunday school every week during the morning. The request was granted, and the first of the expanded morning classes was held Sept. 10, 1922.

White Branch was back again in 1925, this time with the audacious request to allow them to use a piano in the church. Permission was eventually granted, but not until 1933, which gives some idea as to how controversial the move was. Nettle Creek itself did not get a piano until several years later.

One of the reasons White Branch was an early advocate of musical instruments in the church may have been the musical talent of the

Abram Bowman family. Two brothers, Daniel E. and Charles, and their sons, George and Elmer, respectively, formed the Bowman Quartet. They were well known throughout the area of Hagerstown, Mooreland and New Castle for their singing at church services, weddings and funerals. Charles, George, and Elmer led singing at White Branch for many years. They began a musical tradition which has been a strong force in the church for most of its history. Descendants of the Bowman family are still musical leaders in the congregation.

The 1858 church building was completely rebuilt in 1904. Another remodeling program was undertaken in the early 1920s which added a balcony. Electricity was installed in 1927, and a basement was dug in 1936.

The 1950s brought many changes to White Branch. One of the most significant was its organization as a separate congregation. The church had begun taking on more responsibility after Carl Hilbert became the primary pastor in 1939, including keeping its own finances and holding its own elections. Finally in April 1954, a request was made to the General Council to form a committee to study the advisability of dividing the Nettle Creek congregation. That committee reported division would be feasible, but the decision should be left up to the individual groups. A majority voted to reorganize, and the group northwest of Hagerstown voted to retain the name White Branch. The new congregation was officially recognized with the seating of two delegates at the 1955 district conference in Anderson.

After serving faithfully since first being called in 1918, Carl Hilbert resigned as pastor in 1954. Russell McInnis was called as the first full-time, paid pastor for the congregation. He began his service on Sept. 1, 1954.

Plans were laid in 1954 for the construction of a larger church building. The project added several classrooms, a kitchen, and a baptistry and was completed in 1956. Much of the labor was donated, and a large percentage of the cost was paid for with funds raised through the operation of a food tent at the Mooreland Fair over a period of about 20 years.

The same source of funding was used to pay the majority of the cost for a church parsonage which was constructed in 1962.

The centennial of the White Branch congregation was observed at special services in 1958, and Carl Hilbert was honored for his many years of service on Nov. 5, 1972.

A new kitchen was built in 1983. Grace Hilbert had established a kitchen fund a number of years earlier, and it grew slowly with the income from various projects and offerings. The new kitchen was almost entirely planned and financed by the women of the church.

Windfall

Route 1, Box 454A
Sharpsville, IN 46068
 corner Meridian Road and C.R. 350 N.
Membership: 45

Thirty charter members were part of the Windfall Church when it was
organized in May 1896. It was carved out of the southern part of the
Greentown territory, and the first ministers were T.J. Stout, Thomas
Rogers, and F.M. Bogue. Some of the original members had moved to
Indiana from Missouri

The first church building was constructed in 1897 and served the
congregation much in its original form until 1946. In that year, the
members donated all the work for a major remodeling project which
included a new basement and heating system.

Another project in 1967 added a new entry and foyer, classrooms,
an office, and rest rooms. The belfry was removed due to its poor
condition. The church bell was stored until 1987 when it was mounted
on a special base with a memorial plaque listing the names of many of
those who have served the church over the years.

Lucy Blessing gave the church one acre of land adjacent to the
building. The land was used to enlarge the parking lot and create a
recreational area.

The interior of the church was redecorated following a fire in
August 1988.

Windfall was served by the free ministry until 1960 when Thomas Davis was hired as the first salaried pastor.

A recent special event was a homecoming revival Oct. 14-17, 1991.

Yellow Creek
65575 C.R. 11
Goshen, IN 46526
Membership: 180

Yellow Creek Church was formally organized in 1856 from territory that was originally part of the Elkhart Church (now West Goshen).

Some of the first preaching in this area west of Goshen was by Elder John Miller, an early settler on the Elkhart Prairie. He was born in Pennsylvania in 1787 and later moved to Montgomery County, Ohio, where he was called to the ministry. He settled on the Elkhart Prairie in 1835 where he worked with Elder Daniel Cripe in establishing the church in the new territory. The formation of the Yellow Creek congregation under his leadership preceded his death by only a few months. Many current Yellow Creek members are descendants of John Miller.

The fledgling congregation worshipped in homes until the first meeting house was built in 1867 at the same location of the present building. A second meeting house was built in the northern part of the territory at about the same time. This led to the formation of the Elkhart Valley congregation in 1870.

The division of the Old Order Brethren in 1881 was extremely hard on Yellow Creek. Elder Samuel Leer and Benjamin Burkett, a minister in the second degree, left with 11 other church officials. The only official who remained with the original denomination was John Nusbaum, a deacon.

At that time, there was no church polity governing what happened to church property in the case of a division. The story is told locally that Nusbaum attended a meeting with those who were leaving to join the Old Order Brethren. It was agreed that the first person at the church the following day would retain possession.

Nusbaum rose early and rode his horse to the Yellow Creek Church well before dawn. He found the church empty when he arrived and was standing in the doorway when the first of the Old Order representatives appeared. The Yellow Creek building thus remained with the German Baptist Brethren. The Old Order German Baptist Brethren eventually formed the Morningstar congregation and built another meeting house a short distance away where the group is still active.

With this crisis of leadership, elders from the surrounding area pitched in to handle the preaching duties. Nusbaum was called to the ministry in 1883 followed by Hiram Roose in 1884 and Eli Roose in 1887. This nucleus of leadership helped rebuild the shattered congregation at Yellow Creek.

The first Sunday school program was organized in 1882.

A major event in the life of the congregation was the death of Harvey Schwalm who succumbed to typhoid fever in 1922 at the age of 40. He was elected to the ministry at Yellow Creek in 1910 and was the elder in charge and only minister at the time of his death. His funeral was held on a Sunday afternoon and over 2,000 people were in attendance.

The original building was extensively remodeled in 1921. A full basement was added, and the building was turned one-fourth way around. Five Sunday school classrooms were also built.

A number of improvements have followed through the years, including major renovations in 1955 and 1969 which gave the church its present look.

A new parsonage was constructed adjacent to the church in 1964.

Yellow Creek has long been active in churchwide programs. At least 30 people have participated in some type of alternative or volunteer service. One of the first three heifers donated to Heifer Project was given by Bessie Burns, a Yellow Creek member at the time.

The 125th anniversary of the congregation was celebrated Nov. 14 and 15, 1981, with Dale Brown as the guest speaker.

Appendix 1

Research has turned up a long list of names that have been used by Indiana churches since the first Dunkard pioneers entered the wilderness soon after 1800. This list was compiled by Ferne Baldwin, archivist at Manchester College.

The list includes all the names we have been able to find in northern and middle Indiana. We are confident about the completeness of the list in this area. Other churches were organized in the southern part of the state, but research on further names is not yet completed. We believe this is the most complete list of church and meeting house names now available.

Churches marked with • were active in 1991

• *Agape* (1968)—From Pleasant Hill. Located four miles northwest of Fort Wayne on Carroll Road. Northern

• *Andrews* (1855)—Originally named Antioch from Salamonie Territory. Second house—Dora, Ogan's Creek in 1873. Yoked with Markle in 1951. Located in Huntington County. Middle and South/Central.

• *Antioch* (1860)—Originally known as Killbuck. Dora House, Summitville and Pleasant Run all abandoned by 1890. Name changed to Antioch in 1946. Located five miles northwest of Muncie in Delaware County. Split by charismatic movement in 1969. Southern and South/Central.

- *Arcadia* (1856)—From Stony Creek originally known as Cicero Church. Located 1/4-mile east of Arcadia in Hamilton County. Southern and South/Central.

Auburn (1917)—From Cedar Creek and Cedar Lake. Disorganized in 1982. Located in DeKalb County. Northern.

Auton Chapel Mission—Located in St. Joseph County. Northern.

- *Bachelor Run* (1838)—From division of Lower Deer Creek. Lost some members to New Dunker movement 1848; organized Howard 1852; lost 126 to Old Orders 1882, and some to Progressives. Organized Flora 1911. Located five miles southeast of Flora in Carroll County. Middle and South/Central.

- *Baugo* (1868)—From Elkhart (West Goshen) and St. Joseph. Located one mile west and two miles north of Wakarusa in Elkhart County. Northern.

- *Beacon Heights* (1952)—From Lincolnshire. Northern.

Bear Creek—Now Portland, located in Jay County. South/Central.

Beaver Creek (1873)—From Pike Creek and Buffalo. Moved to Buffalo 1930. Name changed to Buffalo in 1932. Located in Pulaski County. Middle and South/Central.

Beaver Dam (1856)—From Squirrel Creek (Roann). Weakened in 1882. Disorganized in 1913. Located six miles west and one mile south of Claypool, Kosciusko County. Northern.

- *Beech Grove* (ca. 1850)—Formerly Stony Creek. Beech Grove and Sugar Creek separated 1878 but later reunited. Located four-and-1/2 miles north of Fortville in Hamilton County. Noblesville organized but closed. Southern and South/Central

- *Bethany* (1856)—From Turkey Creek. Called Solomon's Creek from 1856 to 1912. Organized New Paris 1918; Syracuse 1917; Bethel 1884; Name changed to Bethany 1913. Located four miles south of New Paris in Elkhart County. Northern.

Bethany (1905)—Fifth house built at Ladoga. Disorganized 1921.

- *Bethel* (1884)—From Solomon's Creek. Organized New Salem 1911 and Pleasant View 1915. Located in Milford, Kosciusko County. Northern.

Bethel (1868)—Third house built at Ladoga. Located one mile north of Ladoga.

Bethel—Early congregation in Harrison County. Moved to Disciples of Christ by 1839.

- *Bethel Center* (1886)—Located two miles west of Hartford City in Blackford County. Second house in Hartford City 1895, combined 1916 and separated again 1924. Town house closed 1929. Middle and South/Central.

Berrien (1867)—Northern part of Portage. Organized as Berrien until 1922; name changed to Buchanan 1925. Located in Berrien County, Mich. Northern.

Black River—On Northern District Meeting roll in 1869. Located in Marshall County.

- *Blissville* (1912)—From Pine Creek. Center House organized 1917; Oregon House and Grovertown House in Starke County. Oregon closed ca. 1925. Located seven miles northwest of Plymouth, Marshall County. Northern.

Bloomfield Mission—From Peru. May have been independent briefly.

Blue Creek (1887)—From Walnut Level. Disorganized 1905 to Walnut Level. Located in Adams County. Northern.

- *Blue River* (1852)—Located one-and-1/2 miles south of Merriam. Organized Columbia City 1960. Noble and Whitley counties. Northern.

Bowman School—House of Monticello.

- *Bremen* (1866)—From Yellow River (Mount Pleasant) in Bremen (Marshall County) after 1913. Northern.

Brick—House of Nettle Creek

Bristol Mission—Mission of West Goshen 1908-1913. Located in Bristol. Northern.

Buchanan—Name changed from Berrien in 1925. Disorganized 1963. Northern.

• *Buck Creek* (1845)—From Nettle Creek. Founded Osage Church in Kansas. Located six miles northwest of Mooreland in Henry County. Southern and South/Central.

• *Buffalo* (1873)—Formerly Beaver Creek. Moved to Buffalo 1930. Name changed 1932. Located in Pulaski County. Middle and South/Central.

Burnetts Creek (1898)—Later Burnettsville. Name changed after 1911.

• *Burnettsville* (1898)—Formerly Burnetts Creek, from Monticello. Located in Burnettsville, White County. Middle and South/Central.

Bush Creek—By 1868 but disorganized by 1882. Located seven miles east of Muncie.

Camden (1872)—Became Hickory Grove in 1914.

• *Camp Creek* (1879)—From Yellow River (Mount Pleasant). Located five miles north of Etna Green, Kosciusko County. Northern.

Cart Creek (1914)—From Somerset. Disorganized 1960 to Sweetser. Located three miles north of Sweetser in Wabash County. Middle and South/Central.

• *Cedar Creek* (1853)—Divided in 1873 to Pleasant Hill, Cedar Lake, Little St. Joe, and Cedar Creek. Located four miles southwest of Garrett. Northern.

• *Cedar Lake* (1874)—From Cedar Creek. Formed Auburn 1917; Pleasant Chapel 1921. Located seven miles northwest of Auburn in DeKalb County. Northern.

Christian—Unknown founding date. Disorganized between 1873-1886. Northern.

Center (1917)—Southern Pine Creek organized as Blissville 1917;

northern Blissville organized as Center. Disorganized 1971. Located just east of Walkerton. Northern.

• *Christ Our Shepherd*—District Extension Project. Became a Fellowship in 1991. Located in Greenwood. South/Central.

Cicero—Now Arcadia.

Clear Creek (1850)—Formed Huntington Country and Huntington City. Disorganized 1982. Located in Huntington County. Middle and South/Central.

• *Columbia City*—1875 from Blue River; disorganized 1927. Reorganized 1961. Lost 22 members to independent group 1976. Located in Columbia City, Whitley County. Northern.

Columbus (1860)—Became Lower Fall Creek. Located in Madison County.

• *Communion Fellowship* (1984)—Joint with Mennonite Church. Located in Goshen, Elkhart County. Northern.

Cool Spring (1848)—First meeting house of Ladoga. Located in Montgomery County. Southern.

Courter (1872)—From Mexico. Disorganized 1916. Located in Miami County. Middle.

Copper Creek (1919)—House of Santa Fe. Disorganized 1922 to Plevna and Santa Fe. Located in Miami County. Middle.

Cottage Grove (1875)—House of Four Mile. Southern.

Crest Manor (1877)—From house known as Ulery House located two miles north of South Bend. Became South Bend, then South Bend First 1905. Relocated and changed name to Crest Manor 1963. Northern.

Deer Creek (ca. 1830)—Now Bachelor Run. Southern and South/Central.

Delphi (1920)—From a mission. Disorganized 1930. Some continued to meet and later formed Pittsburg. Located in Carroll County. Middle.

Denmark (1870)—First house of Lick Creek. See Maple Grove. Owen County.

Dora—House of Killbuck, later Antioch.

Dora—Second meeting house of Antioch (Andrews). Located seven miles southwest of Andrews.

Edna Mills—Third house of Rossville 1873-1902.

• *Eel River* (1838)—1838-1852 divided to Manchester, Spring Creek, part of Ogan's Creek. Divided 1913 to West Eel River, Plunge Creek and Eel River. Eel River sometimes called Middle House. Located five miles northwest of North Manchester on S.R. 14, Kosciusko County. Middle and South/Central.

Eight Mile (1852)—From Salamonie. Became Markle in 1902. Located in Huntington County. Middle and South/Central.

Elkhart (1830)—Divided 1837 to create Turkey Creek; 1850 to create Rock Run; Yellow Creek 1856; Little Pine 1950. Became West Goshen, 1915. Located in Goshen, Elkhart County. Northern.

• *Elkhart City* (1897)—From Elkhart Valley. First called Oak Park. Located in Elkhart, Elkhart County. Northern.

• *Elkhart Valley* (1870)—From Elkhart and Yellow Creek. Located two miles south of Elkhart, Elkhart County. Northern.

Elkhart—*We Care Fellowship* (not organized) ca. 1970.

• *English Prairie* (1864)—Originally named Fawn River. Pigeon River was separate 20 years. Located one-and-1/2 miles southeast of Brighton, LaGrange County. Northern.

Fairview (1872)—From North Fork (Pyrmont). Old Orders claimed some. Disorganized 1969. Located two miles north and one mile west of Pettit, Tippecanoe County. Southern and South/Central.

Fall Creek—See Upper Fall Creek and Lower Fall Creek. Southern.

Fawn River—See English Prairie

First Church of the Brethren—See Northview.

Flat Rock (1897)—Disorganized 1901. Located near Monroeville.

- *Flora* (1911)—Called Deer Creek to 1838, then Bachelor Run to 1911. Located in Carroll County. Middle and South/Central.

- *Florence* (1931)—From Shipshewana. Located in St. Joseph County, Mich. Northern.

Fort Wayne (1897)—From Flat Rock District. Name changed to Lincolnshire 1952. Located in Fort Wayne, Allen County. Northern.

Fountain (1906)—Formed as a district project. Sometimes called The Fountain. Located five miles northwest of Holton, Ripley County. Middle and South/Central.

- *Four Mile* (1809)—Divided to Lower and Upper Four Mile, but reunited about 1855. Organized West Florence House 1886; Whitewater House 1908; New Bethel separated 1913. Located in Fayette County. Cottage Grove and Lower Four Mile disorganized in 1933. Located in Union County. Now yoked with Richmond. Southern and South/Central.

- *Goshen City* (1905)—From Rock Run and Elkhart (West Goshen). Northern.

Grace—See Northview.

Greentown (ca. 1875)—Name changed to Plevna. Became Dunkard in 1926. Located north of Greentown, Howard County.

- *Guernsey* (1967)—From Monticello. Operated in own building since 1913. Yoked with Pike Creek. Located seven miles north of Monticello, White County. Middle and South/Central.

Harrison County—A mission ca. 1911.

Hartford City (1895)—Second house of Bethel Center 1924. Separated from Bethel Center, disorganized 1929. Sometimes called Hartford. Middle and South/Central.

Hawpatch (1867)—Name changed to Topeka 1913. Located in LaGrange County. Northern.

• *Hickory Grove* (1872)—From Walnut Level, originally known as Camden. Name changed to Hickory Grove 1914. Located three miles south of Pennville, Jay County. Middle and South/Central.

Highland (ca. 1885)—Closed to Akron 1930. Located two miles south and one mile east of Akron, Fulton County. See Akron.

Hillisburg (ca. 1890)—From Howard. Located 10 miles east of Frankfort. Sometimes called Hillsburg. Located in Clinton County.

• *Howard County* (1852)—From Bachelor Run. Located first on Wild Cat Creek, then 11 miles west of Kokomo, Howard County. In Great Divide about one-third became Old Order. Southern and South/Central.

Huntington Country (1871)—From Clear Creek. Lost members to the Progressives. Disorganized 1924 to Clear Creek. Located six miles northwest of Huntington, Huntington County. Middle and South/Central.

• *Huntington City* (1899)—From Clear Creek, Markle, Salamonie and Huntington Country. Middle and South/Central

• *Iglesia Evanglica Emanuel* (1986)—Hispanic congregation organized with Mennonite Church. Located in South Bend, St. Joseph County. Northern.

Indianapolis—Name often used in records until 1955. See Northview.

Jonesboro—Later Summit or Summitville. Located in Madison County. Southern.

Kempton (ca. 1910)—Located in town of Kempton. Southern.

Kewanna (1890)—Disorganized 1925 to Logansport. Located three miles north of Kewanna, Fulton County. Middle and South/Central.

Killbuck (1860)—Included Dora House, Summitville, Pleasant Run, and house west of Muncie. All abandoned by 1890. Name changed to Antioch 1946. Located in Delaware County. Southern.

- *Kokomo* (1916)—From Howard and Plevna, Howard County. Middle and South/Central.

Ladoga (1826)—Originally known as Racoon Creek District. First meeting house Cool Spring 1848; second house 1861. Little Walnut organized 1892; disorganized 1923. Third house 1869; Bethel 1888. Mount Pleasant organized 1904, then merged with Ladoga 1937. Bethany separate 1894, disorganized 1921. Name changed to Ladoga from Racoon Creek 1904. Disorganized in 1974. Located in Montgomery County. Southern.

- *Lafayette* (1946)—Organized by students and persons moving into Lafayette. Located in Lafayette, Tippecanoe County. Southern and South/Central

Landess—See Landessville.

Landessville (1860)—From Somerset. At first known as West Marion. Organized in 1911 as separate; disorganized 1929. Middle.

- LaPorte (1869)—From Portage. Rossburg House used 1873 to 1923; building in Waterford used 1895-1920. Moved to LaPorte 1923. Located in LaPorte County. Northern.

Liberty (1819)—Originally known as Lost River. Located in Orange County near Orleans. Became part of Hostetler schism; Disciples of Christ by 1830s.

- *Liberty Mills* (1913)—From Eel River. Formerly called Plunge Creek Chapel or East House of Eel River. Located in Wabash County. Middle and South/Central.

- *Lincolnshire* - See Fort Wayne. Name changed to Lincolnshire 1952.

Lick Creek (1852)—First house called Denmark; second house called Maple Grove. Denmark became Progressive; closed 1920. Lick Creek name dropped 1920. Maple Grove disorganized 1966. Located in Owen County. Southern.

- Little Pine (1950)—Formerly Pine Creek House or North House of West Goshen. Located six miles east of Elkhart, Elkhart County. Northern.

Little St. Joe (1873)—From division of Cedar Creek. Disorganized 1914. Northern.

Little Walnut (1892)—A house of Ladoga. Disorganized 1923, most to Ladoga. Located in Putnam County. Southern.

• *Locust Grove* (1955)—A house of Nettle Creek. Located five miles southwest of Hagerstown, Henry County. Southern and South/ Central.

• *Logansport* (1906)—Originally with Adamsboro. Adamsboro closed 1913. Located in Cass County. Middle and South/Central.

• *Loon Creek* (1912)—From Salamonie; had been meeting since 1850. Located five miles southeast of Huntington, Huntington County. Middle and South/Central.

Lost River—See Liberty.

• *Lower Deer Creek* (1830)—Originally known as Deer Creek. Divided to Lower Deer Creek and Bachelor Run 1838; 1848 division to Dunkard Brethren. Flora and Upper Deer Creek separate 1854. 1881 126 members to Old Orders and some to Progressives. Also Nebo House two miles west of Camden. Located in Carroll County. Middle and South/Central.

Lower Fall Creek (1860)—From Upper Fall Creek. First called Columbus. Disorganized. Located five-and-1/2 miles south of Anderson. Southern and South/Central.

Lower Four Mile (1813)—Divided from Four Mile. Reunited about 1855. Southern.

• *Manchester* (1852)—From Eel River. West Manchester separated 1911. Called Walnut Street for a time, now Manchester. Located in Wabash County. Middle and South/Central.

Maple Corner—See Prairie Creek.

• *Maple Grove* (1906)—From Elkhart; later Turkey Creek until 1859, then Union Center. Second oldest house in northern Indiana. Located southwest of New Paris, Elkhart County. Northern.

Maple Grove (1852)—Originally known as Lick Creek. First house Denmark; second house Maple Grove. All Lick Creek until 1916. Denmark discontinued 1920 and name Lick Creek changed to Maple Grove. Disorganized 1966. Located six-and-1/2 miles north of Clay City, Owen County. Southern and South/Central.

• *Marion* (1911)—Originally known as West Marion from Landessville, Grant County. Name changed to Marion about 1960. Middle and South/Central.

• *Markle* (1852)—From Salamonie as Eight Mile. Became Markle 1902. Bought house from Free Will Baptist 1887. Lost some to Progressives. Forced to relocate 1955 to west edge of Markle, Huntington County. Middle and South/Central.

• *Mexico* (1838)—Organized Roann, Beaverdam, Kewanna, Peru, Adamsboro and Logansport, Mud Lake, and Courter. House at Wooleytown. Located in Miami County. Middle and South/Central.

• *Michigan City* (1932)—From mission of LaPorte. Located in Michigan City, LaPorte County. Northern.

Middle House—name used at times for Eel River.

• *Middlebury* (1913)—From Pleasant Valley, first as a house of Pleasant Valley. Located in Middlebury, Elkhart County. Northern.

Middle Fork of the Wild Cat (1845)—Later called Rossville. Southern and South\Central.

Middletown (1917)—From second house of Upper Fall Creek. Disorganized 1965. Located in Henry County. Southern and South/Central.

Milford (1884)—Within Solomon's Creek. See Bethel.

Mississinewa (1841)—Originally met in a house west of Eaton. Established Union Grove House 1885. Bush Creek separate by 1868 but gone by 1882. Name changed to Union Grove 1933. Located in Delaware County. Southern.

Monticello (1865)—From Bachelor Run. Seven houses in 1887: Pike Creek, Burnetts Creek, Paton, Oak Grove, Winamac, Bowman School House and Guernsey. Guernsey and Pike Creek separated 1967;

Burnetts Creek organized 1898; all others disappeared. Located in White County. Middle and South/Central.

* *Mount Pleasant* (1848)—Organized as Yellow River. Name changed to Mount Pleasant 1926. Located five miles northwest of Bourbon, Marshall County. Northern.

Mount Pleasant (1904)—From fourth meeting house of Ladoga. Merged with Ladoga 1937. Located four-and-1/2 miles east of Ladoga, Montgomery Co. Southern and South/Central.

Mud Lake (1896)—From Mexico. Disorganized about 1914.

* *Muncie* (1898)—Started by four churches surrounding Muncie: Mississinewa (Union Grove), Killbuck (Antioch), Upper Fall Creek and Buck Creek. Located in Muncie, Delaware County. Southern and South/Central.

* *Nappanee* (1899)—From second meeting house of Turkey Creek. Located in Nappanee, Elkhart County. Northern.

Nebo House—See Lower Deer Creek

* *Nettle Creek* (1820)—Second oldest in state. Houses included White Branch, Locust Grove, Olive Branch, Brick, Maple Grove. Nettle Creek House was central. Buck Creek organized 1845. Maple Grove closed before 1873. White Branch and Locust Grove separate 1955. Located one mile west and 1/4 mile south of Hagerstown, Henry County. Southern and South/Central.

New Bethel (1913)—From Four Mile. Disorganized 1933. Southern.

* *New Hope* (1891)—Houses near Seymour and near Chestnut Ridge. Located seven miles southeast of Seymour, Jackson County. Southern and South/Central.

New Hope (1865)—Second house of Rossville. Disorganized 1902.

* *New Paris* (1918)—From Bethany. Located in New Paris, Elkhart County. Northern.

* *New Salem* (1911)—From Bethel (Milford). Located five miles southeast of Milford, Kosciusko County. Northern.

Noblesville (ca. 1921)—From Beech Grove. Located in Hamilton County. Southern.

North Fork of Wild Cat (1845)—From division of Wild Cat Territory. Divided to North Fork (Pyrmont) and Middle Fork (Rossville). Forty members left with Old Orders. Located in Clinton County. Middle and South/Central.

• *North Liberty* (1917)—Formerly South Bend. South Bend divided to St. Joseph and South Bend 1868. Name changed to North Liberty 1917, and Oak Grove House became separate. St. Joseph eventually became Crest Manor. Located in North Liberty, St. Joseph County. Northern.

North Manchester—See Manchester.

• *Northview* (1906)—Originally known as Indianapolis; 1917 as First Church of the Brethren; 1923 as Grace Church of the Brethren; 1943 as First Church of the Brethren; 1955 as Northview. Located in Marion County. Southern and South/Central.

• *North Webster* (1852)—Originally known as Tippecanoe and located north of North Webster. Moved to town 1925. Changed name in 1929. Moved to west edge of North Webster 1989, Kosciusko County. Northern.

• *North Winona* (1860)—Originally known as Washington. Sometimes known as North Winona Lake. Three houses. Name changed in 1919. Located two miles northeast of Warsaw, Kosciusko County. Northern.

Oak Grove—Second house of Washington (North Winona).

Oak Grove (1917)—From St. Joseph; also called Whitmer. Weakened when North Liberty organized, and disorganized 1942. Located in St. Joseph County. Northern.

Oak Grove (1870)—Originally known as Palestine. Disorganized 1918. Money from sale used to build Logansport. Located in White County. Middle.

Oak Park—See Elkhart City.

Ogan's Creek (1873)—From Manchester and Andrews. Disorganized 1932. Middle.

Old Stony Creek—Later Beech Grove. Located in Hamilton County.

Old Union—Alternate name for White Branch.

Olive Branch—House of Nettle Creek. Closed 1922.

Olive Branch (1803)—Formed by settlers from North Carolina. Became Hostetler Brethren in 1820s and Disciples of Christ in 1830s. Site between New Market and the Ohio in Clark County.

Oregon—House of Blissville.

• *Osceola* (1895)—From Baugo. Located in St. Joseph County. Northern

Owasco—House of Pyrmont.

Owen County—(Lick Creek) Became Hostetler Brethren and Disciples of Christ.

Palestine (1870)—House of Oak Grove and later Oak Grove. Located in White County.

Palmer's Prairie (ca. 1868)—House of South Bend.

Paton—House of Monticello.

• *Peru* (1912)—With Bloomfield Mission by Santa Fe, Pipe Creek and Mexico. Located in Peru, Miami County. Middle and South/Central.

Pigeon River (1865)—From English Prairie. Disorganized 1910. Located in Steuben County. Northern.

• *Pike Creek* (1887)—House of Monticello. Separate and yoked with Guernsey 1967. Located in White County. Middle and South/Central.

• *Pine Creek* (1854)—From South Bend District as East House. West House closed in 1917; Center and Blissville combined to Blissville 1912; Union 1858. Located in St. Joseph County. Northern.

Pine Creek House—House of West Goshen, now known as Little Pine. See Little Pine

• *Pipe Creek* (1852)—First house near Nead; second house west of

Nead Santa Fe 1865. See Summitville. Located in Miami County. Middle and South/Central.

- *Pittsburg* (1939)—Delphi disorganized 1932. Group continued to meet and organized Pittsburg. Middle and South/Central.

- *Pleasant Chapel* (1921)—From Cedar Lake. Located four miles southwest of Ashley, DeKalb County. Northern.

- *Pleasant Dale* (1899)—From Walnut Level. Blue Creek disorganized to Walnut Level, then Walnut Level disorganized 1913 to Pleasant Dale. Located in Adams County. Middle and South/Central.

Pleasant Grove—See Prairie Creek

Pleasant Hill (1873)—From Cedar Creek; became Agape. Located four miles northwest of Churubusco, Allen County. Northern.

Pleasant Mound—See Wawaka.

Pleasant Ridge—See Wawaka.

Pleasant Run—See Antioch.

- *Pleasant Valley* (1876)—From Rock Run. Divided 1913 to form Middlebury. Schism in 1976 created New Life Christian Center. Located northwest of Middlebury, Elkhart County. Northern.

Pleasant View—House of Rossville. Closed 1915.

- *Pleasant View* (1913)—From Sugar Creek (Tunker), formerly West Sugar Creek House. Located four-and-1/2 miles south of South Whitley, Whitley County. Middle and South/Central.

Pleasant View Chapel (1877)—May have been built in 1877, but organized as a separate congregation in 1915. Disorganized ca. 1921. Located three miles southeast of Milford, Kosciusko County. Northern.

Plevna—formerly Greentown. Became Dunkard Brethren in 1927.

Plunge Creek Chapel (1913)—Became Liberty Mills, formerly East House of Eel River. Located in Kosciusko County. Middle and SouthCentral.

- *Plymouth* (1916)—From Union. Located in Plymouth, Marshall County. Northern.

Pokagon (ca. 1870)—Part of Portage congregation. Project of Northern Indiana Mission Board. Disorganized 1912. Located in Cass County, Mich.

Portage Prairie (1831)—Sometimes called Portage. First house built in northern Indiana, second congregation. Organized Rossburg 1853; Berrien 1867; LaPorte and Pokagon 1870. Some chose Progressives in 1882. Disorganized 1921. Located in St. Joseph County. Northern.

Portage South House—No further information.

- *Portland* (ca.1882)—From part of Bear Creek after Blue Creek organized. Located in Jay County. Middle and South/Central.

Potato Creek (1858)—Later White. Located in White County. Southern.

Prairie Creek (1861)—From Salamonie. Houses at Sugar Grove and Pleasant Grove in Wells County; Maple Corner in Blackford County. All gone by 1943. Middle.

- *Prince of Peace* (1962)—From district mission effort. Located in South Bend, St. Joseph County. Northern.

- *Pyrmont* (1845)—Wildcat Territory divided in 1845 to North Fork (Pyrmont) and Middle Fork (Rossville) of Wildcat. Pyrmont divided to Fairview 1872. Also included Owasco House. Ninety members chose Old Orders. Located in Carroll County. Southern and South/Central.

Raccoon Creek—Later Ladoga

Redwood—A mission near Williamsport in Warren County.

Retreat—An organized church in 1881 with 32 members. Located in Jackson County. Southern.

- *Richmond* (1927)—Yoked with Four Mile 1968. Located in Wayne County. South/Central.

- *Roann* (1855)—From Mexico, originally known as Squirrel Creek. Name changed in 1882. Located in Wabash County. Middle and South/Central.

- *Rock Run* (1850)—From Elkhart (West Goshen). Located four-and-1/2 miles southeast of Goshen, Elkhart County. Northern.

Rossburg—House of LaPorte used from 1873-1923.

- *Rossville* (1845)—Originally known as Middle Fork of the Wildcat. Main house Pleasant View. Also New Hope 1865-1905; Edna Mills 1873-ca. 1902. Combined and named Rossville by 1915. Located in Clinton County. Southern and South/Central.

Salem (1880)—From Union. Last listed in 1955. Located eight miles east and one-and-1/2 miles south of Knox, Starke County. Northern.

- *Salamonie* (1845)—Early spellings Salimony and Salimonie; more recently Salamonie. Organized Markle 1852; Antioch (Andrews) 1855; Prairie Creek 1861; Loon Creek 1913. Forced to relocate 1962 because of dam construction. Located 10 miles south of Huntington, Huntington County. Middle and South/Central.

Sampson Hill (1897)—Last listed 1957. Located near Shoals. Southern.

Santa Fe (ca. 1865)—From Pipe Creek. Organized Copper Creek 1919; disorganized 1922. Santa Fe disorganized 1950. Located two-and-1/2 miles east of Bunker Hill, Miami County. Middle and South/Central.

Shipshewana (1857)—From Rock Run, English Prairie, Topeka and Van Buren. Disorganized 1938. Located in LaGrange County. Northern.

Solomon's Creek (1856)—Original name for Bethany. See Bethany.

Solomon's Creek (1918)—From Bethany. Disorganized 1928. Located northwest of Syracuse, Elkhart and Kosciusko counties. Northern.

Somerset (1848)—Organized Wabash 1859; Landessville 1860; Vernon 1871; Cart Creek 1914. District merged Wabash and Somerset to Wabash Country 1929. Located in Wabash County. Middle and South/Central.

South Bend City—See South Bend Second

South Bend First (1868)—Divided to South Bend and St. Joseph. Ulrey House later organized as St. Joseph Valley and Wenger (1877). Became South Bend, then South Bend First, then Crest Manor. Located in South Bend, St. Joseph County. Northern.

South Bend Second (1905)—A mission of Portage. Called South Bend City after 1950. Disorganized 1986. Northern

• *South Bend Crest Manor* (1877)—From house known as Ulery House located two miles north of South Bend. Became South Bend, then South Bend First in 1905. Relocated and changed name to Crest Manor 1963. Northern.

• *Southside Fellowship* (1965)—Formed with Mennonite Church and General Conference Mennonite Church. Located in Elkhart, Elkhart County. Northern.

South Union—House near Elkhart. No other information.

• *South Whitley* (1913)—Located in South Whitley, Whitley County. Middle and South/Central.

• *Spring Creek* (1870)—From Eel River. Originally called Dodgertown. East House three miles north of South Whitley closed 1895. Located two miles east and 3/4-miles north of Sidney, Kosciusko County. Middle and South/Central.

Springfield—See Wawaka.

St. Joseph Valley (1881)—From St. Joseph and Little St. Joe. Disorganized 1921. From house built as Ulery House. Located two miles north of South Bend. Northern

Squirrel Creek—Now Roann.

Stony Creek (1850)—Houses included Old Stony Creek and Cicero 1860; Beech Grove 1878; Noblesville. See Beech Grove. Located in Hamilton County. Southern.

• *Sugar Creek* (1850)—First house in 1867 built in Dunkard's Corner (Tunker). Second house, West Sugar Creek, became Pleasant View. Located in Whitley County. Middle and South/Central.

Sugar Creek—From Beech Grove. Disorganized to Beech Grove 1902.

Sugar Grove—See Prairie Creek.

Summit—Formerly Jonesboro.

Summitville—Organized as Pipe Creek, then Pipe Creek and Howard attached to Killbuck; then Summitville. Southern.

Sweetser (1960)—From Cart Creek. Disorganized 1975. Most went to Marion. Middle and South/Central

• *Syracuse* (1907)—From Solomon's Creek (Bethany). Located in Syracuse, Kosciusko County. Northern.

Taylor School House—Preaching point of South Bend Whitmer.

The Fountain—See Fountain

Tippecanoe (1852)—Located six miles south of Syracuse. Moved to North Webster 1922. Name changed 1929. Northern.

Topeka (1867)—Originally known as Hawpatch; from Shipshewana. Name changed to Topeka 1913. Disorganized 1931. Located in LaGrange County. Northern.

Tunker—See Sugar Creek

• *Turkey Creek* (1856)—From division of Elkhart (West Goshen). Organized Solomon's Creek 1856; Union Center 1859; Bethel 1884; Nappanee 1898. Located four miles east of Nappanee. Northern.

Ulrey—House of First South Bend organized as St. Joseph Valley.

• *Union* (1858)—From Pine Creek. Divided to Salem 1895 and Plymouth 1916. Disorganized 1929, then reorganized 1949. Northern.

• *Union Center* (1859)—From Turkey Creek. Divided to form Maple Grove 1906. Located northeast of Nappanee, Elkhart County. Northern.

• *Union Grove* (1841)—Originally known as Mississinewa. Name changed 1933. Operated house west of Eaton 1857, and Bush Creek before 1868. Both gone by 1882. Union Grove House organized 1885. Located nine miles north and one mile west of Muncie, Delaware County. Southern and South/Central.

Upper Deer Creek (1854)—From Lower Deer Creek. Disorganized 1967. Located six miles west and one mile north of Galveston, Cass County. Southern.

• *Upper Fall Creek* (1845)—From Nettle Creek. Second house in Middletown. Located two miles east of Middletown, Henry County. Southern

Upper Four Mile—See Four Mile.

Van Buren—Before 1878. Located in LaGrange County.

Vernon—House of Somerset

Wabash Country (1859)—From Somerset. Combined with Somerset in 1929. Disorganized 1987. Located seven miles south of Wabash, Wabash County. Middle and South/Central.

• *Wabash City* (1913)—From mission started by Wabash Country. Located in Wabash, Wabash County. Middle and South/Central.

• *Wakarusa* (1915)—From Baugo. Located in Wakarusa, Elkhart County. Northern.

Waldsmith School House—Preaching point four miles southeast of Whitmer.

• *Walnut* (1864)—From Yellow River (Mount Pleasant). Located southeast of Argos, Marshall County. Northern.

Walnut Level (1866)—Organized Hickory Grove 1882; Blue Creek 1887, disorganized to Walnut Level 1905; Pleasant Dale 1889. Walnut Level disorganized 1914. Located near Petroleum.

Walton (1922)—From mission. Disorganized 1930. See Upper Fall Creek. Located in Cass County. Middle and South/Central.

Washington (early 1860s)—Second preaching point was Oak Grove. Name changed to North Winona 1919. Located two miles northeast of Warsaw, Kosciusko County. Northern.

Waterford—House used by LaPorte 1895-1920.

• *Wawaka* (1854)—Formerly Pleasant Ridge. House also at Weaver. Springfield organized and Pleasant Mound (1874), then combined with Wawaka. Yoked with United Methodist 1972-1981. Located in Noble County. Northern.

Weaver—House of Pleasant Ridge (Wawaka).

Wenger—House of South Bend First.

• *West Eel River* (1913)—From Eel River. Located two miles east of Silver Lake, Kosciusko County. Middle and South/Central.

• *West Goshen* (1830)—Originally known as Elkhart. Name changed 1915. First organization in northern Indiana. Formed Turkey Creek 1838, Rock Run 1850, Yellow Creek 1856, Little Pine 1950.

West Florence—House of Four Mile.

West Lebanon (ca. 1910)—Located on Rush and Decatur county line near Williamstown or Williamsport.

• *West Manchester* (1911)—From Manchester. Located west of North Manchester on Ind. 114, Wabash County. Middle and South/Central.

West Marion—See Marion

West Sugar Creek House—See Pleasant View.

White (1858)—Originally known as Potato Creek. Church burned 1893 and closed for one year. Yoked with Ladoga 1947-48. Disorganized 1953. Located four miles west of Colfax, Montgomery County. Southern and South/Central.

• White Branch (1955)—From Nettle Creek. Located northwest of Hagerstown, Henry County. Southern and South/Central.

White County—See Monticello.

Whitehead—Alternate name for Maple Grove, Elkhart County.

White River (ca. 1821)—Located in Lawrence County and settled from Kentucky.

White Water—House of Four Mile. Located in Fayette County. Southern.

Whitmer (ca. 1868)—House of South Bend. Located in St. Joseph County.

Wildcat Territory (1832)—Located in Carroll and Tippecanoe counties. Divided 1845 to North Fork (Pyrmont) and Middle Fork (Rossville).

Williamsport—Formerly West Lebanon, Warren County.

• *Windfall* (1896)—From Greentown. Located three miles west and 1/2 mile south of Windfall. Southern and South/Central.

Winamac (1875)—Disorganized before 1886. Located in Pulaski County.

Winona Lake—Alternate name for Washington. Name changed to North Winona 1919.

Wooleytown—House of Mexico. Located in Miami County.

• *Yellow Creek* (1856)—From Elkhart (West Goshen). Organized Elkhart Valley 1870. Many leaders became Old Order. Located northeast of Wakarusa. Northern.

Yellow River—Became Mount Pleasant.

Appendix 2

Annual Meetings/Conferences
Held in Indiana

Year	Where Held
1848	Carroll County—Special General Council
1852	Baintertown, Elkhart County
1858	near Flora, Carroll County
1864	Hagerstown, Wayne County
1868	Rock Run, Elkhart County
1878	North Manchester, Wabash County
1882	Arnold's Grove, Elkhart County
1888	North Manchester, Wabash County
1893	Muncie, Delaware County
1900	North Manchester, Wabash County
1913	Winona Lake, Kosciusko County
1916	Winona Lake, Kosciusko County
1918	Goshen City—A Special Conference
1919	Winona Lake, Kosciusko County
1922	Winona Lake, Kosciusko County
1925	Winona Lake, Kosciusko County
1929	North Manchester, Wabash County
1932	Anderson, Madison County
1935	Winona Lake, Kosciusko County
1939	Anderson, Madison County
1945	North Manchester, Wabash County
1978	Indianapolis, Marion County
1981	Indianapolis, Marion County

Appendix 3

District Meetings of
Middle Indiana District 1867-1971

Year	Where Held	Moderator
1877	Monticello	Jesse Myers
1878	Santa Fe	Jacob Flory
1879	Sugar Creek	David Neff
1880	Ogan's Creek	David Bechtelheimer
1881	Upper Deer Creek	Abram Miller
1882	Manchester	Joseph Leedy
1883	Bachelor Run	R. H. Miller
1884	Clear Creek	R. H. Miller
1885	Mexico	R. H. Miller
1886	Prairie Creek	R. H. Miller
1887	Eel River	R. H. Miller
1888	Pipe Creek	R. H. Miller
1889	Salamonie	David Neff
1890	Somerset	David Neff
1891	Bachelor Run	R. H. Miller
1892	Roann	J. S. Snell
1893	Monticello	D. P. Shively
1894	Manchester	D. P. Shively
1895	Landess	D. P. Shively
1896	Mexico	D. P. Shively
1897	Bear Creek	L. T. Holsinger

1898	Pipe Creek	L. T. Holsinger
1899	Bachelor Run	D. P. Shively
1900	Eel River	Daniel Snell
1901	Pleasant Dale	S. S. Ulrey
1902	Mexico	Samuel Leckrone
1903	Monticello	J. H. Wright
1904	Manchester	A. G. Crosswhite
1905	Bachelor Run	Frank Fisher
1906	Pleasant Dale	Daniel Snell
1907	Eel River	Frank Fisher
1908	Mexico	S. S. Ulrey
1909	Monticello	A. L. Wright
1910	Manchester	D. B. Garber
1911	Huntington	Frank Fisher
1912	Flora	J. H. Wright
1913	Camden	Frank Fisher
1914	W. Manchester	J. H. Wright
1915	Mexico	J. C. Murray
1916	Markle	Frank Fisher
1917	Manchester	J. H. Wright
1918	Meeting recalled because of flu epidemic	
1919	Manchester	Frank Fisher (April 3)
1919	Salamonie	I.B. Book (October)
1920	Eel River	Otho Winger
1921	Pleasant Dale	I. B. Book
1922	Flora	Otho Winger
1923	Spring Creek	I. B. Book
1924	Mexico	Otho Winger
1925	Upper Deer Creek	I. B. Book
1926	Burnettsville	Otho Winger
1927	W. Manchester	I. B. Book
1928	Spring Creek	Edward Kintner
1929	Flora	Otho Winger
1930	Huntington	Edward Kintner
1931	Eel River	H. L. Hartsough
1932	Mexico	Otho Winger
1933	Pike Creek	Edward Kintner
1934	Salamonie	J. O. Winger
1935	Manchester	Edward Kintner
1936	Flora	J. O. Winger
1937	Huntington	Edward Kintner
1938	Peru	J. O. Winger
1939	W. Manchester	Edward Kintner

1940	Mexico	T. A. Shivley
1941	Monticello	Edward Kintner
1942	Salamonie	T. A. Shivley
1943	Manchester	Moyne Landis
1944	Flora	Edward Kintner
1945	Huntington	V. F. Schwalm
1946	Manchester	T. G. Weaver
1947	W. Manchester	Clarence Sink
1948	Mexico	T. G. Weaver
1949	Manchester	Russell Bollinger
1950	Spring Creek	Charles Oberlin
1951	Flora	E. Paul Weaver
1952	Manchester	Leonard Custer
1953	Salamonie	E. R. Fisher
1954	Eel River	Howard J. Kreider
1955	Mexico	E. Paul Weaver
1956	W. Manchester	T. Wayne Rieman
1957	Flora	Leonard Custer
1958	Manchester College	Charles Oberlin
1959	Manchester College	R. V. Bollinger
1960	Manchester College	A. Blair Helman
1961	Manchester College	John D. Mishler
1962	Manchester College	W. R. Eberly
1963	Manchester College	Hubert Newcomer
1964	Manchester College	Herbert Fisher
1965	Manchester College	Donald Ritchey
1966	Manchester College	Robert Beery
1967	Manchester College	Paul Thompson
1968	Manchester College	John D. Mishler
1969	Manchester College	Dean Frantz
1970	Manchester College	Paul Hoffman
1971	Kokomo	Arden Ball

District Meetings of
Northern Indiana District 1863-1992

Year	Where Held	Moderator
1863	near Goshen	
—		
1867	Elkhart	
1868	Portage	
1869	Whitehead	D. B. Sturgis

1870	Elkhart Valley	
1871	Solomon's Creek	
1872	Pine Creek	
1873	Elkhart	
1874	Elkhart	
1875	Yellow River	
1876	Rock Run	
1877	—	
1878	—	
1879	Whitehead	
1880	Union	
1881	Turkey Creek	
1882	Cedar Creek	
1883	Washington	W. R. Deeter
1884	Pleasant Valley	W. R. Deeter
1885	Elkhart Valley	W. R. Deeter
1886	Springfield	Jeremiah Gump
1887	Shipshewana	W. R. Deeter
1888	Elkhart	Peter Long
1889	Bethel	Jeremiah Gump
1890	South Bend	W. R. Deeter
1891	Walnut	W. R. Deeter
1892	Yellow Creek	W. R. Deeter
1893	Rock Run	Lemuel Hillery
1894	Turkey Creek	W. R. Deeter
1895	Solomon's Creek	I. D. Parker
1896	Union Center	J. H. Miller
1897	English Prairie	W. R. Deeter
1898	Cedar Lake	A. H. Puterbaugh
1899	Yellow Creek	W. R. Deeter
1900	Bethel	S. F. Sanger
1901	West Goshen	George Zollers
1902	Solomon's Creek	S. F. Sanger
1903	Rock Run	W. R. Deeter
1904	Turkey Creek	S. F. Sanger
1905	Pleasant Valley	W. R. Deeter
1906	Walnut	S. F. Sanger
1907	Pine Creek	Manly Deeter
1908	West Goshen	W. R. Deeter
1909	English Prairie	S. F. Sanger
1910	Union Center	Manly Deeter
1911	Springfield	David Metzler
1912	Solomon's Creek	Manly Deeter

1913	Rock Run	David Metzler
1914	Middlebury	Frank Kreider
1915	Pine Creek	David Metzler
1916	Washington	Manly Deeter
1917	Goshen City	David Metzler
1918	West Goshen	Manly Deeter
1919	Winona Lake	David Metzler
1920	Turkey Creek	Frank Kreider
1921	Bremen	David Metzler
1922	First South Bend	T. E. George
1923	Pine Creek	David Metzler
1924	Elkhart City	T. E. George
1925	Union Center	David Metzler
1926	Yellow River	T. E. George
1927	Blue River	David Metzler
1928	Walnut	T. E. George
1929	Yellow Creek	David Metzler
1930	Nappanee	J. H. Schrock
1931	West Goshen	T. E. George
1932	Pine Creek	H. A. Claybaugh
1933	Bremen	T. E. George
1934	Nappanee	H. A. Claybaugh
1935	Elkhart City	T. E. George
1936	Goshen City	Burton Metzler
1937	Yellow Creek	T. E. George
1938	Plymouth	Edward Stump
1939	New Paris	John Metzler
1940	Camp Mack	A. F. Morris
1941	Camp Mack	H. F. Richards
1942	Camp Mack	G. W. Phillips
1943	Camp Mack	H. F. Richards
1944	Camp Mack	T. E. George
1945	Camp Mack	Eldon Evans
1946	Camp Mack	G. W. Phillips
1947	Camp Mack	Eldon Evans
1948	Camp Mack	James Beahm
1949	Camp Mack	Russel Sherman
1950	Camp Mack	Arthur Keim
1951	Camp Mack	John Metzler
1952	Camp Mack	Eldon Evans
1953	Camp Mack	Harper S. Will
1954	Camp Mack	S. W. Longenecker
1955	Camp Mack	Clarence B. Fike

1956	Camp Mack	Herbert Fisher
1957	Camp Mack	Homer N. Kiracofe
1958	Camp Mack	E. W. Gerdes
1959	Camp Mack	Eldon Evans
1960	Camp Mack	Clarence Stouder, Jr.
1961	Camp Mack	Clarence B. Fike
1962	Camp Mack	Lester A. Young
1963	Camp Mack	Robert Knechel
1964	Camp Mack	John Metzler, Jr
1965	Camp Mack	Clarence B. Fike
1966	Camp Mack	Edgar Petry
1967	Camp Mack	Charles F. Stouder
1968	Camp Mack	Ross Noffsinger
1969	Camp Mack	William Kidwell
1970	Camp Mack	John A. McCormick
1971	Camp Mack	Jack Kline
1972	Camp Mack	Lester A. Young
1973	Camp Mack	E. Bruce Barwick
1974	Camp Mack	Clarence D. Sink
1975	Camp Mack	Clarence B. Fike
1976	Camp Mack	Jeannette Tolle
1977	Camp Mack	Olden D. Mitchel
1978	Camp Mack	J. Earl Hostetter
1979	Camp Mack	Lila McCray
1980	Camp Mack	Paul M. Robinson
1981	Camp Mack	Dana Snider
1982	Camp Mack	Paul Shrider
1983	Camp Mack	Don Jordan
1984	Camp Mack	Susan Weybright
1985	Camp Mack	Arden Ball
1986	Camp Mack	Dorotha Fry
1987	Camp Mack	Paul Nye
1988	Camp Mack	Ruth Angle
1989	Camp Mack	Ed Smith
1990	Camp Mack	Harriet Finney
1991	Camp Mack	Larry Dentler
1992	Camp Mack	Rebecca Bonham

District Meetings of
Southern Indiana District 1863-1971

Year	Where Held	Moderator
1863	near Flora	
—		
1866	Antioch	George Hoover
1868	Actual division into districts	
—		
1877	Howard	Robert H. Miller
1878	Upper Fall Creek	
1880	Middlefork	Eli Caylor
1881	Lower Fall Creek	Hiel Hamilton
1882	Arcadia	Hiel Hamilton
1883	Upper Fall Creek	Hiel Hamilton
1884	Mississinewa	Jacob Rife
1885	Raccoon Creek	Isaac Billheimer
1886	North Fork	Jacob Rife
1887	Lick Creek	William Harshbarger
1889	Four Mile	John H. Caylor
1890	Mississinewa	Jacob Rife
1891	Upper Fall Creek	Robert Goshorn
1892	Howard	Jacob Rife
1893	Nettle Creek	William Harshbarger
1894	Middlefork	L. W. Teeter
1895	Lower Fall Creek	L. W. Teeter
1896	Arcadia	William Harshbarger
1897	Mississinewa	L. W. Teeter
1898	White	L. W. Teeter
1899	Buck Creek	D. C. Campbell
1900	Greentown	L. W. Teeter
1901	Howard	L. T. Holsinger
1902	Nettle Creek	D. F. Hoover
1903	White	L. W. Teeter
1904	Mississinewa	L. W. Teeter
1905	Ladoga	L. T. Holsinger
1906	Four Mile	L. W. Teeter
1907	Pyrmont	J. W. Rarick
1908	Nettle Creek	L. W. Teeter
1909	Rossville	L. W. Teeter
1910	Buck Creek	J. W. Rarick
1911	Ladoga	L. T. Holsinger
1912	Mississinewa	L. W. Teeter

1913	Pyrmont	E. O. Norris
1914	Four Mile	L. W. Teeter
1915	White	Paul Mohler
1916	Nettle Creek	E. O. Norris
1917	Ladoga	J. A. Miller
1918	Buck Creek	E. O. Norris
1919	Rossville	E. O. Norris
1920	Mississinewa	D. W. Bowman
1921	Arcadia	J. A. Miller
1922	Anderson	W. L. Hatcher
1923	Pyrmont	D. W. Bowman
1924	Nettle Creek	D. W. Bowman
1925	Arcadia	O. D. Werking
1926	Buck Creek	D. W. Bowman
1927	Rossville	O. D. Werking
1928	Mississinewa	J. G. Stinebaugh
1929	Pyrmont	O. D. Werking
1930	Four Mile	D. W. Bowman
1931	Nettle Creek	I. R. Beery
1932	White Church	E. R. Fisher
1933	Mississinewa	R. L. Showalter
1934	Rossville	D. W. Bowman
1935	Buck Creek	W. J. Heisey
1936	Anderson	O. D. Werking
1937	Nettle Creek	E. O. Norris
1938	Pyrmont	R. L. Showalter
1939	Upper Fall Creek	R. L. Showalter
1940	Union Grove	J. A. Miller
1941	Rossville	A. P. Musselman
1942	Anderson	R. L. Sink
1943	Buck Creek	D. W. Bowman
1944	Nettle Creek	E. O. Norris
1945	Pyrmont	Lewis Deardorff
1946	Union Grove	A. P. Musselman
1947	Rossville	O. D. Werking
1948	Anderson	E. L. McCullough
1949	Beech Grove	G. L. Wine
1950	Arcadia	Carl Hilbert
1951	Nettle Creek	A. E. Harshbarger
1952	Four Mile	Eldon Petry
1953	Pyrmont	Kenneth Hartman
1954	Buck Creek	Albert Harshbarger
1955	Anderson	Harold B. Statler

1956	Rossville	
1957	Nettle Creek	Elden M. Petry
1958	Richmond	Ralph R. Petry
1959	Union Grove	A. P. Wenger
1960	Pyrmont	Albert Harshbarger
1961	Anderson	Byron Miller
1962	Rossville	Russell McInnis
1963	Kokomo	H. Dale Brubaker
1964	Buck Creek	Robert Tully
1965	Pyrmont	Thomas Davis
1966	Lafayette	Ralph McFadden
1967	Muncie	Ronald Petry
1968	Anderson	John Wagoner
1969	Union Grove	Eldon Morehouse
1970	Kokomo	Paul Kendall
1971	Kokomo	David Markey

Meetings of South/Central District of Indiana 1971-1992

Year	Where Held	Moderator
1971	Kokomo	Moyne Landis
1972	Kokomo	Phyllis Carter
1973	Marion	Robert Tully
1974	Kokomo	A. Blair Helman
1975	Kokomo	John Bunch
1976	Anderson	Ernest Barr
1977	Manchester	David Rogers
1978	Hagerstown	John Mishler
1979	Manchester College	William Eberly
1980	Anderson	John Wagoner
1981	Salamonie	Robert Beery
1982	Manchester	Patricia Helman
1983	Flora	Robert Seese
1984	Peru	Esther Rupel
1985	Wabash	Joan Deeter
1986	Mexico	Terry Shumaker
1987	Northview	Richard Harshbarger
1988	Manchester	Betty Smith
1989	Salamonie	Glen Campbell
1990	Anderson	Helen Wenger
1991	Peru	James K. Garber
1992	Flora	Janet Hildreth

Bibliography

*A Brief Sketch of the Brethren (Generally Known As Dunkards) of
Northern Indiana*
Owen Opperman
1897

A Century of Service 1889-1989
The Church of the Brethren Home
Lester Binnie
Orville and Lois Sherman
C.L. Gottman
1989

*A Short Historical Sketch of the Far Western Brethren of the So-Called
Dunkard Church*
John Clingensmith
1885

Allegheny Passage
Emmert F. Bittinger
1990

Annual Conference Minutes

The Brethren's Family Almanac
(Selected issues)

The Brethren Encyclopedia
The Brethren Encyclopedia, Inc.
1983

The Brethren In Colonial America
Donald F. Durnbaugh
1967

The Brethren in the Western Ohio Valley, 1790-1859
David Barry Eller
Doctoral dissertation, Miami University
1976

Church of the Brethren—Yesterday and Today
Donald F. Durnbaugh, Editor
1986

The Complete Writings of Alexander Mack
Edited by William R. Eberly
1991

European Origins of the Brethren
Donald F. Durnbaugh
1958

Gospel Messenger
(Selected issues)

History of the Church of the Brethren in Indiana
Otho Winger
1917

History of the Church of the Brethren in Indiana
Indiana Historical Committees
1952

History of the Tunkers and the Brethren Church
Henry R. Holsinger
1901

The Indiana Way—A State History
James H. Madison
1986

Indiana to 1816: The Colonial Period
John D. Barnhart and Dorothy L. Riker
1971

Messenger
(Selected issues)

Memories of Manchester
Otho Winger
1940

Otho Winger
Vernon F. Schwalm
1952

Some Brethren Pathfinders
Elder J.H. Moore
1929

The Story of Our Church
J.E. Miller
1941

The Virginia Colony or the Four Mile Church
Merle Rummel

Index

Y